The Most Noble of People

The Most Noble of People

Religious, Ethnic, and Gender Identity in Muslim Spain

Jessica A. Coope

University of Michigan Press
Ann Arbor

Published in the United States of America by the
University of Michigan Press
Manufactured in the United States of America
♾ Printed on acid-free paper

2020 2019 2018 2017 4 3 2 1

A CIP catalog record for this book is available from the British Library.

Library of Congress Cataloging-in-Publication Data

Names: Coope, Jessica A., 1958– author.
Title: The most noble of people : religious, ethnic, and gender identity in Muslim Spain / Jessica A. Coope.
Description: Ann Arbor : University of Michigan Press, 2016. | Includes bibliographical references and index.
Identifiers: LCCN 2016027840| ISBN 9780472130283 (hardcover : alk. paper) | ISBN 9780472122677 (ebook)
Subjects: LCSH: Spain—History—711–1516. | Muslims—Spain—History. | Muslims—Spain—Ethnic identity. | Muslims—Spain—Social conditions. | Umayyad dynasty.
Classification: LCC DP102 .C77 2016 | DDC 946/.02—dc23
LC record available at https://lccn.loc.gov/2016027840

For my mother, Ann Coope,
and for my husband, Stephen Hilliard,
in thanks for their longtime love and support.

Acknowledgments

I wish to thank the University of Nebraska for two semester-long Faculty Development Fellowships that made it possible for me to complete this book. Thanks also to Ben Rader and my other colleagues in the University of Nebraska-Lincoln Department of History for their thoughtful comments on my work over the years.

Contents

Introduction 1

1 The Umayyads 20

2 Arabs 38

3 Christians and Jews 61

4 Gender and Law in al-Andalus 86

5 The Law in Practice: Non-Sharīʿah Views of Gender 107

6 Berbers and Muwallads 128

7 The Banū Qasī and the Northern March 144

Conclusion: Ethnic and Religious Identity 159

NOTES 163

BIBLIOGRAPHY 191

INDEX 207

Introduction

It was said [to Muḥammad]: "Who is the most noble of people?"
[He replied:] "The most pious among them."

—FROM THE ḤADĪTHS, QUOTED BY IBN ḤAZM, *JAMHARAH ANSĀB AL-ʿARAB*

This book is a study of cultural identity in Muslim Spain (called "al-Andalus" in Arabic) during the time of the Umayyads, an Arab dynasty whose continuous rule in al-Andalus began in 756 and ended in 1031. The Umayyads had ruled the entire Muslim Empire, from Spain in the west to modern Pakistan in the east, from 661 until 750. In 750 they were overthrown by the Abbasid family; a surviving Umayyad prince, who had ties in western North Africa through his mother's family, escaped to al-Andalus and became ruler in 756, while the rest of the empire remained under the control of the Abbasids. Al-Andalus was part of the western Islamic world, called in Arabic "al-Maghrib" (literally "the west"), which consisted of western North Africa from Morocco to Tunisia, and most of the Iberian Peninsula.

Although some sections of this book look to periods after the fall of the Umayyads, 1031 is an important transitional date for this study, marking as it did the end of rule by a single dynasty (albeit one that faced frequent challenges) and the beginning of a period of political fragmentation. Paradoxically, 1031 also introduced a brief period of relative cultural stability before the North African Almoravids invaded in 1086. During that period, most people in al-Andalus were Muslim in religion and thought of themselves as Arab in cultural identity, whether that identity was biologically based or adopted. Before 1031 cultural identity was more varied, fluid, and contentious. Christians during the Umayyad period converted to Islam in large numbers. A Christian or Jewish man, although he could not claim to be a part of the Muslim community, could have a kind of honorary Arab identity on the basis of his familiarity with Arab language and culture. Muslim Berbers (indigenous North Africans and their descendants) might see themselves for some purposes as part of the community of all Muslims, while at the same time feeling sufficiently oppressed by the Arab Muslim elite to justify rebelling against them.

The ideology of gender also created unclear boundaries during the Umayyad period. A woman was both part of and not part of her ethnic and religious group. The version of Islamic law dominant in al-Andalus, for example, recognized women as full members of the Muslim community when it came to basic religious observances like prayer and fasting, but placed them under the care of a male guardian for other purposes, like negotiating marriage contracts. Most Muslim religious authorities agreed that men transmitted their religion to their children; children with a Christian mother and a Muslim father were automatically Muslims. Arab tradition treated the transmission of ethnic identity in the same way, so that the child of an Arab father was considered fully Arab, regardless of the mother's ethnicity. While the ambiguity of ethnic and religious identity was resolved in part at the end of Umayyad rule by a general adoption of Arab Muslim culture, the ambiguity of women's place in that culture was not.

In this study I lay out the major conflicts and ambiguities in identity that arose during the Umayyad period. I end the study at a point at which some of those conflicts had been resolved and some remained as loose ends. Among the former were the perceived differences between Muslims who were Arab, Berber, and native Iberian. Although there is some evidence that newcomers to al-Andalus, like some of the Berber groups who arrived only in the late tenth and early eleventh centuries, were still seen as a separate category of Muslim, generally the various categories had merged into a single designation as Arabic-speaking Muslims. Among the latter were ideas about gender, which changed over time but were not resolved by the emergence of a more general Arabic-speaking Muslim culture.

INTENDED AUDIENCE

Although I believe my work will be of interest to scholars who have expertise in al-Andalus, I also intend it for a more general audience, including students and anyone with an interest in the Middle Ages and Islamic history. As I will discuss later in this introduction, it is important that we not see the past only as a reflection of ourselves. Nevertheless, some of the questions about gender, ethnicity, and religious identity that people in al-Andalus faced are still relevant to the world today. Some Muslim countries still use Islamic law to define women's status. The question of what exactly it means to be a Muslim, whether one lives in Tehran or Paris, is a live issue. I have kept specialized theoretical language to a minimum and have tried to explain unusual names and terms as they arise.

SCHOLARSHIP IN THE FIELD

Islamic Studies in Europe and the United States have focused on the eastern part of the Islamic world, traditionally defined as extending from the Nile River to the Oxus River, without much attention to the Maghrib.[1] An argument can in fact be made, if not for neglecting the Maghrib, then at least for treating it as a separate case from that of the east. Although some cities in the Maghrib, including Córdoba and Qayrawān, became important cultural centers, the region was far from the eastern capitals of Damascus and Baghdad. The Muslim invaders of the seventh and eighth centuries who defeated the Berber tribes in North Africa and the Visigoths in Iberia found nothing like the literate cultural traditions of Persia or the heartland of the Byzantine Empire. High culture in al-Andalus consisted of an attenuated Latin intellectual tradition kept alive by the Church. Western North Africa still had remnants of Byzantine urban centers, like Carthage, but much of it was dominated by polytheistic Berber groups unconnected to Byzantine culture. The classical Islamic culture that developed in the ninth-century east, with its legal, literary, and scientific components, evolved partly in response to contact with the older Persian and Byzantine traditions that were indigenous to the region. When that culture diffused to the Maghrib, it came as a borrowed set of norms with few local roots. Also in contrast with the east, relatively few Arabs went west at the time of the original conquests, and as a result large numbers of Berbers in North Africa were quickly converted to Islam and recruited into the military; they made up the bulk of the army that invaded Iberia in 711. Those demographics meant that the Arab conquerors in the Maghrib had to deal with the question of whether non-Arab Muslims were full members of society more quickly than the east did. In conquest-era society, fighting in the army meant that one had a claim to a share of the loot and a place in the community, and Berbers quickly pressed that claim.

In the modern era, the study of al-Andalus has been complicated by the fact that it has taken on an important symbolic role in European history. For European scholars, al-Andalus has at different times represented the confrontation between Islam and Christianity, as well as an idyllic period of coexistence between Muslims, Christians, and Jews. For the Spanish of the nineteenth and first half of the twentieth centuries, the Muslim period was a metaphor for and an explanation of Spain's perceived problems taking its place in the modern world. For many Spaniards of the twenty-first century, living in a Spain that has most definitely joined the modern, forward-looking European world, the period of Muslim dominance and Jewish presence has ceased to be a dark chapter of the past and has become instead a source of pride and a symbol of Spain's history as a cosmopolitan meeting place of cultures. For others in the West, al-Andalus is a part of the debate over Islam. Some see the multicultural nature of Andalusī society as evidence of Islam's essential tolerance; the ever-vigilant anti-Muslim website "Jihad Watch," on the other hand, notes that Osama bin Laden lamented the loss of al-Andalus as a tragedy for Islam, and it takes what he said as a sign that Muslims intend to recapture Spain.[2] Al-Andalus's role in the psyche of the West—its status as both Europe and not-Europe—has separated it from its context in the broader Islamic world and led to its being treated as a unique phenomenon, thus locating it yet one step further from mainstream Islamic Studies.

While al-Andalus's location and the unusual demographics of its invading army make its history unique, it can most usefully be seen as part of the larger Islamic world, and I have tried to conceptualize the region in this book as a variant of that larger world. In spite of its distance from the eastern provinces, al-Andalus shared with them a common religion and, at least in elite circles, came to share a culture. Many social and political institutions that originated in the east also influenced the Maghrib. Scholars like Richard Bulliet and Hugh Kennedy, who mainly study Islam in the Middle East, include al-Andalus in their research as a unique example of Islamic culture, but one still tied to the heartland. Maribel Fierro, Thomas Glick, Janina Safran, and David Wasserstein, all of whose works are cited throughout this book, place al-Andalus within the context of Islamic culture in the Nile to Oxus region, while recognizing its distinctive qualities. Also important are al-Andalus's ties with North Africa, a connection that has been particularly emphasized by Muḥammad ʿĪṣā Ḥarīrī, Muḥammad Ḥaqqī, and ʿAbdulwāḥid Dhanūn Ṭāha.

As in any field, scholars have interpreted the history of al-Andalus in light of their own societies' preoccupations. Their approaches depend on their personal and national background, their discipline (the field includes historians, philologists, and archaeologists), and the period in which they lived or live. The history of the field has been analyzed in detail elsewhere and is beyond the scope of this book,[3] but its general trajectory can be traced here.

Most Spanish scholars of the nineteenth and the first half of the twentieth centuries believed there was a stable Spanish Christian identity that, although threatened by the Muslim invasion, survived intact from the Roman period to the present. Two different approaches to that interpretation can be seen in the works of Francisco Javier Simonet (1829–97)[4] and Isidro de las Cagigas (1891–1956),[5] both of whom wrote about Mozarabs (Christians under Muslim rule in al-Andalus), and both of whom saw the Muslim invaders as an alien force that tried unsuccessfully to destroy Spanish Christian culture. Simonet saw Spanish identity as centering on Christianity; for him, the Mozarabs were the preservers of Spanish culture because of their faith and the institutions of the Catholic Church. Christians in al-Andalus, he suggests, were not influenced by the Muslim invaders, but rather the other way around. Arabs never had much original culture, borrowing instead from conquered peoples, particularly Christians.[6] Writing in the mid-twentieth century, Isidro de las Cagigas also imagined a Christian Spanish culture that was buffeted but largely unchanged by the Muslim presence. Unlike Simonet, however, he saw the essence of Spanish identity as secular rather than religious. For him, Mozarab resistance to conversion and acculturation was an early version of Spanish nationalism.

Americo Castro (1885–1972) offers some contrast to Simonet and Cagigas. He too believed in the existence of a Spanish character, but he saw that character as fluid and heavily influenced by contact with Muslims and Jews.[7] Like Simonet and Cagigas, he did not question the idea that peoples have cohesive national identities but saw borrowing among cultures as an enriching process rather than an existential threat. He also complicated earlier ideas about the unchanging character of the Spanish nation, rejecting, for example, claims that Romans and Visigoths in Spain were in some fundamental sense Spanish.[8]

Scholars of the period who were not Spanish present a more mixed picture. The Dutch orientalist Reinhardt Dozy (1820–83), like Simonet, enthusiastically embraced the notion that Arab culture was inferior to that of Christian Europe and offered no contributions to it.[9] Évariste Lévi-Provençal (1894–1956), a French Islamicist, on the other hand, treated al-

Andalus as part of the larger Islamic world, a world he did not see as inferior to Europe. His vast knowledge of the Arabic chroniclers makes his book *Histoire de l'Espagne musulmane* a key resource to the present time.[10] In some ways he was quite different from the Spanish scholars of the period, and from Dozy, since he was not interested in rendering a judgment concerning the good or bad effects on Spain of the Muslim occupation. He did, however, share with his contemporaries and predecessors a focus on government and institutions, although he devotes considerable space to social and cultural history, particularly in volume three of the *Histoire*.

Scholarship in the later twentieth and early twenty-first centuries dropped the preoccupation with nationalism and national character as anachronistic and reconceived Andalusī society as a network of kinship, tribal, and seigniorial structures with an often thin overlay of central government. Pierre Guichard's work has been particularly important in that respect, focusing as it does on the role of the Arab and Berber tribal system and the relationship of that system to land tenure.[11] Guichard and others, most notably Thomas Glick, have also integrated archeological and anthropological methods with the more traditional text-based methods of history, giving us a better understanding of rural areas and a more nuanced way to talk about the interaction among different religious and ethnic groups.[12]

Another major shift has been away from the history of the state to a more social historical emphasis on relations among different religious and ethnic groups, and between men and women. This is not to say that political history no longer counts; Hugh Kennedy's *Muslim Spain and Portugal* is an outstanding modern entry in that field.[13] Much of the recent scholarship, however, has moved in the direction of social and cultural history, and particularly the history of group identity. Women, who were largely neglected in an earlier scholarship focused on government and politics, became subjects of in-depth research.[14] Scholars of gender have noted that Andalusī society (if not its formal religious law) recognized the reality of same-sex relationships and alternatives to official Islamic views of gender.[15] How ethnic and religious groups in al-Andalus defined themselves, got along with other groups, failed to get along, and borrowed from each other have become central topics in the field, and is the main focus of this book.[16] The goal of this recent scholarship has been to build up a fine-grained model of a society defined largely by family, tribal, ethnic, and religious affiliations.

To some extent these changes represent the growing sophistication of medieval studies as a field and our improved ability to see premodern societies in their own terms rather than as a mirror of our own concerns. It is worth noting, though, that in some sense we have just substituted one set of modern preoccupations for another. Scholars writing in the late nineteenth and the first half of the twentieth centuries were naturally concerned with issues of nationalism and national identity, particularly in light of the world wars. In more recent decades, a revived women's movement, the civil rights movement and the emergence of university Ethnic Studies programs in the United States, and the increasing volume of immigration to Western Europe have all shifted our focus toward group rights and identity. I believe the shift represents a positive change, and that to make sure history remains a relevant discipline we should look to those elements of the past that engage our interest. At the same time, however, we must remember the obvious point that medieval society is not like our own. I have tried throughout this book to emphasize that although Andalusīs cared about group identities, they did not see those identities as we would. And although their society was rigid at times, their perceptions of ethnicity, gender, and religion could also be quite flexible and responsive to new circumstances.

CONTRIBUTION OF THIS STUDY

I see this book as a case study of an Islamic society during a particularly turbulent period of social change. Although my research builds on the work of the other recent scholars of al-Andalus I mention above, it offers some new perspectives on how membership in a particular ethnic or religious group affected people's lives, how the nature of such identities shifted as one moved farther from the metropole of Córdoba, and the extent to which women participated in or were able to transmit those identities. Muslim chroniclers, and historians writing about al-Andalus, generally identify five main social groups in Andalusī society under the Umayyads: (1) Arab Muslims, who occupied the highest social rank and included the Umayyads and their Arab allies and their clients or mawālī (singular "mawlā); the Arabic term for this elite group as a whole was "al-khāṣṣah," the special ones. (2) Muslims of Iberian or Berber origin who had become honorary Arabs and part of the khāṣṣah through the study and acquisition of Arabic language and Arab culture. (3) Muwallads, which is a catch-all term for Muslims who were descendants of Iberian converts and whose origins were, among other possibilities, Celto-Roman, Gothic, or Basque. Muslims fell into this category if they had not broken into the "Arab" elite through ties of clientage or by being recognized as distinguished in their education and knowledge of Arabic. (4)

Muslims of Berber origin, most of whose families came from North Africa in the 700s. They, like Iberian Muslims, could gain elite status, but most did not. (5) Dhimmīs, that is, Christians and Jews living under Islamic rule. A few Christians and Jews were part of the court circle in Córdoba, but most, with the muwallads and the majority of Berbers, formed the great mass of subjects, called in Arabic "al-'āmmah," the ordinary people,[17] or "al-'ajam," those who do not speak Arabic properly. In addition, near the end of the Umayyad period slave troops called ṣaqālibah, mostly from eastern Europe, became a factor in Andalusī politics, and sometimes became regional rulers as Umayyad power collapsed (see chapter 7 and my conclusion).

The sources apply the above categories almost exclusively to men. Of course there were women who were non-Arab Muslims, or who were Jews or Christians living under Muslim rule, but their status had more to do with the identity of the men in their family than with their own attributes; there are for example no recorded cases of non-Arab women who gained honorary Arab status through their scholarship. Women slaves were numerous in al-Andalus, but since they did not fight, none of them could be classified as ṣaqālibah. Women were in many respects not bearers of ethnic or religious identity in Andalusī society.

What is most striking about the society of Umayyad al-Andalus, however, and what this book will argue, is how unstable social categories really were. Being Arab and being Muslim were important sources of prestige for some people, yet the more closely one scrutinizes such categories, the more their meaning collapses. Even gender, the most rigid of the observable social divisions, was ambiguous, as women existed for some purposes within a religious and ethnic group, but were in other ways outside the system of social classification. Identities were fluid and were constantly being negotiated. Non-Arab men could become culturally Arab. The high valuation of Arab and Muslim identity became less important as one moved farther away from the political center at Córdoba; away from Umayyad influence, the categories of Arab Muslim, Berber Muslim, and muwallad, and even of Muslim and Christian, became less clearly defined. Dhimmīs could convert. Women could cross-dress, at least until the authorities ordered them to stop. Some chroniclers portrayed Islamic and Arab identity as related categories, while Islamic law saw them as separate, and indeed as sometimes in conflict: Arab identity called for endogamy (allowing women to marry only within the kin group), male dominance, and pride in one's ethnic heritage, while Islamic law emphasized the equality of all Muslims regardless of ethnicity, did not support the practice of endogamy or tracing relatedness in the male line only, and gave women a range of legal rights, including the right to own and bequeath property. The quotation at the beginning of this introduction expresses the ambiguity of the connection between being Arab and being Muslim. The text from which it is taken, the *Jamharah ansāb al-ʿarab*, is a collection of Arab genealogies confirming the importance of Arab heritage. The author, Ibn Ḥazm, was, however, primarily a religious scholar, and was uneasy enough with the *Jamharah*'s celebration of Arab blood lines to include that quote from the Prophet Muḥammad emphasizing piety as more important than aristocratic heritage.

The particular circumstances of Iberia and the Muslim settlement there made this instability acute. In the mid-eighth century, the Abbasids in the east were making the transition from rule as an Arab elite to being rulers of a multiethnic Islamic state. Although the Abbasids could claim a close kin relationship with Muhammad and identified as Arabs, they came to power largely with the support of non-Arab Muslims in Iran, and at their court they drew heavily on Persian and Byzantine culture and traditions of rule.[18] By contrast, al-Andalus was dominated by the Umayyads, who had always derived their status largely from Arab identity; they lost control of most of the Islamic Empire in part because they were unable to effect the transition to a more universal Muslim rule.[19] In addition, they had moved into an area with a relatively weak indigenous high culture compared to that of the Abbasid east. Those factors made them cling more strongly to Arab identity than the Abbasids did. At the same time, however, the Umayyads were rulers of an area with relatively limited Arab settlement, with a large Berber population, and, as conversion to Islam accelerated in the mid-800s, with a substantial number of Muslims of Iberian descent. The demographic realities of al-Andalus meant that the Umayyads' effort to legitimate themselves by claiming to be Arab aristocrats was not really tenable, and indeed by the time of ʿAbd al-Raḥmān III (r. 912–61) they had moved to a more universal, Islamic justification of rule. In the meantime, however, their claims added to the general instability of Andalusī society, as prominent non-Arab families either found strategies to claim Arab identity or directly challenged the right of the Umayyads to rule.

CULTURAL HISTORY IN THE CONTEXT OF AL-ANDALUS

To the extent that this study belongs to a particular school of historical research, it represents a form of cultural history. The term "cultural history" needs some explanation in the context of al-Andalus. Perhaps the most obvious characteristic of cultural history is that it deemphasizes political and military events, or the operation of economic forces on society, in favor of how people in a particular time and place understood themselves, their society, and the larger world around them. Although it does not ignore events that are focuses of more traditional history like wars or changes of political regime, it seeks to explain how people understood those events rather than to explain their causation. Joyce Appleby et al. give a nice definition of culture as "a society's repertoire of interpretive mechanisms and value systems" and go on to characterize cultural history as follows:

> The historian of culture sought to dig beneath the formal productions of law, literature, science, and art to the codes, clues, hints, gestures, and artifacts through which people communicate their values and their truths.[20]

That description of culture is adapted from definitions used in anthropology and draws ultimately on Clifford Geertz's *Interpretation of Cultures*, in which he describes culture not as a force that determines what happens but as a context in which phenomena can be interpreted. A particular action can be understood only if the observer understands the system of assumptions and symbols that make up the actor's culture.[21] Robert Darnton translates the ideas of Geertz and other anthropologists into a methodology for historians, seeing the cultural historian as an ethnographer of ordinary people:

> Where the historian of ideas studies the filiation of formal thought from philosopher to philosopher, the ethnographic historian studies the way ordinary people made sense of the world. He attempts to uncover their cosmology, to show how they organized reality in their minds and expressed it in their behavior.[22]

This understanding of history carries with it a particular set of assumptions, in part because of its derivation from a case-study approach among anthropologists. One is that cultures are specific and do not necessarily share their symbols or ways of seeing the world with others. Cultural history is therefore not a genre of history that draws broad universal principles of history, of the kind system-builders like Ibn Khaldūn or R. R. Palmer might envisage. The rules I try to abstract for my students in World History courses—plow agriculture leads to a diminution of women's status, urbanization contributes to increased warfare—are generalizations that a cultural historian working in a specific time and place could easily take issue with. A related point is that cultural history emphasizes the otherness of the past. Darnton's *The Great Cat Massacre*, cited above, offers a classic example of "othering" the past, since Darnton's explicit methodology is to focus on what seems unaccountable to us: "When we cannot get a proverb, or a joke, or a ritual, or a poem, we know we are on to something."[23] These tendencies toward seeing cultures as unique and playing up the alienness of the past are of course matters of emphasis rather than strict rules. Cultural historians often describe mutual influence among cultures, a common theme in the historiography of al-Andalus, and may draw broad conclusions from their research. It is nonetheless true that the particular and the weird have a large role to play in this type of history.

I say that this book employs a form of cultural history because of the sources available for al-Andalus, particularly in the Umayyad and early Taifa periods. Those sources allow occasional glimpses of day-to-day life, but they are primarily chronicles, collections of religious law, and court literature, in other words products of literate elites rather than of the ordinary people Darnton calls historians to concentrate on. The particular and the weird do manifest themselves from time to time, in an image of a rebel's head nailed to a city gate or a comment that men in the Umayyad family preferred blond slave girls. Most of the texts I work with, however, are formal rather than anecdotal; and whether they are poetry, chronicles, legal treatises, or works on linguistics, their authors' focus is on the universal rather than the particular. At the same time, within the restrictions the sources present, I do try to focus on the attitudes and assumptions of whatever level of society I can get to.

In some ways William Bouwsma's work on early modern Europe has been the most helpful model for me. Bouwsma works on theology and other texts produced by elites, so not the kind of material preferred by cultural historians. He employs the methods of cultural history, however, looking at the mental strategies societies used to make sense of their world. His understanding of culture has also been helpful to me. In his view early modern literate (and to some extent popular) culture was much influenced by two traditions: Greek science and rationalism, on the one hand, and the biblical tradition, on the other. Those two sources are, he believes, quite incompatible, so that early modern culture functioned largely as a set of rationalizations that allowed people to believe two opposite things at the same time.[24]

Certainly the Andalusī authors I study, with their conviction of Arab superiority and their equally strong belief in the equality of all Muslims, provide a good example of what Bouwsma is talking about.

HISTORY OF RELIGION AND AL-ANDALUS

Bouwsma's work is also relevant to my own in that his main object of study is religion, which he believes is a key avenue for understanding the cultures of premodern societies. This book is also largely concerned with religion as a way of understanding people's world view. Again, however, I am limited by the sources. Where an early modernist like Darnton would be able to focus on popular religion and ritual, my own study is largely restricted to normative religion, that is, religion as it is expressed in official Islamic law. Chroniclers do occasionally mention scenes of popular piety like the enthusiasm of a crowd for a charismatic preacher, but such anecdotes are unusual. I do have some sources pertaining to the way cases were actually adjudicated in Islamic courts, which show that religious law as it appears on the page and religious law as it was practiced were not exactly the same thing. Texts from Sufis (Muslim mystics) provide a radically different view of what a good Muslim should strive for and see gender as less absolute than the law does. Mystical texts were, however, also the product of literate elites and do not necessarily inform us about popular religion.

Islamic law, or Sharīʿah, is one of the major sources for this book, so it might be helpful to characterize it more fully. As is the case with Christianity, the term "Islam" can refer to ritual, practice, and belief, both officially sanctioned and not. Islam, however, is closer to Judaism than to Christianity in that it has an articulated legal system designed to regulate human behavior. The system is derived from the Quran and from the ḥadīths, which are stories about the sayings and deeds of Muḥammad collected in written form in the late eighth and early ninth centuries. The decisions of individual jurists as well as local law and custom also play a role, meaning that there is no single version of Sharīʿah. The law covers religious ritual and practice—how you pray, how you fast, what you do on pilgrimage to Mecca—but it also regulates other areas of life. Those areas include family relationships, for example marriage, divorce, and inheritance, as well as commercial interactions and the proper conduct of warfare. A look at the table of contents of any ḥadīth collection (again, such collections are major components of Sharīʿah) reveals topics that include bathing, dealing with menstrual periods, prayer, religious festivals, pilgrimage, fasting, sales, rents, mortgages, planting crops, freeing slaves, marriage, divorce, hunting and slaughtering animals, warfare, correct dress, inheritance, and punishments for transgression of the law, among many others.

The law and its concern with orthopraxy, or correct practice, is not of course all that Islam is about;[25] Islam, like Christianity and Judaism, has strong traditions in speculative theology, theosophy, and mysticism. Sharīʿah, however, is an important part of Islam, and one that is an excellent source for the cultural historian. Islamic law is produced by religious scholars whose major concern is not popular piety, and it represents an ideal rather than a reality. It nonetheless concerns itself with the mundane and the everyday and asks questions that are relevant to a discussion of group identity and gender in al-Andalus: Can a Muslim perform ablutions with water a non-Muslim has touched? To what extent must a woman who is menstruating be excluded from normal social contact? Can a Christian or Jew serve in the army? (The answers are: 1) yes, 2) she cannot have sexual intercourse or go to a mosque, and 3) no, but the rule was rarely enforced.) In spite of its formality, Sharīʿah can be a source for Appleby et al.'s codes, clues, and hints.

MAJOR THEMES OF THIS WORK

The Articulation of an Arab-Muslim Culture in Córdoba

The first two chapters describe how the Umayyads came to power in al-Andalus and the elite culture they built around them. That culture identified itself as Arab, but the term did not have a precise meaning. Being Arab was partly a matter of blood, at least in the male line, but was also a matter of culture, and particularly of proficiency in Arabic. It also meant following specific Arab family patterns such as endogamy (marriage within the kin group) and the reckoning of genealogy in the male line. Arab identity also included a tradition of manliness and military prowess, meaning that men were the purest bearers of Arab ethnicity.

The elite identified itself as Muslim as well as Arab, and in the 900s Umayyad rulers claimed the title of caliph. Despite the rhetoric of modern radical Islamist groups like the Islamic State, who claimed in 2014 to have re-established the caliphate as a religious office, caliphs historically were largely secular rulers who ran affairs of state and military matters with limited reference to Islamic doctrine. They did, however, have a symbolic religious function as head of the ummah, the community of all Muslims, and had the title of amīr al-mu'minīn, or commander of the faithful. When the Umayyads began calling themselves caliphs, therefore, they were naming themselves the rulers of a universal Muslim community, not just rulers of the Arabs. Muslim identity and Arab identity were often at odds with each other, since Sharī'ah did not recognize ethnic differences among Muslims and did not particularly favor patrilineal kin or the practice of endogamy.

Jews and Christians in al-Andalus

Chapter 3 looks at the legal and social place of dhimmīs, or non-Muslim monotheists, in al-Andalus. The treatment of dhimmīs was one facet of Islamic society in which theory differed widely from practice. The society that the Muslim armies conquered in 711 was made up overwhelmingly of Christians, with a Jewish minority; conversion to Islam was not well underway until the mid-800s. Probably until the mid-900s the Umayyads ruled over a society that was majority non-Muslim. The Muslim world in the centuries after the conquests worked out a system in which dhimmīs were protected by the state; the word "dhimmah," the noun that refers to the legal status of non-Muslims, means something like "covenant guaranteeing protection." Dhimmīs, those subject to the dhimmah, could keep their own religion and had considerable community autonomy. In exchange for those considerations they had to pay a poll tax to which Muslims were not subject, the jizyah. They were prohibited from bearing arms, had to show deference to Muslims in public, and could not serve in government positions that would give them power over Muslims. Non-Muslims therefore had rights and protections, but Islamic law did not give a dhimmī man the full status of "mukallaf," or legally capable (no woman had that status).

Aside from collection of the jizyah, which premodern Islamic states generally insisted upon, regulations pertaining to dhimmīs probably constituted the part of Sharī'ah that was most ignored. In al-Andalus, as elsewhere in the Islamic world, Jews and Christians served in government and the army, and depending on their social status did not always show deference to Muslims. The contrast between the reality and the official theory of their status, however, could put them in danger, as the authorities occasionally invoked the full rules of the dhimmah to bring down powerful Jews and Christians.

Gender in al-Andalus

Chapter 4 lays out the official Muslim view of women, and of the proper relationship between men and women, as envisaged in scripture and Sharī'ah. My argument in the chapter is that women's legal status was a version of the dhimmah. Like dhimmī men, Muslim women did not have the status of adults with full legal rights and responsibilities. Instead they received protection from those who were fully legally competent, that is, Muslim men, reflected in a Muslim man's obligation to present his wife with a dower and to support her financially. In return women were to recognize their subordination to men and show obedience and deference to them. Muslim women, like dhimmīs, also had a fair amount of legal autonomy, especially in the area of property. Women controlled their own property in marriage, including the dower from their husband, could bequeath property, and inherited from their husbands and from their own families. Except in rare circumstances they had the right to refuse a marriage arranged by a father or guardian. Free women were not therefore the property of their fathers or husbands, but neither were they fully autonomous individuals.

The first part of chapter 5 discusses how law pertaining to women worked in practice, in marriage contracts and in Sharī'ah court decisions. The sources suggest that the system did uphold women's rights, particularly their right to property. Later parts of the chapter look at depictions of gender and sexuality in literature and mystical texts. The literature in question was for consumption by elites and does not necessarily tell us about popular perceptions of men and women. It does nonetheless offer an alternative view of gender that is more playful and flexible than anything in Sharī'ah. Mysticism historically offered a greater role to women than normative Islam did; there were a number of famous women Sufis in the middle ages, but no women Sharī'ah court judges. Mystical texts use gender and sexuality as metaphors for the structure of the cosmos and suggest that the feminine side of creation, at least at the symbolic level, is just as positive and indispensable as the masculine side.

Non-Arab Muslims and Their Relationship with the Cordovan Elite

Chapters 6 and 7 look at prominent non-Arab Muslim families, including muwallads and Berbers. Both groups were ambivalent toward the Umayyads, typically oscillating between support for the Cordovan regime and rebellion against it. The degree and nature of opposition to the Umayyads depended on the family in question and on the family's geographical proximity to Córdoba. Chapter 6 begins with a discussion of a powerful Berber family who followed the pattern of cooperation with and revolt against the Umayyads. The rest of the chapter is concerned with an uprising led by a local muwallad ruler in southern al-Andalus, 'Umar Ibn Ḥafṣūn, who seems to have intended to set up an independent state in the south, or possibly to supplant the Umayyads altogether. Although there is a substantial amount of source material for the Ibn Ḥafṣūn revolt, at least compared to sources for most events in al-Andalus, the reasons why a considerable number of people in the region joined the revolt remain difficult to establish. Depending on whose interpretation you read, the uprising had elements of a muwallad protest movement against Arab privilege, a Christian revolt against Islamic rule, and a last attempt by the Visigothic aristocracy to reassert its power. The unrest in the south certainly suggests that people expressed resentment of the Umayyads' authority using a variety of conceptual frameworks.

Chapter 7 explores a different kind of revolt, by the muwallad family called the Banū Qasī in the far north of al-Andalus. The Banū Qasī probably had Visigothic origins, and although they cooperated sporadically with Umayyad policies, they generally ruled in their region of the north without much reference to Córdoba. Where Ibn Ḥafṣūn wanted a more just relationship between the Arab leadership in Córdoba and regional elites, and may have plotted to overthrow the Cordovan regime, the Banū Qasī primarily wanted to be let alone. The society they presided over in the north was one of fluid religious boundaries, with Muslim and Christian families routinely intermarrying and individuals changing their religious affiliation as convenience dictated. Córdoba's preoccupations with Arab ethnicity and religious identity do not seem to have been as important on the northern march.

A WORD ON IBN ḤAZM

Because the works of 'Alī ibn Aḥmad Ibn Ḥazm (994–1064) are a frequent resource for this study, a word on that author is in order.[26] Ibn Ḥazm was from a prominent muwallad family and lived through the transition between the Umayyad period and the Taifa Kingdoms. His father, Aḥmad, was a minister at the court of the later Umayyads; Ibn Ḥazm grew up and was educated at court. During and after the civil war that deposed the Umayyads, he continued to be a strong advocate of their rule and of Arab privilege, often at considerable personal risk; he was imprisoned at least three times for advocating an Umayyad restoration. He also became one of the great polymaths of his day, leaving behind an impressive array of treatises on religious law and a variety of other subjects.

His frequent inclusion in this book is the result of three factors. One is simply the variety and volume of his work. Although he is best known in the West for his treatise on love and friendship, *Ṭawq al-ḥamāmah* (*The Dove's Neck Ring*), he also wrote books on genealogy, Islamic jurisprudence, theology, and Arabic linguistics, as well as a guide to virtuous behavior, and polemical works attacking Christianity, Judaism, and all variations of Islam of which he disapproved, including Shi'ism and Sufism. It is impossible to write a book like this one, focused on Islamic law, relationships among religious groups, and gender, without encountering Ibn Ḥazm. A second reason he is such a valuable resource is that while his opinions almost never became widely accepted, he often provides an interesting counterpoint to mainstream beliefs. Where most Muslims seem to have accepted Jews and Christians as fellow People of the Book (monotheists with a scripture), Ibn Ḥazm condemned all religions other than Islam as mistaken and evil. Where most grammarians assumed the superiority of Arabic as a language, he saw it as merely one among a body of interrelated Middle Eastern languages, with no greater inherent value than any other. Scholars of the Mālikī school of law, the main branch of Islamic jurisprudence in al-Andalus, characterized marriage as a contract of sale; Ibn Ḥazm talked about marriage as a consensual coming together of two individuals, not as the sale of a woman to a man. His often testy critiques of mainstream thought show that there were within Andalusī culture alternative ways of perceiving the issues this book explores. It is also refreshingly unpredictable when and if he will take "my" side in a debate, the side of a liberal modern person. His argument that no language is superior to any other, for example, sounds remarkably modern, while the contention that everyone outside his particular religious group is damned does not.

A final reason for Ibn Ḥazm's frequent appearances in this book is that no one better embodies the contradictory, even schizoid, nature of Andalusī culture. The contradictions begin with his own identity. He was a muwallad, yet he argued for the virtue of being Arab and went further than most Arabs would in excluding the unworthy from that category. At the same time, as a devout Muslim, he believed in the equality of all virtuous believers. He defended Sharī'ah's limitations on sexual behavior, which restricted the expression of men's sexuality to relations with their wives and women slaves. Yet he himself clearly had relationships that were homoerotic, relationships that he discusses in the *Ṭawq al-ḥamāmah*. In one of his later works, on morals and good behavior, he reports that he struggled mightily with an impulse that would flood over him and that only the mercy of God allowed him to resist, possibly hinting of the attraction to men that is more fully articulated in the *Ṭawq*.[27] He grew up at a court that was cosmopolitan in its inclusion of Jews and Christians, yet he purported to despise their beliefs. He is an excellent illustration of Bouwsma's thesis that culture allows people to hold mutually incompatible beliefs while never appearing to perceive the conflict.

IS THIS BOOK RELEVANT TO UNDERSTANDING ISLAM IN THE MODERN WORLD?

As I suggest above, understanding the history of Islamic societies and their beliefs about gender, ethnicity, and religion can be relevant in the modern world. There are, however, also compelling reasons not to read the Islamic world's past too much into the present. Europeans and Americans see their own cultures and societies as evolving and as dramatically different from the past. They perceive the Islamic world, however, meaning in particular the Middle East, to be comparatively static and unchanging. That attitude is evidenced by the uptick in Quran sales that happened in the United States after 9/11, as though reading the Quran would explain the attack on the World Trade Center and the Pentagon. At a recent discussion group my husband attended, a university colleague said he had read the entire Quran in order to understand what the Islamic State's goals were. While it is true that al-Qaeda and the Islamic State claim their actions are dictated by scripture, in fact both groups' reading of scripture is highly selective, and seeking to understand them by reading a seventh-century sacred text, without knowledge of the modern Middle East and Western imperialism, is not likely to be effective. It would be equally misguided to say that one could understand the twentieth-century conflict in Kosovo by reading the Quran and the New Testament. The relevance of the premodern Islamic world to the modern is tenuous. There are occasional cultural survivals, just as a version of the medieval English jury trial has survived in Great Britain and the United States; for example, even in some countries in which Sharīʿah is not the basis for most law, its statutes on family law (mostly meaning law pertaining to women's status) are still in use. Other institutions, like the dhimmah, ended in the nineteenth and twentieth centuries. Perhaps the most important idea to take away from a history about the Islamic world is that it has a history, and that its history, like that of Europe or the United States, has some continuities with and many differences from the present. Another point worth making is that premodern Islamic societies, with their hierarchy of dominant religious group over nondominant and men over women, were in many ways similar to European societies of the same period.

1 ✦ The Umayyads

> Julius Wellhausen, in the title of his famous book, described the Umayyad regime as *Das arabische Reich*, the Arab empire, and held that its passing marked the moment when the Arabs lost control of the movement they had created and the leadership of the *umma* passed to a new élite, some of Arab origin, many others of Iranian or, slightly later, of Turkish descent. Despite the challenges to this picture, it remains basically intact; no one who could not claim Arab descent played a leading role in Umayyad politics or court life, although the talents of non-Arabs in financial or agricultural administration were certainly used. But it was an Arab kingdom in another important sense as well; it was the period when the Arabic language came to dominate the Near East, not in the sense that the majority of the populations became Arabic speaking but in the sense that it became the language of bureaucracy, high court culture, and, above all, the religion of the ruling class. The dominance of Arabic was bound up with the dominance of Islam, which retained its identity and separateness in a society where there were numerous ancient and highly developed religious tradition.[1]

CHRONOLOGY:

661–750: Umayyad rule in the Middle East and al-Maghrib
750–1258: Abbasid rule in the Middle East
711–750, and 756–1031: Umayyad rule in al-Andalus

The quotation above, from Hugh Kennedy, highlights how important Arab culture was during the period of Umayyad rule in the Middle East, and how closely being Arab and being Muslim were linked. Before we examine the specifics of ethnic and religious conflict in al-Andalus, it will be useful to get an overview of Umayyad governance. Although there is much in the Umayyads' history in al-Andalus that is different from their history in the Middle East, the dynasty faced many of the same challenges in both areas. Those challenges included the tensions between Arab ethnic identity and Islamic values, including values relating to gender; the question of how legitimate the Umayyads' claim to religious authority really was; and the problems inherent in supporting Arab cultural traditions while at the same time ruling over a culturally diverse population. The specific incidents of conflict and compromise presented in later chapters were linked to these structural tensions in Umayyad rule.

EARLY UMAYYAD RULE IN AL-ANDALUS

'Abd al-Raḥmān of the Umayyad family, grandson of the caliph al-Hishām (r. 724–43), arrived in al-Andalus in 755.[2] The Umayyads, members of the Prophet Muḥammad's tribe of the Quraysh, and therefore his distant relatives, had been caliphs, leaders of the Islamic community or ummah, since 661. Their empire included the Middle East, parts of central Asia, North Africa, and Spain, all of which they ruled from their capital in Damascus, Syria. In 747, however, a rebellion against their rule began, and in 750 the Abbasid family, also members of Muḥammad's tribe and in fact more closely related to him, came to power.[3] The Abbasids killed most of the Umayyads and ruled as caliphs until the Mongols sacked Baghdad, the Abbasid capital, in 1258. 'Abd al-Raḥmān, one of the few surviving Umayyads, fled from the Middle East to North Africa, taking refuge with the family of his mother, and then to al-Andalus, where powerful clients of the Umayyads were able to ensure his safety.[4]

Al-Andalus at the time of 'Abd al-Raḥmān's arrival was the site of considerable competition for power. A Muslim army of perhaps 12,000, mostly North African Berbers with a small number of Arabs, had conquered the peninsula for the Umayyads beginning in 711. After the conquest, Umayyad-appointed governors ruled in al-Andalus.[5] Most of the Arabs in that early group were from Yamanī, or southern Arabian, tribes. Then in 740 a Berber revolt against Arab privilege in general and Umayyad rule in particular began in North Africa and spread to al-Andalus. Caliph al-Hishām sent an army of 30,000 Syrian troops to North Africa to put down the revolt. Of those, 10,000, led by the general Balj ibn Bishr al-Qushayrī, crossed over to al-Andalus and suppressed the Berbers there. These late-arriving Arabs were mostly from tribes that were originally Muḍarī, or northern Arabian and Syrian. Conflict between Yamanīs and Muḍarīs was widespread in the Islamic empire, and most likely did not in fact go back to ancient territorial conflicts in Arabia; the factionalism probably developed out of the differing political and military interests of various groups involved in the Arab conquests.[6] In any event, the Yamanīs in al-Andalus saw the newcomers as a threat to their power. Balj's troops and the Yamanī early settlers ended up in an armed conflict during which Balj deposed the sitting governor in 741 and became governor himself. He then embarked on policies that favored his newly arrived troops, giving them control of land at the expense of earlier settlers and exempting them from certain taxes. The arrival of Balj and his troops added to the Arab presence in al-Andalus, and more specifically to the presence of northern tribes, many of whom were strong allies of the Umayyads; it also tipped off a damaging round of factionalism.[7]

The Abbasid takeover of 750 had little immediate impact on al-Andalus. Independent governors, not appointed by the Abbasids, continued to rule for the next six years. ʿAbd al-Raḥmān became amīr (a general term meaning ruler or governor) in 756 after a military struggle that pitted the troops of Umayyad allies against those of the reigning governor, Yūsuf al-Fihrī (r. 747–56).[8] As of 756, the Umayyads had lost their role as caliphs and rulers over all Islamic lands, but, with only a short gap during which independent governors ruled, maintained their control over al-Andalus.

The al-Andalus in which ʿAbd al- Raḥmān came to power was troubled, particularly since the coming of Balj, by conflict among Arab factions.[9] A discontent Berber population and a majority population of unassimilated Christian Goths and Celto-Romans contributed to the potential unrest. In many respects, the problems were similar to the ones the Umayyads had faced during their years ruling the Middle East, central Asia, and North Africa. After the death of Muḥammad in 632, Arab Muslim troops came from Arabia into the Middle East and beyond as a foreign invading army and ruled over a population that was, for close to two centuries, mostly non-Muslim. As would later be the case in al-Andalus, factionalism among Arab tribal groups—often representing disputes between old and new waves of settlers—was a common problem. The Arab conquerors began as a ruling military aristocracy, in most areas living in separate military bases or amṣār (singular miṣr), then gradually settled on the land and intermarried with the subject population. While conversion to Islam was mandatory for conquered groups whom Muslims identified as polytheists (such as most

Berber tribes in North Africa), Christians, Jews, and Zoroastrians counted as members of legitimate religions and were not required to convert. They did nevertheless convert, but only gradually, first in urban areas where being Muslim could open up new opportunities in government work and in trade. The Umayyads in al-Andalus faced the same issues as the Umayyads in the Middle East: how to maintain military and political control of a population that was divided not only between rulers and subjects but within the ruling elite itself, how to legitimate their authority, and how and to what extent to maintain an identity for the ruling group separate from that of the subject population.

Despite those basic similarities, however, the Muslim settlement of al-Andalus happened under conditions distinct from those in the Middle East. The defeated Byzantine and Sasanian Persian empires left behind a sophisticated infrastructure in Syria, Palestine, Iraq, and Persia. Cities, religious monuments, governments with the capacity to keep records and levy taxes, all survived; once the military conquest was complete, it was mainly a question of the new rulers plugging into a system that already worked. It was not until the 680s that Arab rulers developed their own cultural style, and that style was often imposed on preexisting institutions.[10] The Umayyad caliph ʿAbd al-Malik (r. 685–705) made Arabic the official language of administration, but Christian and Jewish scribal families continued to run that administration. The Umayyads built the Great Mosque at Damascus, completed between 706 and 715, over a Christian church and with the assistance of Greek craftsmen.[11] ʿAbd al-Malik's Dome of the Rock in Jerusalem, with its location on the Jewish Temple Mount, asserted both a connection with and dominance over an older religious tradition.[12] While Muslims moving into Iberia benefited from some of these same institutions—as a former Roman province the peninsula had cities, roads, cathedrals suitable for refitting as mosques, and trained administrators—the quality of infrastructure was much inferior to that of Byzantine and Sasanian territories.

That difference is explained by the fact that al-Andalus, unlike Syria, Palestine, Egypt, Iraq, and Persia, did not go directly from being part of an empire to Muslim rule. By 500 CE, the Roman Empire in the West had collapsed, and groups of Germanic and other peoples invaded and established kingdoms; in the case of Iberia and, for a time, southern France, the Visigothic tribe dominated. There is considerable difference of opinion as to how effective the Visigoths were as rulers and preservers of the Roman tradition, although by 711 conflicts within the ruling elite and over-dependence on a large slave population had become problems.[13] Whatever the merits of Visigothic administration, however, it is clear that no Germanic regime was able to replicate the complexity of Roman governance, or the Roman sense of a ruler who held a public office rather than seizing territory as a personal possession. The Merovingians in Gaul, contemporaries and military antagonists of the Visigoths, were arguably the more successful dynasty of the two. They nevertheless saw their kingdom as family property rather than a trust they administered for the public good, as is evidenced by their understanding of the tax rolls as a source of personal income.[14] The works of Isidore of Seville and others demonstrate that Latin high culture persisted in Visigothic times, but not at the same level as Greek and Persian literature and scholarship in the former Byzantine and Sasanian provinces. The lack of administrative and cultural complexity in Iberia meant that the Muslim conquerors did not adopt aspects of the local high culture and government as they did elsewhere. When the Umayyads sought models of governance and elite culture, they looked to the Abbasid Middle East and its hybrid of Greek, Persian, and Arab institutions.[15]

Another difference between the conquest of al-Andalus and of the Middle East was the large number of non-Arabs who entered al-Andalus as part of the conquering army.[16] In western North Africa, the dominant group was the indigenous Berber population, divided between farmers and nomads. The Berber tribes became the earliest non-Arab group to adopt Islam in large numbers. In most areas under the early Umayyads, a non-Arab who converted to Islam became a mawlā, or client, of an Arab tribe, meaning someone whom the tribe was obligated to protect but who did not have full equality with members by birth. At that time mawālī probably had to pay a head tax called the jizyah, even though that tax was later levied on non-Muslims only. A mawlā soldier received lower pay than an Arab and did not have a right to share in the booty or to claim conquered land. Because Berbers in the Maghrib were such a vital part of the military, however, making up the majority of the army that conquered al-Andalus, they got better treatment, at least sometimes. Berbers generally had a right to booty and conquered land, and they did not pay the jizyah.[17] This policy was apparently not official or universally observed; Yazīd ibn Abī Muslim Dīnār, appointed by the caliph as governor of North Africa in 720, attempted to reimpose jizyah on the Berbers and was killed by his Berber guard in 721.[18] In some cases, Berber soldiers or their Arab commanders invented genealogies connecting them to Arab tribes, presumably to sidestep the issue of offering privileges to non-Arabs. Arabs were far more likely than Berbers to occupy command positions in the army. Nevertheless, the Berbers' military presence meant that in al-Andalus, as in the rest of the Maghrib, there were large numbers of non-Arab Muslims who had a good argument for demanding equal treatment with Arabs.

A final and important difference between al-Andalus and the Middle East is that the Abbasid Revolution never happened in al-Andalus. That revolution in the Middle East meant more than a shift of power from one dynasty to the other. It entailed a move away from the connection between Muslim and Arab identity to an understanding of Islam as a universal religion without a specific ethnic identity. It meant a greater acceptance, at least in court circles, of Greek and Persian high culture and science.[19] And it included a mode of leadership that emphasized the Persian-style grandeur and distance of the ruler rather than the traditional Arab style, in which the ruler was first among equals. Although the Umayyads in al-Andalus gradually adopted Abbasid court ceremonial and some aspects of Abbasid high culture, they continued for most of their rule to see Islamic and Arab identity as linked aspects of aristocratic culture.

That emphasis on Arab identity was both a strength and a weakness. To be an Arab meant to be able to trace an unbroken line of Arab male ancestors; the female line could be counted in some circumstances but was not crucial. The Umayyads gained social prestige from the fact that they could trace their ancestry back to prominent Arab figures in the pre-Islamic Ḥijāz (western Arabia), and religious prestige from their kinship with Muḥammad's family. 'Abd al-Raḥmān I deliberately styled himself as an Arab shaykh (an elder who led in consultation with other prominent men of his tribe) and invited other Umayyads to immigrate to al-Andalus; they became the Quraysh al-ṣulb, the true descendants of Muḥammad's tribe, and second only to 'Abd al-Raḥmān and his immediate family in precedence.[20] Other Arab families in al-Andalus could also point to distinguished lineages going back to pre-Islamic times, and they formed an aristocracy that was at times a source of support for the Umayyads. Arabs and Berbers in al-Andalus maintained at least a theoretical commitment to the notion of 'aṣabīyah, which can be defined as tribal loyalty. More specifically it means a strong sense of loyalty among men who are agnatic (father's side) kin, a group of men who can trace their common ancestry through the male line for several generations.[21] 'Aṣabīyah also implies a strong commitment to endogamous marriage (marriage among kin), especially for women in the group. While men could and did take wives from outside the kin group, the marriage that Arab society favored for a man was with his bint al-'amm, the daughter of his paternal uncle, or if that alliance was not possible, with another close cousin. Women were prohibited from marrying outside the kin group. Language was another marker of Arab identity. Although many Arabs in al-Andalus spoke Romance, a good command of Arabic remained an important criterion for admission to aristocratic circles and government service.[22]

At its most useful, Arab identity was a source of solidarity and prestige for the Umayyads and their aristocratic followers. It was an ethnic identity that was only partially dependent on biological descent, and was in that respect different from modern ideas of race. The question of who was or was not Arab could be answered in different ways, making the boundaries that set off the ruling elite flexible. A man who was not an Arab by descent but who was an asset to the ruling group could become part of it through a fictive Arab genealogy or by becoming proficient in Arabic and assimilating to Arab culture.[23]

Arab identity was also a source of problems for the Umayyads. They and other Arabs regarded that identity and the principles of ʿaṣabīyah as part of what made them a special and privileged group, but at the same time the Umayyads were trying to establish themselves as rulers of a mixed society, the majority of which was Celto-Roman or Berber, not Arab. Uprisings of Berber and, as more people converted to Islam, muwallads happened for a number of reasons, but one was certainly the ideology of Arab superiority and privilege that the Umayyads and their Arab followers clung to. The Umayyads therefore found themselves in the position of basing their rule's legitimacy largely on their aristocratic Arab identity while claiming the right to rule over a heterogeneous society. The fierce family loyalties implied by the term ʿaṣabīyah could be, and at times were, a source of strength for the Umayyads. Such loyalties could also, however, be a threat to centralized rule.[24]

THE UMAYYAD CALIPHATE IN AL-ANDALUS

The conflict between Arab exceptionalism and the need to assert more universal leadership led the Umayyads to adopt other models of Muslim rule available. Between the period of the early Islamic conquests (seventh and eighth centuries) and the tenth century, Muslim rulers throughout Islamic lands increasingly patterned their courts and bureaucracies on Byzantine and Persian imperial governments. They became more universal and multicultural in their claims to power, more inclined to assert the universality of Islam, and less inclined to base their authority on Arab identity.

Early Umayyad caliphs in the Middle East, although their opponents often accused them of wanting to be kings, in fact ruled over other prominent Arab families as first among equals, and with a limited and decentralized bureaucracy.[25] That situation changed in part under Caliph ʿAbd al-Malik. His rule represented a hybrid between Arab ideas of rule and imperial ideals. As was noted above, he on the one hand continued claims to Arab superiority in his reforms of the bureaucracy by making Arabic the official language of government documents and of the coinage. At the same time, the growing complexity of his administration made it into something closer to Persian and Roman imperial bureaucracies than to the more casual Arab style of government. He invested in monumental building projects that evoked even more connections with imperial traditions, particularly those of Byzantium. The Dome of the Rock's location on the Temple Mount ("al-ḥarām al-sharīf," or "the noble sanctuary" in Arabic), symbolized the superiority of Islam over Judaism, while the Quranic quotations decorating the interior asserted Islam's differences from Christianity. The building was intended to emphasize that the Umayyads' authority derived from Islamic identity rather than an ethnic identity. The use of Byzantine architectural elements showed that the regime was capable of absorbing elements of other cultures for its own purposes.

Although it was ʿAbd al-Malik and the later Umayyads who began the transition to more imperial-style government, the Abbasids truly effected that change.[26] They moved the Islamic capital from Damascus, the center of Umayyad power and the dominance of Syrian Arabs in the army, to the new city of Baghdad, near the Sasanian Persian capital of Ctesiphon. At the center of the new capital was the Abbasid palace, a round structure with four gates at the cardinal compass points, indicating its status as center of the known world.[27] The Abbasids surrounded themselves with poets, writers of literature, geographers, historians, musicians, and philosophers from all ethnic backgrounds, and in particular supported the study of Persian literature. Unlike the Umayyads, who were known by their given names (Muʿāwiyah, Hishām), the Abbasid caliphs took more formal and exalted titles such as al-Manṣūr (the one God aids to victory), al-Mahdī (the savior or restorer of justice), and al-Rashīd (the one who is rightly guided by God). They developed a court ceremonial emphasizing the caliph's magnificence and his separateness from his people.

The symbolism of the move to Baghdad was clear. The Umayyads kept their capital in Syria because members of the family had developed a military power base there in the seventh century, but also because Syria was connected with the original Arab Muslim regime that Muḥammad had established. Syria was one of the earliest objects of Arab conquest, with incursions into the region beginning during Muḥammad's lifetime. Under Caliph Abū Bakr (r. 632–34), a large number of Arabs immigrated to Syria. Geographically it was a sort of continuation of Arabia, with its flat arid lands and mountain ranges to the west; no geographical boundaries divided it from Arabia.[28] Damascus therefore connected the Umayyads with the original Islamic state and with the early conquests. That link with the conquests highlighted the Umayyads' Arab identity. Whatever the true nature of the early conquering armies, during the eighth century it became an accepted part of the Muslim historical narrative that the conquests were Arab in character.[29] In contrast, the Abbasids, while claiming a blood relationship with Muḥammad just as the Umayyads had, adopted a style of leadership drawing legitimacy from its continuity with the Persian imperial tradition.

Beginning in the early tenth century, the Fatimid caliphate in North Africa offered both a challenge to the Umayyads in al-Andalus and another model of Muslim governance. The Fatimids were a Shīʿī dynasty claiming to be direct descendants of Muḥammad through his daughter Fāṭimah and her husband ʿAlī, who was Muḥammad's paternal first cousin. That claim made the Fatimids both members of Muḥammad's family and, because of their alleged descent from ʿAlī, Imāms, that is, Shīʿī leaders, with a divinely inspired right to guide the community.[30] While many Shīʿīs in North Africa did not initially recognize the family's claims to the Imāmate, the Kutāma Berbers did, lending their military assistance to a Fatimid assault against the Aghlabid dynasty in the Tunisian city of Qayrawān. The Fatimids established themselves as rulers of Tunisia in 909, and the movement's leader, ʿUbayd Allāh, declared himself to be caliph, with a right to rule over all Muslims. The Fatimids continued their military expansion, conquering Morocco to the west and, in 969, Egypt to the east. Like the Abbasids, the Fatimids built a new capital city, Cairo (al-Qāhirah), near the older Muslim city of al-Fusṭāṭ. Al-Fusṭāṭ remained an economic and population center, while Cairo housed the caliph and his administration in relative isolation. The Fatimid caliph took on much of the same court ceremonial the Abbasids used, including the practice of the ruler emphasizing his distance from other humans by speaking from behind a curtain during audiences.[31]

From the beginning of their post-756 reign in al-Andalus, the Umayyads continued their traditions of monumental building, beginning with the Great Mosque of Córdoba that ʿAbd al-Raḥmān I constructed, probably over the site of a church.[32] Later they adopted specific elements of Abbasid imperial style. 'Abd al-Raḥmān II, amīr of al-Andalus from 822 to 852, began the process of adopting Abbasid court ceremonial, down to importing a singer and literary figure who was well known at the Abbasid court and buying up some of the Abbasid court's jewelry.[33] 'Abd al-Raḥmān III built a new palace to the northwest of Córdoba, Madīnah al-Zahrā'. The move to new quarters required massive construction, including the building of new roads, the reconstruction of a Roman aqueduct, and the installation of an elaborate sanitation system.[34] Madīnah al-Zahrā' displayed the Umayyads' power and wealth in the style of the Abbasid and Fatimid caliphs and allowed 'Abd al-Raḥmān to remain largely isolated from his subjects.[35] John of Gorze, an ambassador from Emperor Otto I who came to Córdoba in the 970s, commented on the opulence of Madīnah al-Zahrā', with its luxuries that included carpets laid to welcome guests not only in the palace but on the streets immediately outside and on the caliph's remote, formal behavior during the interview John was granted.[36]

In 929 'Abd al-Raḥmān III took the title of caliph.[37] That change broke with the tradition 'Abd al-Raḥmān I and his successors established of using the title amīr, malik (king), or banū al-khulafā' (sons of the caliphs). The appropriation of the title of caliph represented 'Abd al-Raḥmān's desire to enhance his legitimacy in al-Andalus. It was also a claim that he was equal to the Abbasid rulers. The Fatimids probably figured into the decision as much or more than the Abbasids, however. It was they who had taken the title of caliph in 909, thus being the first to challenge the Abbasids' right to that office. The Fatimids were also more clearly a threat to Umayyad power than were the Abbasids. The Abbasids made no serious efforts to establish their rule in al-Andalus. The Fatimids, on the other hand, were a power in North Africa and were pursuing an aggressive expansionist policy during the early part of 'Abd al-Raḥmān's caliphate, which led him to establish defensive bases on the North African coast in Melilla, Ceuta, and Tangier.[38] The Fatimids posed some internal threat as well; in the mosques of his territory south of Córdoba, the rebel leader 'Umar Ibn Ḥafṣūn for a time had the name of the Fatimid caliph read out as the legitimate leader of the ummah, and it is possible that the Fatimids actually sent a fleet to support the revolt.[39]

Whatever the precise reasons for the decision to call themselves caliphs, the shift was the culmination of the Umayyads' attempt to move from Arab ideas of leadership to imperial rule, or, more precisely, to add one on top of the other. It was after the adoption of the title that 'Abd al-Raḥmān III moved his court to Madīnah al-Zahrā'. He took an honorific title, al-Nāṣir, as the Abbasid caliphs did. He ordered the minting of gold coins with his name on them, and during the Friday sermon or khuṭbah, mosques throughout his territory were required to identify him as the legitimate head of the ummah (the worldwide Muslim community) and to ask God to bless him.

Another Abbasid and Fatimid practice the caliph took on, and one with perhaps more serious and practical consequences, was the increased use of mercenary and slave troops. The Umayyads in the Middle East had depended primarily on the traditional military levy of Arab tribal groups. In fact, non-Arab clients of Arab tribes made up part of the army, but the army was at least theoretically Arab, at least outside of the Maghrib. That traditional levy went back to the initial Arab conquests, during which the names of the men participating in the conquest of each region were inscribed in the military roll or dīwān; men enrolled in the dīwān were mustered when the local governor or the caliph needed them, and they were paid from the governor's treasury and entitled to a share of any booty the army won.[40] As we have seen, the situation was somewhat different in the Maghrib because of heavy Berber enrollment in the army. Their status as soldiers and as Muslims was disputed, but for the most part they were treated as part of the dīwān system.[41]

The military's structure changed radically under Abbasid rule. The expectation that Arab tribes who took part in the conquests would form a military aristocracy faded, while the caliphs came increasingly to depend on mercenaries and troops recruited from remote areas. The Abbasid caliph al-Muʿtaṣim (r. 833–42) began the large-scale use of mercenary and slave troops in his army. The army was now made up of recruits who were taken as boys from the border areas of Islamic lands (in the east that meant primarily Turks and Circassians), converted to Islam, and raised in the service of the caliph. They had no connections with the local population. When al-Muʿtaṣim stopped using the traditional dīwān system, he effectively ended the tradition of an Arab army with origins extending back to the conquests.[42]

In al-Andalus the parallel switch to a fully professional and slave army was completed under the Umayyads' chief minister Al-Manṣūr (r. 976–1002), but ʿAbd al-Raḥmān III began the process.[43] Along with Berber mercenaries, large numbers of slave troops came to dominate the army. These slaves, or ṣaqālibah (singular ṣaqlabī), were recruited primarily in eastern Europe.[44] A minority were trained as administrators, but most served in the army. Although they were the caliph's slaves, some ṣaqālibah rose to be highly placed officers, thus cutting out the ruling Arab families who had traditionally taken those commands.

ʿAbd al-Raḥmān III's claim to be caliph was also part of a change in the Umayyads' relationship to Islam, a change that brought both benefits and problems. The Arabic word that is the source of the English word "caliph" is "khalīfah." A khalīfah is a viceroy or, more literally, someone who stands in for someone else, in this case denoting the man who stands in for Muḥammad as head of the ummah. The khalīfah's leadership of the ummah does not mean that he inherits Muḥammad's role as prophet, since according to Muslim belief Muḥammad received God's final, definitive revelation. He does, however, act in Muḥammad's place as administrator and military leader, and he has an obligation to serve the best interests of Islam. Another title of the caliph, "amīr al-mu'minīn," or commander of the faithful, further emphasizes that religious obligation.

JIHĀD

Umayyad claims to religious authority were of course not entirely new at the time of 'Abd al-Raḥmān III. Before their defeat by the Abbasids in 750, the Middle Eastern Umayyads also styled themselves as Islamic leaders in many respects, including in their preoccupation with religious architecture. Their main claim to religious authority in that early period, however, was as leaders of jihād. The term "jihād" is from the Arabic root j-h-d, meaning struggle. It has evolved over time to have a number of meanings, from warfare against nonbelievers to a personal struggle for sanctity. In the twenty-first century the term has retained its meaning of an internal struggle to subdue the self. In the realm of outward social and military action, jihād today means the struggle against unjust and irreligious Muslim rulers, for example al-Qaeda's efforts to undermine Saudi rule, and defensive struggle against non-Muslims who threaten the Islamic world, as in the jihadist struggle against the Soviet Union, and then the United States, in Afghanistan. The concept of jihād as a struggle against impious Muslims can be traced back to the fourteenth century and the arguments of the scholar Ibn Taymīyah that revolt against the Mongol leaders in the Middle East, even though they were nominally Muslims, was legitimate. The idea of jihād as defensive struggle goes back to the ḥadīths and was further elaborated during the Crusades.[45]

During the period of Umayyad rule in the Middle East, however, jihād meant primarily the expansion of Islamic rule. Islamic political theory of the time divided the world into two spheres: the dār al-islām, or house of Islam, referring to regions under Muslim control, and the dār al-ḥarb, or house of war, meaning lands under the control of non-Muslims.[46] The first duty of the caliph was to expand Muslim lands, a policy that the Umayyads pursued vigorously. Between 661 and 750 they had added to the earlier caliphs' conquests of greater Syria, Egypt, Iraq, and Persia by conquering the remainder of North Africa, Spain, parts of modern-day eastern Iran and Afghanistan, the Aral Sea region, and areas of modern-day Pakistan and northern India. The Umayyads also launched unsuccessful attacks against Constantinople in 678 and 717–18.[47] The Umayyads in al-Andalus continued the tradition of jihād as practiced by their predecessors. The amīrs, and later the caliphs, often commanded or sent their sons or other close associates to command summer attacks against Christian areas to the north or in the Balearic Islands.[48]

The premodern Muslim religious ideology of conquest was not the same as that of premodern Christian Europe. From the early medieval expansion of the Frankish kingdom to the Spanish and Portuguese colonization of the Americas, one of the conquerors' goals was to Christianize the newly subdued regions. In the case of early medieval conquests, conversion to Christianity was imposed on everyone in the region as part of a negotiated surrender, and thus lacked the element of personal conviction that modern ideas about religious faith would require; still, conversion was a major goal.[49] In premodern Islamic thought, though, the rationale for conquering the dār al-ḥarb, putting aside the practical issues of material gain and of eliminating a potential enemy, was that everyone was better off under Islamic rule, because an Islamic society was the most just and perfect form of human organization. Conversion to Islam, however, was not an immediate goal of conquest, and in fact a Muslim majority in the Middle East and al-Andalus came about only in the mid-tenth or perhaps even the eleventh century.[50] Men in urban areas had reason to convert if they hoped to gain acceptance among the rulers. There was also a financial reason to convert; at some point, probably before 750, it became the practice for Muslim rulers to collect the poll-tax or jizyah only from non-Muslims.[51] The standard Muslim historiography assumes that Muslims levied jizyah from the time of Muḥammad, and indeed the Quran uses the term (9:29). As has been discussed above, it is in fact not clear when non-Muslims, and only non-Muslims, consistently began to pay jizyah. For much of the 600s and early 700s it was paid irregularly, and non-Arab converts to Islam often continued to pay. Even if collected only erratically, however, jizyah may have offered incentive to convert. There was though no legal necessity for subject peoples to convert, provided the rulers deemed them to be People of the Book.

The People of the Book ("ahl al-kitāb" in Arabic) were religious groups who were monotheists, had a scripture (as the name implies), and believed in a last judgment and in an afterlife. The Quran mentions Jews and Christians as People of the Book, and despite some violence and forced conversion, Zoroastrians were generally included in the category as well, although not always with a status equal to that of Christians and Jews.[52] Expediency may have dictated some decisions as to the legitimacy of religions; in the sixteenth century when the Mughal dynasty conquered northern India, they did not treat Hindus as polytheists, despite what must have seemed like strong evidence that they were, instead incorporating Hindu elites into the ruling aristocracy.[53] The goal of expansionist jihād was Islamic rule, not necessarily religious conversion, and it was a given that a virtuous Muslim ruler pursued jihād.

THE PIOUS OPPOSITION

Although the Umayyads in the Middle East carried out jihād as part of their role as leaders of the ummah, that fact did not convince all constituencies that they were good Muslims, and much of the internal opposition to their rule came in the form of religious resistance. It has been argued that Khārijism (a minority branch of Sunnī Islam) and Shī'ism evolved as part of opposition movements against Umayyad rule. Mainstream Sunnī religious law itself may have developed in resistance to what devout Muslims saw as the secular tendencies of the Umayyad, and later the Abbasid court.[54]

Khārijism and Shī'ism are most clearly opposition movements. The Khārijīs, who were active during the Umayyads' Middle Eastern caliphate and the early Abbasid period, disputed the caliphs' right to rule, arguing that the leader of the ummah should be chosen solely on the basis of his piety, not because of his tribal ties, even if those ties were to the Prophet Muḥammad. Their goal seems to have been the preservation of the early charismatic phase of Islam, with its focus on personal piety and a return to a pure form of monotheism. They did not acknowledge the political, military, and other practical considerations that were part of Umayyad and Abbasid rule, and in particular they resisted the claims of what Fred Donner calls "genealogical legitimation": that is, the belief that Arab identity, or genealogical proximity to Muḥammad, conferred the right to rule.[55] Islam for the Khārijīs was a universal religion based on piety, not politics or kinship. Shī'īs did recognize the importance of genealogy in that they believed that only a direct descendant of Muḥammad through 'Alī and Fāṭimah could serve as leader, or Imām, of the ummah. Like the Khārijīs, however, they saw the Imām's right to rule as tied up with personal piety; descendants of Muḥammad, they believed, had a special charismatic knowledge of God's will. The Shī'is, like the Khārijīs, were contemptuous of the Umayyads and saw them as impious.[56]

Although the Umayyad and Abbasid caliphs were all Sunnī Muslims, Sunnī religious law and doctrine also can be seen as part of an opposition movement against the caliphate. Over time the caliphs supported an increasingly secular court culture in which poets, singers, secular scholars, and artists were likely to hold a higher place than men of religion. Favored subjects at court included adab handbooks (works explaining the proper way to live a cultivated life) and secular philosophy. To the extent that Arabic letters were studied at court, they were studied not to facilitate understanding of religious texts but as part of a celebration of secular, pre-Islamic poetry, with its themes of love and honor.[57] At the Abbasid court, the poet Abū Nuwās (d. 803) wrote poetry celebrating wine and love.[58] The development of Islamic religious and legal studies and of Sufism in urban centers outside the court acted as a balance to and an implied criticism of secular court culture.[59]

THE COLLAPSE OF CENTRAL AUTHORITY

At this point it may be helpful to compare the problems of legitimacy the Umayyads in al-Andalus faced with the experiences of the pre-750 Umayyads and the Abbasids. In the case of the Islamic lands outside of al-Andalus, the Umayyads and Abbasids ruled over a diverse population that only gradually adopted Islam. As the process of conversion accelerated, however, the piety of the caliphs was increasingly called into question, both by opposition movements such as the Khārijīs and the Shī'is and by the development of an alternative tradition of scholarship outside of the court, based on the study of scripture and Sharī'ah and carried out by religious scholars or 'ulamā'. The Abbasids in particular responded by taking on more Islamic trappings, emphasizing the caliph's role as amīr al-mu'minīn. At the same time, however, the late Umayyads and the Abbasids took steps that distanced them from those they ruled, by increasingly adopting a remote, Persian or Byzantine style of rule, which signaled that they were imperial as well as religious leaders. The Abbasids' move to mercenary and slave armies meant that they had troops who were often more efficient and loyal than the armies raised by the dīwān system, but it also broke an important tie between the governed and those in power. Although the Abbasids officially ruled until the Mongols sacked Baghdad in 1258, they in fact became primarily figureheads in the mid-tenth century, when competing Muslim groups pushed them out of power. Ironically, the spread of Islam was another reason for the failure of Abbasid rule. Caliphs made much of their title of commander of the faithful, but Islam does not finally have much place for a largely secular imperial government. Muslims accepted that someone had to carry out the practical function of government, but those functions came to be seen increasingly as separate from religious leadership. The religious life of the ummah flourished outside of the courts.[60]

Many of the same processes affected Umayyad rule in al-Andalus, including the gradual conversion of the subject population to Islam, the dynasty's adoption of elements of imperial governance, and the switch from an army commanded by Arab aristocrats and based on the traditions of the early conquests to a mercenary and slave army. Like the Abbasids, the Umayyads in al-Andalus were gradually pushed out of power. Under Caliph al-Hāshim II (r. 976–1009), the caliph's chamberlain or ḥājib, Muḥammad Ibn Abī 'Āmir al-Mu'āfirī al-Manṣūr, became the de facto ruler. It was he who officially ended the dīwān system, thus continuing the changes to the military that 'Abd al-Raḥmān III had begun.[61] Under Ibn Abī 'Āmir's sons, the Umayyads acted as symbolic rather than real heads of state. The fitnah or civil war that began in 1009, a struggle for power among the Umayyads, the 'Āmirids, various other Arab factions, ṣaqlabī army officers, and recently arrived Berbers, ended with the deposition of the last Umayyad caliph in 1031.[62]

Although the collapse of the Umayyads in al-Andalus had many of the same causes as the end of effective Abbasid rule in the east, the political and social tensions played out somewhat differently in Andalusī society. The introduction of large numbers of Berber mercenary troops, newly imported from North Africa, and of ṣaqālibah into the army caused distinct problems because Arab pride had remained a more important force in al-Andalus than in the east, albeit one that was regularly challenged. Andalusī Arabs were accustomed to positions of leadership in both government and the military, privileges they began to lose with the end of the dīwān system and the use of ṣaqālibah in the army and administration. Arab factions continued to be a force during the civil war of the early eleventh century. Several such factions acted as focuses of Arab pride and discontent with the new order. Among them were the 'Āmirids and their non-Berber clients, who were strongly pro-Arab and anti-Berber.[63] Another group, the Nāṣirids, were the descendants of 'Abd al-Raḥmān III and his supporters; during the fitnah, a number of competitors for the office of caliph were great grandsons of 'Abd al Raḥmān III. Yet another faction, calling themselves the Marwānids (the name of the lineage within the larger Umayyad clan that controlled the caliphate after 684), backed Arab rulers and claimed Umayyad descent. All three groups were strongly opposed to Berber and slave influence in the army and administration.[64] By their dependence on Berber troops and ṣaqālibah, the Umayyads had, in the view of many, betrayed their Arab roots. There had been no Abbasid revolution in al-Andalus, meaning that the move toward a more universal definition of Islam and membership in the ummah was less complete than in the Middle East, and that Arab identity was not as thoroughly displaced as a measure of prestige.

The switch to imperial-style leadership and the distancing of the rulers also had a unique impact in al-Andalus. In the Middle East, the secular, multiethnic culture of the Abbasid court was a milieu with which only a small minority of the population could identify. Still, the court's culture sprang from a combination of Arab roots and the civilizations of the region. There was therefore at least a literate minority of Arabs as well as Greek and Persian-speakers who felt a connection with the court. In the court of al-Andalus, the Arab influence was present, but no native Iberian culture was represented; the Umayyads imitated eastern, Persian and Greek-influenced Islamic culture, but they never included elements of Latin high culture. The Umayyad court, therefore, probably did a more thorough job of alienating its subjects than the Abbasid court did.

No overtly religious opposition movement, like the Khārijīs or the Shī'is, played a major role in al-Andalus, although both had some influence there. And by the time of the caliphate in al-Andalus, the Umayyads were no longer so insistent on Arab prestige; the change can be seen in the fact that 'Abd al-Raḥmān III appointed only two Arabs as head qāḍīs of Córdoba.[65] An important group of 'ulamā', mostly made up of non-Arabs, had developed by that era, with whom the Umayyads generally enjoyed good relations.[66] While many 'ulamā' were part of or close to the ruling elite, however, the group as a whole could act as a source of authority separate from the Umayyads and their clients. As had been the case in eastern Islamic lands, large-scale Islamization was a mixed blessing for the leadership.

Andalusī society after the fall of the Umayyads became more politically fragmented but culturally more united. It was divided into a variety of separate kingdoms, called the party or Taifa kingdoms, headed up by the party kings or mulūk al-ṭawā'if. Even though the rulers were ethnically diverse, including Arab, Berber, and ṣaqlabī heads of state, the societies they ruled over were increasingly Muslim and Arab in culture.[67] There were no kings who called themselves muwallad, suggesting that that category was no longer relevant. The ṣaqlabī Taifas faded fairly quickly, and neither Berber nor Slavic languages seem to have been widely used.[68] And while chroniclers and later historians distinguish among the ethnicities of the various Taifa leaders, there is no evidence that differences in ethnicity were tied to any differences in governance or to the relationship between rulers and ruled.[69] François Clément has suggested that although chroniclers divide the Taifa rulers into Arabs, Berbers, and ṣaqlabī, a more meaningful division is among Taifas controlled by Arabized Andalusī rulers as opposed to Berbers newly arrived from North Africa. That method of classification yields nineteen Arabized regimes and five immigrant regimes.[70] As for non-Muslims, Jews remained an important minority in the Taifa period, but Christians largely converted or emigrated to the north.[71] Many of the ethnic and religious tensions of the Umayyad period faded away. It is to the period of social upheaval and ethnic and religious competition under Umayyad rule, however, that we will now turn, and that will provide the framework for this study.

2 ✦ Arabs

Arabic chronicles of al-Andalus all emphasize the role of Arabs in the region's conquest and subsequent history.[1] The original invasion and settlement in 711, however, was in fact headed up by the Berber governor of Tangier, Ṭāriq ibn Ziyād, with a predominantly Berber army.[2] Ṭāriq was the mawlā of the Arab governor of Qayrawān, Mūsā ibn Nuṣayr, and probably carried out the invasion without orders from Mūsā. In 712 Mūsā arrived in al-Andalus with the Arab jund or army division that he commanded in Ifrīqiyah (central North Africa), which included prominent members of various Arab tribes, among them the Quraysh (the Prophet Muḥammad's tribe). Mūsā met with Ṭāriq in Toledo, a meeting that apparently ended with Ṭāriq abasing himself and apologizing for acting on his own, and Mūsā having Ṭāriq's head shaved. The two commanders then joined forces, but with Mūsā in charge and representing legitimate authority, which is to say Arab authority. From that point on, the ruling class of al-Andalus was predominantly Arab or closely affiliated with Arabs until the collapse of the Umayyad caliphate in 1031, and not until the Almoravid invasion of 1086 did Berbers rule all of al-Andalus.

Arabs may have formed the social elite in al-Andalus, but the question of who qualified as Arab was an open one. Although medieval people believed biological inheritance played an important role in ethnic identity, it was not the determining factor it is today. In al-Andalus, language ability, cultural practices, and religion were also factors, so that individuals could to some degree lose one ethnic identity and acquire another. Men from Christian families not only became government administrators for the Umayyads, positions that were routinely filled by non-Arabs in Islamic lands, but were accepted almost as members of the Arab elite, provided that they spoke and wrote Arabic fluently, converted to Islam, and were circumcised.[3] Rather than being strictly a matter of blood, Arab ethnic identity under the Umayyads was made up of a variety of cultural factors.

This chapter will focus on two of the factors that helped define whether or not a person was Arab. One was biological descent, which was particularly important to the Umayyads and other aristocratic families. Their ideas about biological descent were different from modern ones. In most cases only descent through the male line counted, so that a man could have a Berber or European mother and grandmother but still be considered of pure Arab lineage. The concept of biological descent kept Arabs separate from non-Arabs at least in the short term, since there was no biological route through which one could acquire Arab identity. One could of course take on a fictional Arab lineage, but under most circumstances one could not establish such an identity overnight.

The other sign of Arab identity the chapter will explore is knowledge of Arabic, not in the sense of knowing the colloquial form of the language but of speaking, reading, and writing literary or Classical Arabic, and being familiar with the Classical Arabic learned traditions. Those traditions included secular disciplines like poetry and rhetoric but also scriptural studies and Islamic jurisprudence, meaning that knowledge of Arabic and knowledge of Islam were linked, although often in an uncertain way. Knowledge of the language allowed for a more porous boundary between Arabs and non-Arabs than kinship did. The linguistic piece of Arab identity also drew different boundaries than the biological piece, defining an elite based on education rather than lineage. Non-Arabs who were adept at Arabic language and letters could become honorary Arabs, while the uneducated, even if they were of Arab birth, could be seen as falling outside of the elite group. Taken together, the biological and the linguistic sides add up to a picture of Arab identity that was far from clear-cut, and that allowed for movement in and out of the group.

THE BIOLOGICAL PIECE: ARAB KINSHIP

The seminal work on kinship structures in al-Andalus is Pierre Guichard's *Structures sociales "orientales" et "occidentales" dans l'Espagne musulmane*, first published in 1977.[4] According to Guichard, Arabs and Berbers maintained strict boundaries between themselves and the subject Iberian population by enforcing what Guichard calls a traditional Eastern kinship system, which he contrasts to the Western or European system. Guichard's classification system is on firmer ground when describing Arab rather than Berber kinship, since in the case of Berbers he relies more on modern anthropological studies than on evidence from the medieval period.[5] The basic features of the system are as follows:[6]

1. **Kin groups were patrilineal:** Arab families were organized in patrilineal descent groups. They traced each individual's kinship through the father, not the mother, and viewed themselves as all related through a common male ancestor. 'Aṣabīyah, a strong sense of loyalty to agnatic kin, was a driving social force.
2. **The tribes favored endogamous marriage:** Arab men preferred marriage to a woman from their own patriliny. The ideal marriage was between a man and his bint al-'amm, his parallel cousin on his father's side (father's brother's daughter).
3. **Marriage within the patriliny preserved honor:** Men's honor depended on the chastity and modest behavior of the women in the group. A sister or female cousin who misbehaved compromised the entire lineage's honor; controlling one's women, therefore, was of great importance. Allowing them to marry out of the lineage placed them outside the family's control and increased the possibility that they might cause dishonor. In the anthropological literature, endogamy is generally viewed as a strategy for keeping property within the family. Guichard, however, believes that honor was the chief motive for endogamy.
4. **Marriage with a woman from outside a man's lineage neither increased nor decreased his family's status:** In European societies, a family's prestige rose when a son married a woman of higher social rank. In Arab and Berber society, a woman brought in from outside had no effect on the status of the lineage she married in to. Hence exogamous marriage could not improve a family's prestige.
5. **Women did not inherit:** Under most circumstances women neither inherited nor transmitted property, particularly land.

Guichard contrasts those characteristics of "Eastern" marriage and kinship with the typical "Western" pattern that members of the subject population who were not Arab or Berber followed. Societies following the Western pattern recognized descent through the mother as well as the father. Marriage was usually exogamous rather than endogamous. Among marriage's main purposes was the forming of alliances between families, and a man's marriage to a woman from a higher social class enhanced his family's status. Through dowry and inheritance a woman had at least some control over property and could bring property into her husband's family.

Guichard's assertion that women were disinherited is at least partially incorrect, as we shall see later. A further confusing aspect of Guichard's model is that he applies the term "endogamous" to Arab and Berber men and women alike. A better description of the situation, though, is that endogamy was desirable for men but mandatory for women. While a man's marriage to his bint al-ʿamm might be seen as an ideal, in practice men were free to marry muwallad women or even Jewish or Christian women without dishonor. They could also keep slave women as concubines without compromising the status of any children born to such a union. The point was not to keep unrelated women out but to keep the lineage's women in, to safeguard honor and to reserve the women's reproductive capacities for the lineage's use.[7]

This ideal of Arab kinship practices is best exemplified by Ibn Ḥazm's genealogy of the Arab tribes of al-Andalus, *Kitāb Jamharah ansāb al-ʿarab*. His family were, depending on which source one reads, either Persian mawālī of the early Umayyads or muwallads, and both he and his father served in the Umayyad bureaucracy near the end of the dynasty's reign.[8] He was therefore biologically a non-Arab, but as an adīb, or expert in Arabic letters, a Muslim theologian, and an administrator in the government of an Arab dynasty, he was in some ways more Arab than the Arabs. Writing during and after the collapse of Umayyad power in al-Andalus, he compiled his genealogy most likely with the Umayyads and other important Arab families as his audience. Although there is no guarantee that any genealogies of the period represent the objective genetic reality of who is related to whom, they do tell us what people wanted to believe about their past.[9] Given the political turmoil at the time it was written, the *Jamharah* is perhaps best seen as representing an idealized vision of the Umayyads and of Arab society. Ibn Ḥazm brings his genealogies up to his own time, relating for example the Umayyads' history in al-Andalus from ʿAbd al-Raḥmān I's arrival to the last Umayyad caliph's deposition in 1031.[10] His main focus, however, is not on the time in which he was writing, but on the sixth, seventh, and eighth centuries, that is, on the heroic eras of the Arabian jāhilīyah (pre-Islamic period), the time of Muḥammad, and the Umayyad caliphate before the Abbasid revolution of

750. The *Jamharah* confirms Guichard's contention that Arabs traced their kinship mostly through agnates. It also partially supports his claim that Arabs favored endogamous marriages.

Ibn Ḥazm begins the *Jamharah* by discussing the large blocks into which the Arab tribes were traditionally divided, and ends the work with a catalogue of the major tribal groups who immigrated to al-Andalus and their most famous members.[11] The bulk of the *Jamharah* looks at smaller lineages within tribes of about five to seven generations.[12] Ancestors linking an individual to the lineage's founder are almost exclusively male, making the *Jamharah* primarily lists of fathers and sons.

Ibn Ḥazm does frequently mention women, particularly women from important families of the seventh and eighth centuries. He occasionally treats women as links in a genealogy. There are a few men in the *Jamharah* who apparently identified themselves as sons of their mother rather than their father, probably as a way of sealing an alliance with powerful maternal relatives,[13] and Ibn Ḥazm naturally emphasizes that the children of Muḥammad's paternal first cousin 'Alī were also the children of Muḥammad's daughter Fāṭimah,[14] at one point describing 'Alī and Fāṭimah's daughter Zaynab as "daughter of 'Alī from Fāṭimah daughter of the Messenger of God."[15]

Those cases are, however, unusual. Most of the women Ibn Ḥazm mentions are mothers or wives of important men, are from prominent Arab families, and are identified by the male lineage they were born into, as "so and so daughter of X son of Y son of Z." They are not therefore links in a genealogy but genealogical dead-ends whose children are members of their husbands' lineage. A high-status mother may provide her children with some additional luster, but a mother who is low status does not appear to have an impact on her sons' status. Ibn Ḥazm reports that 'Abd al-Raḥmān I's mother, a Berber woman, was umm walad, that is, a slave who bore her master's child and would be set free after her owner's death.[16] Since the Umayyads were sometime patrons of Ibn Ḥazm's family, it is unlikely that he intended any insult. So although women are not absent from the *Jamharah*, and Ibn Ḥazm sometimes speaks highly of them, they are not transmitters of lineage. Umayyad men often took women of European origin as concubines. Their mothers' background, however, in no way compromised their identity as Umayyads and as Arabs.[17]

Although Ibn Ḥazm does not consistently give the names of men's wives, he often does so, particularly for the seventh and eighth centuries. Whether the marriages he describes are endogamous is open to debate. Some clearly are, particularly within the Umayyad family. Among the Caliph al-Walīd

II's daughters, one married Muḥammad, the son of her father's first cousin Yazīd III. Another daughter of al-Walīd married her father's first cousin 'Abd al-'Azīz.[18] Neither of those marriages was quite the theoretically ideal bint al-'amm pairing, but they were certainly close-kin marriages.

More typical of the families described in the *Jamharah*, however, is the marriage of the sixth-century founder of the Umayyad family, Umayyah al-Akbar b. 'Abd Shams b. 'Abd Manāf to Āminah bint Abān of the Banū Kulayb.[19] While both partners were from what came to be regarded as important Arab lineages, their closest common relative was some dozen generations in the past. In its most basic definition, a patrilineal descent group is a group of kin who are related to one another on the male side and who are all descendants from a common male ancestor. In a loose sense therefore the two are part of the same extended family. In practice, however, descent groups tend to segment every few generations into separate lineages. The larger descent group still recognizes that all its members have a common ancestor, but for practical, day-to-day interactions, the lineage is the most important unit; that is, the smaller patrilineal kin group in which the exact relationship of each member to the others is well known, and in which members recognize specific obligations to each other, for example the obligation to pursue a blood feud.[20] When a group can be said to have segmented is a judgment call, but while two people with an ancestor twelve generations in the past may have recognized that they had common blood, it is unlikely that they saw themselves as actively part of the same lineage.

The marriage of Umayyah and Āminah reflects not so much endogamy as the Arab concept of kafā'ah, or equality of status between spouses.[21] Authorities disagreed as to what constituted equality of status, and to what extent piety, wealth, lineage, and freedom from physical defect should be taken into account.[22] In general, though, kafā'ah meant that women could not marry into families of lower social status, which in turn meant that an Arab woman could not marry a non-Arab. Ibn Ḥazm notes when important Arab men married women from prominent non-Arab families, for example when Caliph Yazīd I married the descendant of a Persian king.[23] For an Arab woman to marry into a non-Arab family, though, however prominent they were, would be a violation of kafā'ah; even the most prominent non-Arab is by definition inferior to an Arab. I have found no examples in Ibn Ḥazm's text of such a marriage. The absence of such examples does not mean that mixed marriages of that sort never happened, but it does mean that the author did not think an account of them was suitable for a work celebrating Arab heritage in al-Andalus.

Ibn Ḥazm further elucidates his views on marriages between Arabs and non-Arabs in his *Naqṭ al-ʿarūs*, a collection of stories and gossip about prominent Arabs. In one section, Ibn Ḥazm describes marriages between illustrious Arab men, including several caliphs, and women who were beneath them socially.[24] Some of the women he mentions may have been Arab, and some were clearly not; one is Jewish, and one is identified as a mawlāh (probably meaning a freedwoman). What Ibn Ḥazm emphasizes, however, is not their ethnic identity but the fact that they are lower class. One is a professional dancer who performs for gatherings of common people; others are identified as the daughter of a gardener and the sister of a fuller. By contrast, when he describes marriages of Arab women to inappropriate men,[25] the men are inappropriate not only if they are lower class (one woman marries her grandfather's mawlā or freedman) but also by virtue of not being Arab. Ibn Ḥazm reports for example that a sister of two recent Umayyad caliphs (Muḥammad II and ʿAbd al-Raḥmān V) married Aḥmad b. Rashīq, a court official from the Banū Shuhayd. The Banū Shuhayd were a successful and wealthy mawālī family of scribes and administrators who had served the Umayyads for generations ("mawālī" in this case means they were the Umayyads' clients).[26] Here Ibn Ḥazm's objection is to the husband's ethnicity, not to his wealth or social prominence.

Ibn Ḥazm may have been unusually particular about whom he would count as Arab; Umayyad mawālī like the Banū Shuhayd, whatever their original background, were generally accepted as part of the Arab elite. Certainly though the sense of Arab superiority and solidarity one sees in the *Jamharah* and the *Naqṭ* can be documented in other sources; a story from a chronicle by ʿAbd al-Malik Ibn Ḥabīb (ca. 791–853) illustrates it well.[27] In the story, one Abū Laylā has a conversation with an early Arab governor of al-Andalus, ʿĪsā b. Mūsā b. Muḥammad b. ʿAlī, whom Ibn Ḥabīb describes as extremely proud and overbearing (jabbār). The governor questioned Abū Laylā about the identity of the fuqahāʾ (singular "faqīh," experts in Islamic jurisprudence) in various major cities of the Islamic world. After Abū Laylā gave each set of names, ʿĪsā asked, "who are they?," and Abū Laylā invariably replied, "mawālī" (in this case meaning non-Arab Muslims). The governor became more and more upset with each mention of a mawlā, until to placate him Abū Laylā named two Arab fuqahāʾ in Kufa. ʿĪsā then said, "God is great," and the conversation ended. The story reflects the fact that Arab aristocrats maintained a sense of superiority in spite of the reality that non-Arabs did much of the heavy lifting in the government and religious establishment.

Ibn Ḥazm's *Jamharah* supports Guichard's thesis that Arabs attached great importance to agnatic kin. With rare exceptions, women in the text, although they themselves are members of their father's lineage, do not transmit membership in a lineage to their children. Men give the lineage its identity and status; thus men can marry women who are foreigners or of lower social rank with limited or no damage to the family honor, while a woman who marries down would disgrace the lineage. As for Guichard's assertions about endogamy for women, the text does suggest that the most powerful families, particularly the Umayyads, preferred to marry a daughter to a close relative when a suitable one was available. Generally though the endogamy that the *Jamharah* depicts is more a tendency for aristocratic Arab women to marry other Arabs of their class. Still, Guichard's general point holds within ethnic and class lines if not always within the lineage. Aristocratic Arab men married other Arabs when possible, and aristocratic Arab women did not generally marry out of their ethnic group.

What the Umayyads and other aristocratic Arabs maintained was by no means a genetically contained system in a modern sense, since non-Arab women were often mothers of even Umayyad princes. It was, however, a pattern that placed boundaries between Arab and non-Arab families and largely excluded intermarriage with European families as a means of forming alliances. It is safe to say that a modified form of endogamy was standard practice among Arab aristocrats during the period of Umayyad rule.

THE CULTURAL PIECE

The second pillar of elite Arab identity was knowledge of what I am going to call Classical Arabic, by which I mean a form of literary Arabic substantially different from the colloquial language, and which Arabic speakers believed was close to the language spoken in Arabia at the time of Muḥammad.[28] Classical Arabic was, and still is, a powerful presence in the lives of those living in Arabic-speaking countries. Since it was not in the middle ages, and is not today, the language of everyday speech, Arabic speakers must in effect master more than one language.[29] Classical Arabic (or as a modernized form of it is sometimes called now, Modern Standard Arabic) is the language of politics, education, and high culture, and is a koiné that is intelligible all over the Arab world. Virtually all Arabic speakers, however, speak an Arabic dialect in their daily lives. The dialects feature structure and vocabulary that are substantially different from Classical Arabic, and from each other;

while most Arabic speakers can understand Egyptian dialect because Egyptian movies and television shows are seen all over the Arab world, Moroccan dialect poses a challenge to people outside that region.[30] In addition, people in many areas use other languages not related to Arabic. Those include spoken languages such as the Berber languages of North Africa and the liturgical languages of non-Muslims, such as Coptic in Egypt. Classical Arabic is taught in secular schools and as part of religious education, and its acquisition is seen as an important part of what makes a person educated. Research into the attitude of Egyptians who study it in school, however, reveals that while learning Classical Arabic is a source of comfort and pride, it is also the focus of anxiety and ambivalence. Many Arabic-speaking Muslims see the acquisition of Classical Arabic as an important component of their religious education and welcome the insights its study gives them into the Quran and other religious texts. On the other hand, they also see the time they spend in school memorizing a complex grammatical system and vocabulary, neither of which has much bearing on how they communicate in day-to-day life, as burdensome and oppressive. Classical Arabic is a cultural marker that people admire, aspire to, and dread.

The situation in the middle ages was just as complicated. In the early days of the conquests, Arabs did not discourage the use of indigenous languages for administrative purposes. Arabic was the language of the conquerors and of Islam, and only in the late 600s did it become the language of government. Even after that shift, much of the indigenous population continued to speak other languages, such as Greek, Syriac, Persian, or Coptic. In most areas, Arabic became more dominant over time, although not always; Persian, most notably, retained its primacy as a spoken language and a language of high culture. Even outside of Persia, people continued to speak languages other than Arabic, for liturgical purposes, in daily life, or both. Spoken Arabic dialects also developed early on, probably by the time of the early conquests,[31] setting up the Middle East's bi- or trilingualism that continues today. Even written Arabic appeared in a variety of forms. Middle Arabic—written Arabic that followed Classical models but incorporated features of spoken dialects—was used throughout the middle ages.[32] The term "Middle Arabic" can apply to the Arabic of authors who did not know the finer points of Classical grammar and made mistakes, but also to a style that deliberately incorporated vernacular elements. The fourteenth-century text of *Alf laylah wa laylah* (*The Thousand and One Nights*), for example, is closer to Middle Arabic than to Classical, although eighteenth- and nineteenth-century editors corrected the language to conform with Classical Arabic.[33] It makes sense that this cycle of often bawdy stories would originally be written down in a vernacular-accented language. Jews and Christians who used Arabic as a written language tended to use versions of Middle Arabic, perhaps because they did not feel the same obligation Muslims did to use a language that was supposedly closer to the Quran. In the case of al-Andalus, a variety of languages were in play: Classical Arabic for government and high culture, Middle Arabic for less formal writing, and Arabic dialect and Romance as spoken languages.[34]

In the linguistically complex situation of the Arab-dominated Middle East and Maghrib, scholars gradually developed an ideology defining Classical Arabic and arguing for its superiority over less formal Arabic and other languages. In its fully articulated form, the argument for the preeminence of Classical Arabic is based on a static understanding of grammar that does not recognize that languages evolve. Or, to be more precise, the model does acknowledge that languages change but classifies any changes as mistakes or signs of degeneration. That theory of an ideal, unchanging Classical Arabic did not evolve all at once but came out of a long tradition of associating correct Arabic with ethnic superiority and with Islamic piety.

The foundational grammarian Sībawayhi (d. ca. 796/180), working in the second half of the eighth century CE (a good one hundred and fifty years after Muḥammad's death and the early conquests), believed in prescriptive grammar—there was a right way and a wrong way to express an idea—drawing his model of correct usage mostly from the contemporary spoken language of Arabian Bedouins. His top three sources for the rules he derived were, first, the current spoken language of the Ḥijāz (western Arabia, including Mecca and Medina), followed by the language of pre-Islamic Arabic poetry, and then lastly the Quran.[35] Perhaps because his priority was the spoken rather than the written word, he recognized the flexibility of language, and that usage often depended on social context.[36] He gave a lower priority to written texts. All usages in the Quran were, by definition, correct Arabic, and part of the reason he favored Ḥijāzī Arabic was that he believed it best represented the language of the Quran. Because the Quran used constructions that were not typical of speech, however, Sībawayhi did not recommend it as a model.[37] In keeping with his focus on language as it was used rather than as it should be, Sībawayhi believed that words have no original or absolute meaning; meaning is a convention between members of a society who need to communicate with each other.[38]

While Sībawayhi's approach to Arabic was generally flexible and descriptive compared with later grammarians, there were aspects of his thought that did not fit well with observable facts. Even though he indicated a preference for the Arabic of Bedouins of the Ḥijāz, in part because it was supposedly closest to the Arabic of the Quran and of the earliest Muslim community, that style of Arabic was already by Sībawayhi's time better represented by the Arabic of eastern Arabia than by the vernacular used in Mecca. The eastern dialect retained features of Quranic language, such as the lack of noun-verb agreement in sentences beginning with the verb, which were no longer current in Meccan Arabic.[39] Even though Sībawayhi saw himself as guided by a living, spoken language, he was already creating something of an artificial construct when he favored Ḥijāzī Arabic.

Some grammarians continued to use Bedouin informants into the tenth century, but by the end of that century, as day-to-day speech drifted away from the ancient ideal, grammatical study was based on written texts,[40] including the Quran, Bedouin poetry, and earlier accounts of Bedouin speech. The lack of living informants contributed to the increasingly normative rather than descriptive nature of grammar. The religious weight of Arabic, which scholars from Sībawayhi on recognized, also pushed the discipline toward the prescriptive. Arabic was the language of God's final and complete revelation to human beings, and if people spoke differently now, it was not because Arabic had changed but because people were speaking incorrectly. Grammarians did recognize that native speakers could creatively manipulate the language, for example by altering word order; instead of following the normal order of verb, subject, direct object, one could correctly use the order direct object, verb, subject in order to emphasize the direct object of a statement (the difference between "Zayd hit ʿAmr" and "It was ʿAmr that Zayd hit"). They argued that such a change, however, is purely accidental or on the surface. Underlying the statement is the true and unchangeable word order, verb, subject, direct object, even though that ideal form is not apparent to the listener. The speaker's ability to make such changes legitimately was limited; foreigners, who could not be trusted to know the underlying structures, made mistakes, not legitimate embellishments.

Grammarians came to see Arabic as superior to other languages and independent from them. Early Arabic grammatical study recognized that Arabic had foreign loan words, but later it became a truism among some scholars that there were no foreign words in the Quran and that what appeared to be loan words in early Bedouin speech could be traced to Arabic roots. That belief required some intellectual gymnastics to sustain, since the Quran clearly does use loan words.[41] Arabic-speaking scholars were not generally interested in learning other languages.[42] Even though Muslim philosophers held Greek culture in esteem, grammarians believed the Greek language was inferior; unlike the Arabs, Greeks had allowed their language to change and deteriorate and spoke a version of Greek that was substantially different from that of the classical period.[43] Rulers of Arabic-speaking lands, however, did face the practical problem of having to communicate with non-Arab rulers, which may explain the high value the Umayyad court in al-Andalus placed on the services of Iberian administrators who were fluent in both Arabic and Latin and could therefore correspond with and act as ambassadors to nearby Christian European states.[44]

Arabic's superiority supposedly came not only from its independence from other languages and resistance to change but from its inherent structural superiority. The North African religious scholar, philosopher, and historian Ibn Khaldūn (1332–1406) summed up the mainline argument for Arabic's superiority, saying that it is grammatically compact and precise in a way that other languages are not.[45] Ibn Khaldūn also followed the consensus of grammarians that the dialect of the Quraysh in the Ḥijāz was the purest form of Arabic and the closest to the Quran, and that Arabic is corrupted by contact with non-native speakers. This inherent superiority meant that translations from Arabic to another language could only be imperfect since Arabic conveyed concepts that no other language could encompass.[46]

Sufism, or Islamic mysticism, was another source of claims for Arabic's special status. Letter mysticism was an important field of study within Sufism; the most famous of the Andalusī Sufis to discuss the mystical meaning of letters was Ibn al-ʿArabī (1165–1240), whose work will be discussed in detail in chapter 5. An earlier Andalusī mystic, Ibn Masarrah (883–931), also made explicit claims about the unique and even magical status of Arabic letters. In his treatise the *Kitāb khawwās al-ḥurūf* (*Book of the Properties of Letters*), he characterizes the cosmos as a book, whose letters constitute the divine creation.[47] In particular he concentrates on the fourteen letters, al-ḥurūf al-muqaṭṭaʿah, that appear without context at the beginning of 29 of the Quran's chapters or surahs; surah 2, for example, is headed by the letters alif, lām, and mīm, a, l, and m, while surah 68 is headed by the single letter nūn or n. What the letters signify is unclear, but they have often been taken to have an esoteric or mystical meaning.[48] Ibn Masarrah assigns particular mystical meanings to the isolated letters, meanings that are in some cases tied to the letter's morphology: alif, for example, because unlike most letters it stands by itself and does not usually connect with other letters in Arabic script, is a sign of God's unity or tawḥīd. Lām also has a special status because it is the only letter with which alif does connect in script, and because it follows alif in the word "Allāh"; Ibn Masarrah calls lām the first veil (al-ḥijāb al-awwal) and connects it to the part of the divine that is hidden.[49] Because the letters' physical morphology affect their meaning, letters written in anything other than Arabic script would not carry the same significance.

CLASSICAL ARABIC AND ISLAM

The impulse to view Classical Arabic as an unchanging, ideal language, subject to damage from the ignorance of outsiders, came from two overlapping groups: the religious scholars or 'ulamā' for whom Arabic was a sacred language and therefore one that could not legitimately change and the governing elite who wanted to demonstrate their cultural distinctiveness and superiority. The earliest works on grammar and lexicography were connected with Quranic exegesis, and religious scholars' enthusiasm for establishing clear rules about Quranic Arabic increased over time.[50] It has been argued that the 'ulamā' became more concerned about grammar and lexicography as contemporary Arabic moved farther away from the Quran's language, but in fact by the time of the early conquests there was probably no group, even among the Bedouin, who spoke anything very similar to Quranic Arabic. The more likely explanation is that as the 'ulamā' elaborated Islamic scriptural exegesis and law, they increasingly saw themselves as upholding a unique and complex religious system in a society that was not yet majority Muslim. At the same time, secular scholars at the caliph's court, and regional courts, developed an Arabic literary tradition. The basis of that tradition, and the marker of membership in it, was mastery of Classical Arabic, and particularly the Arabic of pre-Islamic Bedouin poetry.[51] The court and the world of the 'ulamā' overlapped; the caliphs had a religious role in Islamic society and thus valued the work of religious scholars. And while the 'ulamā' sometimes acted in opposition to the caliphs—for example in the case of a revolt religious scholars instigated against the Abbasids over the caliph's right to make decisions about religious doctrine[52]—caliphs also used scholars as their proxies in urban areas. As time went on, it became more common for rulers to appoint 'ulamā' to major office such as judge (qāḍī). The two groups interacted to form an elite religious and literary culture based on knowledge of Classical Arabic.

In the case of al-Andalus, Maribel Fierro and Manuela Marín argue that the qāḍīs were originally appointed to hear cases involving conquerors and settlers. They were Arab, or perhaps Umayyad mawālī, and their appointment depended on their tribal affiliations.[53] By the ninth century, independent 'ulamā' flourished in a number of cities, including Toledo, Zaragoza, and Seville, and were primarily Berber or muwallad. Also by the ninth century, 'ulamā' had become more closely tied to central authority in Córdoba. A leading 'ālim and center of an important circle of scholars in Córdoba was Ibn Waḍḍāh (d. 900), whose family were mawālī of the Umayyads and whose uncle, al-Ḥārith ibn Bazī', was a military governor and ally of the Umayyads. Ibn Waḍḍāh's group supported the creation of the Umayyad caliphate. Also at the time of Ibn Waḍḍāh it became more common for scholars from all over al-Andalus to study in Córdoba and develop a relationship with the Cordovan 'ulamā'. By the later tenth century, when the Umayyads took the title of caliph, the Cordovan government exerted considerable influence over the appointment of 'ulamā' in other cities. Among the 'ulamā' with connections at court were specialists in grammar. In the period of the caliphate, Abū Bakr al-Zubaydī from Seville, a well-known grammarian, tutored the sons of the caliph al-Mustanṣir (r. 961–76) and became chief qāḍī of Córdoba, a position appointed by the caliph.[54] The Umayyads acted as patrons to the 'ulamā', and in return the 'ulamā' helped shore up the Umayyads' credibility as guardians of religion. Grammarians in particular made the case that Arab cultural identity and Islamic piety were connected.

CRITICS OF THE GRAMMATICAL TRADITION

It is easy for a modern reader to be perplexed by or impatient with the medieval Arabic grammatical tradition, given its complexity and rigidity, and its claim that Arabic is demonstrably superior to other languages. A few medieval scholars were critical as well. In some cases the objections were intellectual in nature, but other critiques had broader social implications, calling into question contemporary assumptions about the nature of the Islamic community and the special status of Arabs within it.

The philosopher al-Farābī (d. 950) rejected the standard classification systems of Arabic grammar; for example, following Greek grammar, he regarded the position of the verb in a sentence as unimportant, while most grammarians of Arabic drew a strong distinction between sentences beginning with a verb and sentences in which the verb appears later.[55] Perhaps because he studied other languages, al-Farābī also rejected the notion of Arabic's superiority. Arabic, like all languages, had its good and bad points. As a philosopher and scientist familiar with the Greek and Persian intellectual traditions, al-Farābī was focused on universal knowledge, not on knowledge conveyed by one particular language or historical tradition, nor did he have any interest in proving the superiority of Arabic.

Another main source of criticism was the Ẓāhirī school of legal thought, which centered in al-Andalus and whose best-known proponent was Ibn Ḥazm.[56] As we have seen, he was a prolific author in many fields, including law and scriptural exegesis, Arab genealogy, and religious polemic against Christianity and Judaism.[57] Although he studied Mālikī law, the dominant madhhab or school of law in al-Andalus, Ibn Ḥazm adopted Ẓāhirism, which can best be described as a technique of interpreting scripture.[58] The Ẓāhirīs leveled a number of criticisms against the grammarians, which, although technical in nature, finally point to an important disagreement about the nature of the ummah.

Ẓāhirism is a method of reading scripture (Quran and the ḥadīths), and interpreting law on the basis of that reading, that favors acceptance of scripture's outer, obvious, generally agreed-upon meaning (its ẓahr, literally its back or visible part) rather than its hidden, esoteric meaning (its baṭn, literally its belly or hidden part). Ibn Ḥazm rejects, for example, readings of the Quran using Hellenistic philosophic techniques, as well as the specialized esoteric interpretations of Shīʿīs and of Sufi mystics. He also disapproves of the use of ra'y (the personal opinion of a legal expert) and of qiyās (analogy) in legal reasoning. It would be easy to conclude that Ibn Ḥazm and other Ẓāhirīs favor a simple-minded, literalist reading of scripture, but that analysis does not do justice to Ibn Ḥazm's concerns. He rejects any use of a specialized language and interpretation, whether philosophical, mystical, or Gnostic, because it is intelligible to only a few people. God's purpose in sending down the Quran, in his view, was to communicate with the whole community of believers, not with a few people possessing special knowledge. Scholars who use ra'y or qiyās in effect create a private meaning for words that by rights have a community function. To find esoteric meanings in the words of the scripture is to distort its primary meaning and purpose, which is communication with a wide audience and the building of community.[59]

Ibn Ḥazm could feel confident that such general communication is possible because of his assumptions about language.[60] For a word to qualify as language, in his view, it must correspond to something that exists. The correspondence can be with an abstraction such as "truth," but it must be an abstraction that is real. In addition, the word must be intelligible to others who speak the same language. That transparency, and the direct correspondence between a word and the material thing or concept it signifies, is guaranteed by the fact that God created language. Ibn Ḥazm takes the passage in the Quran, 2:31, in which God teaches Adam the names of all things, as scriptural evidence that language came directly from God at the very beginning of human society. In addition to quoting scripture, he explains the logic of God's creation of language. Human beings, by definition social beings who live together and cooperate to survive, could not exist without language. Without it they would be unable to communicate to one another the basic concepts about crops, livestock, and how to defend themselves against the elements that would allow the group to cooperate (he does not imagine the possibility that humans might have originally lived as something other than farmers or pastoralists). Clearly, therefore, God must have given people language at the same time he created them, as the Quran says, and he is the reason humans can be confident that words correspond to reality.

Ibn Ḥazm's differences with traditional grammarians are striking. Like the grammarians, he accepts that there is such a thing as a perfect language, in that the original language God gave to Adam was transparent and unambiguous in meaning. In his view, however, there is no reason to think that that language was Arabic or that Arabic is superior to other languages. God revealed the Quran in Arabic not because he particularly favors Arabic but because he wanted to communicate with Arabs. When he wanted to communicate with Jews, he revealed scripture in Hebrew. Furthermore, although God gave humans an original language, language by its nature shifts over time. It is clear, he says, that Syriac, Hebrew, and northern Arabic are all closely related, and that Hebrew and Arabic probably evolved from Syriac. One can see how that evolution took place, he explains, by looking at the example of contemporary Arabic. The Arabic of al-Andalus sounds very different from that of Qayrawān, which is in turn different from that of Khurasān. One need only go a short distance outside of Córdoba to find people who speak an Arabic that is almost a different language. People who are new to the language inevitably make mistakes—he cites the problems Berbers and Galicians have pronouncing Arabic consonants like the glottal scrape, the "sh" sound, and the emphatic "h"—and those variant pronunciations, over a period of time, add up to change.

According to Ibn Ḥazm, change happened even in what grammarians believed were the source of true Arabic, scripture and Bedouin speech.[61] The word "kāfir," in Bedouin speech, meant someone or something that covers something up, so it can mean a farmer, someone who sows seed and covers it up. That is also one of its meanings in the Quran, where it is sometimes a synonym for one who sows (Q. 57:20). For the purposes of

Sharī'ah, however, God shifted the meaning to one who denies God or denies Muḥammad's status as prophet.

Ibn Ḥazm's theory of language is, then, quite different from that of the grammarians. His interest is in the whole community of believers, which includes non-Arabs as well as Arabs. He assigns no special status to Arabic, nor does he see Arabs as possessing any sort of special linguistic wisdom. Arabic is valuable or not valuable insofar as it allows clear communication among believers, and it is subject to change, like other languages. In fact, Ibn Ḥazm's belief in the historicity of texts—that even scripture has a specific intended audience who existed in time—is one of his main differences with the grammarians. He notes, for example, that divine law can change; Jacob was not punished for marrying both Leah and Rachel, although later Jewish law would have forbidden him to marry sisters.[62]

Another Ẓāhirī scholar, Aḥmad ibn 'Abd al-Raḥmān Ibn Maḍā' (d. 1196), who received patronage from the Berber Almohad rulers of al-Andalus, is beyond the chronological scope of this study; his work, however, is related to that of Ibn Ḥazm and helps elucidate Ẓāhirī objections to traditional grammar.[63] Those objections are on the surface quite technical, but, as in the case of Ibn Ḥazm's critique, they are in fact a challenge to the grammarians' assumptions about what language is for and who is included in the discourse community of Islam.

Ibn Maḍā's treatise about grammar, *Kitāb al-radd 'alā al-nuḥāh* (*The Book of Refutation of the Grammarians*), criticizes the elaborate and speculative nature of grammatical study. To simplify his argument considerably, Ibn Maḍā' attacks three aspects of the standard grammatical analysis of Arabic: the concept of the grammatical regent ("'āmil" in Arabic), the related concept of suppressed words, and the search for the root causes of grammatical and morphological rules. 'Āmil, usually translated as "regent," is perhaps better translated as that which produces something else. In Arabic grammatical studies, the concept of the 'āmil is a way of understanding the fact that nouns in Classical Arabic are inflected, taking either the nominative, accusative, or genitive case. So in the sentence "Zayd hit 'Amr," "Zayd" is in the nominative case and "'Amr" is in the accusative, and the verb "to hit" is the 'āmil, the ruling word that forces the nouns into their appropriate cases. The related concept of suppressed words suggests that there is an ideal, standard form for all sentences, and that if an element is missing from a sentence, it is in some sense still present, having been only suppressed or elided. Most commonly it is the 'āmil that is supposed to have been suppressed. For example, in some instances, if one addresses a person directly ("O 'Abd

Allāh"), the name of the person is in the accusative. Since there is no obvious regent to put the proper noun into the accusative (the vocative particle equivalent to the English "O" does not qualify as a regent), there must be an implied or suppressed verb in the sentence acting as ʿāmil. The underlying form of the sentence, therefore, is "[I call] ʿAbd Allāh." Finally, grammarians traditionally strove for a deep level of explanation for grammatical forms, explanations that demonstrated the underlying logic of the language and the wisdom of Arabic speakers.

At the beginning of his treatise, Ibn Maḍāʾ emphasizes his religious objections to those three principles. The idea of implied or suppressed words allows grammarians to read into the Quran words that God did not put there, meaning that they are taking it upon themselves to change scripture.[64] He is particularly incensed by the concept of the ʿāmil, which assumes that words can produce other words. He quotes the Muʿtazilī (rationalist theologian) Abū al-Fatḥ ʿUthmān Ibn Jinnī, who was also critical of the grammarians and who wrote that it is the speaker, not the grammatical regent, that produces the cases of nouns. Ibn Maḍāʾ expands on Ibn Jinnī's statement, saying that it is ultimately God who produces all speech, but agrees that the human speaker is the immediate cause of the words being formed in a certain way.[65] The concepts of the regent and of suppressed words undermine the authority of God and the powers God gave to humans.

Although Ibn Maḍāʾ's argument has religious elements, his main accusation against grammarians is that they have created an elaborate, convoluted system that serves no purpose. At its worst, the system is actively misleading. To say that the utterance "O ʿAbd Allāh" can be understood as identical to "I call ʿAbd Allāh" is to lose the speaker's meaning, since the first utterance does not in fact mean the same thing as the second.[66] Even when grammarians are not actively misleading their audience, their system is mostly useless because of its elaborate search for the causes of grammatical structures. For example, if asked why the name "Zayd" takes the nominative case—that is, the ending "un"—in the sentence "Zayd is standing" (qāma Zayd^{un}), grammarians will give several layers of answers.[67] "Zayd" is in the nominative because it is the subject, and all subjects take the nominative case. The nominative ending is "un" because that is how the Arabs say it. They say it that way because they need to distinguish between the two terms a verb most commonly has regency over: the subject, which takes the nominative, and the direct object, which takes the accusative (the ending "an"). Finally, Arabs use the "an" for the accusative and the "un" for the subject because "an" is "lighter," or easier to pronounce, than "un," and there are more direct objects in speech than there are subjects; verbs normally have only one subject, while they can have multiple objects. Therefore it is logical that the Arabs reserved the easier-to-pronounce "an" as the more common ending, and shows the intelligence of Arabic speakers.[68]

Ibn Maḍāʾ approves of the first two levels of explanation: that all subjects take the nominative and that the nominative is indicated by the ending "un" because that is how Arabs say it. Those two facts can be confirmed by listening to Arabic speakers, and knowing those facts allows a student of Arabic to speak correctly. The rest of the explanation, however, serves no purpose. The statement that Arabs chose "an" as the accusative ending because it is easier to pronounce than "un" does not offer any practical guidance and functions only to make a case that the Arabs are a wise people. Like Ibn Ḥazm, Ibn Maḍāʾ sees language as a practical tool for communication and the study of language as valuable only so far as it furthers the goal of communication. He recognizes no special claims for Arabic as a language, or for the Arabs as a people of particular linguistic abilities. Ibn Maḍāʾ and Ibn Ḥazm cared about correct speech. They were also interested in grammar as a tool for language acquisition, since both were surrounded by non-native speakers. This was particularly true of Ibn Maḍāʾ, whose patrons were Berber.

The Ẓāhirī view of grammar is not a modern view, particularly in its confidence that words reliably correspond to reality. Compared to traditional Arabic grammar, however, it is easier for a modern reader to understand, given its emphasis on communication and its resistance to establishing any hierarchy of languages. The Ẓāhirīs' attitude toward language is also recognizable to the modern reader because of its emphasis on a social context for speech and on any speech act's intended audience, or discourse community; if no one can understand what an utterance means, it is not language.[69]

In the context of al-Andalus, however, the main difference between the Ẓāhirīs and the grammarians was that they envisaged a different audience, and a different purpose, for texts written in formal Arabic. Ẓāhirīs imagined a broad community of believers, some of whom were non-Arabs struggling to learn Classical Arabic. Mainstream grammar addressed an educated elite, primarily people who were courtiers, members of the ulamāʾ, or both. That elite group wrote and, in formal settings, spoke an Arabic based on the model of Bedouin speech of the past and Islamic scripture. Ability in that specialized version of Arabic denoted both Arab identity and distance from non-Arab subject peoples, and from less educated Arabic speakers. For that group, skilled speakers of Arabic took precedence over other believers. Those who considered themselves masters of that type of Arabic vigorously patrolled the borders of their group, looking for those whose membership was suspect.[70]

ARAB, "ARAB," OR NON-ARAB?

Two stories from al-Khushanī (d. 971), author of the *Quḍāt Qurṭubah* (*The Judges of Córdoba*), depict the policing of boundaries between Arab and non-Arab. The first tells the story of the head qāḍī (judge) of Córdoba, Mūsā ibn Muḥammad Ibn Ziyād al-Judhāmī, who was appointed by Amīr ʿAbd Allāh (r. 888–912).[71] Mūsā was descended from Syrian Arabs of the Palestinian jund or army division, probably one of the groups that came in with Balj. The amīr appointed him as head of police, then as the judge of the appeals court, then to the high guard, then to the office of chief qāḍī of Córdoba. One of al-Khushanī's witnesses said that he possessed ḥilm (a quality of personal dignity, self-control, and judiciousness), as is shown by his restraint when a boorish petitioner threw a legal document at him (one needs to imagine large heavy documents with seals).[72]

Whatever his good qualities, however, Mūsā made mistakes in his Arabic. One story circulating among the ʿulamāʾ said that Mūsā was well-mannered and urbane, conspicuous in valor and generosity, and dignified, the only problem being that he was ignorant when it came to expressing himself verbally. One witness said he talked one day about observing the whole fast of Ramaḍān, to the day of al-ʿArafāt. He thus made two ugly mistakes; first, he mistakenly believed that there was a day of ʿArafāt in the month of Ramaḍān as there is in the month of pilgrimage (Dhū al-ḥijjah); second, he used the definite article "al" before the word "ʿArafāt."

The remark about Mūsā's incorrect use of the definite article may seem odd at first glance. Native speakers do not normally misuse the definite article. Given that Arabs generally traced genealogy only through the male line, and that Arab men commonly married Iberian women, Mūsā's family, although technically Arab, may have included generations of Romance-speaking relatives. It is also possible that his family were mawālī of the Umayyads who had arrived as part of Balj's army. Still, clientage to the Umayyads usually meant close association with Arabs and inclusion as part of the elite, so it seems unlikely that he did not speak Arabic as one of his languages growing up. Probably the insult means that he did not use proper Classical Arabic in speech, but instead used more colloquial forms. Perhaps the usage that appears in the ḥadīths, which is "yawm ʿArafāt," without the definite article, was a formal usage, and "yawm al-'Arafāt," with the article, was used more informally; both can be found on the Internet today. The passage goes on to say that he made mistakes forming the plural, another indication that he was not familiar with Classical Arabic.

The claim that he did not understand the Islamic calendar is more difficult to interpret. It seems unlikely that a religious scholar would think that months other than Dhū al-ḥijjah (the month of pilgrimage) would have a Day of 'Arafāt. The Day of 'Arafāt is the ninth day of the month and second day of the ḥajj (pilgrimage to Mecca), on which the pilgrims spend the day in prayer on the Plain of 'Arafāt outside of Mecca. For Mūsā to believe that another month could have a Day of Arafāt would be similar to a Christian believing that each month contained a Feast of the Epiphany, not impossible but unlikely in someone with a reputation for expertise in religious law. Further calling the story into question is the fact that according to al-Khushanī, Mūsā himself went on the ḥajj, although it is not clear whether he went before or after his alleged mistake.

Whatever Mūsā in fact said or did not say, the combination of the two accusations is an interesting one, since the story seems to link together ignorance of Arabic and of Islam. In one sentence, he supposedly demonstrated that he did not know Arabic grammar and that he did not understand the basics of the ḥajj, one of Islam's five pillars. The criticisms of him also suggest that even for someone who was Arab or an Umayyad mawlā, ignorance of Classical Arabic precluded full membership in the Cordovan elite.

A similar linkage between knowledge of Arabic and knowledge of Islam appears in another of al-Khushanī's stories.[73] Aslam ibn 'Abd al-'Azīz, an Umayyad mawlā who became chief qāḍī for the first time under 'Abd al-Raḥmān III, made an obliquely insulting remark about a possible candidate for a judgeship, who according to al-Khushanī was of Iberian parentage. While discussing the candidate, Aslam said, "thank God who made me one of those who say 'there is no God but God.'" The main thrust of the statement is that his possible successor was not a legitimate Arabic speaker. The term al-Khushanī uses to denote the ethnicity of the man's ancestors, "'ajam," is a linguistic designation that originally meant people who spoke Persian rather than Arabic;[74] in al-Andalus, it meant speakers of Romance. The phrase in question is also, however, part of the central confession of faith in Islam, the shahādah or witnessing: "There is no God but God and Muḥammad is his prophet." Aslam's criticism implies that the candidate's lack of legitimacy as an Arabic speaker meant that he was not a legitimate Muslim either.

This is perhaps a good place to say more about the definition of the word "mawlā." The term has a variety of uses, and depending on context it can in fact have the opposite meanings of either "patron" or "client."[75] Generally though it denotes the less powerful party in an unequal relationship between two men; women are not characterized as mawālī, although they could be members of mawlā families. In the period of the conquests and of Umayyad rule in the Middle East the term mawlā referred to a non-Arab and had two common meanings: a freedman or a convert to Islam who became a client of an Arab tribe, who then held a relatively low status in the tribe. The category of mawlā probably emerged from systems of patronage practiced in the Roman Middle East.[76] The term's meanings in al-Andalus are varied and not always identical to usages in the east. At the time of ʿAbd al-Raḥmān I, for example, subordinate branches of an Arab tribe could be referred to as the dominant members' mawālī, in the sense of helpers or confederates, or the term could be used simply to designate supporters of the Umayyads who had no explicit ties of clientage.[77] Most commonly in al-Andalus, however, "mawlā" meant either a freedman or the descendant of a convert who had become a client of the Umayyads at the time of the conquest or, occasionally, of another prominent Arab family. The differences between the two types of clientage were immense. A freed slave remained in an inferior position, while descendants of mawālī who had converted and become clients of the Umayyads were important members of the ruling elite. So while the term "mawlā" in the sense of client suggested low status in the east, in al-Andalus it meant membership in the khāṣṣah and honorary Arab identity.

In the Middle East up to the time of the Abbasid Revolution, becoming a client to an Arab tribe was essential for any non-Arab wishing to convert to Islam. Clientage could involve a hijrah, or move from a rural area or a non-Muslim city to a miṣr, or Muslim military base. Being a mawlā gave legal status and protection to a non-Arab, who took on the Arab lineage of his patron. In a society in which protection came from the kin-group, the new convert had left his behind; as a client his adopted Arab tribe was obligated to pay blood money (diyah) should he cause an injury, and the tribe could collect diyah if another tribe injured him. That original protective function was rendered less important over time as conversion became more common, but the tie remained an important one throughout the period of Umayyad rule in the Middle East.

Originally mawālī were regarded with contempt, as members of conquered peoples. In al-Andalus, however, as has been noted, the term as it was applied to a mawlā by conversion denoted high status. Since the Muslim invaders of al-Andalus lived intermixed with the subject population and never established amṣār, and since the majority of invaders were Berbers rather than Arabs, the issue of clientage for all converts never emerged; Iberian converts were muwalladūn, non-Arab Muslims, or ʿajam, non-Arabic speakers, but not mawālī. Individuals like Aslam who claimed clientage ties were almost always referring to ties with the early Umayyads, usually undertaken before 711 or shortly after. Some mawālī were early Iberian converts who were important enough to be taken on as Umayyad clients; others were members of mawlā families who came over with the first invaders, or with Balj's army, which included large numbers of Umayyad clients. The tenth-century scholar and historian Ibn al-Qūṭīyah, for example, claimed descent from the Visigothic royal family and traced his family's clientage with the Umayyads back to the caliph ʿUmar I (r. 634–44).[78] Clientage with the Umayyads gave the client the status of being Arab; whatever the mawlā's literal genealogy, his ancestor took on a new genealogy at the time of conversion and became part of the Arab ruling class.[79] Maribel Fierro has demonstrated that references to mawālī became much less frequent in biographical dictionaries by the twelfth century, suggesting that mawlā families simply came to be classified as Arabs.[80]

Arab identity, however flexibly it was defined, continued to be important into the period of the caliphate, despite the caliphs' claims of Islamic as well as Arab authority. That identity was based on linguistic ability. It was also based on lineage up to a point, but with some flexibility; a family's ties of clientage to the Umayyads and their longstanding identification with Arab culture could trump what we think of as genetic identity. In al-Andalus, Arab and Muslim identity continued to be equated, as they no longer were in Abbasid society. That equating of ethnicity and religion, however, did not exist in any simple way, nor was it unchallenged. Ibn Ḥazm is a good example of someone who struggled with the question of who was part of the community. As author of the *Jamharah ansāb al-ʿArab*, he celebrates the Arab heritage of the Umayyads and their important allies. Even in the *Jamharah*, however, he struggles to reconcile his enthusiasm for sound Arab lineage with his belief that the community of Islam is not ethnically divided. In his religious works, Ibn Ḥazm defines the community without any reference to ethnicity or language as the Islamic ummah, the community of all believers.

3 ✦ Christians and Jews

By the time the caliphate was established in the tenth century, an elite had emerged in al-Andalus made up of Arab Muslims. The "Arab" part of that identity was fluid, however, and could be extended to those who were not Arab in a strictly biological sense. That status of almost-Arabs included those who were from families of longstanding Umayyad clients and muwallads and Berbers who were civil servants, 'ulamā' connected to the court, or adībs of Arabic literature and culture. Other groups had an ambiguous and sometimes troubled relationship with that elite. Because conversion to Islam happened over a period of at least two hundred years, there continued to be, throughout much of the Umayyad period, large numbers of Christians in al-Andalus, as well as a Jewish minority.[1] Although a few non-Muslims, particularly educated Jews, could claim membership in the ruling group, relations of Christians and Jews with the Umayyad regime were at times strained. This chapter will examine the Umayyad elite's relationship with non-Muslims and will compare the official stance toward nonbelievers as derived from scripture, Muslim theology, and Sharī'ah with the actual treatment of Christians and Jews in al-Andalus. I will suggest that relations between the Umayyad regime and Christians were particularly volatile, most notably in the ninth century. That volatility makes sense given that Christians in the ninth century still constituted the largest part of the population that the Umayyads were attempting to rule, and that the Christian community was in transition, undergoing a period of rapid conversion to Islam.

CHRISTIANS AND JEWS IN MUSLIM SCRIPTURE

According to Islamic scripture as it was interpreted in the Middle Ages, people fell into one of three religious categories. On opposite ends of the spectrum were the muslimūn (Muslims), who possessed God's true and complete revelation, and the mushrikūn (polytheists), who were idolaters and therefore beyond hope of salvation if they did not embrace Islam. In the middle were the ahl al-kitāb (People of the Book), whose beliefs and practices gave them the minimal qualifications for salvation: they had a version of scripture, albeit not as complete as the Quran, they were monotheists, and they believed in prophecy and a last judgment. Which religions qualified for membership in the ahl al-kitāb was open to debate, but the Quran and most later authorities recognized Christians and Jews as People of the Book.

The way Muslims regarded the ahl al-kitāb in the period under study can usefully be divided into three levels. There was what could be called Islam's cosmic view of other monotheists and how they fit into God's plan, as reflected in Muslim scripture, religious polemic, and theology; there was the official legal status of Jews and Christians as reflected in Sharīʿah; and finally there was the actual day-to-day, practical treatment of non-Muslims. Islam's cosmic or theological position on People of the Book, particularly outside of the Quran, was the harshest, while both Sharīʿah's evaluation of them and Muslim regimes' daily treatment of them showed more flexibility and tolerance. The status of non-Muslims is clearest in Sharīʿah, which is not surprising given that a major purpose of Islamic law was to define the status of various groups in Muslim society. In some respects, Sharīʿah lumps People of the Book together with others who were outside the dominant group of free Muslim men; women, children, slaves, and non-Muslims all fell into the category of those with diminished legal status. Compared to those other categories, however, the scriptural and theological treatment of non-Muslim monotheists was less consistent, even within a single text, while the actual day-to-day treatment of subordinate groups was subject to the influence of individual personalities and the political climate of the moment.

The ambiguity of Islam's theoretical, scriptural attitude toward non-Muslim monotheists begins with the Quran, which speaks with two voices on the subject of Jews and Christians. Some verses present God's message in universal terms, emphasizing that God sent the same message to Abraham and all of his descendants, that is, to Jews, Christians, and Muslims.[2] Those verses imply a family relationship among all three religions. Q. 2:62 and 5:72 make the strongest statement of that kinship. 2:62 reads:

Those who believe, and those who are Jews,
And the Christians and the Sabians,
Whoever believe in God and the last judgment
And do righteous work
Shall have their reward with their Lord.
They have nothing to fear, or to grieve about.[3]

Here the Quran affirms that it is righteous work and belief in God that make one eligible for salvation, not membership in a particular sect.

The Quran reiterates elsewhere the idea that Jews and Christians can be saved,[4] but other verses condemn the ahl al-kitāb for being unfaithful even to their own revelations,[5] for wishing ill on Muhammad,[6] and for distorting the truth of the scripture God sent them.[7] In those verses, the Quran speaks of Jews and Christians in a second voice, one filled with frustration at those who did not recognize Muḥammad's teachings. Fred Donner addresses the apparent contradictions in the Quran by suggesting that the earliest ummah—Muḥammad's community in Medina, and perhaps the following two generations—included Jews and Christians, as well as ḥanīfs (Arabian monotheists who were not Jews or Christians, most notably Muḥammad himself).[8] The Quranic verses that are more positive toward the ahl al-kitāb reflect this early community-building, in which what counted was being one of the mu'minūn, the believers, in the sense of believing in God, scripture, and the last judgment, and behaving righteously. The term "muslim" referred to anyone who submitted to God's will, not a member of the sectarian group called Islam. In Q. 2:131, for example, God asks Abraham to submit, and Abraham replies, "I submit [that is, I become a submitter or muslim] to the lord of worlds" (aslamtu bi rabb al-'ālamīn). The more negative verses about the ahl al-kitāb, according to Donner, in some cases represent disagreements with specific Jews and Christians, who mocked and rejected Muḥammad and his teachings. Q 2:105, for example, says:

Neither those who have not believed (kafarū)
Among the ahl al-kitāb
Nor the polytheists (mushrikūn)
Wish that there be revealed to you anything good from your lord.
But God will bestow his mercy on whom he pleases,
For God possesses enormous grace.

Here the Quran condemns not all Christians and Jews but those who do not believe, implying that others are believers. In other negative statements, as in the case of verses that denounce Christian belief in the Trinity,[9] the Quran elucidates specific theological differences between the older religions and Muḥammad's new teachings. Donner argues, however, that the most influential verses for early Muslims were those emphasizing community among all the believers, whatever their sectarian identity. The theological differences became more important later, as the conquests proceeded and the conquerors came to define themselves as a distinct religious (and in part ethnic) group; by the time of Caliph 'Abd al-Malik, that identity had become important enough that the interior of the Dome of the Rock is decorated with early versions of Quranic verses denouncing Christians' belief in the Trinity and in Jesus's divinity.

Donner's argument about the Quran also helps explain the attitude of the ḥadīths toward Christians and Jews. Generally they accept and build on the verses that criticize the ahl al-kitāb and try to position Jews and Christians as separate from and inferior to Muslims. While the ḥadīths probably contain material going back to the Medina community, they were not collected until the mid- to late eighth century. Many reflect the concerns of a Muslim minority attempting to rule over large numbers of non-Muslims and to establish its own religious identity as separate from theirs. One story has Muḥammad saying that Jews and Christians would go to hell if they did not accept what he had been sent (the Quran); in other words, they must convert to be saved.[10] In another story Muḥammad explains that the first chapter of the Quran, which says, "Show us the straight path, the way of those you have favored, not those who have aroused (your) anger, and not those who have gone astray," refers to the Jews (those with whom God is angry) and the Christians (those who have gone astray).[11] At their most generous, the ḥadīths depict God as having decided to give some reward to Jews and Christians, but far more to Muslims:

> Narrated 'Abdullah bin 'Umar bin Al-Khattab: Allah's Apostle said, "Your example and the example of Jews and Christians is like the example of a man who employed some laborers to whom he said, 'Who will work for me up to midday for one Qirat each?' The Jews carried out the work for one Qirat each; and then the Christians carried out the work up to the 'Asr prayer for one Qirat each; and now you Muslims are working from the 'Asr prayer up to sunset for two Qirats each. The Jews and Christians got angry and said, 'We work more and are paid less.' The employer (Allah) asked them, 'Have I usurped

some of your right?' They replied in the negative. He said, 'That is My Blessing, I bestow upon whomever I wish.'"[12]

ISLAMIC RELIGIOUS POLEMIC IN THE MIDDLE AGES

Works of religious polemic and theology mostly confirm the more negative view of Christians and Jews, and in fact call into question whether Jews and Christians have any legitimate place in Islamic society. Theories about People of the Book are not uniformly dismissive: the tenth-century philosopher al-Farābī, who also questioned the superiority of Arabic over other languages, wrote that all religions express the same truths and use the same symbols, although finally only philosophy can grasp pure truth. Ṣā'id al-Andalusī (d. 1070) praised the scholarly achievements of non-Muslims in pursuit of truth.[13] Other writers are not so kind and, while they explore theological issues, can best be characterized as polemicists. Their arguments emphasize three points: (1) Islam is true and other religions' inherently silly beliefs are false. Anyone not intent on denying the truth can see these facts plainly. (2) The Quran at times suggest that Torah and the New Testament are valid revelations. Christians and Jews, however, have corrupted their scriptures beyond recognition, so that whatever truth the Bible may have contained initially has been lost. (3) The Torah and the Gospels, while corrupt, have preserved one truth from their original form: they clearly predict the coming of Muḥammad, meaning that Christians and Jews have no excuse for rejecting his status as prophet.

Ibn Ḥazm was the most prolific Muslim religious polemicist in al-Andalus. His *Kitāb al-faṣl fī al-milal wa al-ahwā' wa al-niḥal* (*The Book of the Final Appraisal of the Religious Confessions, Religious Communities, and Sects*)[14] is a formidable combination of religious scholarship and polemic, in which he condemns the many groups he considers to be heretics or unbelievers. Those groups include all non-Muslims and, within Islam, those who did not support the Umayyad caliphate (Shī'īs and Khārijīs), those who use Greek philosophical models in their theology (Mu'tazilīs and Ash'arīs), Sufis, and any Muslim who believes religions other than Islam have value. His condemnation of Jews and Christians is based on the assertion that Islam is the more rational religion, largely because it lacks the illogic of the other two, for example the Gospel authors' insistence on tracing the genealogy of Jesus through Joseph, even though God is supposed to be Jesus's father.[15]

According to Ibn Ḥazm, Jews and Christians should recognize the truth of the Quran mainly because past generations of their fellow believers have corrupted their own scriptures so thoroughly as to render them both unreliable and ridiculous. This argument that the Torah and the Gospels have been subject to distortion, or taḥrīf, goes back at least to the tenth century and cropped up regularly in Muslim polemics thereafter.[16] According to al-Bīrūnī (d. 1048), for example, the fact that there are four versions of the Gospels and three versions of Torah (the Hebrew version, the Septuagint, and the Samaritan Torah) show that Christians and Jews do not possess a stable version of their scripture, as Muslims do with the Quran. Some Muslim polemicists seem to have been aware of the Talmud, which they claim was also filled with distortions.[17]

Ibn Ḥazm demonstrates the principle of taḥrīf by pointing out the errors in Torah and the Gospels. In his view, the main problem with Torah in its present version, aside from the many obvious inconsistencies and errors of fact, is that it violates the principle of the ʿiṣmah or sinlessness of the prophets.[18] Here Ibn Ḥazm is drawing on several assumptions in Islamic theology. One is that the major male figures in the first five books of the Hebrew Bible (or at least the ones that the Quran also recognizes) are all prophets; women can receive what Ibn Ḥazm calls prophetic inspiration or nubūʾah, as when the angel tells Sarah that she will give birth to a son, but have no prophetic mission or risālah.[19] A second assumption is that prophets are by definition people without sin. Finally, the function of scripture is moral instruction, rather than, say, the recording of a people's history or the exploration of human nature. Given those assumptions, the Hebrew Bible's painfully evocative stories of moral failure—Lot's drunkenness and incest with his daughters, Jacob's theft of the blessing intended for Esau—can appear to Ibn Ḥazm as nothing other than a vulgar practical joke played by earlier Jews on their descendants.

The Gospels do not suffer from the introduction of morally questionable material to the same degree that Torah does, but they do contain their own inconsistencies and absurdities. Ibn Ḥazm regards them as easier to refute than Torah. Jews claim that the Torah they have now is God's word as given to Moses, but Christians admit that the Gospels did not come directly from a prophet but were written at different times by four different men. Mistakes and distortions were therefore likely to be built into the original documents rather than being introduced over time as was the case with Torah.[20] Matthew, according to Ibn Ḥazm, was the earliest gospel author and a student of Jesus; he wrote his gospel in Hebrew nine years after Christ's ascension.

Mark and Luke, who Ibn Ḥazm characterizes as disciples of Peter, wrote their gospels more than twenty years after Jesus's ascension, in Greek. John wrote his Gospel in Greek some sixty years after the ascension and also translated Matthew into Greek. There was, Ibn Ḥazm says, originally a true revelation God gave to Jesus, in the same way that God gave Moses the Torah and later would give Muḥammad the Quran.[21] Except for a few verses, however, it was lost during the three-hundred-year persecution of Christianity. There are numerous contradictions between the Gospels, for example, the details of Peter's denial of Jesus, which differ in the four accounts.[22] The Gospels also depict Jesus as lying. Jesus says that he did not come to change a single letter of Torah, yet elsewhere in the gospels he prohibits divorce, which is clearly permitted under Jewish law.[23] Since Jesus was a prophet, it is absurd to say that he was capable of telling a lie, so the text must have been corrupted.

Christians and Jews should be eager to accept Islam because some of the few valid revelations still present in Torah and the Gospels prefigure the coming of Muḥammad. 'Alī ibn Rabbān al-Ṭabarī (d. 867), a convert from Nestorian Christianity, and Ibn Qutaybah (d. 889) claimed that both Jewish and Christian scripture predicted Muḥammad's mission.[24] Ibn Ḥazm quotes extensively from al-Ṭabarī in his *al-Uṣūl wa al-furū'*. The following example[25] from that text is an analysis of Dt. 33.2, which reads:

> He [Moses] said: The Lord came from Sinai, and dawned from Seir upon us; he shone forth from Mount Paran.

Ibn Ḥazm responds by showing that the passage refers to all three Abrahamic religions:

> It is said in the Torah: God's revelation came from Mount Sinai, rose up from Seir and appeared from the mountains of Paran. The coming of God's revelation from Mount Sinai is His revealing the exalted Torah to Moses, son of Amram on Mount Sinai, according to the people of the book and according to us. Similarly, his rising from Seir must mean the revelation of the pure Gospel to Jesus, son of Mary; the Messiah, now, lived in Seir in the land of Galilee in a village called Nazareth; after this name his followers are called naṣārā [Christians, literally Nazarenes]. And as God's rising from Seir must refer to the Messiah, so His rise from the mountains of Paran must indicate the revelation of the Quran to our lord Muhammad. Paran, now, is a mountain near the noble city of Mecca, for it is said in the Torah

> that Abraham settled Hagar and Ishmael in Paran (cf. Gen. 21.21). The Prophet was the one on whom the book was sent down after the Messiah; "to appear" and "to rise up" have the same meaning, namely to ascend and to become manifest, and is there any religion that has manifested itself the way the Islamic religion has?

The passage is typical of Muslim arguments about the prefiguring of Islam in the Bible in that it grants the Christian contention that the Hebrew Bible contains predictions of Christ's coming. If that is the case, the Muslim argument implies, then Christians must in turn recognize that the Bible also predicts the coming of Muḥammad. Since he is the last and the greatest of the prophets, his revelation trumps any preceding revelations, just as Christians claim their own revelation supersedes that of Judaism.

The polemic of Ibn Ḥazm and others raises the question of whether the People of the Book have any legitimate status in God's plan. For Ibn Ḥazm, at least in his polemical works, his answer comes close to being no.[26] He makes his argument by emphasizing the Quran's negative characterization of Christians and Jews, ignoring the more inclusive verses such as 2:262, and by suggesting that the extent of corruption to which Jews and Christians have subjected their scriptures have rendered those texts without value. In addition, and despite the distortions, earlier scriptures gave plenty of clues as to Muḥammad's identity.

Ibn Ḥazm also dismisses the idea that Jews and Muslims can be believers mu'minūn), that is possessors of faith (īmān), in the section of the *Faṣl* subtitled "The Book of Faith," or "Kitāb al-īmān."[27] His argument is that faith is made up of three parts: belief in the heart (taṣdīq), verbal profession (iqrār), and physical works such as prayer and fasting (a'māl). He rejects the idea that Christians and Jews can be said to have īmān just because they believe in certain truths, like the existence of God or the last judgment. Since they do not follow the physical practices laid out in Islamic law—praying correctly, fasting in Ramaḍān, pilgrimage to Mecca, reciting the Quran—they do not have īmān. Satan himself believes in God but does not have īmān, because he did not perform the work ordered by God. The Quran tells us that God ordered him to bow down to Adam, and he refused.[28] The only correct path to follow is the way of Muḥammad, in all its details. It is not enough to get a few things right, as do the Christians and Jews who recognize the divine mission of Moses or the unity of God, but ignore the rest of Islamic teachings.

Ibn Ḥazm perhaps imagined part of his audience as non-Muslims whose religious beliefs he wanted to refute; he may for example have engaged in religious disputation with Samuel Ibn al-Naghrīlah, a Jew who also grew up in Córdoba and became an important military leader administrator for the Berber regime in Granada after the fall of the Umayyads.[29] His primary target however appears to be other Muslims who regarded Christianity, Judaism, and Islam as more or less similar religions. In that more ecumenical view, all three shared a common set of moral norms that were based on natural law, that is, on an inborn moral compass given by God to all human beings. Those norms could therefore be defended and understood according to the principles of reason. The details of religious ritual were less important, since rituals were arbitrary and not based on natural law, and therefore not subject to rational analysis. Ibn Ḥazm responds by emphasizing just such rituals—what he calls works of the body—as absolutely integral to faith, not as a secondary matter, and denies any role for natural law in religion; human beings receive both moral and ritual precepts through scripture alone, not through reason. By emphasizing the importance of practice he undercuts the basis for regarding the three religions as similar and asserts the particular truth of Islam. He also rejects any claim to equality among the three religions, putting Christians and Jews firmly in their place as inferior and subordinate groups. It is in fact difficult to find in his polemical works any justification for the legally protected status of those religions. The "kitāb al-īmān" equates the word kāfir (unbeliever, a general term for non-Muslims) with the word mushrik, a pagan or idolater.[30] Ibn Ḥazm is not the only Muslim polemicist to use those words interchangeably; Gerald Hawting has suggested that even the Quran employs "mushrik" as a kind of metaphor in its polemic against Christians and Jews, meaning not that they literally worship idols or multiple gods but that their beliefs are as bad as idolatry.[31] Nevertheless, Ibn Ḥazm clearly intends to question whether People of the Book can have any legitimate standing under Islam.

CHRISTIANS AND JEWS IN SHARĪʿAH

Islamic law, which determines the status of subject religious groups, defines the place of Jews and Christians quite differently from the polemicists. Monotheists living in the dār al-islām were, until the modern period, classified as dhimmīs, or protected persons.[32] Sharīʿah regulations pertaining to dhimmīs gave them a place within Islamic society that was both secure and second class. The exchange upon which the dhimmah, or covenant of protection, was based was tribute in exchange for safety and limited autonomy.

Dhimmīs paid a poll tax, the jizyah, which was not required of Muslims. In return, the Muslim authorities guaranteed the safety of non-Muslim monotheists in their homes and possessions, allowed them to keep their religion, and gave each religious community latitude to run its own affairs. Education, internal legal matters, personal status law pertaining to issues such as marriage and inheritance, and questions of religious practice were all left to dhimmī communities to oversee, provided the community's actions did not impinge on the privileges of Muslims or pose a threat to public order. Dhimmīs were also required to identify themselves as non-Muslims by wearing distinctive dress and to acknowledge their inferior status in various ways: they were to conduct their religious services discretely and quietly, to refrain from building new churches and synagogues (although old ones could be repaired), and to give the right-of-way to Muslims when passing them in narrow streets. They were also barred from holding positions of authority over Muslims, and they could not bear arms. Finally, male dhimmīs were forbidden to marry Muslim women, although Muslim men could marry dhimmī women.[33]

Modern scholars have debated whether one can characterize the classical Muslim treatment of dhimmīs as religious toleration.[34] Often such debates are tied up with modern issues of relationships between the Islamic world and Israel, or Islam and the West.[35] Looked at in the context of the premodern world, however, dhimmī regulations were nothing out of the ordinary. The areas conquered by Muslim invaders all had law codes recognizing differing levels of privileges and obligations for various social groups, or, to put it another way, they assigned differing levels of membership in society. Sharī'ah, although it was in some ways more egalitarian than many laws of the time—it did not for example recognize any privileged legal status commensurate with that of European nobles—gave full rights only to adult, free, Muslim men, and imposed disabilities, often couched in terms of the need to offer protection, on women, slaves, and non-Muslims. From the perspective of modern liberal thought, which rejects the notion of differing legal statuses among adults, dhimmī regulations are not truly tolerant. Compared with the position of Jews in premodern Christendom, on the other hand, the treatment of Jews and Christians in Islamic lands looks rather better. While they were not equals with Muslims, Jews and Christians enjoyed protection and a clearly defined legal status. Jews in Christian Europe had no fixed legal position, no comfortable place in the ideology of Christendom.[36] They were therefore more subject to random violence and the whims of rulers.

It is surprisingly difficult to work out how and when Muslim regulations for subject religious groups developed. The initial conquests after Muḥammad's death brought Arabs into contact with Sasanian and Byzantine law, which were important sources of influence. By the late sixth century, the Sasanian government, while promoting Zoroastrianism as the state religion, allowed Jews, Nestorian Christians, and Monophysite Christians to function as largely autonomous communities; each group was subject to its own religious law and paid a poll tax, supposedly in exchange for military protection.[37] Byzantine law as it pertained to the empire's Jewish minority also helped shape the concept of the dhimmah.[38] By the time of Justinian, Jews suffered legal disabilities but were still entitled to protection under the law; pagans and those the emperor deemed heretics, by contrast, were not. Synagogues were protected by imperial authority, Jewish courts were given recognition for internal legal affairs, and Jews retained the right to follow their religion and perform all relevant rituals, including circumcision and the celebration of religious holidays. All civil and military positions of authority were however closed to Jews. They could not preach their religion to non-Jews or circumcise anyone not born Jewish, were forbidden to own Christian slaves, and could not build new synagogues; old ones could however be repaired. Marriage between Christians and Jews was prohibited under Justinian's code,[39] although it is possible that only marriages between Jewish men and Christian women were prosecuted.[40] Dhimmī regulations borrowed in obvious ways from these earlier models.

The earliest systematic treatment of dhimmī law in Islam is Ibn Qayyim al-Jawzīyah's *Aḥkām ahl al-dhimma* from the fourteenth century.[41] Before then we have only limited written Islamic sources. The Quran and ḥadīths—although the Quran in particular contains extensive material about the theological place of Christians and Jews—make only occasional references to specific rules regulating relationships with dhimmīs. The canonical ḥadīth collections, which divide ḥadīths by subjects such as marriage, divorce, prayer, fasting, and pilgrimage, do not contain sections devoted specifically to non-Muslims. The four Sunni Islamic madhhabs, founded in the late eighth century by the jurists al-Shāfiʿī, Abū Hanīfah, Ibn Ḥanbal, and Mālik, respectively, offer scattered references to dhimmīs but no unified code. Compared to many other parts of Sharīʿah, dhimmī regulations developed from a limited scriptural basis and in response to the local laws and customs of the conquered territories.

Diplomatic documents do give some information about the early treatment of non-Muslims. Although most probably come from the postconquest period, they may contain seventh- and early eighth-century material.

The Covenant of ʿUmar purports to date from the period of Caliph ʿUmar I (r. 634–44), and elements of it probably do go back to that time. The Covenant shares characteristics with other capitulation agreements purporting to be from that early period; like a number of other documents, for example, the Covenant prohibits the subject people from sheltering enemies of the Muslims, and it enjoins them to pay tribute and to quarter and feed Muslims for three days.[42] It also states that non-Muslims may not imitate the dress of Muslims, a regulation intended to support the distinctive status of the conquerors.[43] It seems likely, however, that the full document dates from considerably later than the time of ʿUmar, and that many of the details of the text reflect a gradual working out of the rules.[44] Versions of other capitulation agreements come from ninth-century historians but may also contain earlier material.[45] Those agreements invoke the rules of the classical dhimmah contract only on occasion—many, for example, do not mention jizyah—and, like the Pact of ʿUmar, seem more concerned with promises from the subject population to help equip and quarter Muslim troops. While such early agreements certainly influenced later law pertaining to dhimmīs, it is clear that the classical rules of the dhimmah evolved only gradually, and that early practice was inconsistent. Even the basic transaction of the dhimmah—non-Muslims pay tribute in exchange for protection—was not consistently enforced. At the time of ʿUmar I, it was unclear whether Christian Arabs should pay jizyah or be exempt because of their ethnic identity, suggesting that the question of whether one's legal standing was based on religion or ethnicity was still to be determined.[46] Even by the time of Umar II (r. 717–20), the status of converts was unclear, and many non-Arab converts to Islam still paid jizyah.[47]

Al-Andalus, unlike most Muslim lands, did not go directly from imperial to Muslim control, but was ruled by the Visigoths at the time of the conquest. Germanic law, however, does not appear to have had a direct impact on the treatment of dhimmīs. Visigothic and Frankish law adapted some Roman laws concerning Jews that also found their way into dhimmī regulations.[48] In Frankish Gaul, building new synagogues was prohibited, and Jews were not allowed to proselytize. They could generally not own Christian slaves, although that regulation varied by time and place. Intermarriage was forbidden. Jews were banned from any office in which they would hold authority over Christians. More than Roman law, however, Germanic law focused on maintaining boundaries between Jews and Christians. Christians could not eat with Jews and were not to celebrate the Jewish Sabbath or work on Sundays. Christians could not associate with Jews during Holy

Week. The regulations against mixing suggest that Jews and Christians were in fact in regular social contact, and that Church and royal authorities feared the influence of Judaism as a threat to Christian orthodoxy.

Visigothic law contained many of the same features, including the prohibition against intermarriage,[49] but added regulations that were far more hostile toward Jews than those of the Frankish system. At various times Visigothic law prohibited basic Jewish observations such as circumcision, celebrating Passover, or separating meat and dairy products. Starting with King Sisebut (r. 612–21), the Visigothic monarchy also periodically ordered that all Jews either convert to Christianity or be expelled from the kingdom.

It is not clear why the Visigoths, in contrast to the Franks and other Germanic groups, were so hostile to Jews. Various theories have been put forward, some emphasizing the monarchy's political and economic motives.[50] For whatever reason, a key aspect of Visigothic ideology, particularly after the Visigothic leaders converted from Arianism to Catholicism and developed a strong alliance with the Catholic Church, was the building of a purely Christian society, making the Visigoths ahead of their time in their vision of a pure Christendom and their willingness to persecute Jews to get it. Also impossible to know is how much influence their laws actually had, or to what extent they represented the views of the subject population, particularly in Spain's Romanized cities.[51] In a premodern society in which rulers had limited influence, it is uncertain how a rule like the prohibition against separating meat and dairy could be enforced. The Inquisition in late medieval Spain could enforce such regulations for Jewish converts to Christianity only through a haphazard system of neighbors informing on each other, but there is no evidence of even such an imperfect mechanism at work in the early Middle Ages. Like much early medieval law, Visigothic anti-Jewish legislation can perhaps best be seen as the regime's mission statement rather than as a reflection of reality. In any event, the legislation does not appear to have had any influence on rules for dhimmīs in al-Andalus.

Rules regulating marriage among dhimmīs and between dhimmīs and Muslims provide an exception to the lack of early sources for dhimmī regulations. Marriage regulations will be covered in some detail in chapter 4, but it should be noted in the current context that legal opinions regarding dhimmī marriages and interfaith marriages are numerous in the early work of all four madhhabs and, like all dhimmī regulations, give Jews and Christians limited autonomy while emphasizing the superiority of Muslims.[52] All of the founding jurists except for Mālik recognize the legitimacy of Christian and Jewish marriages; Mālik classifies them as a form of concubinage, but one the Muslim state should tolerate.[53] All four madhhabs allow a Muslim man to marry a dhimmī woman and to sleep with Christian or Jewish slave women, but they strictly prohibit a dhimmī man from marrying a Muslim woman (and since dhimmīs cannot keep Muslim slaves, the opportunity for a dhimmī male to sleep with a female Muslim slave should never arise). These rules are perhaps connected with Arab ideas of female endogamy—we marry your women but do not give you ours—but also represents the power gradient in a male-centered society in which women are in part commodities: men in the dominant group have sexual access to the women of subordinate groups, but not the other way around.[54]

Outside of rules concerning marriage, which appear in the foundational legal works, there is no early set of texts one can look to as a model for the dhimmah, with the exception of Roman and Sasanian law codes. Whether or not the conquerors had direct access to those codes, one can imagine that in Byzantine and Sasanian areas the religious leaders who negotiated with the conquerors, and then became mediators between their communities and the Muslim rulers, taught them how to treat embedded religious communities according to preconquest practices.[55] That process, along with the scattered references to non-Muslims in the Quran, ḥadīths, and early works of jurisprudence, formed the basis of the classical system. Al-Andalus imported that system from the East, without original contributions to dhimmī regulations from the Visigothic codes.

CHRISTIANS AND JEWS: THE PRACTICAL REALITY

The actual experience of Christians and Jews in al-Andalus bore some relationship to the legal and theological place of dhimmīs in Islamic society, but only up to a point. Although many parts of Islamic law came to have practical influence on the lives of Muslims in al-Andalus, for example in the area of inheritance and property rights for women, dhimmī law in al-Andalus and indeed throughout the Muslim world always remained a statement of Muslim society's ideals rather than a reflection of its realities. Particularly before the majority of the population converted to Islam, the question of Muslim society's relationship with non-Muslims in the population was obviously of great importance. Treatment of dhimmīs, however, was inconsistent, and Sharīʿah regulations were imposed unevenly. Some were almost never enforced. It was for example common before the modern period for non-Muslims to serve in Islamic governments, despite the supposed prohibition against dhimmīs having power over Muslims. Other rules, like those pertaining to dress, were upheld only occasionally; some devout Christians in ninth-century Córdoba criticized Christians who dressed like Muslims, suggesting that dhimmīs did not consistently follow the rules.[56] Only the collection of jizyah and the prohibition against a non-Muslim man marrying a Muslim woman seem to have been regularly enforced.

The evidence from al-Andalus, such as it is, bears out that pattern of inconsistent enforcement. Sources for the treatment of non-Muslims in al-Andalus present problems, first because they are limited and second because the type of available information about Christians is different from that for Jews. The evidence concerning Jews is largely biographical and consists of examples of Jews who became prominent in government, the military, and as scholars. Information about prominent individual Christians is also available, but there is additional evidence for the broader Christian community, at least in and around Córdoba, that does not exist for Jews. The years for which we have information about Jews and Christians during the Umayyad period are also different; most evidence for Christians pertains to the ninth century, while Jews appear in the sources as socially prominent figures only beginning in the second half of the tenth century. Those differences in the type and the chronology of sources for the two groups make it difficult to compare their treatment.

The way information about Jews and Christians is distributed is partly a matter of which sources happened to survive. The distribution does however make some sense if one looks at the social history of al-Andalus. At the time of the conquest, Christians formed the bulk of the subject population. It is natural, therefore, that they feature in sources pertaining to the ninth century, when the Umayyads were still establishing power over their territory. There is by contrast very limited evidence of large Christian communities by the end of the eleventh century. That lack of evidence by itself is not meaningful, but taken in combination with Bulliet's theory about conversion rates and the evidence for emigration of Christians to the Christian kingdoms in the north, there are grounds to believe that the Christian population was greatly diminished by the 1000s,[57] with the exception of the area around Toledo.[58] While there are stories of prominent Christians at the court of the ninth-century Umayyads, there are fewer for the period of the late Umayyads or of the Taifa kingdoms. Jews, however, as a minority population, were not under as much pressure to convert, and Spanish Christian kingdoms did not invite them to immigrate. They continued as a distinct group through the late Umayyad and the Taifa periods. For reasons that will be explored presently, they were connected to the Muslim scholarly community and thus took part in the cultural flourishing of the tenth and eleventh centuries.

Let us look now in more detail at the surviving evidence for dhimmīs in al-Andalus. As usual, we have limited information for the eighth century, but the sources do consistently suggest that most of the Iberian Peninsula submitted to the Muslim armies and agreed to capitulation treaties similar to those employed in the Middle East; the pact (ʿahd) with Tudmir, for example, called for its inhabitants to pay tribute and to refrain from aiding enemies of the Muslims, in exchange for which the Muslims would protect their lives and property and allow them to keep their religion.[59] By the ninth century the Umayyads had developed an administrative structure for the Christian community—that is, for the vast majority of their subjects—that included a number of officials, such as the Count (qūmis) who oversaw the region, the head judge (qāḍī al-ʿajam), and various tax collectors.[60] All were probably appointed by the Muslim ruler, with varying degrees of consent from the community. Bishops were also appointed by, or at least with the consent of, the ruler and were responsible for ensuring the good behavior of Christians under their jurisdiction.

References in the sources to ninth-century Christian officials usually present them as controversial among the Muslim population, the Christian population, or both. The Christian Count Rabīʿ ibn Theodolfo served as chief of the personal guard of Amīr al-Ḥakam I (r. 796–822) and was also in charge of tax collection in Córdoba.[61] Rabīʿ was unpopular with Christians and Muslims alike, and his prominent role in the amīr's regime, in addition to al-Ḥakam's violent suppression of dissent, fueled a major revolt in one of the Cordovan suburbs. Al-Ḥakam responded by killing large numbers of the rebels (Muslims and Christians), then destroying the suburb and exiling its inhabitants. He also eventually had Rabīʿ crucified as a concession to the protesters.

Christian officials continued to be controversial figures later in the century. Samson, abbot of the monastery of Pinna Melaria, describes a number of such officials active around the middle of the ninth century in his *Apologeticus*.[62] As the title suggests, Samson's work is a polemical one, written specifically to condemn Christians who worked for the Muslim government. It is an important source for the activities of Christians within the Umayyad administration. Samson had at one time been associated with the court himself and had translated letters from the amīr to the king of France from Arabic to Latin, a type of job commonly entrusted to bilingual Christians.[63] Samson was however accused of passing military secrets to the Franks and was dismissed from court. At or near the same time he was accused of blasphemy by a fellow Christian, Bishop Hostegesis of Malaga, and was brought up on charges before a Church council in 862. Samson characterizes Hostegesis as a close associate of the Umayyads. Not surprisingly, given the bishop's accusations against him, and Samson's forced exile from government service, he devotes considerable space in the *Apologeticus* to denouncing Hostegesis and other Christians he sees as too closely connected with the Muslim court. He treats Hostegesis as a collaborator with an enemy occupying force, saying that the bishop took a census of Christians in his diocese and turned them over to the court to be used as tax rolls, and on one occasion missed vespers because he was waiting to meet with an important courtier of the amīr. Although Samson treats both these pieces of information as outrages, collecting tax information and waiting on the pleasure of important administrators were doubtless normal activities for a bishop under Islamic rule.

Three relatives of Hostegesis were also figures at court: his father, Avurnus, who had converted to Islam; an unnamed uncle who was a former bishop of Granada; and Servandus, a relative of Hostegesis by marriage. Samson accuses them, as well as other Christian or recent converts to Islam at court, of various immoral deeds, including stealing from the Christian community, constant drunkenness, and engaging in sexual relations with the palace eunuchs. Looking beyond Samson's overwrought polemical tone, we see in Hostegesis and his relatives a family that had gravitated toward government service and become assimilated to the urbane, or corrupt (depending on one's point of view), culture of ninth-century Islamic courts.[64] Such families of civil servants, Christians or recent converts to Islam, were also fixtures of the Abbasid administration in the East, for example the Nestorian Christian Banū Jarrah family.[65] Whether or not Hostegesis's relatives actually had sex with eunuchs, Samson's accusation is a way of saying that they were part of an elite court culture that he had turned against.

Another family of civil servants was headed up by the Christian scribe Qūmis ibn Antonian ibn Julian,[66] whose son ʿUmar and nephew ʿAbd Allāh also went into government service. Ibn Antonian was an important figure at court under the rule of Muḥammad I (r. 852–86) and was known for his eloquence in both Arabic and Latin, skills that allowed him to write diplomatic letters for the government. He had the distinction of being the first important administrator to take Sunday off from work, so that he could go to church, and under his influence it became common for civil servants of all religions to take that day off.[67] After the death of ʿAbd Allāh ibn Umayyah ibn Yazīd, who was head secretary of the civil service,[68] the amīr said that if only Ibn Antonian were a Muslim, he would want no one else to replace ʿAbd Allāh. When Ibn Antonian heard what Muḥammad said, he converted and became head secretary.

Many people were offended by his advancement, particularly the powerful administrator and military leader Hāshim ibn ʿAbd al-ʿAzīz.[69] Hāshim, who prided himself on his heritage as a mawlā of the Umayyads, disliked the idea of a dhimmī or muwallad outranking Arabs; the term he uses for those more deserving men is "rijāl al-ajnād," literally "men of the armies," by which he meant men from Arab and mawālī families who were officially registered in the dīwān system. He and others accused Ibn Antonian of fabricating his conversion to Islam while continuing to live as a Christian—a charge amounting to apostasy, which was punishable by death—and of various other crimes. The constant hounding may have contributed to Ibn Antonian's death soon after his promotion. After Ibn Antonian died, Hāshim found witnesses to testify before the qāḍī that he had died a Christian and that his property should go to the state treasury rather than to his family, since an apostate cannot transmit property.[70] The qāḍī, however, ruled that there was no evidence to support Hāshim's claim and allowed Ibn Antonian's family to inherit his estate. His heirs, who are not specified, would also have had to be Muslims to inherit,[71] suggesting that at least some members of Ibn Antonian's family also converted when he did, or before. His son's name, ʿUmar, is clearly Muslim.

The stories of Ibn Antonian and of the courtiers Abbot Samson describes, some of whom had decidedly uncomfortable relations with the Christian community, their Muslim colleagues and superiors, or both, took place in the context of a mid-ninth-century Christian protest movement against Muslim rule, sometimes called the voluntary martyrs' movement.[72] Between 850 and 859, Sharīʿah courts in Córdoba ordered the execution of forty-eight Christian men and women, mostly on the charge that they made insulting remarks about Islam or the Prophet Muḥammad. Some, in spite of their hostility to Islam, had in the past been connected with the Umayyad court. A handful were executed for apostasy because they were children of one or more Muslim parent (usually a Muslim father and Christian mother), making them legally Muslim, yet claimed publically that they were Christian. Such families probably reflect the fact that Christians were beginning to convert to Islam in increasing numbers, but that male converts still married within their former community. The martyrs actively sought execution, often by walking into a mosque and denouncing Muḥammad as a false prophet or adulterer. Those who had a Muslim father had only to make a public declaration of their Christianity, or attend church openly, to draw charges of apostasy.

Since I have written about this movement elsewhere I will not go into detail about it here, but a few points will help clarify the position of ninth-century Christians in the civil service. The martyrs' movement was a small movement that mostly represented the interests of a particular group of clergy, and of men and women who lived at or were associated with Cordovan monasteries. They saw Muslim rule as a profound crisis for Christianity, something to be vigorously resisted rather than accommodated. Some scholars have overestimated the martyrs' importance; Simonet, for example, took them as evidence of broad Christian resistance to Muslim rule, while in fact most Christians seem to have regarded the martyrs as dangerous troublemakers who were undermining relations with the Muslim authorities. Although the movement was small, and strongly associated with local monasteries, it drew in people with ties to Muslims. As we have seen, Abbot Samson, who was an advocate of the martyrs, at one point worked for the Umayyad administration. The martyrs included a member of the amīr's guard and a former *exceptor rei publicae*, or tax collector, in charge of taxation of Christians.[73] The priest Eulogius, the leader and main chronicler of the movement, had Muslim friends at court.[74] Other martyrs came from Muslim or partially Muslim families and were often denounced to the authorities as apostates by their own relatives.

Despite the limited support the movement received from Christians, it disrupted the Christian community as well as relations between Christians and the Umayyad state. Christians were divided between the minority who defended the martyrs and the majority who opposed them, and, among Christian leaders, between the martyrs' supporters and those who continued to work for the Umayyads. Samson's *Apologeticus* is evidence of how deeply some of those hostilities ran. The Muslim authorities saw the movement as a serious threat, perhaps because it involved some former officials, and because it uncovered the instability of families in the process of conversion. People who are willing to die to make a point are, under any circumstances, unsettling. Muḥammad I retaliated by arresting clerics, including the bishop of Córdoba, whom he regarded as responsible for the behavior of his community, dismissing Christians (but not Jews) from administrative posts, and destroying churches and monasteries built since the Muslim invasion.[75] The latter two measures were required by Sharīʿah anyway but were not common practice. The execution of fewer than fifty people over the course of nine years does not constitute a mass movement. The movement did however inspire Muslim distrust of Christians; Ibn Antonian, despite his high rank, ultimately fell victim to the Muslim suspicion of Christians and of converts that the movement provoked. Mikel de Epalza argues that the decline of the Christian Church in much of al-Andalus had to do less with the phenomenon of active conversion to Islam than with the Muslim government's lack of interest in establishing and maintaining enough bishoprics to keep the Church running.[76] The martyrs' movement was probably a factor in that decline in government support.

According to the *Vita Johannis Abbatis Gorziensis*, both Christians and Jews were still working for the Umayyads when John arrived in Córdoba in 953 as an envoy from Otto I of Germany to ʿAbd al-Raḥmān III. John's mission was to deliver certain letters to the caliph, but there was concern among administrators at the palace that the letters contained material that would offend the caliph, including denunciations of Islam;[77] ʿAbd al-Raḥmān had apparently made insulting remarks about Christianity in letters to Otto I, and Otto was now settling the score. Jewish and Muslim civil servants visited John and his delegation to brief them on local customs, and also to talk John out of delivering the potentially inflammatory letters.[78] John, Bishop of Córdoba, told John of Gorze that if the letters angered the caliph, he might retaliate against Christians under his rule. John of Gorze, who according to his biographer came to Córdoba specifically to be martyred,[79] was unimpressed and refused to give up the letters. He berated Bishop John for being lukewarm in his faith, particularly because he was circumcised and followed Islamic food laws.[80] Bishop John explained that Christians had to make compromises to survive. Finally the caliph decided to send an ambassador to Otto I asking him to withdraw the letters. The ambassador was Recemundus, a Christian civil servant fluent in Arabic and Latin.[81] In exchange for various gifts from the caliph, including the bishopric of Granada, Recemundus agreed to take on the assignment, and succeeded in convincing Otto I to instruct John not to deliver the letters. John's mission having been discharged, he and his entourage were feted at the palace and sent back to Germany.

In addition to the information John's biographer offers, there are a few records about Christians for the tenth century. Sources tell us of a handful of tenth-century Christians executed under similar circumstances to those of the ninth-century martyrs of Córdoba. The head qāḍī of Córdoba questioned a Christian in 920 who was guilty of denouncing Islam and probably ordered his execution.[82] A Christian inscription refers to the martyrdom of a woman named Eugenia in 923.[83] A Christian named Vulfura, along with another woman named Argentea, who was probably the daughter of the muwallad rebel ʿUmar Ibn Ḥafṣūn, were executed in 931.[84] We also know that the ḥājib (chamberlain) al-Manṣūr, who ruled as a regent for the Umayyads during the last part of the tenth century, used Christians in his army and paid them well;[85] the army by this time was made up of slave troops and mercenaries rather than Arabs and their clients. The picture these limited sources offer is of a continuing Christian presence in the administration; Recemundus had a lengthy career at court and went on to be an ambassador to the Byzantine Empire. It appears though that tensions also continued. The churchmen and administrators who met with John of Gorze may have exaggerated the threat John's letters posed to Cordovan Christians; at one point John was told that the entire Christian community might be killed if ʿAbd al-Raḥmān read the letters, a claim that would have appeared far-fetched to anyone familiar with the dhimmī system or with the nature of the Umayyads' tax base. Still, the issuance of the threat and the occasional flair-up of martyrdoms suggest that harmony did not always prevail.

For the Jewish community as a whole in the Umayyad period we have even less information available than for Christians. The sources do however give a picture of several Jewish administrators and scholars who became part of the Umayyad elite.[86] While much of what is known as the Golden Age of Jewish letters in Iberia happened after the Umayyad period, in the later eleventh and twelfth centuries, its origins go back to the tenth and early eleventh century. The Jewish administrator Ḥasday ibn Shapruṭ (915–70) served under ʿAbd al-Raḥmān III as the Umayyad-appointed head of the Jewish community, as a court physician, and as a diplomat, undertaking missions to the Byzantine Empire and Christian Spain. He also, with the help of Greek-speaking scholars from the Byzantine Empire and Sicily, translated a major Greek medical work, the *De materia medica* of Dioscorides, into Arabic.

A devotee of Hebrew letters as well as Arabic, Ḥasday became patron to the poet Dūnash ibn Labrāṭ (920–90). Dūnash was among the earliest of the Jewish poets in al-Andalus (to which he came from Baghdad by way of North Africa) to write secular poetry in Hebrew; Jews in both Muslim and Christian lands had a long tradition of writing religious poems, or piyyuṭim, in Hebrew, but Hebrew was not widely used for poetry that did not have a religious theme. Dūnash also introduced elements from Arabic poetry into his own Hebrew compositions. For example, he appropriated the muwashshaḥah, a form of poetry normally written in Classical Arabic, and adapted it to Hebrew.[87] An important Jewish literary figure at the end of the Umayyad period and the beginning of the Taifa kingdoms was Samuel Ibn Naghrīlah (993–1056), mentioned above, who became head of administration and a military leader under the Taifa king of Granada. In addition to being a key administrator, he was a scholar, writing Hebrew poetry, a Hebrew lexicon, various religious commentaries, and religious polemic. Later well-known Jewish scholars in al-Andalus included the courtier and poet Solomon Ibn Gabirol (1021–53 or 1058); the poet and scholar of Hebrew and Arabic poetics Moses ibn Ezra (ca. 1055–1138); the poet, philosopher, and physician Judah ha-Levi (ca. 1065–1141); and, of course, Maimonides (ca. 1137–1204).

Two observations can be made about the tradition of Jewish scholarship and government service going back to Ḥasday ibn Shaprūṭ and Dūnash ibn Labrāṭ. The presence of Jewish courtiers confirms what we know from the *Vita Johannis Gorziensis*: that Jews as well as Christians held positions in Umayyad administration, and that they could serve important roles as civil servants and diplomats, as we see in the cases of Ḥasday and Recemundus. In other ways, though, the experience of Jews and Christians at the Umayyad court diverged from one another in the ninth century. Jews in al-Andalus developed a bilingual, Arabic and Hebrew, literary culture that both maintained Jewish cultural distinctiveness and incorporated the traditions of Classical Arabic, making educated Jews part of the dominant culture defined by Arabic literacy. In contrast, there is no evidence that Christians developed anything like that hybrid literary culture.

Hebrew ceased to be a common vernacular language in the second century CE, when Aramaic became the dominant spoken language among Jews in the Middle East.[88] Biblical Hebrew, however, and a modified Second Temple version of it, known as Rabbinic or Mishnaic Hebrew (in recognition of the fact that the oral law or Mishnah was eventually committed to writing in this type of Hebrew), were still used in Jewish education. After the Muslim invasions, Jews continued to use various styles of Hebrew, some more similar to Biblical Hebrew and some to Rabbinic Hebrew, for writing; merchants and other travelers may also have used Hebrew as a common spoken language.[89] Jewish education throughout Islamic and Christian lands probably followed a pattern established in the late ancient world. Boys were taught basic religious practices and Hebrew prayers at home. Around age four to six they began school, learning Biblical Hebrew and reading the Bible. At age ten they began studying Mishnah, then Talmud at age thirteen. At fifteen boys either left school or began study in an advanced academy or Yeshiva; a Yeshiva was most likely established in Córdoba in the tenth century.[90] In the years after the conquests, Jews in Islamic lands developed a pattern of using both Hebrew and Arabic as written languages. Sa'adiyah ben Yosef, for example (892–942), who was Gaon or head of a Talmudic academy in Iraq, used a modified form of Biblical Hebrew for religious poetry, while writing philosophical treatises in Arabic.[91]

It was in al-Andalus, however, that a multilingual Jewish culture really flourished, beginning in the tenth century. In al-Andalus, advanced study for Jews also included the study of Arabic language, and of philosophy and science written in Arabic. Elaine Miller describes the Jewish community of al-Andalus as displaying multiglossia,[92] a variant of the more common term "diglossia." Generally "diglossia" describes language patterns among groups who use a high version of a language for writing and for speaking in formal settings and a low (in terms of the social prestige it carries) version of the same language for day-to-day speech; I used "diglossia" in chapter 2 in connection with Arabic speakers who switch between Classical and colloquial depending on the circumstances. The linguistic situation of Jews in al-Andalus was however more complicated than diglossia. Jews used a variety of languages as "high," namely Biblical Hebrew, Rabbinic Hebrew, and Middle Arabic. Colloquial Arabic and Romance were the "low" or spoken languages. Their use of high languages was mostly determined by genre. Poetry, both secular and religious, was in Hebrew. Scriptural exegesis also employed Hebrew. Prose works on philosophy, science, theology, and even works on Hebrew linguistics and grammar were in Arabic, although there were exceptions; some tenth-century works on Hebrew grammar were written in Hebrew, while Maimonides wrote his *Mishnah Torah* in Rabbinic Hebrew.[93]

Norman Roth and others have characterized the revival of Hebrew in al-Andalus as a response to the Muslim elevation of Arabic as an ideal literary language and a marker of social status. And in fact the rejection among Jewish poets of Rabbinic in favor of Biblical Hebrew, the Jewish parallel to Classical Arabic, as well as the intense interest in establishing a grammar and linguistics of Hebrew suggest an attempt to build a high literary cultural parallel to but independent of Classical Arabic and Arab identity. Samuel Ibn Naghrīlah emphasized his illustrious descent from the Levites, while a character in one of Judah ha-Levi's works (written in the twelfth century, well after the Umayyad period) described Hebrew as the best of languages, although somewhat deteriorated on account of the Jews' exile, and as the original language of Adam and Eve.[94] Both claims seem to be responses to assertions of Arab linguistic and genealogical superiority. On the other hand, some parts of this Jewish literary flowering can be best described as appropriations of Arabic high culture rather than a challenge to it. It is true that Jews never adopted the ornate language of Classical Arabic, instead writing their poetry in Hebrew and their prose in Middle Arabic. Their secular Hebrew poetry, however, employed Arabic verse forms, and their scientific and philosophic scholarship was written in Arabic and was influenced by Arabic sources. The result was a new Jewish high culture in al-Andalus that was in some ways independent of the dominant Arab-Islamic culture but in other ways firmly tied to it.

By the tenth century Jews had begun to develop a place at the Umayyad court that would over time make them a more integral part of the Muslim court and administration than Christians ever were. Jewish administrators in the late Umayyad and Taifa periods continued to suffer from the same insecurities all dhimmī civil servants were subject to, since their positions of authority were finally not legitimate under Sharīʿah; some Muslims questioned the right of Samuel Ibn Naghrīlah to hold high office, particularly after he was accused of writing polemic critical of the Quran,[95] and his son Yūsuf, also an administrator, was forced to flee Granada in the wake of anti-Jewish riots.[96] Some of the credit for the pogrom in Granada goes to the Arab poet and faqīh Abū Isḥāq (d. 1066), who wrote poems denouncing Ibn Naghrīlah and Jews in general, calling them unbelievers and apes who should be among the lowest of the low, but who instead rule over Muslims.[97] In spite of the incident in Granada, though, Jews seem to have become the favored group among the dhimmah; from the tenth century on, there are no reports of Christians who commanded the power and respect of Ibn Naghrīlah in Granada. For the purposes of our inquiry into dhimmī status in al-Andalus, the important question is why Jews succeeded in carving out a place (however risky) for themselves in the Muslim elite, both politically and culturally, while Christians did not.

There are certainly cultural and religious factors one can point to in explaining why Jews in al-Andalus ultimately had more access to elite status than Christians. Jews under Islam, starting in Iraq, had begun using Arabic as a scholarly language as early as the ninth century, setting a precedent for later scholars in al-Andalus. Hebrew and Arabic are related languages; thus it was easier for Jews to adapt Arabic poetic forms to Hebrew than for Christians to have done so to Latin. With its unambiguous commitment to monotheism and well-defined religious law code, Judaism is in its theology and practice closer to Islam than Christianity is, perhaps making it easier for Jews and Muslims to study together. Cultural and religious reasons, however, do not fully explain why Jewish courtiers succeeded where Christians failed; it does not explain why a Christian like Ibn Antonian, an admired figure at court and a master of both Arabic and Latin, could not have begun a tradition of Christians in al-Andalus writing poetry in Latin based on Arabic models and Christian theology in Arabic. The more compelling distinctions between Jews and Christians were political. Christians formed, perhaps until the end of the Umayyad period, the majority of the population, and Christian states to the north were a direct threat to al-Andalus, making the large Christian population a potential fifth column. In addition, the Umayyads had been unnerved by the Cordovan martyrs' movement, even if it had never reached the status of a revolt. Jews in the elite were a safer proposition than Christians.

Dhimmī status in al-Andalus, as elsewhere in the Islamic world, was consistent only at the theoretical level. The theological status of dhimmīs was well worked-out in polemical and theological sources, while clear rules for their treatment developed over time in Sharīʿah. In practice, however, the situation of dhimmīs depended on whether they were Jews or Christians, and on the particular political context of the moment. The uncertain status of Christians in particular, and the tensions between Christians and the Umayyads in the ninth and tenth centuries, form part of a picture of a society in transition and subject to conflict.

4 ✦ Gender and Law in al-Andalus

The following two chapters will exam the status of women—primarily Muslim women—in al-Andalus, in terms of the society's norms for women as they were laid out in Sharīʿah, the very different ideals depicted in literary and mystical sources, and the actual treatment of women in Sharīʿah courts. Unlike some of the ethnic and religious tensions this book analyzes, the ambiguities of women's position in society were not resolved with the end of the Umayyad period. Women's status, however, did change under the Umayyads, because of the large-scale conversion of Christians to Islam, and with the establishment of Sharīʿah courts as an important social force. Changing ideas about gender were a part of the social transformation that occurred in ninth- and tenth-century al-Andalus.

For medieval and early modern Europe, sources detailing official norms for the behavior of men and women, including sermons, law codes, and books of moral instruction, are relatively plentiful. Information about the many ways in which men and women actually behaved and related to each other, however, is more difficult to come by, although by the later Middle Ages and the Early Modern period a greater variety of material becomes available. A similar imbalance in the types of sources affects the study of gender in the premodern Islamic world. A great deal of normative Islamic material survives, but fewer sources either give us a more secular set of norms or offer stories about gender relations as they actually occurred, particularly in the period before 1000. The Sharīʿah sources are detailed and clear about certain aspects of gender identity, for example in setting out the norms for men's and women's obligations in marriage. Sharīʿah, however, represents an ideal, and we cannot always tell how much attention people in different regions and periods actually paid to its rules. Less overtly normative literature—the poetry of rulers' courts, for example—can be a rich source for understanding social norms, but such literature may describe behavior that was limited to a small elite. Chronicles and biographies are more likely to give accurate glimpses of something approaching real behavior, but their authors' primary objective is the description of battles, politics, and heroic or pious behavior, and not of ordinary social situations.

There is, however, enough material to allow us to tease out some of the meanings of gender in al-Andalus. This chapter will examine Islamic law and will use marriage regulations and regulations regarding inheritance as examples of what Sharīʿah has to say about the meaning of masculinity and femininity, the rights and duties of Muslim men and women, and proper relations between the sexes. It will also offer some comparisons between Sharīʿah and Visigothic law. Christians probably continued to use Visigothic law for issues of personal status, so it is important to understand what changes women would have experienced as they and their families converted to Islam. The next chapter will explore how the rules of Sharīʿah were carried out in real life, and will also examine sources that are not intended to be normative, including literature and mystical texts.[1]

SUBORDINATE GROUPS IN SHARĪʿAH

Women, like dhimmīs, constitute a subordinate category of person in Sharīʿah. Sharīʿah is typical of premodern legal systems in which only men in the dominant social group (in this case, free Muslim men) enjoy full legal rights. In Sharīʿah, only such men are fully "mukallaf," or legally capable.[2] Under Sharīʿah and other premodern codes, groups outside of the dominant one, including members of nondominant religions, foreigners (in some societies), slaves, women, and minors, have diminished legal capacity, meaning that they have obligations, limitations on their actions, and recourse to legal protection that all differ from those of dominant-group men. Despite various modern disputes among European and Middle Eastern societies as to which religions, or which regions, have traditionally treated women better, there is not finally much to choose from among societies in premodern Eurasia; the concept of equality before the law, and certainly the concept of women having a claim to such equality, is modern.

Historically under Islamic law free Muslim women were not treated as slaves, but neither were they fully competent legal persons. There are, as Kecia Ali points out, some important parallels between the status of married free women and that of slaves; men had extensive rights over the actions and the sexuality of both their female slaves and their wives, although the control was less absolute in the case of wives.[3] Another parallel can be drawn between the status of free Muslim woman and free dhimmī men. Muslim society offered women, like Jewish and Christian men, the society's protection, as well as freedom from key obligations, in exchange for submissive behavior and some limitations on their ability to act as independent persons before the law. It would be unwise to insist too strongly on the similarities in status, since the fact that free Muslim women shared a household with free Muslim men and bore their children obviously made their relationship with the dominant group different from that of dhimmīs. There are, however, some interesting parallels.

Sharīʿah offered both dhimmīs and Muslim women legal rights and protections, although at a lesser level than that afforded to Muslim men. They were protected against arbitrary violence or seizure of their goods. Muslim women, married or unmarried, could, like dhimmīs, own and bequeath property, although Muslim wives and daughters inherited proportionally less from spouses and parents than men did. Women and dhimmīs could buy and sell and engage in other commercial activities.[4] Both were restricted in the professions they could pursue, however, dhimmīs by the rule (not consistently enforced) that they could not hold positions of power over Muslims, and women primarily by the rules of modesty incumbent on middle- and upper-class households.

Also like dhimmīs, the essential contract between Muslim society and women was protection and freedom from certain obligations in exchange for deferential behavior. Dhimmīs received legal and physical protection from the authorities and were excused from military duties. In exchange, they paid jizyah and agreed to the rules outlined in chapter 3, most of which were designed to show subservience toward Muslims. A Muslim woman was also theoretically protected, either by a husband or, if she was unmarried, by her walī or guardian.[5] That role would normally be filled by her father or, in his absence, by a brother or other close agnatic kinsman. A woman's birth family, if they had the means to do so, supported her financially before marriage, and her husband was similarly obligated after.[6] Women were also excused from certain religious duties, including attendance at Friday services, which was obligatory for men, and were under less pressure than men to complete the ḥajj.[7] In exchange for those protections and dispensations, women occupied a lower place than men. They were to obey their husband or walī, behave modestly, and accept restrictions on their legal capacity; women had limited ability to arrange their own marriages, divorce, get custody of their children after a divorce, or to act as witnesses.

It is possible to see the rules for dhimmīs and for women as expressing anxiety about the potential threat posed by subject groups. The ban on military service for dhimmīs, however imperfectly it was enforced, originally meant that dhimmīs could not arm themselves to attack or defend against Muslims. In the long term, however, it also meant that that they were not part of the dīwān system and therefore not full members of society. In the same way, women's freedom from certain religious obligations meant that they were not full participants in the ummah. Women and dhimmīs were supposed to limit their presence and obtrusiveness in public space. Dhimmīs were to restrict their building of churches and synagogues, refrain from public processions or rituals, and make space for Muslims in public streets. The ninth-century historian and jurist Ibn Ḥabīb says that women should stay home. If they do go out they should cover themselves and walk to the side of the street rather than down the middle.[8] That last recommendation echoes the rule that dhimmīs should make way for Muslims on the street; both dhimmīs and women were to keep out of the way. In addition, both were feared as a possible source of ritual pollution. The prayers of a menstruating woman were not valid, and she was prohibited from entering a mosque.[9] Ibn Ḥabīb presents conflicting views as to whether or not a Muslim could purify himself for prayer with water a dhimmī had washed in, concluding that one could do so only if no alternative was available.[10]

Regulations for both groups express fear that dhimmīs and Muslim women would try to pass as Muslim men. Regulations against Christians and Jews dressing like Muslims go back to the Pact of ʿUmar.[11] What evidence there is for al-Andalus suggests that the rule was not well enforced, but that Christians who appeared to be Muslims continued to be a source of anxiety. Manuela Marín reports the case of the bearded woman of Tudela in the early eleventh century, who dressed as a man in order to travel freely. The qāḍī told her to put on women's clothing and to travel only in the company of a close male relative.[12] Ibn Ḥabīb seems preoccupied with the possibility that women will cross-dress. He relates the story of a pious man who found his wife with her hair arranged in a masculine style and her robe belted, and instantly pronounced her divorced. Women, he says, should wear necklaces and use kohl and henna so that they do not look like men.[13] In that same passage, Ibn Ḥabīb says that men should not dress as women, but he devotes far less space to that prohibition. Also of concern to him is the possibility of slave women dressing to look like free women.[14] Put in that context, his anxiety can be interpreted as fear that members of a lower caste will try to infiltrate a higher one and enjoy its privileges, the same anxiety that is evident in rules against dhimmīs dressing as Muslims.

Perhaps the key difference between the status of dhimmī men and the status of Muslim women was that dhimmī men could change their identity through conversion to Islam; converts might in fact meet with discrimination, but they were legally equal to men who were born Muslims. Women, however, had inherent physical characteristics that curtailed their legal status. Islam borrowed from Judaism the concept that menstruation and vaginal bleeding or discharge after childbirth were ritually impure (as did European Christianity well into the early modern period, with its practice of churching women after childbirth).[15] Women who were menstruating or experiencing postpartum bleeding could not say required prayers, fast, enter a mosque, or recite or handle a Quran; during such times they were not able to participate in the essential practices of Islam.[16] Women were also believed to have moral disabilities that disqualified them from full legal standing, including uncontrolled sexuality and a tendency toward sin that was stronger in women than in men.

WOMEN IN SCRIPTURE

The Quran, although it is often assumed to be the source of misogynist ideas in Islam, does not suggest that women are more flawed than men. One of the key verses about women's status in marriage is 4:34, which says:

> Men are the caretakers (qawwāmūn) of women,
> Because God has favored some over others [God favors men over women],
> And because they [men] provide [for women] out of their assets.
> Therefore the righteous women are obedient and are guardians of that which is concealed
> Because God guards [the concealed].
> And as for those women from whom you fear disobedience (nushūzahunna), admonish them
> And leave them alone in their beds

> And beat them (iḍribūhunna),
> But if they [then] obey you,
> Then do not look for a way to oppress them.

The verse makes it clear that God favors men over women and goes on to say that husbands may punish disobedient wives by beating them. It does not however attribute any inherent faults to women as a group. The verse admonishes women to be modest and obedient and foresees the possibility that some will be neither, but it does not suggest that bad behavior in women is inevitable. In fact, the first half of the verse, while asserting the superiority of men, refers primarily to the differing economic statuses of men and women; men take precedence in marriage because they support their wives.

It is the ḥadīths that attribute weakness and sinfulness to women as a class. Muḥammad in the ḥadīths says that since women are made from a rib, any woman is bound to be crooked. If you try to straighten her out entirely she will break, so to get some use from her you have to tolerate crookedness (ʿiwaj) in her.[17] Those ḥadīths refer to the biblical story in which God creates Eve from Adam's rib, a story about women's dependent nature that is absent from the Quran. In another ḥadīth, Muḥammad sees in a vision that the majority of people entering hell after the last judgment will be women.[18] The ḥadīths suggest that, while men as individuals may have good or bad characteristics, women are defective as a category. The concept of women's natural inferiority is developed more thoroughly in ninth- and tenth-century legal sources. Ibn Ḥabīb says that one should be patient with women, for every day and night that a man is tolerant of the evil of his wife's character, he will receive the same rewards as a martyr.[19]

WOMEN IN SHARĪʿAH

Sharīʿah in the Middle Ages recognized Muslim women as believers who were entitled to many of the same rights as men and were bound by many of the same obligations. At the same time, women were subject to legal disabilities that made their legal standing different from men's. Sharīʿah's rules concerning marriage and inheritance offer examples of both the similarities and differences between men's and women's status. Marriage and inheritance laws give men notable advantages over women. At the same time, they preserve women's rights within the family and are particularly concerned with giving women financial security. For al-Andalus, which was dominated by the Mālikī madhhab, the major legal sources are Mālik's late eighth-century *Muwaṭṭa*[20] and the ninth-century compilation of his and his followers' legal opinions collected by Saḥnūn, *al-Mudawwanah al-kubrā*. I will also be making some references to Ibn Ḥazm's views on marriage in *al-Muḥallā bi-al-āthār*.[21] Although his legal opinions never became normative in al-Andalus, they offer some interesting contrasts with Mālikī opinion.

It is not clear how early in al-Andalus's history its 'ulamā' were in fact in contact with the Mālikī school of law centered in Medina. The traditional argument among Muslim scholars is that contact between al-Andalus and Medina dates from the early days of Umayyad rule in Spain. From the time of 'Abd al-Raḥmān I, according to this argument, it was common for scholars from al-Andalus to study with Mālik and his followers in Medina, in part because the other main centers of legal study were in Iraq, in the heartland of Abbasid power, and were therefore not the first choice of scholars whom the Umayyads supported. Scholars continued to study in Medina in the time of 'Abd al-Raḥmān's successor Hishām I (r. 788–96), during whose reign the legal expert Ziyād b. 'Abd al-Raḥmān Shabṭūn brought back to al-Andalus a complete version of Mālik's *Muwaṭṭa'*.[22] Later scholars introduced into al-Andalus the *Mudawwanah al-kubrā*. The Umayyad amīrs by the time of 'Abd al-Raḥmān II (822–52) supported the Mālikī school above all others, with Mālikī legal experts numbered among the rulers' advisers at court.[23] Other scholars, however, including Fierro and Marín, have argued that the claims of early contact with Mālik and his students may or may not be historically accurate.[24] Whether or not the stories of specific individuals having contact with the Medina school of law are literally true, however, or just a way of explaining the importance of that madhhab, it is clear that by the mid-ninth century Mālikī law had a substantial influence on Andalusī jurists. Ibn Ḥabīb, whom 'Abd al-Raḥmān II recruited from Granada, says that in al-Andalus Mālik's decisions must always take precedence over those of other authorities.[25] Even if not all Sharī'ah was specifically Mālikī as early as the ninth century, Sharī'ah of some kind already played an important role. In the 850s the Christian martyrs of Córdoba were tried and executed for defaming the Prophet and other crimes, all in accordance with Sharī'ah.[26] So while we cannot say with certainty that every corner of al-Andalus was governed by Mālikī law by 850, it is reasonable to assert that at least a version of it was in use in urban areas quite early on.

WOMEN AND MARRIAGE IN SHARĪʿAH

The Islamic law of marriage prevalent in al-Andalus expressed a tension between two ways of defining marriage. On the one hand, the marriage contract had elements of a contract of sale, in which the woman was the property; the active parties in the exchange were the woman's father or guardian and the prospective husband. On the other hand, marriage contracts were largely devoted to ensuring the bride's financial security, and many Sharīʿah regulations envisaged marriage as a set of mutual obligations between husband and wife. Generally, Sharīʿah leaned more toward the idea that husband and wife were both active parties to the marriage, albeit with the understanding that a woman entered into matrimony as the inferior partner. Tensions between the concepts of the wife as property and the wife as a party to the contract were not fully resolved, however, and produced some interesting ambiguities.[27]

The right to arrange and give permission for a marriage was technically at least restricted to men. Mālik assumes that a girl or woman's father or other walī would negotiate the terms of her marriage, although there is no reason why her mother or other family members, a matchmaker, or the girl herself could not be involved in testing the waters before an actual contract was negotiated. No marriage could take place, however, unless the walī gave his permission.[28] The potential bride also had to agree to the match under most circumstances.[29] Those general rules—no marriage without the walī's permission or (mostly) without the bride's consent—were made more complicated by the law's recognition of different classes of walīs and potential brides. Fathers, as opposed to other kinds of walīs, had special authority; according to Mālikī opinion, the father of a virgin, but no other walī, could force her to marry, and only a father could marry off a girl before she reached menarche.[30] Mālikīs also made distinctions among potential brides according to their social class and sexual status. Most important was the difference between a virgin and a woman who had had intercourse in marriage but was now divorced or widowed. The woman who had experienced licit relations with a man was called a thayyib, and the fact of her sexual initiation automatically brought her closer to the status of an adult male, in the same way that widowhood conferred increased independence on premodern European women. While a virgin's permission could be expressed by her silence when her walī informed her of his plans for her marriage—if she did not protest, the marriage was valid—a thayyib had to give her spoken consent.[31] And although the *Mudawwanah* says that no woman could marry without permission from her walī, one opinion that is raised but rejected suggests that a thayyib of low social status who arranged her own marriage, including a black woman, a convert, or a freedwoman, was less culpable than a more respectable woman would be.[32] It was the duty of the walī to ensure kafā'ah and thus prevent the family from being humiliated, but a women at the bottom of the social hierarchy by definition could not be humiliated.[33] There is no suggestion, however, that a virgin from even the lowest levels of society could marry without a walī's permission.

Mālikī rules about the role of the walī in marriage, and the need for his daughter or ward's consent, illustrate the tension between marriage as a property transaction and marriage as a contract between the spouses. In the *Mudawwanah*, opinions waver between emphasizing the woman's ability to refuse an unwanted marriage and the walī's right to dispose of a daughter or ward. One opinion states that once a woman became a thayyib, even if her husband divorced her immediately afterwards, she was legally responsible for herself. That opinion, however, is followed by the statement that a walī who thought his thayyib daughter or ward was likely to disgrace herself could forcibly retake control of her.[34] Ibn Ḥazm seems equally ambivalent about the balance between the walī's rights and his sense that females are autonomous persons. In the *Muḥallā* he asserts absolutely that no female, virgin or thayyib, can marry without her walī's permission, but he goes on to defend the necessity of obtaining the potential bride's consent, even in the case of a virgin. He quotes from the Quran, 6:164: "Each soul can lay responsibility for its actions nowhere but on itself" (wa-lā taksibu kullu nafsin illā 'alayhā).

Mālikī opinions also suggest that the concept of women as property was strongest in families of status and means. Women's actions did not matter as much if they did not reflect well or badly upon a socially significant network of male kin. Freedwomen, recent converts to Islam (probably slaves or freedwomen who converted to improve their social position and chances for marriage), and women of sub-Saharan African background (most likely freedwomen or their descendants) were unlikely to be imbedded in such networks. Ibn Ḥazm acknowledges that some authorities allow a thayyib to arrange her own marriage[35] and also give that power to low status women, such as black women, poor women, converts, or freedwomen.[36] He insists, however, that the rule requiring a walī's permission applies to all females, virgin or thayyib. Furthermore, he sees any distinction between high and low status persons as un-Islamic. He points out that all of the prophets were poor, while evil-doers like Haman and Pharaoh were rich, and that one of Muḥammad's wives was both black and a freedwoman, in spite of which no one was more favored in the early ummah than she (it is not clear what wife Ibn Ḥazm is referring to here).[37]

Some of the confusion over the role of the potential wife in marriage negotiations goes back to the earliest Islamic texts. Muḥammad's first wife, Khadījah, was a respected figure in Islamic history, revered as a person of high moral character and as one of the key supporters of Muḥammad's prophetic mission. She did not, however, adhere to the standards of female behavior Sharī'ah later set out. She was a widow who owned her own business; the earliest biography of the prophet, called the Sīrah, which is a mixture of eighth- and ninth-century material, reports that Khadījah was first Muḥammad's employer and then later proposed marriage to him ('ariḍat 'alayhi nafsahā, "she offered herself to him").[38] The narrator goes on to say that one of Muḥammad's paternal uncles then went to Khadījah's father to formalize the proposal; the father agreed and married her to Muḥammad. The historian al-Ṭabarī (d. 923) follows the Sīrah, leading with the story that Khadījah proposed to the prophet herself but also including other accounts claiming that her father or her uncle married her to Muḥammad.[39] Unlike the Sīrah, al-Ṭabarī's history presents the story of her father making the marriage not as a continuation of the narrative in which Khadījah proposes to Muḥammad but as an alternative version of events. It is possible that the presence of Khadījah's father or uncle represents a later addition aimed at bringing Khadījah's story into conformity with Islamic ideals as they developed in the late eighth and ninth centuries.[40] In any case, Khadījah remained in the tradition as a sort of super thayyib, financially independent, entrepreneurial, and free to arrange her own marriage.

At the heart of Shar'īah's ambivalence about women's status in marriage was the dower, called ṣadāq or mahr. The dower was a transfer of property from the husband to his new wife and was supposed to represent a significant percentage of the husband's worth. The rules of ṣadāq illustrate the tendency of Mālikī Sharī'ah to treat marriage as a commercial exchange, but also the law's concern with protecting women's financial rights. Mālikī law is clear that no marriage is valid without a ṣadāq that is appropriate to the bride's status, and that a walī who fails to negotiate a proper amount is guilty of a serious infraction. Mālikīs prohibited shighār marriage, or marriage of exchange, in which two men agree that each will marry his daughter to the other and neither man will pay ṣadāq.[41] Shighār marriage was impermissible because it was a contract negotiated by two men for their own benefit, treating the daughters as property to be exchanged. From the Mālikī authorities' point of view, such an arrangement tipped the balance too far in favor of men's property rights and away from considerations of the bride's well-being. Once a marriage contract was complete, the walī had no right to renegotiate a lower dower. The only exception occurred in the case of a virgin daughter whose walī was her father. Then he had the right to accept a lower ṣadāq if the husband divorced his wife immediately, or if the walī felt it would be in his daughter's interest to release the new husband from part of his obligation. The father of a virgin could also take over management of the ṣadāq if he felt his daughter was incompetent to manage it herself. No walī other than a father could negotiate a lower dower or control the dower of a virgin, and not even a father could do either of those things if his daughter was a thayyib.[42]

Mālikī law also concerned itself with the quality of the dower offered. It had to consist of items with an immediate value, including money, animals, income from land, or slaves. Things that had only a potential value—date palms that had not yet born fruit or the promise of sheep or goats or camels expected to be born the following year—were not permissible.[43]

Dower in Mālikī law was closely tied to the consummation of the marriage. If for example the husband did not name an amount at the time the marriage contract was negotiated—a practice Mālikī law allows but does not encourage—his wife could refuse to consummate the marriage until he specified the ṣadāq.[44] If two sisters married two brothers, then accidently slept with the wrong brothers on their wedding night (a mix-up that is at least plausible in the case of brides and grooms who had not met before marriage), the two women underwent a three-month waiting period to make sure they were not pregnant, then each returned to her legal husband. Each, however, was owed ṣadāq not by her legal husband but by the brother who actually had sex with her.[45]

Ibn Ḥazm brings some of the ambiguities of Islamic marriage law to light when he criticizes Mālik's ideas about dower.[46] His main objection is to what he sees as Mālik's characterization of marriage as a transfer of property. For example, Mālik set the minimum ṣadāq at four dinars, because four dinars was the minimum value of goods a thief must have stolen in order for the authorities to amputate his hand.[47] Ibn Ḥazm interprets this minimum (which he reports as three rather than four) as meaning that Mālik saw marriage as an amputation or alienation of the woman's sexual organs. Mālik's reasoning, says Ibn Ḥazm, represents a false analogy.[48] There is no comparison between theft, which is a sin, and marriage, which is a pious act, and in which no literal amputation takes place. He also criticizes Mālik for prohibiting ṣadāq from including items that are not licit media of exchange but that may be given as a gift or as inheritance. Examples include items that have not reached their potential value, such as trees that have not yet borne fruit and domestic animals not used for food or transportation, such as dogs or cats.[49] In addition, he says, Mālik is wrong to say that a man cannot consummate his marriage before the ṣadāq is paid. Those rules imply that marriage is a commercial transaction, a purchase of one human being by another. In fact, marriage is a mutual and voluntary exchange of body for body; one person is not purchasing the body of another. Because the marriage is not simply an economic transaction, it is wrong to set a minimum amount of ṣadāq.[50] He says that the dower can include up to one-half of what a man owns, but it does not matter how small that amount is; if a man is poor he can offer one grain of wheat or skills that he possesses, such as the ability to teach his wife part of the Quran. Here Ibn Ḥazm is referring to ḥadīths in which Muḥammad allows a poor man to offer only an iron ring to his bride or the promise that he will teach her verses of the Quran as her dower.[51] Ṣadāq, Ibn Ḥazm implies, is not a payment but is similar to a gift given out of love or an inheritance set up to benefit a family member.

Ibn Ḥazm is correct that Mālikī ideas about ṣadāq suggest that marriage is a type of sale in which a man purchases a set of rights over a woman, and in particular rights over her sexual and reproductive functions. Marriage law and the law of commercial transactions were closely related in Mālikī law. If, for example, a couple married but then disagreed about the amount of ṣadāq agreed to, the dispute was settled by what was in effect commercial law. If the couple had not yet had sex, then the wife's word as to the amount prevailed; it was then up to the husband either to pay what she asked or refuse to pay, in which case the marriage became invalid. If they already had sex, however, his word prevailed.[52] Here the *Mudawwanah* invoked the rules of the marketplace. If the marriage was not consummated, then the sale was not final; the goods—that is, the woman's sexual services—had not been handed over. In such a case the seller's word prevailed; the buyer could either pay the price named or the deal became invalid. After consummation, though, the sale was final and the goods had been delivered. In that case the buyer's word prevailed and the seller could not demand a higher price.[53]

As much as a modern reader may prefer Ibn Ḥazm's apparently more humanistic understanding of marriage, it is important to note who, in Mālik's view, was doing the selling. There is no doubt that Mālikīs saw marriage as a sale. It is also clear that, in spite of the walī's important role, it was the woman who was intended to benefit from the sale. It was she who could ask her husband to set a firm amount for the dower before she slept with him, and she who received the dower. Mālikī rules about the quality of the dower—nothing of only potential value, no dogs or cats—helped make sure that wives had some financial independence, particularly in the event of divorce. It is an unsentimental view of marriage, but there are possible advantages to making women's well-being dependent on set rules of property transfer rather than on their husbands' affection.

Once married, a wife's primary duties were obedience and deference to her husband. She was also obligated to have sex with him when he wanted, unless she had a compelling reason (such as illness) to refuse. Men, however, had reciprocal obligations. In addition to the payment of dower, a husband was required to support his wife during their marriage; as long as she was married, the wife could not be asked to pay her own expenses out of her ṣadāq or other personal resources. Mālikī opinion emphasized that a husband's obligation to support his wife was absolute provided that they were both of age and had consummated the marriage. Poverty was not an excuse, and even if the woman fell ill and was unable to have sex, the husband could not withdraw support.[54] Ibn Ḥazm says that a wife has a claim on her husband for clothing and housing, but that he has no similar claim on any of her property. He defines proper support as a man maintaining his wife at the same level of prosperity that he enjoys, feeding her what he eats and clothing her as he clothes himself.[55] A man also owed his wife physical intimacy, although Ibn Ḥabīb says that she should be content with sex once a month.[56]

A marriage ended with the death of either party or with divorce. The Sharīʿah term for divorce is ṭalāq, which more specifically means a man's dismissal of his wife. No aspect of marriage law was more clearly favorable to men; a man could divorce his wife simply by stating three times that she was dismissed.[57] While some Islamic countries in the modern period require that a man send his wife and the local authorities a written declaration of the divorce, traditional Sharīʿah makes no such provisions; if a man said it, it was done. He was not required to give any reason. Once a man dismissed his wife, he was obligated to support her for three months. That three months was her ʿiddah or waiting period, mandated to determine whether or not she was pregnant.[58] After the three months, any minor children from the marriage continued to receive support, but hers came to an end. She was then free to remarry or could return to her natal family. A women could petition a Sharīʿah court for a divorce on the grounds of desertion, impotence, or brutality. If a court accepted such a petition, it normally resulted in a khulʿ

divorce, in which the woman had to either forgo any deferred portion of her dower or refund a part of the dower she had already received, in return for her freedom. It is not possible to say how readily a woman could obtain a khulʿ divorce, but Ibn Ḥabīb sets a high standard of proof for spousal abuse. He says that if a thayyib comes to a judge complaining that her husband beat and raped her, but there is no blood, then there can be no presumption of brutality; she was probably simply not showing him due deference.[59]

Mālikī Sharīʿah, however, did build in some restraints on men's freedom to exercise their rights. A man could dismiss his wife at will, but consequences would ensue. Any part of the dower not yet paid must be handed over to the wife immediately; the delayed portion of ṣadāq was in effect support for the woman in the event of divorce and could result in considerable expense for the husband. Once a man divorced his wife, he could not remarry her until she had been through her ʿiddah, been married to another free Muslim man or a Muslim slave whose master gave him permission to marry,[60] been divorced by him, and then completed another ʿiddah. A man could not, therefore, divorce a wife in a fit of anger, then easily remarry her later. Even Ibn Ḥabīb believed in limitations on a husband's right to punish his wife physically; he prohibits hitting a woman in the face or disfiguring her and presumably would grant a divorce to a woman who suffered such treatment.[61] Other factors external to Sharīʿah no doubt limited men's arbitrary behavior. A woman's birth family could also play an important role in protecting her. Under most circumstances, a man could beat his wife without legal consequences, but he might face repercussions from her male relatives.

In Islamic law there is no term that specifically means infidelity in marriage. "Zināʾ" is the legal term for any unpermitted sexual intercourse, which includes the concepts of adultery and fornication.[62] Men traditionally had more options for legal sex than women, since they had access (at least theoretically) to multiple wives and slave women, while women could sleep only with their husbands. Punishment for zināʾ could be severe. When the evidence against a couple was clear, Mālik recommended stoning, even though he recognized that stoning was a practice from Torah that does not appear in the Quran. In cases where the evidence was less persuasive, or if the guilty parties confessed and repented, Mālik preferred lashing. Both parties were to be punished equally.

Although there is evidence from many periods that men and women were not in practice punished equally for sexual misconduct, it is worth noting that Sharīʿah mandates that they should be. Sharīʿah understands zinā' as a crime against God's law that is just as reprehensible in men as it is in women. A man could theoretically have more legitimate partners than his wife could, but any woman outside of his wives and the slave women of his household were off limits. In that respect Sharī'ah shows similarities to canon law, which sees unpermitted sex as a sin against God, and is quite different from Roman law, which on other issues is an important source for Islamic jurisprudence. Under Roman law, adulterium was a property crime against a man. A married woman who had an affair and the man with whom she had it were both guilty of infringing on her husband's rights over her sexual capacities. A married man who had an affair did not infringe on his wife's rights over his body, since she had none.[63]

In spite of the walī's important role in Islamic marriage, Sharī'ah in al-Andalus treated marriage primarily as a set of mutual obligations between a man and his wife or wives. Men and women did not have equal status in marriage in that men had more freedom and control. They also, however, had responsibilities toward their wives, including financial support, sex, and some degree of considerate treatment.

Islamic marriage law, of course, affected only Muslim women, except in the case of mixed marriages. Although there is little evidence about personal status law for Jewish and Christian women, it is likely that Jews followed their own marriage regulations,[64] while Christians continued to use Visigothic law in the form of the *Forum iudicum*.[65] Since large numbers of Christians converted to Islam in the ninth and tenth centuries, it is important to assess how women's status in marriage changed as they moved from Visigothic law to Sharī'ah.

ISLAMIC AND VISIGOTHIC MARRIAGE LAW

Marriage regulations in Sharī'ah and the Visigothic code differed in some respects, but they also shared a number of characteristics. Some of the similarities between the two systems may be explained by the fact that both the Germanic and Muslim conquests included Roman territories, making Roman law an important source for both groups. Anthropologist Jack Goody, however, has argued that there are basic continuities among marriage patterns throughout premodern Eurasia, and not only in territories of the former Roman Empire; Sharī'ah and Visigothic law are just two instances of a much larger system.[66]

The Eurasian systems were patrilineal. The importance of paternal versus maternal kin differed from society to society, but status and, often, key property were passed down in the male line. Because the production of legitimate children was important to men, female sexuality was strictly controlled. Women's sexual misbehavior could call paternity into question, and could also, to a greater or lesser extent depending on the particular society, be a source of shame and humiliation for their male relatives. Daughters could be valuable on the marriage market as means to make alliances and advance the family's social position, but not if their sexual conduct was in doubt. Men, on the other hand, had more sexual freedom, through such institutions as concubinage, slavery, and, in some cultures, polygyny. Women were divided between those who were fair game for men to approach, usually including the poor, slaves, and prostitutes (all of whom could occupy overlapping categories), and women who were respectable, meaning that they had male relatives with enough power and resources to protect them. A respectable woman's sexuality and reproductive capacities were controlled by men, first by her father and other male relatives, then by her husband.[67] We see traces of the distinction between respectable and not-respectable women in the Mālikī opinions discussed above regarding the walī's role in marriage negotiations. The fact that some Mālikīs allowed marginal women—particularly freedwomen and the poor—more freedom in negotiating their own marriages may have to do with the perception that they were not properly controlled by male relatives as higher status women were.

While these systems upheld male prerogatives, they also were guided by the fact that men had female relatives who must be protected and made financially secure, both for reasons of familial affection and because it would bring shame on a family if a female member fell into poverty. In the premodern Eurasian societies Goody discusses, dowry (paid by the bride's family) or dower (paid by the groom or his family, as was the case with ṣadāq), or some combination of the two, was an essential part of marriage, setting apart legitimately married women from concubines. According to some anthropologists, dower is equivalent to bride price, a payment made by the groom's family to the bride's family, meaning that dower systems are fundamentally different from systems requiring dowry; dowry goes to support the wife, while dower enriches her birth family, usually her father. Goody, however, sees dowry and dower in Eurasia as having the same goal, namely to create a conjugal fund primarily for the wife's support. Roman law, for example, required a dowry, called in Latin the "dos," to be paid by the bride's family to the groom.[68] The husband could control his wife's dowry during the marriage and could keep profits deriving from his investment of the dowry. But he was obligated not to decrease the fund's value and to use income from the fund to support his wife in a suitable fashion. His wife reclaimed the dowry if he divorced her or died. Dower, in Goody's view, has the same purpose, and he uses the biblical story of Jacob's marriages to Leah and Rachel to support his point.[69] In ancient Israelite marriages, the groom paid a dower or mohar (a cognate with the Arabic word mahr) to his bride, part of which was due immediately and part if the couple divorced. Mohar was the main subject of the marriage contract, a document concerned primarily with protecting the bride's interests, as it was later under Islam. Because Jacob could not afford to pay dower, he worked for Leah and Rachel's father (and his maternal uncle) Laban. His work for Laban, however, was not simply a bride price he paid to Laban for his daughters. He was also working to earn a portion of Laban's flocks while undertaking some biblical genetic engineering to get the largest possible number of animals. The flocks he earned served as a conjugal fund to support not only himself but Leah, Rachel, and their children.

Sharīʿah and Visigothic law share in these general characteristics of the Eurasian marriage system. The formation of a conjugal fund was important in both legal traditions. As we have seen, dower was a fundamental requirement under Sharīʿah for a marriage to be legitimate. Visigothic law, like Roman law, called for a dos to be negotiated at the time a couple became engaged.[70] In the Visigothic case, however, the dos was a dower rather than a dowry, paid by the groom to the bride, although the bride's family often gave gifts to the couple as well.[71] The dos was under the wife's control during her lifetime. She was required to bequeath three quarters of it to the couple's children, but, in the absence of children, she could dispose of it as she pleased.

As in Sharīʿah, the marriage of a young woman was largely in the hands of family members. The power to betroth a child was called "potestas de coniunctione," and it was wielded first by the child's father, then his widow, then by the child's adult brothers, and then by a paternal uncle. A father or other guardian could marry off a girl or young woman against her will, although there is some doubt that a woman over twenty could be forced.[72] A woman betrothed by her father who ran off and married another man could be forcibly brought back and handed over to the original fiancé.[73]

Another continuity between the two law codes, and with Goody's Eurasian model, is their concern with sexual propriety, although here Visigothic law was more heavily influenced by Roman precedents than was Sharīʿah. Adulterium in the Visigothic codes is similar to the idea of zinā' in the Islamic system.[74] The term "adulterium" was used in Visigothic law to describe not only adultery but any kind of sexual misconduct; it appears where one might expect to see the Latin word "stuprum." Visigothic law prohibited adulterium for men as well as women, and a conviction on the charge of adulterium could result in execution for both men and women. Despite this theoretical similarity between male and female sexual impropriety, however, Visigothic law followed the Roman tradition by making infidelity at least partly an issue of men's property rights. If the woman of a couple guilty of adulterium was married, both she and her partner were punished. They could be executed after a trial, or the offended husband had the right to kill the errant wife and her lover if he caught them in the act, or the court could hand over the couple to the husband to do with as he liked. A woman could be punished for adulterium even if neither she nor her partner were married. Her partner had the option of marrying her if he wished, which rendered her once again respectable, but if he did not want to marry her, she but not he was guilty of a crime. In addition, as in Roman law, the father, brother, or other male relative of a female guilty of adulterium had the right to kill her to preserve the family's honor.[75]

Visigothic law did not condone either divorce at the will of the husband or concubinage, but it did recognize the existence of both practices. While one statute prohibits divorce except in the case of the wife's adulterium,[76] another decrees that no man could marry a free woman claiming to have been repudiated by her husband until he had proof that the husband really divorced her; proof could consist either of the testimony of witnesses or a written instrument recording his repudiation.[77] This statute recognizes divorce at the will of the husband as a current practice, if not one the kings or the Church favored. Another statute points to concubinage as a known practice as well when it says that a man having sex with a free or slave concubine of his father or brother is guilty of adulterium.[78]

Like Sharīʿah, the Visigothic code prescribes a waiting period before a widow or divorcee could remarry, pointing to the systems' interest in assigning paternity accurately. Visigothic law prohibited a widow to remarry within the first year after her husband's death.[79] Although Islamic law generally called for only a three-month waiting period, Mālik was stricter than other authorities and made no allowances for women with irregular periods. If a woman did not have regular periods, her ʿiddah was nine months; if she had not had a baby by the end of the nine months, she must still do an additional three-month ʿiddah.[80] A year waiting period was therefore not unknown under Sharīʿah.

It is possible that women who converted from Christianity to Islam experienced restrictions, like veiling, that they had not faced under Visigothic law.[81] Their husbands would also have had the right to marry multiple wives, although polygamy does not seem to have been prevalent outside of a few elite Arab families,[82] and a woman could stipulate in her marriage contract that her husband was not allowed to take a second wife (see chapter 5). In many ways, however, including women's access to dower, attitudes toward women's sexual behavior, and the role of the father or other guardian in arranging marriages, the Islamic and Visigothic marriage systems were fairly similar.

WOMEN AND INHERITANCE LAW IN SHARĪʿAH

Islamic inheritance law in al-Andalus was of a piece with the law of marriage; it assigned women a lower status than men but also guaranteed the economic interests of women and girls. Within each category of the deceased's relatives (children, parents, siblings), females inherited less than males. If for example a man died leaving behind a son and a daughter, the son inherited twice as much as the daughter. Following the same pattern, if the deceased's parents survived him or her, the father received twice what the mother received. It is important to note, however, that daughters and other close female kin could not be disinherited.

As was discussed in chapter 2, Pierre Guichard has argued that Arabs and Berbers in al-Andalus generally disinherited females in order to preserve property in the male line. If that was sometimes the case, it was done without reference to Sharīʿah, which supported the concept of patriliny and the favoring of male kin only to a limited extent. Sunni inheritance law (but not Shīʿī law) did favor agnatic kin over cognates (mother's side kin) as heirs;[83] Mālik was especially strict on this point, excluding some of the cognatic heirs (maternal aunts and uncles, for example) that other law schools allowed to inherit in the absence of agnatic kin.[84] Generally, though, Sharīʿah did not distinguish between agnates and cognates. Incest regulations say that a man may not marry his female ascendants (mother, grandmother, etc.) or descendants (daughter, granddaughter, etc.), his aunts or their ascendants, his sisters, or his siblings' descendants (nieces, great nieces, etc.). He is also prohibited from marrying certain affines (kin acquired through marriage): he cannot marry anyone such that his wife, if she were a man, could not marry them (the wife's ascendants or descendants, her aunts, her nieces, or her sisters), nor can he marry wives of his ascendants or descendants (thus a man cannot marry his father's divorced or widowed wife).[85] So while works of genealogy like Ibn Ḥazm's *Jamharah* saw the individual as part of a patriliny, incest regulations in Sharīʿah described each person as a member of a kindred, that is, of a group of his or her closest family members, made up of cognatic, agnatic, and affinal kin.[86]

To simplify the matter somewhat, Mālikī inheritance law (like that of the other Sunni schools of law) classified the deceased's primary heirs into two categories: agnatic heirs and Quranic heirs, the latter term referring to those heirs whose right to inherit a specific share is mentioned or implied in the Quran. Agnatic heirs are the deceased's father's side kin and include females as well as males; a man's daughters, sons' daughters, and sisters or paternal half-sisters all inherit as agnatic kin. While there is some overlap between the two categories of heirs (a daughter inherits from her father as both agnatic kin and as a Quranic heir), the Quranic heirs are generally cognatic kin such as the deceased's mother, maternal half-brothers and half-sisters, and maternal grandmother. In addition, spouses inherit from each other as Quranic heirs.

There are three aspects of this system that are of particular interest: property can be transmitted to cognates as well as agnates, women can both inherit and transmit property, and husbands and wives can inherit from each other (and in fact cannot be excluded from inheriting). Those characteristics mean that women, while generally inheriting less than men, cannot be closed out of inheritance altogether. Let us look at the hypothetical case of a marriage between two free Muslims that ends in the death of the husband. During the marriage the wife's father dies. Sharīʿah guarantees that she will inherit a portion of his estate, the size of which depends on what other relatives are in line to inherit, and in particular on whether or not she has brothers, who must by law inherit twice as much as she. Next the woman's husband dies. At that point she receives the deferred portion of her ṣadāq, plus, as specified in the Quran, one-eighth of his estate if the couple has surviving children and one-fourth if they do not. When the wife herself dies, her estate will go primarily to her children if she has them, who are her husband's agnatic kin (but not hers). Set shares, however, will also go to her father and mother if they survive her. If she dies without surviving children, her brothers, sisters, paternal grandfather, and both grandmothers may inherit. The ṣadāq she received from her husband, her one-eighth to one-fourth of his estate, and her share in her father's estate could very possibly go to people who are neither her husband's nor her father's agnatic kin. Inheritance is not, then, strictly patrilineal, even though, as we saw in chapter 2, Arab families regarded themselves for some purposes as part of a patriliny. As Jack Goody points out, a society can trace its family history according to patrilineal principles while still practicing diverging inheritance.[87]

WOMEN AND INHERITANCE IN VISIGOTHIC LAW

In the case of inheritance, Visigothic law was more flexible and egalitarian than Sharīʿah, and women making the transition from Christianity to Islam would lose substantial property rights. There were some restrictions in the *Forum iudicum* on how men and women could dispose of their property. Anyone who had surviving children or grandchildren could not disinherit any of them and could not use more than one-third of his or her estate to increase the share of a favored child or grandchild. In addition, women could not alienate more than one-fourth of their dos away from children or grandchildren and could not give the dos she received from one husband to children of a different husband.[88] Otherwise, however, the Visigothic code allowed men and women considerably more discretion as to how they disposed of their property than Sharīʿah did. Visigothic law was also more favorable to women and mother's side kin; the codes do not distinguish between agnatic and cognatic kin as heirs and mandate that sons and daughters must inherit equally from their parents.[89]

Sharīʿah, like other premodern Eurasian legal systems, envisages a society that is male-dominated and largely patrilineal. That patrilineal family structure, while it did not have as negative an effect on women as Guichard supposes, did restrict women's inheritance rights. Because of the focus on succession in the male line, women were subject to strict control by their male relatives and husbands to prevent sexual indiscretions. In practice if not in theory, women were punished more harshly for having sex outside of marriage. To some extent women were a medium of exchange between men. On the other hand, Sharīʿah limited men's arbitrary exercise of power over women, largely by giving women property rights through dower and inheritance, rights that Sharīʿah courts appear to have taken seriously. There is a tendency in Islamic legal thought toward seeing women primarily in light of their usefulness to men, but another that recognizes them as human beings. A comparison between Sharīʿah and the *Forum iudicum* suggests that women's legal status in marriage would not have changed all that much, although their ability to inherit and bequeath property would have declined significantly.

5 ✦ The Law in Practice

Non-Sharīʿah Views of Gender

Chapter 4 examined the gender system as it was represented in the version of Islamic law that was probably current in al-Andalus by the ninth century, with some comparisons to the Visigothic code. The Sharīʿah-based system describes Muslim men and women as sharing a common humanity and religious identity, but also as distinct in their inherent characteristics, their manner of dress, their legal and financial standing, their sexual freedom, and their capacity to be full participants in their religion. Sharīʿah itself cannot, however, tell us how women were treated in fact or how closely their treatment adhered to the law.

WOMEN'S LEGAL STATUS IN PRACTICE

Fortunately we have at least limited sources that can illuminate how Sharīʿah was applied to women. One source from al-Andalus is the notarial formulary of Ibn al-ʿAṭṭār (d. 1009).[1] This formulary contains templates of marriage contracts for practical use. A look at what they have to say on the subject of dower suggests that the rules of Mālikī law were generally followed, but with some important exceptions that benefited women.

The most fully sketched out of the model marriage contracts is similar to those in other parts of the Islamic world and includes several basic elements that make the contract legal.[2] The model contract asserts that the groom will deliver the contract to his new wife. It next indicates that there must be a ṣadāq that the groom will deliver to the bride's walī, which the walī will use to provide the furnishings the bride will need in her new home. A specified amount will be delivered immediately, while a deferred amount must be paid within a stipulated period of months or years. This particular model contract is to be used in cases in which the bride is a virgin. Next, any stipulations (shurūṭ) limiting the groom's rights must be spelled out. The template lists several possible shurūṭ that are likely to appear in contracts: the husband may not take a second wife or a slave concubine, or maintain in the household any slave who has given birth to his child (an umm walad, whose child would be born free and a legitimate heir to his or her father).[3] If the husband violates any of these stipulations, the wife has the option of requesting a divorce. Further stipulations that may be included prevent the husband from being absent for more than six months, unless he goes on the ḥajj. If he does travel to Mecca, he cannot be gone for more than three years, and he must ensure that his wife is fed and housed in his absence. He cannot move her away from their current place of residence without her permission, and he may not prevent her from visiting relatives. In another possible stipulation, to be included if the bride is from a wealthy and distinguished family, the husband acknowledges that his new wife's high social status means she has always had servants and has not been required to see to her own needs; he understands that he will have to provide servants for her. Finally, witnesses must affirm that the contract is an accurate record of the oral agreement that the groom and the bride's walī have entered into. As is the case with all legal documents under Sharī'ah, the actual transaction is the spoken agreement between the parties involved; the contract merely documents that transaction.[4]

The contract distills a number of Sharī'ah's principles regarding marriage, including the role of the walī and the central importance of the ṣadāq. In other respects, though, the contract deviates from Mālikī Sharī'ah. Most importantly, Mālik did not allow the bride or her walī to place stipulations in a marriage contract, since they had the effect of limiting the authority God had given men in marriage; he says that even if a stipulation is included in the marriage contract, saying for example that the husband may not move his wife away from her village, he has the right to do so anyway.[5] Ibn al-'Aṭṭār's formulary, however, suggests that stipulations were in practice quite ordinary.[6] They appear in marriage contracts from other Islamic societies, including the early Ottoman Empire; it has been suggested that Sharī'ah courts became more inclined to support men's legal privileges in the nineteenth century, partly under the influence of European colonialism, than they were in the premodern period.[7]

The limits the formulary's stipulations put on men's privileges clearly benefitted married women. Although scripture permitted polygyny, Islamic texts as far back as the ḥadīths recognized that a second wife damaged the status of the first wife; Muḥammad is reported to have forbidden his cousin and son-in-law 'Alī from taking a second wife in addition to Muḥammad's daughter Fāṭimah, saying that "she is part of me; what alarms her alarms me, and what hurts her hurts me."[8] A wife's ability to prevent a second marriage, or a long-term liaison between her husband and a slave concubine, gave her a powerful tool for shaping her life and that of her family. The prohibition against moving a wife away from her home was also crucial, since her family could offer her protection and support. The fact that men regularly signed away some of their privileges suggests that Muslim women in al-Andalus, particularly if their families were wealthy, had powers in marriage that went beyond those that Sharī'ah specified.

Also of interest is the acknowledgment that if the bride comes from a family that is accustomed to having servants, the groom, assumed to be of similar status, will furnish her with servants in their home. In this clause the template recognizes the principle of kafā'ah, the social and economic equality of the groom to the bride (discussed in chapter 2). A man could marry someone of a lower social status, but a woman could not. Religious authorities were ambivalent about the concept of kafā'ah. It was widely enforced, yet it goes against a foundational principle of Sharī'ah: that all free adult Muslims are members of the ummah and, allowing for differences in status between men and women, are equal before the law. It follows that a man's piety, not his birth or income, should determine his ranking as a prospective husband. The *Mudawwanah* communicates some of this ambivalence, offering in one place the opinion that a woman may marry someone below her (dūnahā) socially or economically, including a non-Arab, provided he is her equal in religion.[9] Elsewhere, however, the *Mudawwanah* relates the story of a divorced woman who came to Mālik and told him that her ex-husband was negotiating a marriage between their daughter and the husband's brother's son. The daughter was wealthy and therefore entitled to a large dower, but her father had negotiated a relatively modest one, presumably as a favor to his brother and nephew. Mālik, who generally did not allow women to be involved in official negotiations for a marriage contract, says the woman has the right to object to her daughter's inappropriate dower.[10] The formulary's templates suggest that in practice, the rule of kafā'ah was observed, and without the ambivalence the topic generated for religious scholars.

Collections of legal rulings (fatwās) also tell us that in addition to the dower and the husband's support, a woman normally received a gift from her own family at the time of marriage, usually consisting of items for the household and for the bride's personal use. That practice is not specified in Sharī'ah, so mention of a gift from the bride's family (as opposed to a portion of the ṣadāq that the bride's father uses to purchase household furnishings for her) is not normally included in marriage contracts. It seems, however, to have been common throughout medieval Islamic lands, particularly among upper-class families with the resources to donate a substantial gift for their daughters' support.[11] The gift could represent a form of early inheritance that allowed families to work around the restrictions Sharī'ah placed on women's inheritance.[12] Such gifts from the bride's family frequently appear in al-Andalus.[13] Ibn Ḥabīb issued a ruling in the case of a father who made a gift of clothing and household furnishings to his newly married daughter, then, when he visited her at her new home, found that the goods were missing. According to Ibn Ḥabīb's ruling, if the bride was a virgin at the time of marriage, she is not responsible for the missing items. If she was a thayyib, she is.[14] That fatwā and others tell us something about the usual contents of the gift, along with confirming Sharī'ah's view that thayyibs were closer than virgins to having full legal responsibilities. Mālikī opinions state that while the house and most of its contents, including slaves, are presumed to belong to the husband unless his wife can produce evidence that she owns them, certain furnishings are assumed to be hers: lanterns, the bread basin, the bed, the cushions, and the carpets.[15] That assumption may stem from the fact that such items were a normal part of the endowment from the wife's family. It appears that women's economic resources in marriage, at least in the case of well-to-do families, exceeded what was laid out in Sharī'ah.

Another glimpse of women's actual legal status comes from records of Sharī'ah courts. Guichard's model of "eastern" kinship assumes that women were mostly disinherited, particularly in the case of land, despite what Sharī'ah says to the contrary. There is evidence, however, that Sharī'ah's inheritance rules did carry weight in al-Andalus. Sources from Sharī'ah courts and faqīhs suggest not that Arab and Berber women were automatically disinherited, but rather that a tension existed between Sharī'ah and men's desire to control property. Confirming Guichard's model in part, men were particularly interested in preventing women in their families from inheriting land, often going to court and claiming that the land belonged to a living male relative rather than to the deceased.[16] On the other hand, Sharīʿah courts did defend women's rights to property. One of Ibn Ḥabīb's fatwās involves a brother and sister who had inherited property from their parents.[17] When the sister died before her brother, he claimed that her heirs had no right to inherit from her, because she never asked for her share of the property (presumably when their parents died). Because of her silence, he argued, the property belongs to him and his heirs. Ibn Ḥabīb, however, ruled that the sister's silence did not negate her rights to family property, and that her heirs therefore must inherit their share.

A number of the lawsuits the Andalusī legal expert Ibn Sahl (d. 1093) describes in his *Dīwān al-aḥkām al-kubrā* involve family members, women as well as men, suing each other in Sharīʿah courts over inheritances.[18] Since Ibn Sahl is interested in lawsuits rather than the routine dispersal of property, the cases he describes often feature male and female heirs fighting for their rights. In one instance, a husband challenges the right of his deceased wife to bequeath a one-third interest in her house to her sister. In another, a wife inherits property from her husband. He leaves behind two sons by another woman who have disappeared; the sons' creditors demand a share of the widow's inheritance.[19] Women's rights over their property are, then, frequently challenged. In no instance, however, do the judges and faqīhs involved assume that being female is an impediment to inheriting or bequeathing property.

A particularly interesting example involves a complex dispute over farm land. A woman named Hashīmah complained to the court that her paternal first cousin was attempting to seize land she legitimately inherited from her father, Saʿīd b. Muzayn.[20] The cousin asserted that his family had purchased the property before Saʿīd's death. The matter apparently dragged on for some time. Ibn Sahl, who is interested in the legal questions suits raise rather than the outcomes, does not tell us who finally got the property. Nevertheless, the case gives us important information. One of the qāḍīs hearing the case was Muḥammad b. Salmah, who was chief qāḍī of Córdoba and died under the reign of ʿAbd Allah (888–912), making the early tenth century the latest possible date for the proceedings.[21] The Banū Muzayn, as Ibn Sahl calls Hashīmah's extended kin group, were an Arab family whose members included a noted faqīh and a governor of Toledo under Al-Ḥakam I who eventually settled in Córdoba.[22] As in Guichard's model of the Arab family, Hashīmah's paternal male cousin seemed to regard himself as having rights over her as her paternal first cousin, and he was perhaps trying to bully her out of property that was legitimately hers. In contrast to what one would expect from Guichard's model, though, Hashīmah was not powerless; she took the case to a Sharī'ah court. The various legal experts commenting on the matter were concerned with the facts in evidence and whether witnesses were properly deposed. Even though the case involved real property, however, they do not assume that the male cousin's rights take precedence over Hashīmah's.

MEN AND WOMEN IN LITERARY SOURCES

Sharī'ah in al-Andalus assumed that men and women were essentially different and that sexuality needed to be carefully controlled and limited to marriage (and, in the case of men, to the relationship between a master and a female slave). Practices that challenged those norms, like homosexuality or any expression of female sexuality outside of marriage, were prohibited. Other types of sources from the period, however, viewed gender differently. Literary sources elided the differences between the sexes, either by depicting men and women as similar in their essential natures or by presenting male narrators who regarded male and female erotic partners as more or less interchangeable. Mystical literature came closer to Sharī'ah's view that men and women were fundamentally different, but it saw their differences as representing a cosmic rather than a social reality. This section of the chapter will begin with a discussion of Ibn Ḥazm's treatise on love, *The Dove's Neck Ring*, which will establish some of the common themes of Andalusī literature as it pertains to gender, followed by an analysis of Arabic and Hebrew love poetry. The final section will focus on gender in mystical literature. It is not my intention in this chapter to offer a general survey of Andalusī literature and mystical texts but rather to select examples that offer a counterpoint to the previous chapter's discussion of gender.

IBN ḤAZM'S *ṬAWQ AL-ḤAMĀMAH*

Ibn Ḥazm composed *The Dove's Neck Ring*, or *Ṭawq al-ḥamāmah*, in either 1022 or 1027.[23] At that point he was in his late twenties or early thirties and was living in Játiva, more or less in exile, as Umayyad rule in Córdoba was breaking down. The full title of the work is *Ṭawq al-ḥamāmah fī al-ulfah wa-al-ullāf.* "Ulfah" means friendship, love, or intimacy, and "ullāf" means people who are one's intimates, including close friends or lovers. Although the *Ṭawq* is often characterized as a treatise on love, it is more accurate to say that it is a treatise on intimacy. Love, erotic attraction, and friendship are all addressed.

The *Ṭawq* is a prose treatise incorporating poetry. It is connected to a long history of Arabic love poetry that purports to date back to pre-Islamic Arabia.[24] More specifically, it formed part of a series of treatises on love going back to Muḥammad ibn Dāwūd al-Ẓāhirī's *Kitāb al-zahrah* (*Book of the Flower*), written around 900.[25] Ibn Ḥazm's treatise is unusual, however, in that the author does not rely on traditional stories about lovers but instead draws on his own experiences and those of his contemporaries, although some parts may of course be fictionalized. That emphasis on contemporary events makes the *Ṭawq* a valuable source, since it includes anecdotes about life in al-Andalus at the end of the Umayyad period. To give just one example, he adopts at one point a theme from early Arabic poetry. In that traditional poetry set among Bedouins, the lover, who was separated from his beloved when their two tent-groups went their different ways, mourns the loss at the site of the abandoned campground. In the *Ṭawq*, however, Ibn Ḥazm's mourning is for the site of his old family home that was destroyed during the political unrest surrounding the Umayyad state's collapse.[26] Its contemporary orientation also makes the *Ṭawq* more entertaining than most such treatises; instead of material about lovers drawn from traditional literature, Ibn Ḥazm gives us gossipy anecdotes about the great and the near-great of al-Andalus. It is from him, for example, that we learn of the preference for blonds among men of the Umayyad family, a preference which Ibn Ḥazm shared. So long-standing was this Umayyad predilection for blonds (presumably slave women of European descent), he tells us, that all the descendants of ʿAbd al-Raḥmān III, with one exception, were blonds.[27]

Ibn Ḥazm's treatise does have obvious limitations as a source for understanding Andalusī society. Beyond the question of how much is fictionalized, there is no evidence that it was widely circulated or particularly struck a chord with contemporaries. While some scholars in the eastern and western Islamic worlds were aware of it in the two or three centuries after the author's death, it survives today in only one manuscript dating from 1338, suggesting that interest in it was limited. And certainly Ibn Ḥazm's views on any subject cannot be taken as typical. He seems to have had a reputation as an eccentric during his lifetime; Ibn Sahl apparently wrote a treatise about him called *al-Tanbīh ʿalā shudhūdh Ibn Ḥazm* (*A Warning Against the Eccentricity of Ibn Ḥazm*).[28] Even with those limitations, however, the *Ṭawq* is important in that it shows that a view of gender different from that of Sharīʿah was conceivable in al-Andalus. Moreover, it suggests that someone could hold Sharīʿah's view of gender and an alternative view at the same time. As we have seen in previous chapters, Ibn Ḥazm was himself a faqīh. And while his opinions on women's status and their relationship with men did not always match those of the dominant Mālikī madhhab, his legal writing recognized the same distinct roles of and hierarchy between men and women that the Mālikīs asserted. His legal writings also characterize homosexuality as a violation of God's law, and one that calls for strict punishment.[29] In the *Ṭawq*, on the other hand, he depicts women as similar in many respects to men and is sympathetic to homoerotic, if not homosexual, relationships. The hierarchy between Muslims and non-Muslims, which he insists on so strongly in his polemical works, is likewise much attenuated in the *Ṭawq*. Despite the contempt he shows for Judaism in the *Faṣl*, the Ibn Ḥazm of the *Dove's Neck Ring* depicts himself sitting in the shop of a Jewish doctor in Almería, watching people on the street and speculating companionably with his friend on the love life of passersby.[30]

Although it is possible to explain the unique tone of the *Ṭawq* in chronological terms—he wrote it before his later preoccupation with law and theology, and before his polemical attack on Ibn Naghrīlah—his awareness of genre may be a better explanation. I do not refer only to the fact that different genres demand that one adopt different rhetorical conventions, so that bitter polemics about the failings of other religions or exhortations to wifely obedience would be out of place in a genre devoted to the themes of love and attraction. The different genres Ibn Ḥazm wrote in also touched on different aspects of his life, particularly since the *Ṭawq* has a strong autobiographical element. The *Muḥallā*'s section on marriage is about hierarchy and duty and the shape that Islamic society should take. The *Ṭawq* is about emotions and intimacy. The author's statement that he prefers blonds, which seems perfectly natural in the *Ṭawq*, is hardly something he would put in a legal or theological treatise. As for Ibn Ḥazm's easy companionship with the Jewish doctor in Almería, it may be that the formal attitude he took toward Judaism in his polemical works was different from his attitude toward non-Muslims in his personal life. Polemic is a type of performance, requiring a stance that admits of no nuance; in a treatise on love and desire, nuance is central.

Nuance, or perhaps ambivalence, is a key feature of the *Ṭawq*'s depiction of women. Manuela Marín argues that Ibn Ḥazm's anecdotes about women are just more of the usual, emphasizing women's weak-mindedness and susceptibility to passion.[31] In some respects she is right. At one point, Ibn Ḥazm states that he has a poor opinion (sūʾ al-ẓann) of women, which he attributes to his inborn sense of ghayrah. "Ghayrah" means a man's jealousy or his sense of honor, particularly the aspect of honor that is increased or diminished by the good or bad behavior of the women in his family. The term goes back a long ways; it does not appear in the Quran but can be found in the ḥadīths, where, for example, one of Muḥammad's followers known for his ghayrah says that if he saw a man with his wife, he would strike him with his sword.[32] By characterizing himself as having ghayrah, Ibn Ḥazm places himself in a long tradition of men viewing women primarily in terms of how they affect men's prestige, and as beings who are likely to behave badly, especially in sexual matters.

Women's power to dishonor men is evident in Ibn Ḥazm's story about Saʿīd ibn Mundhir ibn Saʿīd, a qāḍī in Córdoba. He was in love with one of his slave girls and decided to manumit and marry her. She demanded that he cut his beard in order to gain her favor. He did so, then freed her and proposed marriage to her. She did not accept, but instead accepted the proposal of his brother. Saʿīd, who as her former owner was now her walī, gave his permission for the match.[33] The story appears in a section of the treatise about how passion makes the lover submissive to his beloved, so its main point is probably not that women are manipulative but rather that people put aside their dignity when in the grips of passion. There is, however, some implication in the story that Saʿīd's freedwoman has emasculated him. Beards are an obvious marker of masculinity in the middle ages for both Muslims and Christians; for a soldier, a long beard meant that he had never been taken captive or humiliated by an enemy. In the twelfth- or early thirteenth-century *Cantar de mio Cid*, for example, the Cid reminds his enemy Count Don García that he, the Cid, has a luxuriant beard that had been touched by no one. In contrast, Don García, after the Cid defeated him, had been thoroughly plucked by the Cid's servants, so that "there was not a boy there who did not tear a wisp out."[34] Muslim religious authorities generally recommend keeping the beard long, primarily to distinguish Muslims from pagans. In the *Muḥallā*, Ibn Ḥazm quotes a ḥadīth in which Muḥammad says, "do the opposite of the pagans: trim the mustaches and leave the beard."[35] In addition to being a marker of religious identity, beards in Islamic thought also served to distinguish men from women. Al-Ghazālī (d. 1111), a distinguished legal scholar, philosopher, and mystic, wrote at the end of the eleventh century that plucking the beard is a major evil: "for the beard is the ornament of man. . . . It is one of the signs of perfect creation, and distinguishes men from women."[36] The slave girl's request that Sa'īd cut his beard implies that she was undermining his identity as both a Muslim and a man.

The concern about becoming feminine also surfaces in a story about an acquaintance of Ibn Ḥazm who took his relationship with a young man too far, by allowing the affair to become public knowledge and, probably, allowing it to become sexual.[37] Ibn Ḥazm says that his acquaintance, when he let his relationship with the young man get out of control, "uncovered his head and showed his face . . . and unveiled his countenance" (kashafa ra'sahu wa-abdā wajhahu . . . wa ḥasara muḥayyāhu). Uncovering the face and showing oneself in public was of course a source of shame and dishonor for women, not men. The man in the story has symbolically made himself into a woman.

In spite of the anxieties about honor and gender roles that the *Ṭawq* expresses, it is not simply a literary version of Ibn Ḥabīb's treatise on women. In the world of the *Ṭawq* it is possible for men to feel deep love for women, rather than regarding them as an important but troublesome resource to manage. Ibn Ḥazm recounts his first experience of profound love, when he was less than twenty, with a slave-girl named Nu'm.[38] He was devoted to her and, when she died, was so distraught that he went months without changing his clothes. He says that he would have given up limbs to have her back, calling her "pure, and white like the sun." Women can be similarly devoted to men. One young woman, the niece of a qāḍī of Córdoba, loved her husband so intensely that when he died, she spent the night before his burial wrapped with him in his shroud.[39]

Women can also be good friends and confidants, an assertion Ibn Ḥazm makes in the same section in which he notes his own suspicion of women.[40] The lover, according to Ibn Ḥazm, needs a helping friend to see him through the ordeals of love. The confidant must be a person of restraint and dignity (jalīl al-ḥilm) and refined in manners (ṭayyib al-akhlāq). A male friend can fulfill that role, but so can a woman, and in some ways a woman may be superior. Women, he says, are more likely to keep a secret for lovers than men are. He relates one story in which a wealthy woman discovered that a young man in her family was in love with one of her slave-girls. She tortured another slave-girl, who was a friend of the first girl and knew about the liaison. Even though she tortured the girl beyond what a man could endure, the girl would not divulge what she knew. He also tells the story of a pious elderly woman, whom he characterizes as honorable, as knowing the Quran by heart, and as an ascetic (jalīlah, ḥāfiẓah li-kitāb allāh, nāsikah), who came across a letter written by a young man to a slave-girl with whom he was infatuated. She promised to keep the couple's secret. Older women in general, he says, because they no longer desire men and are presumably not competing with other women for men's attention, can be very generous to younger women. It is not unusual to see a pious older women working to find a good marriage for an orphan girl or lending her clothes and jewels to a poor bride.

Elsewhere, Ibn Ḥazm denies the common perception that women are more likely to give into sexual temptation than men.[41] This discussion takes place in one of the last sections of the *Ṭawq*, on disobedience to God's laws of sexual behavior.[42] He has, he said, often heard people claim that restraint of the passions is a trait of men but not of women. But in fact, he says, women and men are equal in these matters. Virtue is to a large extent a matter of keeping oneself away from temptation; given enough temptation, men and women will both fall into sin. His point is illustrated in a story from his own life that he relates earlier in the treatise.[43] The story is about a beautiful slave-girl who was raised in the household of Ibn Ḥazm's family. He fell in love with her, but she, a virtuous girl, refused each of his advances. He describes a party at his family's home at which he pursued the slave-girl constantly, but she moved away whenever he tried to talk with her. She, not he, was the strong one who protected her virtue, and she did so by refusing to put herself in a situation in which he might be able to tempt her.

The *Ṭawq al-ḥamāmah* is hardly a piece of feminist rhetoric. It describes the world from a masculine point of view. Unlike some of the period's authors of love poetry, Ibn Ḥazm does not always make a distinction between an active lover and a passive beloved, but almost all of his stories are told from the perspective of a man pursuing love (which helps explain his apparent silence on the question of lesbian love).[44] Despite the masculine orientation of the treatise, however, it does offer some interesting contrasts with Sharīʿah's depiction of women. It would be unfair to say that Sharīʿah does not grant women their humanity; in fact, it is careful to condemn practices that treat women as mere items of exchange between men. Sharīʿah does not, however, grant women much agency. Agency belongs to men, who are responsible for fulfilling their obligations to women and enforcing their obedience. Women are presented not as subhuman but as substantially different from men, as people to be controlled but not understood. In the *Ṭawq*, the two sexes are psychologically more similar. Passion can lead either sex into foolish or immoral behavior. At the same time, both men and women are capable of restraint and of profound love and sacrifice. Perhaps more strikingly, both are capable of being generous friends and advisers, suggesting that women can have value in ways that are not tied to sexuality or reproduction.

Louis Crompton has argued that just as the *Ṭawq* does not make a psychological distinction between the way men and women experience love, it does not distinguish between the love men feel for women and the love they feel for other men.[45] While most of the stories in the *Ṭawq* are about men and women, Ibn Ḥazm includes several stories about love between two men and does not suggest that that kind of love is different from any other. In his section on the importance of the eyes as gateways to love, he describes in a poem how, at a social gathering, he never took his eyes off of a man he was in love with.[46] Interestingly, given Ibn Ḥazm's own scholarship on the nature and origins of language, he employs a simile from grammar. He says, "I send them [my eyes] where you turn, and however you move, [so that you are] like a noun (manʿūt) in grammar with its adjective (naʿt)." The words he uses are technical terms in Arabic grammar; "manʿūt" means a substantive accompanied by an attribute, and "naʿt" means a quality or descriptor. His gaze can no more cease to follow the man he loves than an adjective can decide it will not follow the noun it modifies.[47] Given that grammarians of Arabic in that period saw syntactic connections between words as shaped by unchanging rules that are in a sense built into the cosmos, his grammar analogy, which sounds a bit silly in English, conveys in Arabic a deeper sense of inevitability and commitment.

At times when Ibn Ḥazm is discussing his general observations about love, rather than recounting specific anecdotes, he seems to use the masculine pronoun in a generic way, suggesting that the object of the (male) lover's affection may be male or female. That generic usage occurs in his section on the importance of love letters in maintaining a romantic affair.[48] A letter, he says, can act as a man's tongue when speech fails him, and receiving a letter can be as exciting as a face-to-face meeting. It is of course possible to become too excited about a letter; he describes one lover who put his beloved's letter on his penis, a practice Ibn Ḥazm disapproves of (although he reports it anyway). The terms he uses for "lover" and "beloved" ("al-muḥibb" and "al-maḥbūb") are both masculine, and, in view of Ibn Ḥazm's untroubled shifting back and forth between stories of opposite-sex and same-sex love, it is likely that he intended the masculine pronouns as default or neutral terms; the correspondence could be with a male or female beloved. Crompton refers to Ibn Ḥazm's flexibility as to the gender of the beloved as his "romantic bisexuality" and comments that Western readers may find that flexibility unsettling.[49] His observation is borne out by the fact that A. R. Nykl, in his translation dating from the early 1930s, helpfully translates all of the masculine pronouns in this section referring to the beloved as feminine, explaining in a note that "I translate 'she' where the text warrants it."[50] In fact, the text does no such thing.

For all his ease with hetero- and homoerotic relationships, however, Ibn Ḥazm does not go so far as to condone overtly sexual relationships outside of what was permitted by Islamic law. Near the end of the treatise, the section on "The ugliness of disobedience" ("qabḥ al-maʿṣiyah," meaning in this case disobedience to God's law on sexual matters) denounces those who give in to the passions and praises those who are ruled by the intellect and are thus drawn to that which is truly good and beautiful, which apparently does not include actual sex.[51] He says proudly that he has never taken off his undergarment (mi'zar) to engage in illicit sex.[52] It is possible that he added this section of the treatise mainly to deflect criticism, but in fact the only overtly sexual relationship of which he speaks with approval in the treatise is his own youthful affair with the slave-girl Nuʿm. She, assuming she was his own slave, was licit for him under Sharīʿah. Ibn Ḥazm observes social norms by limiting most of the heteroerotic liaisons he describes to those between free men and slave-girls; although a few stories mention married couples, respectable unmarried women do not appear in the *Ṭawq*. A slave woman was of course owned in a literal sense, and her owner was both her only legitimate sexual partner and a walī who could arrange her marriage. Still, she was not under the protection of male relatives whose honor could be violated in the same way a brother's or father's honor could be. Slave women were, therefore, independent operators to whom Ibn Ḥazm could assign agency as he would to a man without disturbing anyone's sense of ghayrah.

The author's own attachments to men seem to have been erotic but not sexual, and, as was discussed above, he condemns relationships between men that become sexual. Ibn Ḥazm's other writings show that his legal position on sex between men is more forgiving than that of most jurists, who consider homosexuality to be form of zinā' and decree that practitioners should be stoned to death. Ibn Ḥazm's conclusion in his legal writing is that sex between two men is a grave crime but not zinā', and that it should not carry a mandatory death sentence; it can be punished according to the discretion of a qāḍī, possibly by lashing.[53] Still, his position is hardly an endorsement of homosexuality. In light of the full range of his writings, it seems reasonable to take Ibn Ḥazm's word for it that he kept his underwear on and did not write his treatise to condone sex outside the confines of Sharīʿah. What is significant about the *Ṭawq al-ḥamāmah* is not that it argues for sexual liberty but that it has a capacious vision of love, in which the gender of those who love and are loved is not of primary importance.

GENDER IN ANDALUSĪ POETRY

The Andalusī poetry of the period—as opposed to the mixture of poetry and prose that makes up the *Ṭawq*—presents a complicated landscape. Much of the poetry associated with the Umayyad and Taifa courts is unsatisfying as a source for contemporary attitudes about gender, even in court circles, since it is based on traditional conventions of love poetry and can therefore be formulaic and emotionally distanced.[54] The poetry of the period, however, does express, in perhaps less spontaneous ways, the same themes we saw in the *Ṭawq*, including the power of the beloved over the lover and the pain of being apart from the beloved. The famous "Nunīyah" (poem rhymed in the letter "n") of Ibn Zaydūn (d. 1071), which is part of a cycle of poems that is traditionally thought to be about the Umayyad princess Walladah, is about the pain of separation. It depicts the beloved woman as a noble and exalted creature who rules over the lover; the poet refers to her as one who is without peer and who has no associate in any quality (wa-mā shūrikta fī ṣifah). The use of a verb from the root sh-r-k, the root of the word "shirk," idolatry or the associating of something with God, suggests that the beloved is almost divine in her lover's eyes.[55]

Two forms of poetry that originated in al-Andalus, the muwashshaḥah and the zajal, were written for elite audiences but were probably influenced by popular Romance and vernacular Arabic songs of the region. The muwashshaḥah was written in formal Arabic but always ended with two lines in a vernacular language, either colloquial Arabic or Romance, which usually represented the speech of the beloved woman or boy. The zajal was written entirely in vernacular Arabic, often with Romance words thrown into the mix.[56] Zajals could be quite smutty. In one poem, Ibn Quzmān (d. 1160) writes,

> Hardly had I beheld that leg
> And those two lively, lively eyes,
> When my penis arose in my trousers like a pavilion, And made a
>   tent of my clothes.
> And since I observed that a certain 'son of Adam' was dilated
> The chick wished to hide in the nest.
> "Where are you taking that *pollo* [chicken, written in Romance], for
>   an immoral purpose?"[57]

Muwashshaḥāt were more formal than zajals but also more free-wheeling than traditional Middle Eastern poetic forms. In a homoerotic muwashshaḥah of Ibn ʿUbāda al-Qazzāz (active in the second half of the eleventh century), the beloved (a boy) is described in conventional terms as a gazelle, a full moon, and a lily:[58]

> I loved a new moon unique in its beauty borrowing from the gazelle
> its glances and (slender) neck.
> A full moon that shone in shapely proportion was proud of its
> beauty, desiring no increase.
> Grace had adorned him; his figure was graceful.
> A full moon that conquered with evident charm, cheek down
> curling over a jasmine (complexion),
> A lily placed in line with a well-guarded rose; when it appeared it
> (proudly) trailed the edges of beauty's robe.

In the last two lines of the poem, however, the boy who is the object of love speaks in colloquial Arabic to rebuff the lover's advances, saying that the lover will never taste the tempting morsel (qūqū). Jewish courtiers writing in Hebrew also explored the themes of homoeroticism and homosexuality in muwashshaḥāt.[59] One Hebrew poem by Ibn Gabirol uses language similar to Ibn ʿUbada's to describe the beloved boy, invoking the images of the moon and of vegetation:

> His cheeks are like apples of gold in a setting of silver, and a word
> fitly spoken.
> The moon is shamed when he sees the light of his cheeks, and the
> sun sets in his face.
> His breast is like golden pomegranates fastened with silver; would
> that I could suck his pomegranates![60]

The casual inclusion of homoerotic themes provides a link between this type of poetry and the *Ṭawq*. The fact that the poems are about love between mature men and boys, however, points to a major difference, since the *Ṭawq* is more concerned with love between men who are equals as friends, if not always social equals. The difference may perhaps be explained by Ibn Ḥazm's personal experiences, but it also reflects his interest in portraying the subjective sense of union and companionship that comes with love. Even the muwashshaḥāt, which usually gave the beloved the last word in their final lines, emphasized the subjectivity of the lover, but not that of the beloved.

The literature of love produced in court circles may not record widely accepted gender norms. It does, however, suggest that relationships between men and women, or men and men (or boys), could be seen in ways that had little to do with duty or the maintenance of social structure, and everything to do with private pleasure and intimacy.

GENDER IN SUFI TEXTS

Mystical texts, although they are obviously religious in nature, demonstrate a view of religion, and of gender, that is distinct from that of Islamic law. Where Sharīʿah addresses gender in the context of how the family and society should function, Sufi texts use gender as a metaphor, either to express the intense relationship of the Sufi with God or to describe the nature of God or the cosmos. Poetry using the metaphor of erotic love to depict the bond between the mystic and his or her beloved God, like that of Jalāl al-Dīn Rūmī, has not survived in the Andalusī tradition. We do, however, have a body of writing from the mystic Ibn al-ʿArabī (1165–1240), who used gender as a metaphor in his cosmological and theosophical writings.

The term "Sufism" covers a wide variety of beliefs and practices within Islam. It can refer to the practices of ascetics like Rābiʿah of Basra, to those seeking annihilation of their individuality in God like al-Junayd, to charismatic preachers like al-Ḥallāj, or to students of theosophy and cosmology like Ibn al-ʿArabī. In the North African tradition, the term "Sufi" is synonymous with "walī," meaning in this context a friend of God or a saint; God grants walīs the ability to perform miracles. The Sufi tradition in al-Andalus was more limited and developed later than in most other areas of the Islamic world. There were examples in the ninth and tenth centuries of men acclaimed as ascetics (zuhhād), who fasted and prayed or recited the Quran continually.[61] Women could also be known as ascetics (zāhidāt) and Quran readers (muqri'āt).[62] By the second half of the tenth century, saints' miracles, or karāmāt, were attributed to some mystics.[63] Such claims were controversial, however, since they could be put to political use. In 901 the Umayyad Ibn al-Qiṭṭ, a descendent of the amīr Hishām I, led a movement of Nafzah Berbers in Mérida. His stated goal was jihād against Christian Zamora, but he also claimed to be the Mahdī, or messiah, and was widely believed to perform miracles; his claims made him a distinct political threat to his kinsman, the amīr ʿAbd ʿAllāh. His claim to being the Mahdī, as well as his association with a Berber movement, suggests a connection with the various messianic Shīʿī movements in North Africa at the time.[64] Ibn al-ʿArabī gives a lengthy account of holy men, and holy women, in al-Andalus, suggesting that the recognition of exceptionally pious and ascetic men and women as walīs had become widespread by the late twelfth century.[65]

Ibn Masarrah, whose letter mysticism was discussed in chapter 2, was a muwallad who died in 931 and was probably an important link between the earliest mystics, whose practice focused on asceticism, and Ibn al-ʿArabī, who saw mysticism as a road to understanding the structure and meaning of the universe. The foundational modern work on Ibn Masarrah is an early twentieth-century study by Miguel Asín Palacios.[66] According to Asín Palacios, Ibn Masarrah drew on the works of the pseudo-Empedocles, whom Muslim philosophers placed in the tenth century BCE as a contemporary of David and Solomon, but who in fact represented late antique Neoplatonic thought. Asín Palacios argues that there are two central tenets of that Neoplatonic thought as Ibn Masarrah understood it. The first is that God created the universe by an emanation of the first substance (al-jawhar al-awwal) that was purely spiritual but became degraded and formed material reality as well, meaning that the world we see around us is a mix of the more exalted spirit and the more degraded matter. The second and related concept is the existence of a universal spirit, of which all human souls originally were part. Human beings are a mixture of that pure soul with impure matter and must struggle to purify themselves so that their souls can return to the universal soul after death. Asceticism plays a major role in purification.[67] According to Asín's account, Ibn Masarrah founded a school of legal practice or madhhab. One of its leaders, Ismaʿīl ibn ʿAbd Allāh al-Ruʿaynī, a contemporary of Ibn Ḥazm, taught that property beyond what was necessary to sustain you for a day was not truly yours, and he believed in either holding all women in the community in common or at least in mutʿah marriage, a form of temporary marriage for a set period of time that was allowed in early Islam but was later permitted only under Shīʿī law. He denied the resurrection of the body and taught that the soul is rewarded or punished immediately after death.[68]

How much truth there is in Asín's description of Ibn Masarrah is open to debate, given how inconsistent the information in the primary sources he uses actually is.[69] The work of Pilar Garrido Clemente makes a good case that Ibn Masarrah was a much more conservative figure than Asín suggests. According to her research, his thought did have some Neoplatonic elements; his *Risālah al-iʿtibār*, or *Letter of Interpretation*, for example, sees humans as beings who have descended from God into the material world, and who can, through the mystical study of scripture, ascend and return to God.[70] Much of his piety seems to have been more conventional, however.[71] He wrote a summary and commentary on *al-Mudawwanah al-kubrā*, suggesting that he saw himself as a Mālikī. During a trip to Medina, he visited the house of one of Muḥammad's wives, Maria the Copt, and took measurements of an upstairs room in which Muḥammad was said to have prayed, so that he could recreate the room when he returned to Córdoba. This last story suggests a traditional pietistic outlook—he wanted to imitate the Prophet—rather than any radical position.

Furthermore, although some of his followers were under suspicion at the end of ʿAbd al-Raḥmān III's reign, Ibn Masarrah himself was never accused of impropriety during his lifetime. Ibn Ḥazm did later accuse him of being a Muʿtazilī.[72] Muʿtazilism was a movement in ninth-century urban Islam, centering in Baghdad, which held that logic and rational argumentation based on Greek models had a legitimate place in theology and that God had created human beings with extensive free will and responsibility for their actions.[73] In al-Andalus, however, the term was used more broadly to mean something like "free-thinker." While it would not quite be fair to say that Ibn Ḥazm classified anyone who disagreed with him as a Muʿtazilī, he did use the term in a general way to describe Muslims who were more open to the use of speculative theology than he was, which meant virtually everyone with an interest in that field. The accusations against al-Ruʿaynī—that he believed in communal property and the sharing of women—are standard accusations against communities deemed heretical, and they are leveled at such communities in both the Islamic and Christian traditions.[74] It does seem likely, though, that Ibn Masarrah practiced asceticism and imitation of Muḥammad's actions, and that he believed a mixture of meditation and rational thought could lead to knowledge of God and the universe.[75]

Ibn Masarrah's interests represent a bridge between the ascetics and miracle workers of the ninth and tenth centuries and the most famous Sufi scholar of al-Andalus, Ibn al-ʿArabī (1165–1240). Ibn al-ʿArabī wrote about the holy people with whom he associated, but most of his writing can be classified as theosophy. In developing his ideas, he often used images of gender, and specifically images of the male and female body. He saw both as sacred and as corresponding to various aspects of the divine; the male body in particular he associated with language.

There is an argument against including Ibn al-ʿArabī in this study since he lived so much later than the Umayyad period, but his views on gender provide a particularly interesting contrast with Sharīʿah. In the first place, he recognized the authority of women mystics and the importance of religious education for women. Additionally, in his mystical texts, he presents gender as complementary, at least on the symbolic level; the male and the female principles are both essential parts of the cosmos. What, if anything, his theoretical ideas about gender or his warm regard for women mystics tells us about the period of this study is admittedly debatable. His ideas may represent a continuation of mystical ideas and practices that go back to Umayyad times but are poorly documented for that period. His views of gender, and the presence of women Sufis in al-Andalus, could also point to a later development of women's mysticism that opened up at least some spiritual paths to women well after the Umayyad period. In any event, I present an analysis of his work here to suggest another possible way in which Andalusīs understood gender.

Ibn al-ʿArabī refers to God as al-wujūd, that which exists, or al-ḥaqq, the real; nothing else truly exists or has reality.[76] Before the creation of the cosmos, al-wujūd existed as a completely self-contained being. It longed, however, to express itself, and it did so with speech. Al-wujūd spoke its names, which denote its multiple attributes: the Merciful, the Compassionate, the Wrathful, the Destroyer, the Victorious. As God spoke his names, the cosmos came into being. Before that act of speech the names were undifferentiated and contained within the divine being, but as God spoke the names emanated outward and became differentiated, thus creating the diversity of the created world. The universe was created because of God's desire to express his nature, and it is supported by a network of his words. Ibn al-ʿArabī illustrates this concept of words as an active force in the cosmos in a story he tells about one of his teachers, a woman in her nineties, who could use the words from the first chapter of the Quran as a charm. For her the words became an active presence, like a daemon or jinnī that could do her bidding. In one case, in order to help a woman whose husband had deserted her, she sent the words after the errant husband, and they physically forced him to return home.[77]

Ibn al-ʿArabī develops this idea of language as the basis of creation when he discusses the image of the pen (qalam) and tablet (lawḥ).[78] The pen and tablet are images that appear in the Quran in the context of God's revelation of the Quran to human beings. Quran 68:1, for example, talks about an archetypal pen of revelation, and 85:22 describes the Quran as inscribed on a tablet. In both cases the image is of revelation coming specifically through the written word, as something God writes. Ibn al-ʿArabī takes this image of writing much farther and connects God's inscribing of words as the actual process of creation, not just of the Quran, but of everything. The pen, which Ibn al-ʿArabī equates with intellect, was the first thing God created; the tablet emerged out of the pen as an emanation.[79] God spoke to the pen, which then wrote God's words on the tablet, thus bringing the cosmos into being; it inscribed on the tablet "everything that was and that is and that will be and that is not but could have been had God willed it."[80] The pen and the tablet are gendered in Ibn al-ʿArabī's thought; the active pen is masculine, while the passive tablet on which it writes is feminine. More specifically, they are related to the male and female body, corresponding to the penis and the womb respectively.[81] Pen and tablet undergo a marriage, and the signs the pen places on the tablet are like semen deposited in the womb.[82]

This image of insemination suggests the sacredness of the human body and of sexuality as a symbol of God's creative act. And indeed in the final chapter of his *Bezels of Wisdom*, Ibn al-ʿArabī discusses the symbolism of relations between men and women.[83] He first sets up a correspondence between God's love for his creation and a man's love for a woman. The intense desire of God's names to express themselves led to his creation of the cosmos; his love and desire drew him to abandon his perfect unity and create, by speaking his names, the fragmentation and variety of the world. In the same way, women draw men away from their intellectual and spiritual life and into the world of physical life and change.

He then sets up a second correspondence between God's love for human beings and man's love for woman. Just as man was created out of God, woman was created out of man; a man is drawn to a woman because the whole is always drawn to one of its parts, as God is drawn to man. Contemplating women, who are below men and created from them, can benefit men spiritually because it reminds them of their own servitude and incompleteness in relationship to God. Finally, he argues that man stands in the same relationship to woman as God does to nature. God created the cosmos by injecting his works into the formless void of nature. In the same way man initiates creation by injecting his seed into woman.

The relationships among, and distinctions between, men and women, God and man, and God and nature are symbolically present in the pen and tablet. The pen is a symbol of God's unity; it contains latent versions of the cosmos' diversity, but that diversity only manifests itself when the pen writes on the tablet.[84] The pen's unity is similar to a man's integrity, while the tablet's multiplicity is echoed in a woman's place in the natural world of change and variety. In addition, the female tablet is passive and its existence and meaning are dependent on the active male pen; the tablet is an emanation of the pen, just as Eve is an emanation of Adam on the physical plane.[85]

Ibn al-ʿArabī's understanding of the feminine in some ways parallels that of the jurists. Women are below men in the hierarchy of creation and stand in relation to men as men stand in relation to God. In addition, the feminine is passive by nature; for Ibn al-ʿArabī the feminine is without form or meaning until the masculine writes meaning into it, while for the jurists women are (mostly) passive in their social and sexual relationships with men: "The man is the one who marries, the one who takes a concubine, and the woman is the one who is married, who is taken as a concubine."[86] In other respects, Ibn al-ʿArabī presents a very different idea of gender relations. His writing shows us women who are admirable teachers and ascetics, as advanced in their spirituality as men. In his more abstract theosophical works, masculine and feminine exist in a hierarchy, but also as essences that complement and complete each other. The masculine may be superior to the feminine, but it also longs for the feminine and has no way of completing its process of self-expression without her. In many respects, Ibn al-ʿArabī's masculine and feminine principles have more in common with the lovers in the *Ṭawq al-ḥamāmah* than with the husbands and wives described by jurists.

No literary, mystical, or legal work from al-Andalus shows a modern belief in equality of the sexes; all sources see at least some elements of hierarchy between men and women, and all differentiate between the roles of men and women and the meaning of masculinity and femininity. Looking at a variety of sources, however, allows us to see a range of attitudes toward masculinity and femininity. The legal materials envisage strict social roles for men and women and place men and women largely in the relationship of guardian to ward. Poetic and literary sources show a more flexible attitude toward gender, emphasizing the mutual dependence of the sexes and the potential for women to share men's virtues. Those sources also suggest the possibility of love and sexuality between men, clearly not a part of Islamic legal thought. Finally, mysticism emphasizes the complementary relationship between the masculine and the feminine as much as their hierarchical relationship.

6 ✦ Berbers and Muwallads

I began this book by naming five distinct social groups in Umayyad al-Andalus: Arab Muslims, Berber Muslims and muwallads who through clientage or education became honorary Arabs, muwallads who did not have elite status, nonelite Muslim Berbers, and dhimmīs. In fact, though, the most important division was between a small ruling group and everyone else. That elite, or khāṣṣah, was made up of prominent Arab Muslims who could trace their ancestry back to the early days of Islamic rule in al-Andalus, Muslims of Iberian or Berber origin who had become honorary Arabs through ties of walā' (clientage) or the study and acquisition of Arabic language and Arab culture, and a few dhimmīs who occupied key administrative positions. The larger group made up of everyone else (al-'āmmah) included Arab families who had lost elite status (or never had it),[1] ordinary muwallads and Berber Muslims, and almost all dhimmīs.

Although Arab ancestry was an important route to membership in the khāṣṣah, we have seen that there were a number of routes to quasi-Arab status even if one was not Arab by blood. Jews and Christians in the ninth and tenth centuries could hold important government appointments. Distinguishing oneself as a member of the 'ulamā' was a path to high status. Ties of walā' with the Umayyads also made one part of the elite. The tenth-century grammarian and historian Ibn al-Qūṭīyah, for example, came to prominence partly because of his status as a historian and a scholar of the Arabic language. He was also helped, however, by the fact that he was descended from the marriage of the Visigothic princess Sarah to an Umayyad mawlā.[2] In the same way, the renowned Berber faqīh Yaḥyā ibn Yaḥyā Ibn

Kathīr al-Laythī was reported to have studied with Mālik in Medina and was an important figure at the court of ʿAbd al-Raḥmān II.[3] His family also identified themselves as linked to the Arab aristocracy through a tie of alliance (ḥilf) with the Banū Layth. While the two men were able to associate themselves with the elite because of their respective ties of walāʾ and ḥilf, the combination of those ties with scholarly distinction made their claim that much more powerful.

While some dhimmīs and non-Arab Muslims rose to positions of prominence, most did not and were perceived as outside the Arab Muslim power structure. The elite's authority, however, did not go unquestioned. Chapter 3 outlined some of the tensions between Muslims and dhimmīs. The following two chapters will look at challenges from non-Arab Muslims to the idea of Arab superiority and to the connection between Muslim and Arab identity. This chapter will examine the challenge an important Muslim Berber family posed to Umayyad rule and will then focus in more detail on a major muwallad uprising in the south.

BERBERS: THE BANŪ DHĪ AL-NŪN

Until 750, the Umayyads, as sole caliphs, ruled both al-Andalus and North Africa. By the second half of the 700s, the Umayyads controlled only al-Andalus, and despite Abbasid claims, much of the North African Maghrib was independent, ruled by the Idrisids in northern Morocco and the Rustamids in western Algeria.[4] Al-Andalus and North Africa were, however, culturally and economically linked both before and after 750.[5]

An example of that link is the Berber uprising of 740–41, which began in North Africa and spread to al-Andalus. As we saw in chapter 1, Berbers were a crucial element of the Muslim armies in North Africa and al-Andalus yet were often not given the same status as Arab fighters. They were sometimes subject to the jizyah and, under some governors of North Africa, were required to produce an annual levy of slaves. In 741, Berbers assassinated the Umayyad governor Kulthūm ibn ʿIyād al-Qaysī and killed many of his troops.[6] The insurrection spread to al-Andalus, where Berbers in northern al-Andalus revolted and marched south. The Arab general Balj ibn Bishr, who had lost many troops to the Berber uprising in North Africa, crossed over at the behest of the Andalusī governor and put down the Berber revolt near Toledo.[7] That uprising set a pattern of Berber insurrection against the Umayyads.

Whatever the full range of reasons for the Berber uprising, they were at their most obvious level protests against the ill-treatment they received from Arabs in power. The influence on Andalusī Berbers of Berber revolts in North Africa is clear and unsurprising, given the frequency of migrations between al-Andalus and North Africa.[8] Shī'ī and Khārijī ideologies that were popular in North Africa may also have played a part in the Andalusī revolts.[9] Khārijism in particular was widespread in North Africa and often expressed itself in political terms, as a struggle for independence.[10] Exactly what role religion played in the revolts is difficult to determine, however, since Sunni Muslim chroniclers looking back at the revolts tend to judge any religious component against the standard of Sunni Islam. Sources say, for example, that the revolt led by the Berber Shaqyā al-Miknāsī, which 'Abd al-Raḥmān I put down in 776, was inspired by Shī'ism. Eduardo Manzano Moreno, however, has suggested that the revolt was largely led by Shaqyā's mother, Fāṭimah, and was related to Berber political uprisings in North Africa led by women, such as al-Kāhinah's revolt against the Arabs in the early 700s, rather than to a tradition of Shī'ī dissent.[11]

Explaining revolts as religious movements could serve as a way for the chroniclers, who were generally Umayyad sympathizers, to trivialize the causes of Berber discontent. Arabic chronicles explain the Berber movement surrounding Ibn al-Qiṭṭ in 901, for example, as an outbreak of hysterical millenarianism.[12] According to al-Rāzī by way of Ibn Ḥayyān, Ibn al-Qiṭṭ ibn Hishām ibn Mu'āwiyah al-Qurayshī, a descendant of the amīr Hishām, emerged under the tutelage of a troublemaker named Abū 'Alī al-Sarrāj, who styled himself as an ascetic and was intent on fomenting rebellion. With al-Sarrāj's support, Ibn al-Qiṭṭ arrived in the region of Mérida. There he insinuated himself with local Berber tribes, prophesying and preaching jihād and denigrating the current Umayyad amīr, 'Abd Allāh. He claimed to be the Mahdī and the guardian ('āṣim) of the Muslims, finally inciting the tribes to go on a holy war against the city of Zamora, in order to return it to Muslim hands. The enterprise at Zamora concluded badly after key tribal leaders deserted the siege, and Ibn al-Qiṭṭ's head ended up on the city wall. What is most interesting about al-Rāzī's account, however, is its condescending tone and his portrayal of the Berbers as dupes who were easily blinded and led astray by the rhetoric of Ibn al-Qiṭṭ and al-Sarrāj. For him there is no possible cause for the jihād against Zamora except the Berbers' childish credulity.

In contrast to the stories of Berber dissent, the chroniclers also record many cases of Berbers supporting the Arab elite. During the emirate, the

Berbers played an important role in defending the marches against Christian incursions, with the result that the amīrs often granted iqṭāʿ land (which gave the holder usufruct from land in exchange for military service) to Berber families.[13] In the tenth century, ʿAbd al-Raḥmān III made heavy use of Berber military allies. He also appointed Berbers to important administrative positions; he made Muḥammad ibn ʿAbd Allāh Ibn ʿAbī ʿĪsā, a descendent of Yaḥyā ibn Yaḥyā, chief qāḍī of Córdoba and used him as an ambassador to the marches, where the notables upon whom the caliph depended for military support were often Berber.[14] The limitation of the chronicles is that they evaluate the behavior of Berbers in terms of whether they supported the Umayyads or not; the only two types of Berbers are those who are obedient and those who are not. Reading beyond those categories, however, it becomes clear that during the Umayyad period a number of areas in al-Andalus were evolving as Berber societies whose formation was not under the political control of Umayyad Córdoba.

Chroniclers divided Berber tribes arriving in al-Andalus into Butr and Barānis. The term Barānis seems to have referred to North African tribes who had assimilated to Byzantine culture and were Christian before their conversion to Islam. The Butr tribes were pagan before their conversion and less connected to urban Byzantine culture.[15] Arabs characterized the majority of the Berbers in al-Andalus as Butr, emphasizing their historical distance from urban life and monotheism. The association of Berbers with paganism may be exaggerated, since Christianity and Judaism would have been familiar to most North African Berbers in the period just before the advent of Islam.[16] The characterization of tribes as Butr may have been a way for the chroniclers to talk about the fact that areas in which Berbers settled were often not heavily populated by Arabs, and that Berber societies were not always subject to the norms of Arab Córdoba. The pro-Arab chroniclers' disdain for many Berbers also obscures the fact that the relationship between Berbers and Arabs was complex, in that Berbers were able to pick and choose what they took from the Arab elite; their own leading families might embrace Arab Muslim culture, while maintaining political independence from Córdoba.

The Berber family known in the Arabic sources as the Banū Dhī al-Nūn is in some way typical of prominent Berber groups, in that they were at different times allies of the Umayyads, rebels against them, and an independent elite who ruled without reference to them. According to Ibn Ḥayyān, the ancestor who first came to al-Andalus was al-Samḥ.[17] The family settled in Santaver, near Cuenca. Ibn ʿIdhārī tells us that the family's original name was Dhannūn, which was a common Berber name, but that it was later mistakenly written as Dhū al-Nūn, an Arab name.[18] The change was no doubt in line with the family's gradual assimilation to Arab culture. The earliest mention of the Banū Dhī al-Nūn in al-Andalus, from the period of Amīr Muḥammad I, places them as allies of the Umayyads. At that time, Mūsā Ibn Dhī al-Nūn is reported to have cared for a favorite eunuch of the amīr's who fell ill on his way home from a campaign. In return the amīr made official Mūsā's control of the area around Santaver (asjala lahu 'alā nāḥiyah), later giving him a castle in the region as an iqṭā', and accepted one of Mūsā's sons as a hostage. The taking of a hostage was meant to ensure good behavior on the part of the family in question. Provided that good behavior was forthcoming, the hostage was treated as an honored guest, which usually meant a trip to Córdoba and an education in Arab courtly culture.[19]

Other periods found the Banū Dhī al-Nūn acting independently of the Umayyads. Mūsā's son, also called Mūsā, the one who had been a hostage at Cordoba, took over the region of Huete in his own name.[20] Starting in 874 he made two attacks on Toledo (strictly without Umayyad permission), which led to the Banū Dhī al-Nūn's sporadic control of that city until the muwallad Banū Qasī conquered it in 897.[21] Despite their strong presence in the area, the Banū Dhī al-Nūn did not regain control of Toledo itself until around the time of the caliphate's collapse.[22] Mūsā died in 907, dividing the family's territory between his three sons.[23] They maintained the family's pattern of occasional cooperation with the Umayyads. Al-Fatḥ ruled the city of Uclés and worked to expand his territory at the expense of the Umayyads and of local leaders. 'Abd al-Raḥmān III's army defeated the second son, Yaḥyā, who along with his family was taken to Córdoba in 933; 'Abd al-Raḥmān III pardoned him, after which he remained loyal to the Umayyads. The third son, Muṭarraf, generally cooperated with the Umayyads.

After the collapse of Umayyad power in 1031, al-Andalus fragmented under the control of Arab, ṣaqlabī, and Berber dynasties, some of the latter being recently arrived Berber groups. The Banū Dhī Nūn, as one of the Berber dynasties whose presence in al-Andalus went back to the period of the conquests, continued to do what they had been doing anyway, that is ruling the area around Toledo. Although their efforts to control Toledo in the past had met with resistance on the part of its muwallad leadership, those tensions seem to have lessened by 1031; Pierre Guichard speculates that the steady Arabization of the peninsula had smoothed over differences of ethnicity among Muslims.[24] That may be true, although Ibn 'Idhārī is very clear in his identification of the family as Berber, and in his view as rather obscure Berbers who had no important historical role until the Umayyads lost power.[25] In any event, they were in the Taifa period a major political force in the central peninsula, in spite of repeated conflicts with the Arab Banū Hūd in the region.[26]

The story of the Banū Dhī al-Nūn reflects the general pattern of Umayyad rule: close control of the area around Córdoba, with more sporadic and looser rule outside that area, often in the form of alliances with families holding regional power. Despite the chroniclers' efforts to define the exercise of Berber authority as an act of either obedience to or defiance of the Umayyads, much of the family's history unfolded independently of Córdoba. After 1031, the Banū Dhī al-Nūn's power no longer came with the official imprimatur of the Umayyads, but its nature did not really change.

MUWALLADS: THE ʿUMAR IBN ḤAFṢŪN REVOLT

The ninth- and early tenth-century revolt of ʿUmar Ibn Ḥafṣūn, his family, and his allies represented at least as great a threat to the Umayyads as any Berber revolt. The nature of the threat was first of all geographic; the center of the uprising was the province of Rayyah in southern al-Andalus, putting Ibn Ḥafṣūn within striking distance of Córdoba. As in the case of the on-again off-again revolt of the Banū Dhī al-Nūn, the uprising spanned a long period of time, from 879 to 928; but while the Banū Dhī al-Nūn's goal was primarily to maintain their independence, expanding their territory as possible, Ibn Ḥafṣūn's actions suggest an intent to destroy Umayyad power and form a new state in southern al-Andalus.[27]

The revolt at its greatest extent encompassed much of the southern-most part of al-Andalus, from the Mediterranean in the south to the Guadalquivir Valley in the north. The population of that area was made up primarily of Christians and Muslims who were Berber or muwallad. The terrain is mountainous, and despite the presence of important cities like Ronda, Malaga, and Algeciras, the area at the time was largely rural in comparison with the Guadalquivir Valley. Although each province was technically run by an Umayyad governor, power in rural areas was concentrated in the hands of powerful families who held castles (ḥuṣūn; the holder of a castle is called a ṣāḥib in the Arabic sources, plural aṣḥāb), to which local people could retreat during times of danger.[28]

ʿUmar Ibn Ḥafṣūn's family were well-to-do muwallads from the area of Ronda who converted to Islam at the time of Ibn Ḥafṣūn's great-grandfather

Ja'far.[29] The thirteenth-century historian Ibn 'Askar says that Ibn Ḥafṣūn's ancestor Alfonso was a Visigothic count.[30] When he was young, Ibn Ḥafṣūn killed a man in a fight and had to flee to the mountains, where he became a bandit. After the local governor had him arrested and flogged, he decamped for Ifrīqiyah, specifically to the city of Tāhart, the capital of the Rustamid dynasty in what would now be western Algeria. There he became the apprentice of a tailor who also had roots in Rayyah.[31] The fact that he was in contact with at least one other person from al-Andalus suggests that the choice of Tāhart was not arbitrary, but may reflect trading or other connections between Malaga and that part of Ifrīqiyah. He returned to al-Andalus where, with the help of his paternal uncle, he established himself at the fortress of Bobastro with a private army, which began conducting raids on neighboring areas around 879 or 880. Ibn Ḥafṣūn succeeded in setting himself up as the local authority and tax collector in defiance of the Umayyads. He was able to expand his geographic reach over time and became increasingly aggressive in his attacks on the Guadalquivir region. After his death in 917, his sons continued the revolt. The last surviving son, Ḥafṣ, surrendered to the Umayyads in 928.

There is some difference of opinion as to how much of a threat Ibn Ḥafṣūn's revolt actually posed to the Umayyads. Lévi-Provençal believed that Ibn Ḥafṣūn was finally an opportunist who did not have the temperament or the organizational skills to conduct a sustained campaign against Córdoba.[32] An argument can be made that the revolt was in fact haphazard. As was the case with most of the local uprisings against the Umayyads, Ibn Ḥafṣūn's revolt stopped and started, punctuated by periods of peace with Córdoba. In 883 he surrendered to the Umayyad army and was taken to Córdoba. There he was given an important position in the military, in keeping with the Umayyads' policy that it was safer to bring troublemakers into the tent than to leave them outside. Shortly after his surrender he fought as a commander in the Umayyad army against the Banū Qasī on the upper march. Soon afterwards, however, he fled Córdoba and returned to Bobastro.[33] In 887 Ibn Ḥafṣūn negotiated peace with the amīr al-Mundhir, although he quickly violated the terms.[34] And while at times he took aggressive action against the Umayyads, long periods of the revolt were much more passive and consisted of Ibn Ḥafṣūn and his followers going to ground in their various castles to ride out Umayyad sieges. The fact that, in 898 or 899, he converted to Christianity also calls into question how seriously he can be taken as a leader. Whatever the motivation for his conversion, it resulted in the immediate loss of many Muslim allies and an overall weakening of his position.[35]

Contemporaries and near contemporaries, however, took Ibn Ḥafṣūn seriously. Ibn ʿIdhārī characterizes him as the arch-rebel (kabīr al-thuwwār).[36] Particularly during the reign of Amīr ʿAbd Allāh, Ibn Ḥafṣūn recruited increasing numbers of followers among holders of castles in southern al-Andalus. ʿAbd Allāh, unable to mount a successful attack against the rebels, simply gave up at one point, appointing Ibn Ḥafṣūn as governor of the province of Rayyah and returning to Córdoba.[37] Ibn Ḥafṣūn then extended his raids to the area near Córdoba, attacking estates that were important food sources for the capital.[38] Those attacks suggest that he did not simply wish to be left alone in Rayyah, but that he wanted to conquer the Umayyads' center of power. His alliances were at some points very broad, including Christians, muwallads, Berbers, and Arabs.[39] In 898 Ibn Ḥafṣūn explored the possibility of an alliance with Muḥammad ibn Lope of the Banū Qasī, a powerful muwallad family on the northern march; an agreement never materialized, but if it had the Umayyads might have found themselves threatened from both north and south.[40]

Even when he was not actively pursuing campaigns in the Guadalquivir Valley, Ibn Ḥafṣūn continued to be a drain on the Umayyads' resources. His core of support was the network of aṣḥāb in the area. The aṣḥāb were the local authorities; the more they participated in the revolt, the less control of the region the Umayyads had, and the less tax revenue they received. In addition, even though the Umayyads were at some points able to keep Ibn Ḥafṣūn and his followers contained, it was difficult to end the revolt decisively, since many of the castles in question could withstand lengthy sieges. Judging from the site archaeologists believe is the ruins of Bobastro, with its high elevation and limited access, anyone defending a siege there would have been almost impossible to dislodge; Ibn ʿIdhārī calls it the most impregnable fortress in al-Andalus without exception.[41]

Ibn Ḥafṣūn's revolt shows us that the Umayyads were weak at times, and that in spite of their claims to be "sons of the caliph," their right to rule al-Andalus was far from universally acknowledged. It is less clear what the revolt tells us about the society and culture of the period, although a number of theories have been advanced in an effort to find a deeper historical meaning in the rebellion. The theories divide roughly into those that emphasize Ibn Ḥafṣūn's Christian and Visigothic roots and those that emphasize his place in the Islamic world.

Spanish scholars in the late nineteenth century and the first half of the twentieth focused on Ibn Ḥafṣūn's Christian and Iberian identity, seeing his rebellion as either a Christian uprising against Islam or a proto-nationalist movement against foreign occupation.[42] The idea of Ibn Ḥafṣūn as a Spanish nationalist has been widely rejected as anachronistic, but the focus on his pre-invasion roots continues in the work of Manuel Acién Almansa and Thomas Glick, both of whom see the uprising as a final attempt by the old Visigothic aristocracy to assert its power.[43] They argue that although the Visigothic aristocracy did not maintain a presence in cities after the conquest, the invaders made deals with great Visigothic families in rural areas, encouraging them to convert to Islam and become honored mawālī, while allowing them to maintain their local power and estates. The Banū Qasī in the north (assuming they were in fact Visigothic in origin, as they claimed) are a good example of a family who maintained its preconquest elite status. Those old families ran their rural estates as "feudal" holdings in the sense that regional authority, including the right to collect rents, remained within the family, rather than being held by the state. The Cordovan state began to assert its rights during the time of ʿAbd al-Raḥmān II, appointing its own governors and insisting that the income previously collected locally as rents was in fact taxation owed to the central government. Rebellions ensued; many local warlords and landholders who were not of Visigothic origin revolted as well, of course, but the old Visigothic families were key players in the struggle against centralization. In this scenario, Ibn Ḥafṣūn's revolt represents the last gasp of Visigothic resistance.

The sources certainly give us reasons to link Ibn Ḥafṣūn to the Christian and Visigothic past. As was mentioned above, Ibn ʿAskar says that the family was originally Visigothic, and they fit Acién Almansa's model of a rural dynasty controlling its area of influence as a private estate. Ibn ʿIdhārī reports that Ibn Ḥafṣūn gave out gold armbands to his followers.[44] Muslim leaders distributed booty to their followers, but the specific gift of gold armbands seems intended to invoke a Germanic past. Probably after his conversion in 899, Ibn Ḥafṣūn had two new churches built in Bobastro.[45] The style of the churches is similar to that of churches built in León at around the same time. Some features, however, such as the use of three apses, appear in much older Spanish churches dating to the Visigothic period. It would be unwise to draw too many conclusions about the architecture as a deliberate symbol of cultural loyalty—maybe, as far as Ibn Ḥafṣūn was concerned, that was just what churches looked like—but it is possible that he was deliberately linking himself to the Visigothic past.

Then there was the family's conversion to Christianity in 899. Although they always had Christian followers, it is difficult to see how the conversion benefitted them politically, since most of the aṣḥāb they depended on were muwallads, many of whom went over to the Umayyads' side after 899; in addition, the conversion meant that Ibn Ḥafṣūn was no longer simply a rebel but an apostate and an object of jihād. Cagigas suggests that Ibn Ḥafṣūn converted because of pressure from the many Christians who fought in his army, a possible reason but one that does not explain his willingness to alienate his more powerful muwallad allies. Another possibility is that the conversion came out the family's cultural orientation rather than out of practical concerns. There is some evidence suggesting that Ibn Ḥafṣūn's Christianity was deeply felt; his decision to build two new churches was expensive as well as a deliberate flouting of Sharī'ah, which prohibited the construction of new churches and synagogues. After he defeated Ibn Ḥafṣūn's son Ḥafṣ, 'Abd al-Raḥmān III reportedly had 'Umar Ibn Ḥafṣūn exhumed and the corpse taken to Córdoba to be crucified; the body was found at Bobastro buried in the Christian style, his head turned toward the east and his arms crossed over his chest.[46]

It is also possible that the family had in some sense been Christian all along. Ibn 'Idhārī maintains that there really was no conversion; Ibn Ḥafṣūn had been a secret Christian his whole life, and now he simply acknowledged the fact openly.[47] The actions of Ibn Ḥafṣūn's daughter Argentea also support the theory that the family had been strongly identified with Christianity prior to 899.[48] Although Ibn Ḥafṣūn's son Ḥafṣ is usually cited as the last rebel in the family, it is really Argentea who was the last member of the family to create a nuisance for the authorities. After her father's death, Argentea traveled to Córdoba with her brother Ḥafṣ when he went there to take up his position in the army of 'Abd al-Raḥmān III, accompanied by other family members and citizens of Bobastro. There she was executed as an apostate in 931.

It is the Latin *Vita* of Argentea, written in the late 900s, that makes the best case for the family's Christian identity.[49] Although the *Vita* says that Argentea left Bobastro for Córdoba with family members after the Umayyads defeated her father, it does not identify her father as a muwallad rebel, but says that Argentea was from a noble Christian family who raised her to be devout.[50] As a girl she devoted herself to asceticism and longed to be a martyr. When she arrived in Córdoba she immediately sought out other virgins with whom she continued her ascetic practices for several years. Her opportunity for martyrdom came with the arrival of a Christian preacher from France named Vulfura, who had come to al-Andalus to be martyred. He preached publicly, urging his listeners to become Christian, a violation of Sharīʿah regulations against People of the Book proselytizing to Muslims, and was arrested and imprisoned. Argentea visited him in prison and was herself arrested. Although the *Vita* author does not say so, the charge against her was most likely apostasy. As the daughter of a Muslim she was legally Muslim herself, but apparently the authorities in Córdoba were willing to overlook the matter of her apostasy as long as her religion remained private. By visiting Vulfura, however, she acknowledged both that she was a Christian and that she was in sympathy with his preaching. Her religion became a public matter. When she refused the qāḍī's offer of a chance to renounce Christianity and affirm that she was a Muslim, she was executed, as was Vulfura.

One has to approach the *Vita* with some skepticism, and in fact it has been argued that the *Vita* is a formulaic fiction based on martyrs' stories from the Roman period, bearing no connection with ʿUmar Ibn Ḥafṣūn.[51] Admittedly the information about her saintly behavior in childhood may be formulaic, but the details—the military defeat of her father, her coming to Córdoba with her brothers from Bobastro (or Bibistrense in the Latin)—make it plausible that the story is indeed about ʿUmar Ibn Ḥafṣūn's daughter. The use of rhetoric from Roman-era martyrs' stories is also typical of Eulogius's accounts of the martyrs of Córdoba and is quite appropriate for those martyrs who came from Muslim families. Their crime was simply being Christian, since anyone with a Muslim father was legally obligated to practice Islam; like the Roman martyrs, they professed their faith and refused opportunities to renounce it.

Argentea's story suggests some interesting connections between Ibn Ḥafṣūn's family and the martyrs' movement in Córdoba eighty years earlier. To give one example, among the martyrs in the 850s was a woman named Nathalia, who was from a Muslim family and therefore, by law, a Muslim.[52] After her father died, however, her mother married a man who was a secret Christian, who convinced mother and daughter to convert. At her baptism, Nathalia secretly took the Germanic name Sabigotho, perhaps to invoke the preconquest Christian past, as Ibn Ḥafṣūn may have done with his gold armbands. Later she married Aurelius, also a secret Christian from a Muslim family. After the beating and arrest of the Christian merchant John in 851 on charges of publicly insulting the Prophet Muḥammad, Sabigotho and Aurelius decided to adopt a more ascetic way of life and, later, to seek martyrdom. Sabigotho and another secret Christian friend, Liliosa, attended church with their faces uncovered; the combination of their attendance at church and their putting aside the veil demonstrated publicly that they were Christian. The two women and their husbands were arrested and executed as apostates. Argentea seems to have been deliberately imitating the actions of earlier Christian women who were legally Muslims, like Sabigotho and Liliosa. The fact that after arriving in Córdoba she was able to find likeminded ascetics, probably in a monastery, suggests that religious dissent in the capital had not entirely died out by the time of Ibn Ḥafṣūn's revolt. Perhaps Ibn Ḥafṣūn's profession of Christianity was not so much a tactical move but a radical act of reclaiming the family's history, as well as the history of earlier Christian protests.

There are, then, some good arguments for seeing Ibn Ḥafṣūn in the light of his Christian and Visigothic roots, and for seeing his cultural orientation as being northern, toward Christian Spain and western Europe. There are also, however, convincing reasons for seeing him primarily as part of the Muslim world and as culturally oriented to the south, toward North Africa. Among modern scholars, Muḥammad 'Īsā Ḥarīrī in particular argues that Ibn Ḥafṣūn's uprising was directly linked to the Berber revolts that began in North Africa and spread to al-Andalus.[53] The Berber movements were informed by Shī'ī and Khārijī ideology, and according to Ḥarīrī, Ibn Ḥafṣūn was particularly influenced by Khārijī thought. From Ḥarīrī's perspective, the uprising was essentially a muwallad revolt that, like contemporary Berber movements, had as its goal the formation of a new Islamic state in which all Muslims would be equal, and in which Arabs would have no special precedence.

Ḥarīrī's thesis is supported by the fact that Ibn Ḥafṣūn spent time in a part of North Africa that was ruled by Khārijīs. As we have seen, when he fled al-Andalus as a young man to avoid trouble with the law, he went to Tāhart, the capital of the Rustamid dynasty. Khārijism, as discussed in chapter 2, developed in the seventh century, during the early part of the Umayyads' reign in the Middle East. Its doctrine evolved in opposition to Umayyad rule, emphasizing that religious devotion rather than ethnic or family identity determined membership in the ummah, and that the ruler should be selected solely on the basis of his superior piety, regardless of his genealogy. The particular group of Khārijīs whose doctrine spread to western Algeria were the Ibāḍīs.[54] The Ibāḍī movement began in Basra, Iraq, in the seventh century. Preachers from Basra traveled to North Africa and gained many followers among the Zanātah and Nafūsah tribes. Among the preachers was the Persian mawlā 'Abd al-Raḥmān Ibn Rustam, who had spent much of his life in Qayrawān. The Abbasids suppressed an Ibāḍī uprising in central North Africa in 761, at which point Ibn Rustam fled to Tāhart, where he was elected Imām (the term for head of the ummah that both Khārijīs and Shī'is used instead of caliph) by his followers. Tāhart became the capital of a small Rustamid state that survived until the Fatimids conquered it in 909. Ibn Ḥafṣūn maintained ties with North Africa throughout most of his career. In the 880s he applied to the Aghlabids (an Arab dynasty who ruled Ifrīqiyah from the late 700s until 909, ostensibly in the name of the Abbasids) for military assistance against the Umayyads and was turned down.[55] Later he ordered that leaders of Muslim congregations recognize the Fatimids rather than the Umayyads as legitimate rulers. He asked the Fatimids for military help, and according to one version of events, they responded by sending a fleet of ships to his aid, although the ships were turned back by the Umayyad navy.[56] His appeal to the Fatimids came after his conversion to Christianity in 899. In addition to Ibn Ḥafṣūn's North African connections, and the links between North African and Andalusī Berber movements, Ḥarīrī notes that there were at least some 'ulamā' in al-Andalus who were influenced by Khārijī thought; he does not, however, claim that they had any direct influence on Ibn Ḥafṣūn.

Ḥarīrī freely admits that, among the small bits of information we have about Ibn Ḥafṣūn's motivations, there is no specific evidence that he identified himself as a Khārijī. Nor do the sources depict him as having a special belief in the true ummah as a community of the pious or in rule by the most devout. On the other hand, there is some evidence that Ibn Ḥafṣūn saw his revolt as a struggle for the equality of non-Arab Muslims. Ibn 'Idhārī preserves what purports to be a quotation from a speech Ibn Ḥafṣūn gave to a crowd of followers:

> How often have the powers that be treated you harshly, taking your property, burdening you beyond what you can bear; the Arabs humiliate and subjugate you. But I want to avenge you, and bring you out of your bondage.[57]

Here Ibn Ḥafṣūn equates the oppressive authority of the state specifically with Arabs. Ibn Ḥayyān also tells us that the revolt was based on a joining together of muwallads and Iberian Christians (al-'ujmah) against the Arabs.[58] Since most of Ibn Ḥafṣūn's followers were muwallads and Berbers, admittedly with some disgruntled Arabs in the mix,[59] one can argue that the Khārijī principle of equality among Muslims was an important part of the rebels' ideology. The fact that Christians also played a role in the revolt does not weaken the case for Khārijī influence. Elizabeth Savage has suggested that from its origins in southern Iraq, the Ibāḍī movement had Christian as well as Muslim supporters, particularly among Nestorian Christians who, like Muslim Ibāḍīs, were often engaged in long-distance trade.[60] In North Africa as well, Ibāḍīs found support from Christian Berbers; Savage argues that the North African revival of Donatist Christianity in the seventh and eighth centuries, with its emphasis on the Church as a community for the righteous only, gave common doctrinal ground to Christians and Ibāḍī Muslims. Tāhart in the ninth century had a substantial Christian population, and the Rustamid Imāms used Christians in their personal guard.

There is an interesting passage in Ibn 'Idhārī that suggests that Ibn Ḥafṣūn wanted to appeal, if not to Khārijī sentiments, then at least to Muslim cultural practices.[61] The passage comes immediately after the quotation given above from Ibn Ḥafṣūn's speech. Ibn 'Idhārī goes on to denounce Ibn Ḥafṣūn's followers as wicked scoundrels. He admits, however, that they were devoted to him and lists several reasons for his popularity beyond his promise to liberate them from oppression. One of his practices, noted above, was to honor loyal followers with gold armbands. Another source of his popularity was his treatment of women:

> He was, along with his wickedness and sinfulness, strong in his sense of honor (al-ghayrah), protecting that which is sacred and forbidden (al-ḥurmah), and that is part of what drew people to him.

The terms Ibn 'Idhārī uses make it clear that he is talking about Ibn Ḥafṣūn's attitude toward women. "Ghayrah," discussed in chapter 5, refers to a man's sense of honor as it pertains to the behavior of women. "Ḥurmah," from the same root as ḥarīm, means that which is sacred or taboo and also refers by implication to a woman or wife. The passage continues with an example of how Ibn Ḥafṣūn's ghayrah caused him to abhor women who acted too independently:

> Women in his day used to take money and goods from town to town on their own, without anyone in God's creation stopping them. His penalty was the sword . . .

In other words, his punishment was the death penalty, although is not clear from the passage whether the death penalty applied to the women who were traveling and conducting business on their own or to the people with whom such women did business, or both. Ibn ʿAskar also mentions Ibn Ḥafṣūn's ghayrah, saying that he punished with death (al-sayf, meaning the sword) any of his men who reached out his hand to a woman, even if it was only because she was accepting a trinket from him.[62]

Ibn Ḥafṣūn's ghayrah does not particularly suggest a connection with Khārijism. One of the primary criticisms mainstream Muslims had of the Khārijīs was that they did not have a proper sense of honor toward women; among other signs of laxness, they allowed women to fight in battles, citing the precedent of women who had gone into battle with Muḥammad. That practice, allowing as it did a public role for women, was strictly prohibited in mainstream Islam by the time of the Umayyads.[63] The Ibāḍīs had notable women supporters in the Middle East, including women from the Muhallab family, a powerful Arab family who had settled in Khurasān,[64] although it is not clear if women played a similar role in the North African Ibāḍī movement. Even though Ibn Ḥafṣūn's display of ghayrah does not connect him with Khārijism, it suggests that, sincere or not, he was playing to a specifically Muslim audience; the belief that women moving around freely and handling their own affairs posed a threat to society was certainly reflected in Sharīʿah as it was understood in al-Andalus.

Both images of Ibn Ḥafṣūn, as the Christian Visigothic rebel and as the muwallad struggling for equality among Muslims, are in their way convincing. Both, however, are based on limited evidence, the veracity of which is difficult to evaluate, and each undercuts the other. In light of the conflicting evidence it is tempting to embrace Lévi-Provençal's characterization of Ibn Ḥafṣūn as a cynical opportunist who tried on different identities as they suited his purposes. Still, given how long and at what cost he fought against the Umayyads, it seems likely that he had a plan or vision that went beyond simply making it up as he went along. What the vision was, however, we do not know.

The revolts of Berber families like the Banū Dhī Nūn and of the muwallad ʿUmar Ibn Ḥafṣūn demonstrate how politically chaotic al-Andalus was in the eighth and ninth centuries. Despite efforts at state-building, the Umayyads' actual control of al-Andalus often amounted to a firm grip on the area around Córdoba, a constant battle to retain control of Seville and of the southern coast, and, in the region of Toledo, a series of face-saving summer campaigns and offers of governorships to de facto regional princes. The Ibn Ḥafṣūn revolt was perhaps the most threatening, both because it targeted areas near Córdoba and because the family directly attacked Umayyad assumptions about Arab Muslim supremacy. The rebellions also show the instability of ethnic and religious identity in the period. The Banū Dhī al-Nūn at times sought to be part of the Cordovan elite, beginning with their adoption of an Arab name and later in their intermittent alliances with the Umayyads. At other times, as opportunities in their region presented themselves, they became opponents of Córdoba. Ibn Ḥafṣūn's revolt moved between an assertion of the rights of non-Arab Muslims to be important political players and a complete abandonment of Muslim identity as family members converted to Christianity.

7 ✦ The Banū Qasī and the Northern March

At its most ambitious, the revolt of Ibn Ḥafṣūn and his family and allies threatened the Guadalquivir Valley and the heartland of Umayyad power. It developed in areas over which the Umayyads expected to have at least some direct control. Those participating in the revolt also seem to have accepted the social norms that were current in Córdoba: Ibn Ḥafṣūn recognized a difference between muwallads and Arabs and between Christians and Muslims, and he used those differences to defy Umayyad authority. Farther from the geographic center of the Arab Muslim elite, though (however imperfectly that elite was defined), such categories had less meaning, and distinctions between ethnic and religious identity seem to have been not so much blurred as ignored. The ongoing political resistance of the Banū Qasī, a muwallad family on the northern march, illustrates some of the cultural differences between the capital and the distant border regions.

By the time of ʿAbd al-Raḥmān III, the Umayyads understood the northern frontier of al-Andalus as falling into three rough divisions: the lower, middle, and upper marches.[1] The frontier between al-Andalus and the Christian north (always ill-defined by modern standards) followed the Duero river in the west, then in the east rose north of the Ebro river to include the Ebro plains up to about the 1,000 meter line; the hills and valleys beyond that point were part of the Christian kingdoms. All three marches were, in comparison with the citied heartland of the Guadalquivir Valley, rural and had small Arab populations; they were controlled largely by Berbers and muwallads. The presence of what cities and towns there were on the marches, and the Arab population, increased from west to east. To the west, the lower march had Mérida as its principle town; otherwise the area was largely made up of rural villages punctuated by castles. Powerful landlords in the area were primarily muwallad and Berber, with the majority of the population made up of muwallad or Christian farmers and Berbers who were farmers or pastoralists. The middle march centered on the larger city of Toledo, most of whose leading families were muwallads. The city ruled over a rural muwallad, Berber, and Christian farming population, along with some Berber pastoralists. In the northeast, the upper march was a more urban and ethnically mixed region that included the city of Zaragoza and a number of smaller but significant towns like Tudela, Huesca, Calatayud, and Tortosa. Powerful Arab, Berber, and muwallad families vied for supremacy in the region.

The Arabic term "thaghr" (plural thughūr) is usually translated as frontier or march, in contrast with the demilitarized province or kūrah (plural kuwar). The thaghr bordered non-Muslim lands (the dār al-ḥarb), while the kūrah did not. The kūrah had a governor (walī or ʿāmil), while the thaghr had a qāʾid or military commander. The thughūr were taxed at a lower rate than the kuwar, paying the ʿushr or one-tenth of income rather than the more substantial land tax or kharāj. Relative to the kūrah, the thaghr was more independent and was not expected to participate in military campaigns that did not affect its particular region.[2]

That distinction between thaghr and kūrah became stable by the time of ʿAbd al-Raḥmān III; before that period, terminology was more fluid. The term thaghr was sometimes used for areas that were not directly in contact with the dār al-ḥarb, but whose ruling families were involved in defense and had a relationship with regions that really were on the frontier. An example is the territory of the Banū Dhī al-Nūn who, from their base around Santaver, periodically helped the Umayyads defend border regions.[3] The territory included in the three major thughūr also differed over time, although the designation of the upper or far march (al-thaghr al-aʿlā or al-thaghr al-aqṣā) seems consistently to have meant the region along the Ebro river centering on Saragossa.[4]

In the Abbasids' lands, the thaghr was strongly connected with the idea of jihād.[5] Frontier towns often featured volunteer jihadists and the construction of ribāṭs, which were paid for by established waqf funds. While the Umayyads in al-Andalus, like the Abbasids in the east, styled themselves as jihadists and embarked most years on the summer campaign or ṣāʾifah, rulers of the marches were not always reliable allies, fighting with the Umayyads only sporadically. As we will see in the case of the Banū Qasī, the culture of the upper march in particular was not focused on religious militancy, and Umayyad power over the region was too weak to compel regular participation in jihād.

The story of ʿAbd al-Raḥmān ibn Marwān al-Jillīqī illustrates the contentious nature of the Umayyads' relationship with provincial leaders on the marches.[6] As the name "al-Jillīqī," "the Galician," suggests, Ibn Marwān came from a family with roots in northwestern Iberia; by the ninth century, they were a prominent muwallad family living on what was at that time called the nearer march (al-thaghr al-adnā), around the area of Mérida and Badajoz. ʿAbd al-Raḥmān's father, Marwān ibn Yūnis al-Jillīqī, rebelled against Córdoba in 816/17, then apparently made peace with the Umayyads in the time of the amīr ʿAbd al-Raḥmān II, who made him governor of Mérida—probably, as happened repeatedly in the ninth century, offering the emirate's legitimation to a provincial family who were already de facto rulers. After Marwān's death, his son took over as ruler of Mérida and staged a major rebellion against the Umayyads in the 860s. In 868 the amīr Muḥammad I put down the revolt, and Ibn Marwān and his followers agreed as part of the terms of surrender to come to Córdoba and serve in the amīr's army. While in Córdoba, however, Ibn Marwān got into a dispute with the army general and court official Hāshim ibn ʿAbd al-ʿAzīz, the powerful Umayyad mawlā who had challenged the authority of the Muslim convert Ibn Antonian. Ibn Marwān left Cordoba, created a new stronghold for himself in Badajoz, and continued in a more or less permanent state of revolt until his death in 890. Badajoz remained under his family's control until ʿAbd al-Raḥmān III conquered it in 929/30. The on-again off-again alliance of Ibn Marwān and his family with the Umayyads, the family's periodic open rebellions against central authority, and the regime's intermittent attempts to integrate the family into the Cordovan power structure were all typical of the relationship between the Umayyads and the great families of the marches.

Ideally, from the Umayyad point of view, the powerful families of the marches, whether muwallad, Berber, or Arab, functioned as Muslim allies against the Christian kingdoms and principalities to the north. In the ninth century, the major Christian states were (moving from west to east) Asturias-Leon, including the towns of Leon, Burgos, and Oporto; Navarre, whose urban center was Pamplona; and the Spanish March (the future Catalonia), which included the city of Barcelona.[7] The Christian north was ethnically diverse and included Galicians, Asturians, Cantabrians, Basques, Gascons, and Franks, as well as families who continued to identify themselves as Goths. Although the threat from the north became acute only in the eleventh century, as Umayyad rule collapsed, Christians did make incursions south in the eighth and ninth centuries as well. In the late eighth century, for example, the Umayyads lost Pamplona, which was subsequently controlled by Franks, by a Gascon and Frankish alliance, and later by local Basque families.[8] At times aristocratic families on the marches did act as good Muslims, defending the borders and waging jihad against the infidel north; in 856, the Banū Qasī leader Mūsā ibn Mūsā led a summer raid against Barcelona.[9] Often, however, prominent Muslims on the marches were unreliable jihadists. Particularly on the upper march, the border, to the extent that there was such a thing, was porous, and the great families on either side formed a society that crossed religious lines.

The history of the Banū Qasī illustrates the complexities of society on the borders, and of that society's relationship with Córdoba.[10] Ibn Ḥazm says that the family's founder, Cassius (rendered as Qasī in Arabic), was count of the northern marches in the time of the Visigoths. After the Muslims conquered al-Andalus, Count Cassius traveled to Syria, where he converted to Islam at the hands of the Umayyad caliph al-Walīd (r. 705–15).[11] The family's original stronghold was just to the north of the Ebro, across the river from Tudela.[12] In the course of the eighth and ninth centuries, however, they came to control a large territory on both sides of the eastern Ebro River, a territory that included at various times Pamplona, Huesca, Zaragoza, Borja, Tarazona, and Arnedo. The family also, for a brief time in the mid-ninth century, controlled Toledo, away from their main center of operations.[13] As was the case with many of the ruling families in border regions, the Banū Qasī acknowledged the authority of the Umayyads only intermittently.

Some details of this narrative have been called into question. Fierro, among others, dismisses the story that Cassius was a count as a way for the family to aggrandize itself through a fictitious pedigree.[14] Manzano Moreno, on the other hand, makes a case that Cassius really was a Visigothic count and was part of a continuity of rule along the northern frontier; he had manned the borders against the Basques in Visigothic times and continued to do so after the Muslims arrived.[15] Fierro also finds it unlikely that Cassius traveled to Syria to convert. According to her, it is more plausible that he became the mawlā of an Arab family that settled in the north and only later became, or claimed to become, an Umayyad mawlā.[16] To me the claim that Cassius was a count seems reasonable; he likely had some status that gave him the authority and resources to move smoothly into the role of defender of the march for the Umayyads. On the other hand, as Fierro suggests, the claim that a frontier official traveled to Damascus to be converted by the caliph himself seems more dubious.

Even if the family were mawālī, converted at the hands of the caliph, that fact seems to have been largely irrelevant to their political dealings. Ibn Ḥazm, who refers to the Banū Qasī as muwallads but also makes the claim that they were mawālī of the Umayyads and therefore had a kind of Arab identity, says that in the days of the factional divide between the Yamanīs and the Muḍarīs in the eighth century, they were grouped with the Muḍarīs. Their affinity with the Muḍarīs presumably reflects the fact that it is the faction the Umayyads were part of. Other than this one reference, however, there is no evidence that the Banū Qasī ever behaved or were treated like Umayyad mawālī. Mawālī like Hāshim ibn 'Abd al-'Azīz enjoyed a level of prestige comparable to that of well-born Arabs—for all intents and purposes they were Arabs—and were integrated into the Cordovan power structure. The Banū Qasī, for all that they were occasional allies of the Umayyads, were far from Córdoba and were not part of that inner circle. They seem to have related to the Umayyads in the same way Ibn Marwān and leaders of other powerful muwallad families did.

The Banū Qasī's power and territory were at their height at the time of Mūsā ibn Mūsā ibn Fortún ibn Qasī (ca. 790–862), the great-grandson of Cassius.[17] By Mūsā ibn Mūsā's time, the Banū Qasī's pattern of occasional cooperation with the Umayyads between periods of revolt was well-established. His father, Fortún, had rebelled against the Umayyads in the early ninth century, primarily over control of Zaragoza. That issue reemerged in 840/41 when 'Abd al-Raḥmān II attempted to appoint the governors of Tudela and Zaragoza. Since the Banū Qasī regarded those cities as part of their territory, Mūsā ibn Mūsā fought vigorously against the appointees and defeated the amīr's troops who were supporting them, taking the general commanding the Umayyad force, Ḥārith ibn Bazī', prisoner. In 843 'Abd al-Raḥmān appeared in person at the head of an expedition against the Banū Qasī, whom he defeated; Mūsā ibn Mūsā was forced to surrender Ḥārith and swore obedience to the amīr. In exchange, the amīr appointed Mūsā ibn Mūsā as the official governor of Arnedo, a town he already controlled. In 844 Mūsā ibn Mūsā rebelled again; the amīr's forces besieged him at Tudela, forcing him to capitulate and taking his son Lope as a hostage. Later in 844, when Vikings landed near Seville, Mūsā ibn Mūsā led troops to assist the amīr. 'Abd al-Raḥmān released Lope, who also fought against the Vikings. After 'Abd al-Raḥmān died in 852, Mūsā ibn Mūsā continued to expand his territories in the Ebro Valley; Muḥammad I made him the official walī of the upper march, probably as a way of saving the Umayyads' dignity in the face of the inevitable.

Mūsā ibn Mūsā died in 862 from injuries sustained during a battle with the Banū Sālim Berbers, the leaders of Guadalajara. After his death, the family's relations with the Umayyads improved briefly as Mūsā's sons, Lope, Muṭarraf, Fortún, and Ismā'īl, laid low and consolidated their power in the north. By 871, though, the alliance deteriorated as badly as ever; Muṭarraf proclaimed himself governor of Tudela in defiance of the amīr, and Ismā'īl did the same in Zaragoza. Muḥammad I led an expedition to the north where he defeated Muṭarraf, brought him back to Córdoba, and had him crucified along with his three sons, Muḥammad, Lope, and Mūsā, certainly a low point in relations between the Umayyads and the Banū Qasī. The pattern of alternating rebellion and quiescence resumed, until the family lost the last of its major castles in 929, and 'Abd al-Raḥmān III reasserted Umayyad power over the region.

While the power struggles along the upper march most obviously represented a potential military threat to Córdoba's control of the north, the area is also of interest for the ways in which it was culturally and socially different from the Umayyad heartland. Distinctions among religious and ethnic groups seemed to matter far less than they did in Córdoba.

We can see some of this indifference to the cultural and social concerns of Córdoba in the Banū Qasī's relationships of kinship and military alliance. Their major allies in the areas were the Iñiga family, a Christian Basque family from around Pamplona.[18] The first of the Iñiga family to appear in the sources is called Wannaquh in Arabic, or Iñigo Arista.[19] He had two sons, Fortún and Iñigo Iñíguez; the latter, whom the Arabic sources call Wannaquh ibn Wannaquh (probably derived from Enneco, the Basque version of the name Iñigo), became ruler of Pamplona sometime between 810 and 820. After Iñigo Arista died sometime around 780, his widow married Mūsā ibn Fortún Ibn Qasī and became the mother of Mūsā ibn Mūsā, making Mūsā the half-brother of Iñigo Arista's sons Fortún and Iñigo Iñíguez; they fought with him against the Umayyads during his revolt in the early 840s. 'Abd al-Raḥmān's campaign of 843 was directed against the Iñigas as well as the Banū Qasī. Fortún was killed in battle and his head sent to Córdoba as a trophy; Iñigo Iñíguez agreed not to leave the principality of Pamplona and to pay the amīr 700 dinars a year. Iñigo Iñíguez's son García, who took over the principality of Pamplona after his father's death in 851 or 852, was married to Mūsā ibn Mūsā's (presumably Muslim) daughter Oria or Aurea; they had a son, Mūsā Garcés. Mūsā ibn Mūsā's son Muṭarraf married Velasquita, a daughter of García by another wife.[20] Ibn Ḥazm also notes that Mūsā ibn Mūsā arranged the marriages of his (Muslim) nieces, the daughters of his brother Lope, to members of the Iñiga family.

The most obvious questions that the frequent marriages between the Iñigas and the Banū Qasī raise pertain to religion. As far as can be determined, among Muslims in al-Andalus, only aristocratic Arab families (and perhaps elite Berber families, although that is difficult to determine) enforced strict endogamy for women. Other groups did not see female endogamy as desirable or practical and used marriages to seal alliances; they were Muslims but followed what Guichard would call a European kinship pattern. It is not surprising, therefore, that muwallads like the Banū Qasī would use daughters as bargaining chips, and indeed we can sometimes see them handing out daughters for strategic purposes. In the early 860s, when it seemed likely that there would be hostilities between the Banū Qasī and the Banū Sālim Berbers of Guadalajara, Mūsā ibn Mūsā offered his daughter to the Banū Sālim leader Izrāq (or Azrāq) ibn Mantīl, telling Izrāq, according to Ibn al-Qūṭīyah, that his daughter was the most beautiful in al-Andalus and should be married only to the most beautiful young man in al-Andalus, who was none other than Izrāq.[21] Despite the flattery, Mūsā ended up attacking Izrāq in Guadalajara when he feared Izrāq was colluding with the Umayyads against him. In another instance, Mūsā ibn Mūsā's son gave one of his daughters as part of a peace agreement with 'Abd Allāh ibn Khalaf ibn Rāshid, the governor of Boltaña, but then later attacked him and seized the town.[22]

Giving one's daughters to other Muslim families, as in the examples above, is one thing; giving them to non-Muslims, as was the case when the Banū Qasī married their daughters to the Iñigas, is something else again, and it certainly violates a major principal of Sharī'ah family law, which is that Muslim women are a resource for the ummah. Muslim men took resources from the unbelievers by marrying Christian or Muslim women (although not pagans). Muslim women, however, could under no circumstances be given to non-Muslims, whether or not they were People of the Book, and for a Muslim woman to marry outside the faith was an act of apostasy. Aside from the intermarriages with the Iñigas, a Banū Qasī daughter named Urraca was married to Fruela, the son of Alfonso III of Asturias-León, sometime around 900.[23] This casual shuffling of daughters between Christian and Muslim families calls into question how important religious identity was on either side of the frontier.

It is also worth noting that the Christian families involved seemed to have no qualms about marrying daughters to Muslims, or at least not to prominent ones. Aside from the marriages outlined above, there were kinship ties between the Iñiga family and the Umayyads. Fortún Garcés, who ruled Pamplona from 882 to 905 and was the great-grandson of Iñigo Arista, was captured (before he was ruler of Pamplona) by the amīr Muḥammad I and, along with his daughter Iñiga or Onneca, was held for some time in Córdoba. There Iñiga married (or at least became part of the ḥarīm of) the future amīr ʿAbd Allāh, taking the name Durr, or pearl. Her status as a captive, and the fact that Durr is a common slave name, suggest that she was a slave concubine rather than one of the official wives.[24] That status, however, did not affect the position of her offspring; her son with ʿAbd Allāh, Muḥammad, while he did not become amīr himself, was the father of ʿAbd al-Raḥmān III, meaning that Iñiga was the grandmother of the first Umayyad caliph of al-Andalus. Iñiga's daughter by a previous marriage, Tota or Ṭūṭah, became queen of Navarre; she traveled to Córdoba to arrange an accord with ʿAbd al-Raḥmān III, who treated her as an honored relative.[25]

The practice of northern Christians giving their daughters in marriage to Muslims is perhaps less striking than the fact that Muslims in that region married their daughters to Christians, given that there are plenty of references to marriages between Muslim men and Christian women in the sources for the martyrs of Córdoba. There is an important difference, however. In Córdoba, the Christian families involved were most likely interested in marrying up into the Muslim-dominated hierarchy. The northern women in question, however, were aristocrats, whose families were equals of the Muslim families, such as the Banū Qasī, with whom they married (Iñiga's marriage to an Umayyad is the exception, since she was a captive, however honorably treated). There marriages may have come out of political expediency, but they also are more likely than the marriages in Córdoba to represent a free choice on the part of Christian families, rather than a response to social pressures.

Members of the Banū Qasī, while they remained predominantly Sunni Muslim, sometimes changed religions. Ibn Ḥazm reports that Lope ibn Muḥammad ibn Ismāʿīl became a Shīʿī while he was in central North Africa. Two other Banū Qasī sons became Christian. Unfortunately we do not know the context of those conversions, but they do suggest a certain fluidity of religious identity. As we have seen in the case of some Berber uprisings, and in the rebellion of ʿUmar ibn Ḥafṣūn, claiming Shīʿī identity was a way to defy, or at least annoy, the Umayyads, so there is a context for that conversion. The claiming of Christian identity also showed defiance, or at least a disconnect, with Cordovan power, and probably also had to do with the family's close ties to Christians; Ibn Ḥafṣūn would later use a similar shift to Christianity as a way to separate himself from the Umayyads. The Banū Qasī's casual attitude toward religious identity, as well as the family's often open hostility toward Córdoba, undermines any notion that they acted as Umayyad mawālī.

The family's naming practices are also suggestive of a social group that extended across the border and across religious lines. Generally once an Iberian family converted to Islam, subsequent generations of boys were given standard Muslim, or at least Arabic, names. In 'Umar Ibn Ḥafṣūn's family, for example, men had Arabic names going back to the great-grandfather, Ja'far, who was the original convert. Before Ja'far the family had Romance or Latinate names, for example Damian and Alfonso. It is true that Ibn Ḥafṣūn's daughter Argentea had a Romance name, but no Romance family names for boys are recorded. Banū Qasī sons, however, were split between a majority who had Arabic names like Muḥammad or Ismā'īl and a minority with Romance names like Lope or Fortún, a name also used by the Iñigas (the name Cassius never reappears in the family). Sons of the same father might end up with a mixture of Romance and Arabic names, so for example the sons of Mūsā ibn Fortún Ibn Cassius included Mūsā and Muṭarraf but also Lope and García (although David Wasserstein has suggested that the name "Lope" or "Lubb" was a rare case of a Romance name that Muslims broadly adopted).[26] Naming patterns do not therefore seem to represent the practices of different branches of the family. It is possible that the sons of Mūsā ibn Fortún with Arabic names and those with Romance names had different mothers with different religious or ethnic backgrounds. Perhaps the most obvious explanation, though, is that the family chose to preserve traditional family names, and names they shared with the Iñigas, without regard to their origin. We have very few girls' names from the family, but it is interesting that the two we do have—Aurea and Urraca—are both Romance names.

To what extent we are looking at a unique concept of religious identity that prevailed in the north, one in which boundaries between religions were less defined than in Córdoba, is hard to determine. Lévi-Provençal believes that the fluidity was quite pronounced and goes so far as to suggest that the much-married Iñigo Iñiguez may have been polygynous, in imitation of his Muslim relatives among the Banū Qasī.[27] There is no way to verify this theory, however, nor for that matter is it clear that the Banū Qasī men married more than one wife at a time. More generally, it is impossible to say what the religious sensibilities of the population as a whole were along the northern march. Presumably most people on both sides of the Ebro were Christians at the time of the Banū Qasī; if Bulliet's theory about conversion rates is correct, then Muslims had not been in control of the upper march long enough for any widespread conversion to Islam to have taken place on the southern side of the frontier.[28] But although we can say that most people in the region were probably Christians, the texture of what being a Christian meant to them is not something we can recover. It does appear, however, that there was an aristocratic culture and system of kinship alliances in the north that superseded religious identity.

Arabic-speaking chroniclers writing about the Umayyad heartland often mention language: the Christian administrator whose Arabic was impeccable, the Muslim qāḍī whose grasp of Arabic grammar was sadly inadequate. No such issues are raised about the north. The sources give no indication that the Banū Qasī, in spite of Ibn Ḥazm's assertion that they were Umayyad mawālī, saw themselves as part of the Arab and quasi-Arab elite, nor do we know if the family, or at least the men, spoke Arabic or were educated in Arabic letters. Maribel Fierro claims that they were in fact conversant in Arabic language and culture.[29] Her assertion, however, is based on a passage from Ibn al-Qūṭīyah that is open to interpretation.[30] In the passage, the courtier Umayyah ibn 'Īsā Ibn Shuhayd reports that in Córdoba, at the house where hostages were kept (dār al-rahā'in), he heard hostages from the Banū Qasī reciting a poem by the pre-Islamic Arab poet 'Antarah. Ibn Shuhayd chastises the teacher of the hostages, saying that he should not be teaching the enemies of the caliphs poetry like that of 'Antarah that inspires heroism; instead he should teach them only the wine poetry of Ḥasan ibn Hānī' (Abū Nuwās) and other jokers (ahzāl) like him. Ibn Shuhayd's story does not tell us if the members of the Banū Qasī were reciting from a tradition they already knew or being taught that tradition for the first time. Fierro may be correct in concluding that they came to Córdoba already literate in Arabic. The whole point of bringing enemies to the capital, however, was to integrate them into the Umayyads' service, as was attempted in the case of Ibn Marwān and, later, members of 'Umar Ibn Ḥafṣūn's family. Education in Classical Arabic would have been part of that process. In addition, the fact that the Banū Qasī hostages were working with a teacher (mu'addib) suggests a tutorial rather than a salon. What Ibn Shuhayd overheard could have been part of an ultimately unsuccessful effort to bring the northern rebels in line with the Umayyads' worldview.

The Banū Qasī do not, then, appear to have acted as members of the Arab elite. In particular they did not show any interest in the endogamous marriage practices of that elite. At the same time, they do not seem to have had any sense of superiority based on their Gothic identity and were happy to marry daughters and sons to Berbers, Basques, or to whomever expediency dictated.

There are some useful contrasts to be drawn between the Banū Qasī and ʿUmar Ibn Ḥafṣūn that can give us an idea of how geography, and specifically distance from the capital, affected culture. In Ibn Ḥafṣūn's world it mattered whether you were Arab or muwallad, Muslim or Christian; when he became Christian (or admitted to being a Christian, depending on how one looks at the situation), his political and legal status changed dramatically. On the northern march, those boundaries were less important. That contrast can perhaps best be seen in the lives of the Banū Qasī's daughters as opposed to the fate of Ibn Ḥafṣūn's daughter Argentea. Under Sharīʿah, a Muslim woman who married a Christian man was guilty of apostasy. The Banū Qasī nevertheless regularly married their daughters to Christians, correctly anticipating that there would be no repercussions. Argentea's own act of apostasy, however, led to her death at the hands of a Sharīʿah court. In southern al-Andalus, the rules of the Islamic polity applied. In the north, they intruded only minimally.

NON-ARAB MUSLIMS IN THE ELEVENTH CENTURY: THE SHUʿŪBĪYAH

I have argued throughout this book, following Wasserstein and others, that the Umayyad period in al-Andalus was a time of particular tensions about ethnicity and religious identity. But by the end of the tenth century, as the Umayyads increasingly identified themselves as Muslim rather than Arab leaders, and as the majority of the Christian population converted to Islam and took on aspects of Arab culture, those tensions faded. The evidence does not suggest that they played an important role in the Taifa period. Furthermore, after the Umayyads lost power and the Christian north began to seize Muslim lands in the eleventh century, culturally ambiguous areas like the Ebro Valley region were eliminated from Muslim rule, leaving a core of al-Andalus in which most people were Muslims and Arabic-speaking. Muslim elites generally identified themselves with Arab culture and often adopted Arab genealogies. Thus François Clèment distinguishes only two classes of Taifa leadership: Arabized leaders, made up of those claiming biological Arab descent along with old Berber families and ṣaqālibah, and non-Arabized leaders, meaning newly arrived Berbers.[31]

One piece of evidence that could potentially contradict this view of the Taifa period is the *Risālah* of Ibn García, written in the mid-eleventh century.[32] The *Risālah* is an example of shu'ūbī literature, a polemical literature that originally appeared under the Abbasids in the late eighth century. Its original authors were primarily Persians and other non-Arab Muslims at the Abbasid court who argued that non-Arab Muslims had a noble and dignified history equal to, if not superior to, that of Arabs.[33] To what extent the shu'ūbīyah can be connected to a real political movement, rather than a literary exercise on the part of Persian courtiers, is debatable, but in its original incarnation it does seem to have served as a way for Persian and other non-Arab elites to express their claim to a place in the Abbasid system, and to reject the idea that Islam was inevitably associated with Arab identity. The authors' proof text was the Quran, sūrah 49:13. Ibn Ḥazm used a paraphrase of this same verse from the ḥadīths (somewhat unconvincingly) at the beginning of his book on Arab genealogy, the *Jamharah*, to temper his claims for Arab superiority:

> O people, we have created you
> from a male single male and female,
> and we have made you into groups (shu'ūb)
> and tribes (qabā'il) that you may come to know one another;
> truly the noblest (akram) among you
> before God is the most righteous (atqā) among you;
> truly God is all-knowing, all seeing.[34]

Although commentators differed in their interpretation of that verse, Persian exegetes generally took "qabā'il" as referring to the Arabs, who calculated relatedness through genealogy, and "shu'ūb" as 'ajam (non-Arabs) or mawālī (in the eastern sense of non-Arab Muslims, not the Andalusī sense of honored clients), who understood relatedness to mean coming from a common city or region.[35] To shu'ūbī authors, the verse demonstrated that both groups were equally part of God's creation of humankind and was the basis for an argument that tried to break the link between nobility and the possession of an Arab genealogy.

Ibn García, writing in the mid-eleventh century, was part of a smaller and later version of that movement. His full name in Arabic was Abū 'Āmir

Ibn Gharsīyah al-Bashkunsī, and, as the name suggests, he was (according to Ibn Saʿīd) a Basque; he was captured as a child, converted to Islam, and educated at the Taifa court in Denia.[36] The rulers of Denia at that time were ṣaqālibah, and the *Risālah* may have been a response to the work of a poet at the court of Almería praising the lineage of Almería's Arab ruler.[37] Despite the fact that his background was quite different from that of the eighth- and ninth-century shuʿūbī authors, he adopted their polemics without much adjustment, arguing for the superiority of Byzantine and Persian culture over the culture of Arabs, characterized in the *Risālah* as goat-milkers and herders of mangy camels. Ibn García also argues that Muslims who were descendants of Christians had an edge over Arab Muslims, in that their ancestors were at least monotheists rather than pagans. Those of Christian ancestry were descended from Sarah, the legitimate wife of Abraham, rather than Hagar, a slave. All the shuʿūbī authors, including Ibn García, purport to show the inferiority of Arab identity, yet they use Classical Arabic and imagery from Arabic poetry to do so, suggesting that they were in fact arguing for their fitness to be part of Muslim, Arabic-language culture.

The *Risālah* might then suggest that conflicts over the connection between Arab and Muslim identity continued well into the eleventh century. Gören Larsson argues that this is in fact the case, and that Ibn García's intention was "to formulate and legitimize a non-Arab alternative to Arab rule."[38] For Larsson, the treatise is about the rights of non-Arab Muslims in general to have a role in Muslim society equal to that of Arabs, making Ibn García's work similar in intention to the earlier shuʿūbī literature in the east. Wasserstein, on the other hand, sees the *Risālah* as a work by a freed slave, a ṣaqlabī, in the service of the ṣaqlabī rulers of Denia, and believes he is arguing for the inclusion of the ṣaqālibah in the dominant Arabic-Muslim culture of al-Andalus. The culture in which Ibn García wanted full membership was defined by Arabic language and literature but was no longer linked to Arab identity in a genealogical sense, including as it did groups like the established Berber families of the peninsula.[39] Other than newly arrived Berbers, the ṣaqālibah were the only Muslims who continued to stand out as a separate group.

The difference of opinion about Ibn García's intentions is understandable given how difficult it is to know exactly what he was up to, or how he understood his own position in Andalusī society. Taken at face value, the *Risālah* says that people of Persian and Byzantine background are superior to Arabs, an argument that is not relevant in the context of al-Andalus; Ibn García was Basque, not Byzantine or Persian. It is also not clear that he fits the category of ṣaqlabī, as Wasserstein assumes. David Ayalon has argued forcefully that in Andalusī society the term ṣaqālibah referred only to slaves taken from east of German-speaking lands, and that slaves from Galicia, the Basque Country, and other parts of western Europe counted as a different group altogether.[40] His argument depends, however, on his interpretation of a fairly ambiguous passage from the tenth-century geographer Ibn Ḥawqal, which in any case may not have applied to the situation in the eleventh century. The question of Ibn García's identity in his society cannot be fully resolved.

Surviving refutations of the *Risālah*[41] do nothing to clarify its meaning any further. The responses range chronologically from the 1080s, within decades of the *Risālah*'s writing, to the early thirteenth century,[42] and none of them addresses directly the conditions of Andalusī society any more than Ibn García does. The refutation of Abū Yaḥyā Ibn Mas'adah, an Almohad courtier writing around one hundred years later, is primarily a polemic against Christianity, as though the *Risālah* were a defense of Christianity rather than a defense of non-Arab Muslims.[43] Along with denouncing Christian beliefs and practices—he claims that Christians place Judas's authority above that of Abraham and Noah[44]—he attacks Sarah, the mother of the Christians, saying that she was loaned out as a sexual partner to an Egyptian prince. In addition, he asserts that Sarah was a partner in an incestuous marriage between uncle and niece,[45] apparently relying on a story in Talmud that conflates Sarah with Abraham's niece Yiskah, the daughter of Abraham's brother Hārān.[46] The other refutations seem equally disconnected from the social realities of al-Andalus, and from the *Risālah* itself.

Ibn García's language therefore is symbolic of a problem he perceived in Andalusī society, rather than a literal description of that problem. Most likely Wasserstein is correct in interpreting the *Risālah* as a plea for the inclusion of freedmen in the Arabic-speaking Muslim community. Even if Ibn García's society would not have classified him as a ṣaqlabī, he was a freed slave, and his masters were certainly ṣaqālibah. A Basque freedman and the ṣaqālibah may well have been among the last non-Arab Muslims who stood out as different in al-Andalus. He does not seem to be mounting a defense of muwallads, a term that was rarely even used by the eleventh century;[47] the sources do not classify any of the Taifa rulers as muwallads. He was not a muwallad himself, since he was not a descendent of Iberian converts to Islam. Ibn García says that he is speaking on behalf of "ma'shar al-mawālī," the community of the mawālī, which Monroe seems to accept as a term for non-Arab Muslims in general. The term mawālī would in fact have had that meaning in the ninth-century Abbasid east. As we have seen, however, the system of tribal clientage for converts used in the east did not exist in al-Andalus after the earliest period of the conquest, and the word mawālī was mostly used to designate elite families. These facts suggest that Ibn García was either simply lifting the term out of the eastern shuʿūbī literature or was using it in the other sense in which it commonly occurred in al-Andalus, which was to refer to freed slaves. In any event, it is most likely that Ibn García was pleading the case of a very limited community of freedmen in al-Andalus, and that the *Risālah* does not represent any widespread continuation of the Umayyad period's ethnic conflicts.

Conclusion

Ethnic and Religious Identity

The Muslim elite in the Umayyad period, in both al-Andalus and in the Middle East, connected being Arab with being Muslim and believed that Arab Muslims deserved a higher social status than either non-Arab Muslims or dhimmīs. In al-Andalus, however, the Umayyad ideal of a "unitary state dominated by Arabs," to use Thomas Glick's phrase,[1] was always a shaky one, given the relatively small number of Arabs attempting to rule over a large non-Arab subject population. The ideal became even less viable as time went on, for several reasons.

Membership in the army had traditionally been an important source of Arab prestige. By the time of ʿAbd al-Raḥmān III, however, the Arab army had been largely eliminated, as new waves of Berbers were brought in to fight in the caliphs' army, along with ṣaqālibah from eastern Europe. The use of Berbers led to the Umayyads' downfall in a direct way, in that Berber soldiers led periodic revolts in the capital in the early 1000s.[2] In a less direct sense, however, the loss of the Arab army weakened Umayyad legitimacy, which was based in part on the family's claim to lead an Arab social and military aristocracy. The dismantling of the dīwān system that the ʿĀmirid chamberlain al-Manṣūr completed did away with an important site of Arab privilege.

The porous nature of Arab identity also, in the long term, undermined the significance of that identity, since the ability to trace Arab bloodlines was only one factor in being Arab. Because adopting Arabic culture did not require one to be biologically Arab, it was possible for Arabic written culture to spread to educated elites throughout al-Andalus. Vernacular Arabic, along with Romance, became a standard spoken language and developed characteristics distinguishing it from other dialects by the tenth century.[3] In a sense, everyone, or at least a large part of the population, became culturally Arab. When everyone is Arab, the distinction loses its significance.

Finally, change came about because of al-Andalus's increasingly strong identity as an Islamic society. The growing importance of Islam meant not only that a majority of the population converted to Islam, as it probably did by 950 or 1000. It also meant that ʿAbd al-Raḥmān III, when he took the title of caliph, decided to base his legitimacy more on his role as commander of the faithful than as the leader of an Arab aristocracy. The deepening of Islamic identity can also be seen in the spread of Mālikī jurisprudence and the widespread use of Sharīʿah courts. Although the Quran and, to a lesser extent, the ḥadīths grew up in an Arab environment, Sharīʿah did not on the whole support the idea of Arab superiority. Ibn Ḥazm's ambivalence about Arab prestige is telling. The *Jamharah* celebrates Arab families, but even in that work he admits that Islam acknowledges religious virtue over ethnic identity. In his religious and legal treatises, he emphasizes that Islam does not give precedence to any ethnic or economic group, and in his theories about language and grammar he gives no special place to Arabic as a sacred language.

As the nature of the army changed, the amīr became the caliph, and more Iberians converted to Islam, the line between Arab and non-Arab grew increasingly less clear. By the end of the Umayyad regime, Arab lineage was no longer an accurate marker of high social status, nor was being Muslim as strongly associated with being Arab. The Party or Taifa kingdoms that replaced Umayyad rule were all ruled by Muslims, but by Muslims who variously identified themselves as Arab, Berber, or ṣaqlabī, and the distinction between Arab Muslims and muwallads seems to have broken down. The cultural side of Arab identity survived; Andalusīs spoke Arabic (in addition to Romance) and the Taifa courts supported Arabic poetry and literature. Membership in an identifiable Arab lineage, however, became less important.

GENDER IDENTITY

Changes in women's status and ideas about gender do not correspond neatly with the political shift from Umayyad rule to the Taifa system. There were, however, some shifts in gender relations that were part of the general cultural changes in the Umayyad period. Christian women whose families converted to Islam would have found themselves subject to Sharīʿah's personal status regulations. Some of those regulations, particularly regarding marriage, were not all that different from Visigothic law. Islamic inheritance law, however, would have represented a step down for women in their ability to inherit and transmit property, and other Islamic cultural norms, in particular middle- and upper-class ideas about feminine modesty and veiling, probably led to greater restrictions for women moving from Christianity to Islam.

For Muslim women, the increasing influence of Sharīʿah courts was beneficial. Although Mālikī inheritance law sometimes privileged agnatic over cognatic relatives, it did not support the patrilineal Eastern family pattern that Guichard identifies, instead seeing the individual as part of a kindred, in which both mother's-side and father's-side relatives were important. And while Mālikī Sharīʿah unquestionably gave women a subordinate position in society and in marriage, it also guaranteed women property rights in the form of inheritance, including the inheritance of land. It also guaranteed married women a dower and the right to financial support from their husbands.

CULTURAL FLUIDITY

One feature of Umayyad-era society I have tried to emphasize was its cultural instability and the possibilities that instability created for individuals to change their religious and ethnic identity. Dhimmīs converted to Islam. Men became Arab, either through fictive genealogies or by reinventing themselves culturally. Some strict gatekeepers, like the Umayyad mawlā Hāshim ibn ʿAbd al-ʿAzīz, tried to hold the line, regarding converts and non-Arabs as suspect, although the super-purist Ibn Ḥazm might in turn have questioned Hāshim's credentials as an Arab. In a period of rapid conversion and Arabization, however, the demographic realities made such distinctions increasingly irrelevant.

That cultural fluidity and opening of opportunity can be contrasted with some of the more rigid social systems that prevailed in later Andalusī and Christian Spanish history. The Almoravids, the Berber group who controlled al-Andalus from the late 1000s until 1163, were much more hostile to dhimmīs than the Umayyads or Taifa kings were, regarding non-Muslims as enemies of Islam and not as potential converts.[4] The Christian rulers who had conquered most of al-Andalus by 1212 initially treated Muslim and Jewish subjects in ways analogous to Muslim treatment of dhimmīs. Alfonso VI, after conquering Toledo in 1085, allowed Muslims freedom of worship,[5] and Alfonso X's thirteenth-century *Siete Partidas* spells out both legal disabilities and legal rights of Jews and Muslims.[6] In the eleventh and twelfth centuries, Spanish Christians continued to accept the idea that conversion of Jews and Muslims was possible and desirable, and the thirteenth-century Spanish Church regarded religious conversion as its major mission. Raymond Penyafort, who became minister general of the Dominicans in 1238, supported the founding of language schools to teach Arabic and Hebrew in order to facilitate the work of Christian preachers.[7] By the mid-fifteenth century, however, an essentialist theory of religion had evolved, holding that someone who was born Jewish or Muslim would always in some sense maintain their former religious identity, even after baptism. Many city statutes from the mid-1400s, for example, prohibited conversos (converts from Judaism to Christianity) from holding any high office, implying that conversion did not finally change one's core identity. The authors of those statutes, who saw themselves as protecting Christian society's purity of blood, or "limpieza de sangre," perceived religion as a fixed, biological reality in a way that offers a sharp contrast with earlier medieval thought.[8]

All of this is not to say that Umayyad al-Andalus was a paradise of multiculturalism. It was as much a period of violence and social upheaval as a period of tolerance. The shifting nature of religious and ethnic identities, however, did make that time an unusually rich environment for social mobility and change.

Notes

INTRODUCTION

1. See for example one of the classic works in the field, Marshall G. S. Hodgson's *The Venture of Islam* (Chicago and London: University of Chicago Press, 1974), 3 vols., which covers the Maghrib in less detail than the Nile to Oxus region.

2. "In 1492 We Lost Everything," "Jihad Watch," http://www.jihadwatch.org/2005/03/in-1492-we-lost-everything.html

3. James T. Monroe, *Islam and the Arabs in Spanish Scholarship (Sixteenth Century to the Present)* (Leiden: Brill, 1970); Alex Novikoff, "Between Tolerance and Intolerance in Medieval Spain: A Historiographic Enigma," *Medieval Encounters* 11, no. 1 (2005), 7–36; Kenneth Baxter Wolf, "*Convivencia* in Medieval Spain: A Brief History of an Idea," *Religion Compass* 3, no. 1 (2009), 72–85.

4. *Historia de los mozárabes de España, deducida de los mejores y más auténticos testimonios de los escritores cristianos y árabes* (Madrid: M. Tello, 1897–1903); *Glosario de las voces ibéricas y latinas usadas entre los mozárabes* (Madrid: Est. tip. de Fortanet, 1888).

5. *Los mozárabes* (Madrid: Consejo Superior de Investigaciones Científicas, 1947–48), 2 vols.

6. *Historia de los mozárabes*, introduction, liv.

7. *España en su historia: Cristianos, moros y judíos* (Buenos Aires: Editorial Losada, 1948).

8. *The Spaniards: An Introduction to Their History* (Berkeley and Los Angeles: University of California Press, 1971), 174–208. Simonet thought that the Romans in Iberia were sources of Spanish Christian culture, but not the Visigoths, whom he viewed as collaborators with the Muslim invaders. *Historia de los mozárabes*, introduction, lv–lvi.

9. *Histoire des musulmans d'Espagne* (Leiden: Brill, 1932), 3 vols.

10. (Paris and Leiden: Brill, 1950), 3 vols.

11. *Structures sociales "orientales" et "occidentales" dans l'Espagne musulmane* (Paris: Mouton, 1977). In this book page references will be to the Spanish translation of the book, *Al-Ándalus: estructura antropológica de una sociedad islámica en Occidente* (Granada: Universidad de Granada, 1995). On Guichard see also Thomas Glick, *From Muslim Fortress to Christian Castle* (Manchester and New York: Manchester University Press), preface.

12. Glick, *Islamic and Christian Spain in the Early Middle Ages* (Princeton: Princeton University Press, 1979); Glick and Oriol Pi-Sunyer, "Acculturation as an Explanatory Concept in Spanish History," *Comparative Studies in Society and History* 11, no. 2 (1969), 136–54; Guichard, "El problema de la existencia de estructuras de tipo "feudal" en la sociedad de al-Andalus," in *Estructuras feudales y feudalismo en el mundo mediterráneo*, ed. Pierre Bonnaisse (Barcelona: Crítica, 1984), 117–45; Guichard, "Le problème des structures agraires en Al-Andalus avant la conquête chrétienne," in *Andalucía entre Oriente y Occidente (1236–1492): Actas del V Coloquio Internacional de Historia Medieval de Andalucía*, ed. Emilio Cabrera (Córdoba: Diputación Provincial de Córdoba, Servicio de Publicaciones, 1988), 161–70.

13. (London and New York: Longman, 1996).

14. See, among many others, María Jesús Fuente Pérez, *Velos y desvelos: cristianas, musulmanas, y judías en la España medieval* (Madrid: Esfera de los libros, 2006); Gloria López de Plaza, *Al-Andalus: Mujeres, sociedad, y religión* (Málaga: Universidad de Málaga, 1992); Manuela Marín, *Mujeres en Al-Andalus* (Madrid: Consejo Superior de Investigaciones Científicas, 2000); and Celia del Moral, *Árabes, judías, y cristianas: mujeres en la Europa medieval* (Granada: Universidad de Granada, 1993).

15. Camilla Adang, "Ibn Hazm on Homosexuality: A Case-Study of Záhiri Legal Methodology,"*Al-Qantara* 24, no. 1 (2003), 5–31; Louis Crompton, "Male Love and Islamic Law in Arab Spain," in *Islamic Homosexualities: Culture, History, and Literature*, ed. Stephen O. Murray and Will Roscoe (New York: New York University Press, 1997), 142–57; Norman Roth, "Deal Gently with the Young Man: Love of Boys in Medieval Hebrew Poetry of Spain," *Speculum* 57, no. 1 (1982), 20–51.

16. A small sample of this literature includes Jessica Coope, *The Martyrs of Córdoba: Community and Family Conflict in an Age of Mass Conversion* (Lincoln: University of Nebraska Press, 1995); Glick, *Islamic and Christian Spain*; Maria Menocal, *The Ornament of the World: How Muslims, Jews, and Christians Created a Culture of Tolerance in Medieval Spain* (Boston: Little, Brown, 2002); Dolores Oliver Pérez, "Una nueva interpretación de 'árabe,' muladí,' y 'mawla' como voces representivas de grupos sociales," in *Proyección Histórica De España En Sus Tres Culturas: Castilla y León, América y El Mediterraneo*, ed. Eufemio Lorenzo Sanz (Valladolid: Junta de Castilla y León, 1993), 3:143–55; Janina M. Safran, *Defining Boundaries in al-Andalus: Muslims, Christians and Jews in Islamic Iberia* (Ithaca: Cornell University Press, 2013); and Ragnhild Johnsrud Zorgati, *Pluralism in the Middle Ages: Hybrid Identities, Conversion, and Mixed Marriages in Medieval Iberia* (London and New York: Routledge, 2012).

17. "al-'āmmah" is the term Egyptian translators of the Harry Potter books use for "Muggles."

18. Hodgson, 1:272–79, 280–314; Ira M. Lapidus, *A History of Islamic Societies*

(Cambridge: Cambridge University Press, 1988), 67–97; M. A. Shaban, *The Abbasid Revolution* (Cambridge: Cambridge University Press, 1970), 35–52.

19. Hugh Kennedy, *The Prophet and the Age of the Caliphates: The Islamic Near East from the Sixth to the Eleventh Centuries* (London and New York: Longman, 1986), 117–23; Lapidus, 67–80; Shaban, *Islamic History: A New Interpretation* (Cambridge: Cambridge University Press, 1971), 166–89.

20. Joyce Appleby, Lynn Hunt, and Margaret Jacob, *Telling the Truth About History* (New York: Norton, 1994), 218.

21. Geertz, "Thick Description: Toward an Interpretive Theory of Culture," in *The Interpretation of Cultures* (New York: Basic Books, 1973), 3–30.

22. Darnton, *The Great Cat Massacre and Other Episodes in French Cultural History* (New York: Vintage Books, 1985), 3.

23. Darnton, 5.

24. William Bouwsma, *A Usable Past: Essays in European Cultural History* (Berkeley and Los Angeles: University of California Press, 1990), 1–16.

25. Talal Asad, "The Idea of an Anthropology of Islam," *Qui Parle* 17, no. 2 (2009), 1–30.

26. See chapter 1 for bibliography on Ibn Ḥazm.

27. *Al-Akhlāq wa al-siyar fī mudāwāt al-nufūs*, ed. Ṭāhir Aḥmad Makkī (Cairo: Dār al-maʿārif, 1981), 45–46.

CHAPTER 1

1. Kennedy, *The Prophet and the Age of the Caliphates*, 117.

2. For the arrival of ʿAbd al-Raḥmān I see Lévi-Provençal, *Histoire*, 1:95–117; Pedro Chalmeta, *Invasión e islamización: La sumisión de Hispania y la formación de al-Andalus* (Madrid: Editorial MAPFRE, 1994), 349–87; Hugh Kennedy, *Muslim Spain and Portugal: A Political History of al-Andalus (London and New York: Routledge, 1996)*, 30–38; and ʿAbdulwāḥid Dhanūn Ṭāha, *The Muslim Conquest and Settlement of North Africa and Spain* (London: Routledge, 1989), 234–53.

3. For the Abbasid Revolution see Hodgson, 1:241–79; Shaban, *Abbasid Revolution*; Lapidus, *Islamic Societies*, 54–80; Kennedy, *Age of the Caliphates*, 124–33.

4. Lévi-Provençal, *Histoire*, 1:98–99.

5. For the period of the governors see Kennedy, *Muslim Spain*, 18–29; Ṭāha, 183–218; and Lévi-Provençal, *Histoire*, 1:34–53.

6. The exact nature of the original Yamanī- Muḍarī split is not clear. See Hodgson, 1:227–29; Shaban, *Islamic History*, 120–24; Lapidus, *Muslim Societies*, 59; Fred M. Donner, *Narratives of Islamic Origins: The Beginnings of Islamic Historical Writing* (Princeton, NJ: Darwin Press, 1998), 104–11. Patricia Crone, *Slaves on Horses* (Cambridge: Cambridge University Press, 1980), 42–45, sees the split as factionalism within the army, not connected to any real tribal identities in the broader society. See also Gerald R. Hawting, *The First Dynasty of Islam: The Umayyad Caliphate A.D. 661–740* (London and Sydney: Croom Helm, 1986), 34–40, who demonstrates that tribes under the Umayyads switched their identity between southern and northern depending on political exigencies.

7. Kennedy, *Muslim Spain*, 23–29.

8. Kennedy, *Muslim Spain*, 30–38; Lévi-Provençal, *Histoire*, 1:51–53, 101–4.

9. Dolores Oliver Pérez notes that the pro-Umayyad chroniclers sometimes use the term "Arab" in a pejorative sense, meaning people who behave like tribesman competing for power with the state instead of supporting it. "Una nueva interpretación de 'arabe.'"

10. For the process of adapting preexisting institutions and imposing an Arab cultural stamp, see Hodgson, 1:187–240; Lapidus, *Muslim Societies*, 54–64; Kennedy, *Age of the Caliphs*, 82–122.

11. Lapidus, *Muslim Societies*, 85.

12. Oleg Grabar, "The Umayyad Dome of the Rock in Jerusalem," *Ars Orientalis* 3 (1959), 33–62; Grabar, "The Meaning of the Dome of the Rock," in *The Medieval Mediterranean: Cross-Cultural Contacts*, ed. Marilyn Chiat and Kathryn Ryerson (St. Cloud, MN: North Star Press of St. Cloud, 1988), 1–10; Nuha N. N. Khoury, "The Dome of the Rock, the Ka'ba, and Ghumdan: Arab Myths and Umayyad Monuments," *Muqarnas* 10, *Essays in Honor of Oleg Grabar* (1993), 57–65.

13. Roger Collins, *Early Medieval Spain: Unity in Diversity, 400–1000* (London: Macmillan, 1983), 87–143, emphasizes the continuing prosperity of cities and cultural continuities with the Roman Empire under the Visigoths. Taking the opposite view is Chalmeta, *Invasión*, 68–72, who sees Visigothic rule as on the verge of collapse by 711.

14. Gregory of Tours, *The History of the Franks*, trans. Lewis Thorpe (London: Penguin Books, 1974), 296–98 (Book V.34).

15. For the development of that mixed high culture see Hodgson, 1:280–314, and Lapidus, *Muslim Societies*, 81–97.

16. Kalid Yahya Blankinship, *The End of the Jihād State: The Reign of Hishām Ibn 'Abd al-Malik and the Collapse of the Umayyads* (Albany: State University of New York Press, 1994), 67–73.

17. Blankinship, 136–40.

18. Blankinship, 57–67.

19. Ahmad Dallal, "Science, Medicine, and Technology," in *The Oxford History of Islam*, ed. John Esposito (Oxford: Oxford University Press, 1999), 155–214; Howard R. Turner, *Science in Medieval Islam* (Austin: University of Texas Press, 1995), 1–35.

20. Chalmeta, *Invasión*, 359–67.

21. Guichard, *Estructura antropológica*, 55–140.

22. 'Alī ibn Aḥmad Ibn Ḥazm, *Jamharah ansāb al-'arab* (Beirut: Dār al-kutub al-'ilmīyah, 2001), 443, mentions an Arab lineage outside of Córdoba that does not speak Romance (al-laṭīnīyah), "neither the women nor the men." He clearly regards them as an anomaly. See also Julián Ribera y Tarragó, *Disertaciones y opúsculos* (Madrid: Impr. de E. Maestre, 1928), 2 vols., 1:27–56.

23. Coope, *Martyrs*, 84–90. Eduardo Manzano Moreno, *Conquistadores, emires y califas: los omeyas y la formación de al-Andalus* (Barcelona: Crítica, 2006), 159–66, sees the discourse about ethnicity in Umayyad al-Andalus as primarily a way to talk about social status.

24. Guichard, *Estructura antropológica*, 459–557.

25. Blankinship, 79–81; Kennedy, *Age of the Caliphates*, 82–90.

26. Hodgson, 1:280–84; Lapidus, *Muslim Societies*, 83–89.

27. Janina M. Safran, *The Second Umayyad Caliphate: The Articulation of Caliphal Legitimacy in al-Andalus* (Cambridge, MA: Harvard University Press, 2000), 53–54.

28. Donner, *The Early Islamic Conquests* (Princeton: Princeton University Press, 1981), 91–110.

29. Donner, *Narratives*, 177–78.

30. On the Fatimids, see Jamil M. Abun-Nasr, *A History of the Maghrib in the Islamic Period* (Cambridge: Cambridge University Press, 1987), 59–75; Michael Brett, *The Rise of the Fatimids: The World of the Mediterranean and the Middle East in the Fourth Century of the Hijra, Tenth Century C.E.* (Leiden: Brill, 2001); Heinz Halm, *The Empire of the Mahdi: The Rise of the Fatimids* (Leiden: Brill, 1996); Hodgson, 2:21–28; Kennedy, *Age of the Caliphs*, 315–45.

31. Safran, *Second Caliphate*, 70 and 75.

32. Safran, *Second Caliphate*, 61–67

33. Coope, *Martyrs*, 7–8; Kennedy, *Muslim Spain*, 44–54; Lévi-Provençal, *Histoire*, 1:263–72.

34. Antonio Vallejo Triano, "Madīnat al-Zahrā': Transformation of a Caliphal City," in *Revisiting al-Andalus: Perspectives on the Material Culture of Islamic Iberia and Beyond*, ed. Glaire D. Anderson and Maria Kosser-Owen (Leiden: Brill, 2007), 3–28.

35. Kennedy, *Muslim Spain*, 98–99; Lévi-Provençal, *Histoire*, 2:110–17; Safran, *Second Caliphate*, 52–60.

36. John, Abbot of St. Arnulf, *Vita Johannis Abbatis Gorziensis, Auctore Iohanne Abbate S. Arnulfi, Monumenta Germanica Historica, Scriptores . . . in usum scholarum*, 4 (Hanover, 1841), 375–77.

37. Kennedy, *Muslim Spain*, 78–79, 87–95; Safran, *Second Caliphate*, 19–37; Lévi-Provençal, *Histoire*, 2:110–17.

38. Kennedy, *Muslim Spain*, 96

39. Kennedy, *Muslim Spain*, 95–97. For possible Fatimid engagement in Ibn Ḥafṣūn's revolt, see Muḥammad Muḥammad Ibrāhīm Zaghrūt, *Al-'alaqāt bayna al-umawīyīn wa al-fāṭimīyīn fi al-andalus wa al-shamāl al-ifrīqī* (Cairo: Dār al-tawzī' wa al-nashr al-islāmīyah, 2006), 47–57.

40. Blankinship, 42–46; Shaban, *Islamic History*, 34–45. See also Fred Donner, *Conquests*, 221–50; Donner is not convinced that the armies were organized tribally.

41. Blankinship, 67–73, 82–91, 136–40, 193–95.

42. Hodgson, 1:481–83; Kennedy, *Age of the Caliphs*, 159–60; Lapidus, *Islamic Societies*, 127.

43. Kennedy, *Muslim Spain*, 85–95; Lévi-Provençal, *Histoire*, 2:122–30. The regime had used slave troops as early as 'Abd al-Raḥmān I, but not as extensively as the later Andalusī Umayyads. See Chalmeta, *Invasión*, 359–67.

44. Not everyone agrees with this characterization of the ṣaqālibah. See chapter 7.

45. For a good introduction to the history of jihād see John L. Esposito, *Unholy War: Terror in the Name of Islam* (Oxford: Oxford University Press, 2002), 26–70, and Michael Bonner, *Jihad in Islamic History: Doctrines and Practice* (Princeton:

Princeton University Press, 2006), 1–19. For jihād and the Crusades see Carole Hillenbrand, *The Crusades: Islamic Perspectives* (London and New York: Routledge, 2000), 89–255.

46. For a discussion of how those terms were used in al-Andalus, see Safran, *Defining Boundaries*, 168–208.

47. Blankinship, 1–9 and 11–35.

48. Abū Marwān Ḥayyān ibn Khalaf Ibn Ḥayyān al-Qurṭubī, *Al-Muqtabas min anbā' ahl al-Andalus*, ed. Maḥmūd 'Alī Makkī (Beirut: Dār al-kitāb al-'arabī, 1973), 2–3, for example, describes the amīr 'Abd al-Raḥmān II's campaign to subdue Majorca and Minorca and extract booty from them.

49. See for example the terms Charlemagne imposed on the Saxons after he defeated them. Einhard, *The Life of Charlemagne*, in *Einhard and Notker the Stammerer: Two Lives of Charlemagne*, trans. Lewis Thorpe (New York: Penguin Books, 1981), 61–63.

50. Richard W. Bulliet, *Conversion to Islam in the Medieval Period: An Essay in Quantitative History* (Cambridge, MA: Harvard University Press, 1979), 124–25.

51. See Hawting, *First Dynasty*, 76–81, and Blankinship, 82–91.

52. Jamsheed K. Choksy, *Conflict and Cooperation: Zoroastrian Subalterns and Muslim Elites in Medieval Iranian Society* (New York: Columbia University Press, 1997), 69–109. There was some question as to whether Muslim men could marry Zoroastrian women. See Zorgati, 104–6.

53. Lapidus, *Muslim Societies*, 452–63.

54. Hawting, *First Dynasty*, 1–20.

55. Donner, *Narratives*, 98–111.

56. For brief introductions to Shī'ism see Hodgson, 1:372–84; Lapidus, *Muslim Societies*, 115–19; and David Pinault, *The Shiites: Ritual and Popular Piety in a Muslim Community* (New York: St. Martin's Press, 1992), 11–57.

57. Hodgson, 1:444–72.

58. In his poem "The Wretched Pause," he describes wine and the barmaid serving it: "Golden-hued, it mingles water and froth, / As it pours from the hand of a slim-waited beauty, / Who resembles a willow branch, flaunting its graceful bearing." Trans. Nancy Coffin, "Princeton Online Arabic Poetry," http://www.princeton.edu/~arabic/poetry/

59. Hodgson, 1:315–58.

60. For the collapse of Abbasid rule see Hodgson, 1:473–95; Lapidus, *Muslim Societies*, 126–36; Kennedy, *Age of the Caliphates*, 158–351.

61. David Wasserstein, *The Rise and Fall of the Party Kings: Politics and Society in Islamic Spain, 1002–1086* (Princeton: Princeton University Press, 1985), 41–42.

62. For the Umayyad dynasty's collapse see Lévi-Provençal, *Histoire*, 2:291–345; Hugh Kennedy, *Muslim Spain*, 109–34; Manzano Moreno, *Conquistadores*, 471–503; Peter C. Scales, *The Fall of the Caliphate of Córdoba: Berbers and Andalusis in Conflict* (Leiden: Brill, 1994); María Jesús Viguera Molíns, Luis Molina Martínez, Muḥammad Jallāf et al., *Los reinos de taifas: al-Andalus en el siglo XI* (Madrid: Espasa Calpe, 1994), 31–38; and Wasserstein, *Party Kings*, 55–81.

63. Some of those clients were not biologically speaking of Arab ancestry but had

come to be regarded as part of the more general category of Arabs in the sense of Arabic-speaking, educated scholars or courtiers. For the ʿĀmirid faction, see Bruna Soravia, "A Portrait of the ʿĀlim as a Young Man: The Formative Years of Ibn Ḥazm, 404/1013–420/1029," in *Ibn Ḥazm of Córdoba: The Life and Works of a Controversial Thinker*, ed. Camilla Adang, Maribel Fierro, and Sabine Schmidtke (Leiden: Brill, 2013), 25–49.

64. Scales, 110–14.

65. Maribel Fierro, "Los cadíes de Córdoba de Abd al-Rahman III (r. 300/912–350–961)," in *Cadíes y cadiazgo en Al-Andalus y el Magreb medieval*, ed. Rachid El Hour and Rafael Mayor (Madrid: Consejo Superior de Investigaciones Científicas, 2012), 69–98.

66. Maribel Fierro, *Abderramán III y el califato omeya de Córdoba* (Donostia-San Sebastián: Nerea, 2011), 17–20; Fierro, "Mawālī and Muwalladūn in al-Andalus (Second/Eighth—Fourth/Tenth Centuries)," in *Patronate and Patronage in Early and Classical Islam, ed. Monique Bernards and John Nawas* (Leiden: Brill, 2005), 195–245.

67. Pierre Guichard and Bruna Soravia, *Les royaumes de taifas: apogée culturel et déclin politique des émirats andalous du Xie siècle* (Paris: Geuthner, 2007), 133–36. Guichard, *Al-Andalus frente a la conquista cristiana: los musulmanes de Valencia*, trans. Josep Torró (Valencia and Madrid: Biblioteca Nueva, Universitat de València, 2001), 207–35, notes that the population of Valencia by the end of the twelfth century self-identified as Arab, speaking Arabic and claiming Arab genealogy.

68. Viguera et al., 70–72, and Wasserstein, *Party Kings*, 116–17, 164–74.

69. *Pouvoir et légitimité en Espagne musulmane à l'époque des taifas, Ve-Xie siècle: l'imam fictif* (Paris: Editions L'Harmattan, 1997), 13–16.

70. *Pouvoir*, 205–18.

71. Wasserstein, *Party Kings*, 227–34.

CHAPTER 2

1. Chalmeta, *Invasión*, 32–62.

2. This chronology is recounted in Chalmeta, *Invasión*, 126–32 and 163–83; Ṭāha, 84–109; and Kennedy, *Muslim Spain*, 3–16. Major primary sources for the conquest include the *Akhbār majmūʿa fī fatḥ al-Andalus*, trans. Emilio Lafuente y Alcántara (Madrid: Bibliofilo, 1984); *Crónica del Moro Rasis*, ed. Diego Catalán and María Soledad de Andrés (Madrid: Editorial Gredos, 1974); *Crónica mozárabe de 754*, ed. and trans. José Eduardo López Pereira (Zaragoza: Anubar, 1980); ʿAbd al-Malik Ibn Ḥabīb, *Kitāb al-taʾrīkh* (Beirut: Dār al-kutub al-ʿilmīyah, 1999); and Muḥammad ibn ʿUmar Ibn al-Qūṭīyah al-Qurṭubī, *Taʾrīkh iftitāḥ al-Andalus*, ed. ʿUmar Fārūq al-Ṭabbāʿ (Beirut: Muʾassasah al-maʿārif, 1994). See Chalmeta, *Invasión*, 29–66, for a thorough discussion of the primary sources.

3. Coope, *Martyrs*, 56–61 and 80–90.

4. All references in this book are to the Spanish translation cited in the introduction.

5. For example, *Estructura antropológica*, 77–85. Guichard's arguments about

Berber kinship are more plausible when they are based on Islamic-era place-names; see 285–458. See also Scales, 152–72.

6. Guichard, *Estructura antropológica*, 55–140.

7. Scales's otherwise excellent critique of Guichard reflects this confusion when he says that the Umayyad lineage's status was not affected when men had children by their slave women, then later makes the contradictory point that the family's position was damaged because men sought mates outside the lineage. The real issue is not whether men marry outside the group, but whether women do so. See Scales, 117–31.

8. For information on his life and works, see Theodore Pulcini, *Exegesis as Polemical Discourse: Ibn Hazm on Jewish and Christian Scriptures* (Atlanta: Scholars Press, 1998), 1–11; Ghulam Haider Aasi, "Muslim Understanding of other Religions: An Analytical Study of Ibn Hazm's *Kitab al-fasl fi al-milal wa-al-ahwa' wa al-nihal*" (PhD dissertation, Temple University, 1987), 4–53; W. Montgomery Watt and Pierre Cachia, *A History of Islamic Spain* (Edinburgh: University of Edinburgh, 1965), 128–31; and *Encyclopedia of Islam*, ed. C. E. Bosworth et al. (Leiden: Brill, 1995), s.v. "Ibn Hazm."

9. Donner, *Conquests*, 20–28.

10. Ibn Ḥazm, *Jamharah*, 93–103.

11. Ibn Ḥazm, *Jamharah*, 7–9, 463–86.

12. This arrangement into tribe and clan is common in genealogies of the period. Clan and tribal identity could shift over time in response to political changes. See Donner, *Conquests*, 20–34, and W. Robertson Smith, *Kinship and Marriage in Early Arabia* (London: Cambridge University Press, 1885), 1–58.

13. For example, in the case of two sons of Sa'sa'ah b. Mu'āwiyah, who called themselves the Banū Salūl after their mother, Salūl bint Dhuhl. Ibn Ḥazm, *Jamharah*, 271–72.

14. *Jamharah*, 37–38.

15. *Jamharah*, 68.

16. *Jamharah*, 93.

17. Lévi-Provençal, *Histoire*, 1:266–68.

18. *Jamharah*, 91–92.

19. Ibn Ḥazm, *Jamharah*, 280. See 271–72 for more on Āminah's family, and 78–80 for that of Umayyah.

20. Robin Fox, *Kinship and Marriage: An Anthropological Perspective* (London: Penguin, 1974), 122–45; Smith, 35–58

21. Donner, *Conquests*, 28–34, and note 49.

22. Amalia Zomeño, "Kafā'a in the Maliki School: A Fatwā from Fifteenth-Century Fez," in *Islamic Law: Theory and Practice*, ed. Robert Gleave and Eugenia Kermeli (London: I. B. Tauris, 1997), 194–204.

23. *Jamharah*, 89.

24. Ibn Ḥazm, *Naqṭ al-'arūs*, ed. C. F. Seybold, trans. Luis Seco de Lucena (Valencia: Universidad de Valencia, 1974), Arabic 160–61, Spanish 94–95.

25. *Naqṭ*, Arabic 161, Spanish 95–97.

26. Kennedy, *Muslim Spain*, 65, 113; Marín, *Mujeres*, 417–29. See also Ibn Ḥayyān, ed. Makkī, 26–28, and Makkī's note 86.

27. *Kitāb al-ta'rīkh*, 157–58.

28. I am using the term for convenience, with the understanding that some linguists would see it as too imprecise; see for example Jonathan Owens, *A Linguistic History of Arabic* (Oxford: Oxford University Press, 2006), 2–5.

29. See Niloofar Haeri, *Sacred Language, Ordinary People* (New York: Palgrave Macmillan, 2003), 37–48, and Kees Versteegh, *The Arabic Language* (New York: Columbia University Press, 1997), 189–208.

30. Versteegh, *Arabic Language*, 130–47.

31. Versteegh, *Arabic Language*, 93–113.

32. Versteegh, *Arabic Language*, 114–29.

33. David Pinault, *Story-Telling Techniques in the Arabian Nights* (Leiden: Brill, 1992), 12–16. See also *The Arabian Nights Encyclopedia*, ed. Ulrich Marzolph and Richard van Leeuwen (Santa Barbara, CA: ABC-CLIO, 2004), 2 vols., 2:620–21.

34. On the use of Romance in al-Andalus among both Iberians and Arabs, see Ribera y Tarragó, 1:27–56.

35. M. G. Carter, *Sībawayhi* (London and New York: I. B. Taurus, 2004), 39.

36. Carter, 56–61.

37. Carter, 44–46.

38. Carter, 69–72.

39. Carter, 40–42; Versteegh, *Arabic Language*, 37–52.

40. Versteegh, *Arabic Language*, 53–73.

41. Versteegh, *Landmarks in Linguistic Thought III: The Arabic Linguistic Tradition* (London and New York: Routledge, 1997), 11–22.

42. Bernard Lewis, *The Muslim Discovery of Europe* (Princeton: Princeton University Press, 1982), 71–88.

43. Versteegh, *Landmarks*, 52–63.

44. Comes (Count) Ibn Antonian, an important official of Iberian origin in the Umayyad court under the amīr Muḥammad I (r. 852–86), was valued for his fluency in the two languages. See Ibn Ḥayyān, ed. Makkī, 142. In the tenth century, the Christian official Recemundus was similarly valued for his ease with diplomatic correspondence in European languages and was sent as an ambassador to the Constantinople. See Liutprand of Cremona, *Antapodosis*, ed. Joseph Becker, in *Monumenta Germanica Historica, Scriptores . . . in usum scholarum* (Hanover: 1915), 1–158.

45. Abū Zayd ʿAbd al-Raḥmān Ibn Khaldūn al-Ḥaḍramī, *Al-Muqaddimah*, trans. Franz Rosenthal (New York: Pantheon Books, 1958), 3 vols., 3:320–67.

46. Versteegh, *Landmarks*, 52–63.

47. Pilar Garrido Clemente, *Estudio, traducción y edición de la obra de Ibn Masarra de Córdoba: La ciencia de las letras en el sufismo* (Salamanca: Ediciones Universidad de Salamanca, 2008), 251–72.

48. See Faruq Sherif, *A Guide to the Contents of the Qur'an* (Reading, UK: Garnet Publishing, 1995), 45–47.

49. *Kitāb khawwās al-ḥurūf*, in Garrido Clemente, Arabic 198–202 and 208, English 290–97 and 308.

50. Hodgson, 1:254–56; Lapidus, *Muslim Societies*, 90; Versteegh, *Landmarks*, 11–22.

51. Hodgson, 1:296–98; Kennedy, *Age of the Caliphates*, 119–20; Lapidus, *Muslim Societies*, 89–91.

52. Lapidus, "The Separation of State and Religion," *International Journal of Middle Eastern Studies* VI (1975), 363–85.

53. "La islamización de las ciudades andalusíes a través de sus ulemas (s. II/VIII-comienzos s. IV/X," in *Genese de la ville islamique en al-Andalus et au Maghreb occidental*, ed. Patrice Cressier and Mercedes García-Arenal (Madrid: Casa de Velázquez, Consejo Superior de Investigaciones Científicas, 1998), 65–97.

54. Khaḍr Mūsā Muḥammad Ḥamūd, *Al-naḥū wa al-nuḥāt: al-madāris wa al-khaṣā'is* (Beirut: 'Ālam al-kutub, 2003), 173.

55. Versteegh, *Landmarks*, 76–87.

56. See Sharaf al-Dīn 'Abd al-Ḥamīd Amīn, *Ibn Ḥazm al-Andalusī wa naqd al-'aql al-uṣūlī* (Kuwait: Dār su'ād al-ṣabaḥ, 1995), 61–75, and my discussion of Ẓāhirism and Ibn Ḥazm, "With Heart, Tongue, and Limbs: Ibn Hazm on the Essence of Faith," *Medieval Encounters* 6, nos. 1–3 (2000), 101–13.

57. For the latter, see, in addition to Pulcini, Camilla Adang, *Muslim Writers on the Hebrew Bible: From Ibn Rabban to Ibn Hazm* (Leiden: Brill, 1996).

58. Ẓāhirism is sometimes characterized as a madhhab (school of religious law) but is really more of a methodology. See Versteegh, "Ibn Maḍā' as Ẓāhirī Grammarian," in Adang and Fierro, *Ibn Ḥazm of Cordoba*, 207–31. Ibn Ḥazm never became an opponent of the Mālikī madhhab, although he disagreed with Mālikī 'ulamā' on a number of points.

59. Amīn, 65–75; Roger Arnaldez, *Grammaire et théologie chez Ibn Hazm de Courdoue: essai sur la structure et les conditions de la pensée musulmane* (Paris: J. Vrin, 1956), 73–87.

60. Ibn Ḥazm summarizes his views on the origin and development of language in *al-Iḥkām fī uṣūl al-aḥkām*, ed. Muḥammad Aḥmad 'Abd al-'Azīz (Cairo: Maktabah 'Ātif, 1978), 2 vols., 1:34–40. See also Arnaldez, 37–47 and 73–87.

61. Ibn Ḥazm, *Al-faṣl fī al-milāl wa al-ahwā' wa al-niḥal*, ed. Muḥammad ibn 'Abd al-Karīm al-Shahrastānī (Beirut: Dār al-ma'rifah, 1975), 5 vols., 3:211.

62. Adang, *Muslim Writers*, 216–22.

63. For this analysis I am using the treatise on grammar by Ibn Maḍā', *Kitāb al-radd 'alā al-nuḥāh*, ed. Shawqī Ḍayf (Cairo: Dār al-ma'ārif, 1982), and the English translation by Ronald G. Wolfe in his PhD dissertation, "Ibn Maḍā' al-Qurṭubī and the Book in Refutation of the Grammarians" (Indiana University, 1984), 144–269. I will cite pages for both the Arabic treatise and the translation. For general background on Ibn Maḍā' and his work see Versteegh, *Landmarks*, 140–52, and Versteegh, "Ibn Maḍā'," in Adang and Fierro, *Ibn Ḥazm of Cordoba*.

64. Ibn Maḍā', 71; Wolfe, 145.

65. Ibn Maḍā', 77; Wolfe, 153–54.

66. Ibn Maḍā', 79–80; Wolfe, 159.

67. Ibn Maḍā', 130–31; Wolfe, 252–54.

68. George Bohas discusses the concept of light and heavy sounds, as well as the levels of grammatical explanation, in "Aspects of Debate and Explanation Among

Arab Grammarians," in *The Early Islamic Grammatical Tradition*, ed. Ramzi Baalbaki (Aldershot, UK: Ashgate, 2007), 169–86.

69. Edward Said comments on Ẓāhirism's connections with modern linguistic thought in *The World, the Text, and the Critic* (Cambridge, MA: Harvard University Press, 1983), 36–39. He gives incorrect dates for Ibn Maḍā'.

70. John Wansbrough, *Quranic Studies: Sources and Methods of Scriptural Interpretation* (Oxford: Oxford University Press, 1977), 96–106, discusses the uses of Classical Arabic to enforce social boundaries.

71. Muḥammad ibn al-Ḥarīth al-Khushanī, *Historia de los jueces the Córdoba por Aljoxani*, ed. and trans. Julián Ribera y Tarragó (Madrid: Imprenta Ibérica, 1914), Arabic 161–63, Spanish 200–202. See also Ibn al-Qūṭīyah, 133.

72. Ribera's translation implies that al-Khushanī's source is criticizing him for being too lenient with the man, but the context makes it more likely that the story is an example of Mūsā's ḥilm.

73. Arabic 182–88, Spanish 225–34.

74. Lévi-Provençal, *Histoire*, 1:77.

75. For an introduction to the term, see *Encyclopedia of Islam*, ed. C. E. Bosworth, E. Van Donzel, B. Lewis, and Charles Pellat (Brill: Leiden, 1991), s.v. "mawlā"; Crone, *Slaves on Horses*, 49–57; Crone, *Roman, Provincial and Islamic Law: The Origins of the Islamic Patronate* (Cambridge: Cambridge University Press, 1987); and David Pipes, "Mawlas: Freed Slaves and Converts in Early Islam," in *Muslims and Others in Early Islamic Society*, ed. Robert Hoyland (Aldershot, UK: Ashgate, 2004), 277–322.

76. Crone, *Roman, Provincial and Islamic Law*, 77–88.

77. Dolores Oliver, "Sobre el significado de 'mawla' dentro de la historia de al-Andalus," *Al-Qantara* 22 (2001), 321–44.

78. Ḥamūd, 172–73.

79. Oliver argues for the positive status of mawālī in al-Andalus as honorary members of an Arab tribe, particularly in the early period of Islamic rule there.

80. "Mawālī and Muwalladūn."

CHAPTER 3

1. Bulliet developed an ingenious system for estimating the impact of conversion on particular areas of the Islamic world based on biographical dictionaries, which often list the genealogy of their non-Arab Muslim subjects back to the original convert in the family. See pp. 124–25, where he estimates that about half the total conversions to Islam in al-Andalus had happened by 961 (the year of 'Abd al-Raḥmān III's death), and more than 80 percent by 1105 (the year before the Almoravid dynasty officially came to power). He thinks at least 80 percent of the population converted overall.

2. For example Q. 2:136.

3. In this chapter I am following Abdullah Yusuf Ali's translation, with some modifications (Elmhurst, NY: Tahrike Tarsile Qur'an, 1988).

4. See for example Q. 2:112, 2:356, and 3:114.
5. 2:89.
6. 2:105.
7. 3:71, 5:14.
8. "From Believers to Muslims: Confessional Self-identity in the Early Islamic Community," *Al-Abḥāth* 50–51 (2002–3), 9–53.
9. For example Q 4:171 and 5:76. 5:76 occurs shortly after a verse asserting that Jews, Christians, and Sabians can be saved (5:72), so following Donner's argument, 5:76 may be taken as a kind of restriction on 5:72: People of the Book can be saved except for those who make specific theological claims that cast doubt on God's unity.
10. *Ṣaḥīḥ Muslim*, Book 1, no. 325.
11. *Ṣaḥīḥ al-Bukhārī*, Book 12, no. 749.
12. *Ṣaḥīḥ Bukhārī*, Book 36, no. 469. The ḥadīth appears to be influenced by the Gospel story about the laborers in the vineyard, Matt. 20.1–6.
13. Pulcini, 45–54.
14. This translation of the title is by Samuel M. Behloul, "The Testimony of Reason and Historical Reality: Ibn Ḥazm's Refutation of Christianity," in Adang and Fierro, *Ibn Ḥazm of Cordoba*, 457–83.
15. *al-Faṣl*, 2:12. A Spanish translation of part of the *Faṣl* can be found in Miguel Asín Palacios, *Abenhazm de Córdoba y su historia crítica de las ideas religiosas* (Madrid: Ediciones Turner, 1984), 5 vols.
16. See Hava Lazarus-Yafeh, "Some Neglected Aspects of Medieval Muslim Polemics against Christianity," *The Harvard Theological Review* 89, no. 1 (January 1996), 61–84, and Pulcini, 29–43.
17. Adang, *Muslim Writers*, 227–331. Later Christian polemic (thirteenth century) against Judaism made a similar point about Talmud being a corrupt text that has distracted Jews from true Torah. See Jeremy Cohen, *The Friars and the Jews: The Evolution of Medieval Anti-Judaism* (Ithaca: Cornell University Press, 1982), 51–76.
18. Pulcini, 57–95. Ibn Ḥazm defends the absolute obedience of the prophets to God's will in *al-Faṣl*, 4:9–21.
19. *al-Faṣl*, 5:17–19.
20. *al-Faṣl*, 2:2–7. See also Pulcini, 134–38.
21. Muslim polemicists generally understood Christian scripture as originally a revelation given directly to Christ, although it was later corrupted into what Christians call the Gospels, which by Muslim standards were unreliable ḥadīths about Jesus lacking verifiable isnāds (chains of oral transmission). See *al-Faṣl*, 1:211–12.
22. *al-Faṣl*, 2:48–49.
23. *al-Faṣl*, 2:21–24. Ibn Ḥazm takes the position that Jesus always followed Jewish law, and that later Christians like Paul were at fault for abrogating it, for example by rejecting circumcision.
24. Adang, "Some Hitherto Neglected Biblical Material in the Work of Ibn Hazm," *Al-Masaq* 5 (1992), 17–28.
25. Quoted in Adang, "Biblical Material," her translation.
26. He sums up his views of Jews and Christians in *al-Faṣl*, 3:214–15 and 222–23.

In his legal works such as *al-Muḥallā*, he does recognize the legitimacy of dhimmī status; see Adang, *Muslim Writers*, 249–55.

27. See *al-Faṣl* 3:188–259, particularly 3:194–95 and 226–27. The rest of my discussion of Ibn Ḥazm in this chapter draws on the "Kitāb al-īmān."

28. Q. 2:34; *al-Faṣl*, 3:223–24.

29. See Adang, *Muslim Writers*, 67–69, and Fierro, "Ibn Ḥazm and the Jewish Zindīq," in Adang and Fierro, *Ibn Ḥazm of Cordoba*, 497–509.

30. *al-Faṣl*, 3:222–23.

31. "Shirk and 'Idolatry' in Monotheistic Polemic," in *Dhimmis and Others: Jews and Christians and the World of Classical Islam*, ed. Uri Rubin and David J. Wasserstein (Tel-Aviv: Eisenbrauns, 1997), 107–26.

32. A concise summary of the position of dhimmīs can be found in Mark R. Cohen, *Under Crescent and Cross: The Jews in the Middle Ages* (Princeton: Princeton University Press, 1994), 52–74. Full-length works include Antoine Fattal, *Le statut des non-Musulmans en pays d'Islam* (Beirut: Imprimerie catholique, 1958); Bernard Lewis, *The Jews of Islam* (London and New York: Routledge, 1984); A. S. Tritton, *The Caliphs and Their Non-Muslim Subjects* (London: Frank Cass, 1970); and Bat Ye'or, *The Dhimmi: Jews and Christians Under Islam* (London: Association of University Presses, 1985).

33. Unlike the other three main schools of Sunni law, Mālikī law disapproves of marriages between Muslim men and dhimmī women. See Mālik ibn Anas and Abū Sa'īd 'Abd al-Salām Saḥnūn ibn Sa'īd ibn Ḥabīb al-Tanūkhī, *Al-Mudawwanah al-kubrā* (Beirut: Dār al-Sādir, 1990–1999), 6 vols., 2:306–10.

34. See Cohen, 3–14.

35. Bat Ye'or, for example, cites Muslim ideas about jihād and dhimmī status from the time of Muḥammad and the middle ages as support for her polemic against modern Islam. See her *Eurabia: The Euro-Arab Axis* (Madison, NJ: Farleigh Dickinson University, 2005), particularly 163–75 and 190–208.

36. Cohen, 30–51.

37. Michael G. Morony, "Religious Communities in Late Sasanian and Early Muslim Iraq," in Hoyland, *Muslims and Others*, 1–23.

38. Andrew Sharf, *Byzantine Jewry from Justinian to the Fourth Crusade* (New York: Schocken Books, 1971), 19–41.

39. David Nirenberg, *Communities of Violence: Persecution of Minorities in the Middle Ages* (Princeton: Princeton University Press, 1996), 130.

40. See Solomon Katz, *The Jews in the Visigothic and Frankish Kingdoms of Spain and Gaul* (Cambridge, MA: Medieval Academy of America, 1937), 88.

41. Cited in Cohen, 53.

42. Tritton summarizes the various extant versions of the Covenant, 5–17. See also Fattal, 60–69.

43. Albrecht Noth emphasizes that the regulations on dress were not intended to impose new styles on non-Muslims but rather to make sure that non-Muslims would continue to dress in their customary fashion, instead of trying to pass as part of the ruling elite. See his "Problems of Differentiation between Muslims and Non-Muslims," in Hoyland, *Muslims and Others*, 103–24.

44. See Cohen, 54–55; David M. Freidenreich, "Christians in Early and Classical Sunnī Law," in *Christian-Muslim Relations: A Bibliographical History: Volume I (600–900)*, ed. David Thomas (Leiden: Brill, 2009), 99–114; Safran, *Defining Boundaries*, 10–17; and Tritton, 5–17.

45. Fattal, 34–57.

46. Tritton, 89–99.

47. See Hawting, *First Dynasty*, 76–81.

48. Bernard S. Bachrach, *Early Medieval Jewish Policy in Western Europe* (Minneapolis: University of Minnesota Press, 1977), 3–26 and 44–65; Katz, cited above; and Norman Roth, *Jews, Visigoths and Muslims in Medieval Spain: Cooperation and Conflict* (Leiden: Brill, 1994), 7–38. See also P. D. King, *Law and Society in the Visigothic Kingdom* (Cambridge: Cambridge University Press, 1972), in particular 131–46, and scattered references in E. A. Thompson, *The Goths in Spain* (Oxford: Clarendon Press, 1969).

49. The Visigothic *Forum iudicum*, Liber III, titulus IV, discusses interfaith marriage and sexuality. It uses the term "adulterium" as a general term for prohibited sexual behavior, parallel to "stuprum" in Latin or to "zinā'" in Arabic. In *Fuero juzgo en latin y castellano*, Real Academia Española (Madrid: Ibarra, 1815). See also Nirenberg, 130–33.

50. Roth, *Jews, Visigoths and Muslims* discusses and rejects most current theories. See also Bachrach, "A Reassessment of Visigothic Jewish Policy, 589–711" *American Historical Review* 78, no. 1 (February 1973), 11–34.

51. John Boswell suggests that the cultural life of urban areas was not much affected by Visigothic laws against either Jews or homosexuals. See *Christianity, Social Tolerance, and Homosexuality* (Chicago: University of Chicago Press, 1980), 174–76.

52. Fattal, 127–43.

53. Fattal, 127–29.

54. Boswell notes this same power gradient in fourteenth-century Christian Aragon, where Jewish or Muslim men sleeping with Christian women were severely punished, while Christian men had access to Jewish and Muslim women. *The Royal Treasure: Muslim Communities under the Crown of Aragon in the Fourteenth Century* (New Haven: Yale University Press, 1977), 343–53.

55. Morony imagines how that process might have worked in Iraq.

56. Coope, *Martyrs*, 55–56.

57. Mikel de Epalza, "Mozarabs: An Emblematic Christian Minority in Islamic al-Andalus," in *The Legacy of Muslim Spain*, ed. Salma Khadra Jayyusi (Leiden: Brill, 1992), 149–70.

58. Reyna Pastor de Togneri, "Problèmes d'assimilation d'une minorité: Les Mozarabes de Tolède (de 1085 à la fin du Xiiie siècle)," *Annales* 25e Année, no. 2 (March–April 1970), 351–90. Epalza cautions that many of the Christians in Toledo after the 1085 Christian conquest were converts from Islam, and that the Toledan Christian population under Islam may not have been as large as we have assumed.

59. Chalmeta, *Invasión*, 209–20; Lévi-Provençal, *Histoire*, 1:30–33.

60. Simonet, 69–138.

61. Robert Hillenbrand, "'The Ornament of the World': Medieval Córdoba as a Cultural Center," in Jayyusi, *Legacy*, 112–35 (see 114–15 for Count Rabīʿ); Kennedy, *Muslim Spain*, 42–44; Lévi-Provençal, *Histoire*, 1:165–69, 196.

62. Book II, *praef.* The *Apologeticus* appears in *Corpus scriptorum muzarabicorum*, ed. Juan Gil, 2 vols. (Madrid: Instituto Antonio de Nebrija, 1973), 2:506–658. See also Coope, *Martyrs*, 56–61.

63. Bernard Lewis, *Muslim Discovery of Europe*, 71–88

64. See Hodgson, 1:280–314, on the formation of that culture in contrast to what he calls the piety-minded culture of the urban ʿulamāʾ.

65. Lapidus, *Islamic Societies*, 128–29.

66. His story appears in Ibn Ḥayyān, ed. Makkī, 138 and 142, Ibn al-Qūṭīyah, 120–21, and al-Khushanī, Arabic 130–34, Spanish 159–64. Regarding his name, see Lévi-Provençal, *Histoire*, 1:289, and Ibn Ḥayyān, Makkī's note 310. Makkī and Lévi-Provençal follow majority scholarly opinion in saying that Qūmis is the Arabic transliteration of the title Comes (Count) rather than a proper name, since the proper name it most resembles, "Gomez," would more likely be transliterated as "Ghūmis." The sources do not however always use the definite article as one would expect if "Qūmis" were a title; also Ibn Antonian's son ʿUmar was called ʿUmar ibn qūmis (rather than ʿUmar ibn al-qūmis), a construction that treats "Qūmis" as a proper name.

67. Ibn Ḥayyān, ed. Makkī, 138.

68. The sources call this position "kitābah al-ʿulyā" or "kitābah al-ʿuẓmā." It was subordinate to the head of the entire administration, the ḥājib.

69. See Ibn al-Qūṭīyah, 122–32 passim, and Kennedy, *Muslim Spain*, 65–71.

70. Fattal, 141.

71. Fattal, 137–38.

72. For the martyrs movement, see Edward Colbert, *The Martyrs of Córdoba (850–859): A Study of the Sources* (Washington, DC: Catholic University of America Press, 1962); Coope, *Martyrs*; and Kenneth Baxter Wolf, *Christian Martyrs in Muslim Spain* (Cambridge: Cambridge University Press, 1988). The Latin primary sources can all be found in Gil, *Corpus scriptorum muzarabicorum*; they are Eulogius of Córdoba, *Documentum martyriale* (2:459–75), *Epistulae* (2:495–503), *Liber aplogeticus martyrum* (2:475–95), and *Memoriale sanctorum* (2:363–459); Paul Albar, *Epistulae* (1:144–270), *Indiculus luminosus* (1:270–315), and *Vita Eulogii* (1:330–43); and Abbot Samson's *Apologeticus.*

73. See Coope, *Martyrs*, xv–xvii, for a roster of the martyrs and their social connections.

74. Coope, *Martyrs*, 35.

75. Coope, *Martyrs*, 31–32.

76. See note 57 in this chapter. Simonet, 662, questions whether even large cities like Seville and Toledo really had a functioning bishop or just a titular bishop living elsewhere.

77. According to Lévi-Provençal, *Histoire*, 2:154, the letters berated the caliph for allowing pirates from al-Andalus to operate off the coasts of western Europe.

78. *Vita Johannis*, 371–73.

79. *Vita Johannis*, 370.

80. Abbot Samson also indicates that Christians at court were circumcised.

81. *Vita Johannis*, 374–75; Simonet, 606.

82. Al-Khushanī, Arabic 186–87, Spanish 231–33.

83. Enrique Flórez et al., *España Sagrada*, 52 vols. (Madrid, 1747–1918), 10:462–65.

84. Flórez, 10:465–71, 564–70. See chapter 6.

85. Simonet, 629–30.

86. For this section I rely on Jane S. Gerber, *The Jews of Spain: A History of the Sephardic Experience* (New York: The Free Press, 1992), 60–89; Elaine R. Miller, *Jewish Multiglossia: Hebrew, Arabic, and Castilian in Medieval Spain* (Newark, DE: Juan de la Questa, 2000); Norman Roth, "Jewish Reactions to the *'Arabiyya* and the Renaissance of Hebrew in Spain," *Journal of Semitic Studies* 23, no. 1 (Spring 1983), 63–84; Roth, *Jews, Visigoths and Muslims*, 73–112; Arie Schippers, *Spanish Hebrew Poetry and the Arabic Literary Tradition: Arabic Themes in Hebrew Andalusian Poetry* (Leiden: Brill, 1994), 41–71; and Angel Sáenz-Badillos, *A History of the Hebrew Language*, trans. John Elwolde (Cambridge: Cambridge University Press, 1993), 161–266.

87. The Arabic and Hebrew muwashshaḥah in al-Andalus were unusual forms of poetry in that the body of the poem was written in the formal literary language, but the two lines closing the poem were in a vernacular language, either colloquial Arabic or Romance. See James Monroe, "*Zajal* and *Muwashshahah*: Hispano-Arabic Poetry and the Romance Tradition," in Jayyusi, *Legacy*, 398–419.

88. Sáenz-Badillos, 166–73.

89. Sáenz-Badillos, 202–9.

90. Miller, 50–52. Roth, *Jews, Visigoths, and Muslims*, 80, questions the existence of a Yeshiva in Córdoba at that time.

91. Sáenz-Badillos, 214–19.

92. Miller, 28–31.

93. Miller, 118–23.

94. Roth, "Jewish Reactions," 71, 72–76.

95. Wasserstein, "Ibn Ḥazm and al-Andalus," in Adang and Fierro, *Ibn Ḥazm of Cordoba*, 69–85, says that the polemic was in fact by a Muslim who was declared a heretic, Ibn al-Rāwandī.

96. Roth, *Jews, Visigoths and Muslims*, 89–108.

97. James T. Monroe, *Hispano-Arabic Poetry* (Berkeley and Los Angeles: University of California Press, 1974), 27–28, 206–13.

CHAPTER 4

1. The best overview of gender in Islam is Leila Ahmed, *Women and Gender in Islam* (New Haven and London: Yale University Press, 1992). Also of interest for Islam in general are Amira El Azhary Sonbol, ed., *Women, the Family, and Divorce Laws in Islamic History* (Syracuse, NY: Syracuse University Press, 1996); Abdelwahab Bouhdiba, *Sexuality in Islam*, trans. Alan Sheridan (London and New York: Rout-

ledge and Kegan Paul, 1985); M. E. Combs-Schilling, *Sacred Performances: Islam, Sexuality, and Sacrifice* (New York: Columbia University Press, 1989); and Sachiko Murata, *The Tao of Islam: A Sourcebook on Gender Relations in Islamic Thought* (Albany: State University of New York Press, 1992). For gender relations specifically in al-Andalus, the best is the previously cited book by Manuela Marín, *Mujeres en al-Andalus*. See also Marín, "Marriage and Sexuality in al-Andalus," in *Marriage and Sexuality in Medieval and Early Modern Iberia*, ed. Eukene Lacarra Lanz (New York and London: Routledge, 2002), 3–20, and López de la Plaza, *Al-Andalus: mujeres, sociedad, y religión*.

2. See Ibn al-ʿAṭṭār, *Formulario notarial y judicial Andalusī del alfaquí y notario cordobés m. 399–1009*, trans. Pedro Chalmeta and Marina Marugán (Madrid: Fundación Matritense del Notariado, 2000), 1–3.

3. *Marriage and Slavery in Early Islam* (Cambridge, MA: Harvard University Press, 2010), 1–28.

4. Marín, *Mujeres*, 253–311.

5. Leila Ahmed traces the role of male guardianship back to pre-Islamic Mesopotamia and Greece; see *Women and Gender*, 20 and 30.

6. See *al-Mudawwanah*, 2:254–63 on support.

7. López de la Plaza, 44–62.

8. Abd al-Malik ibn Ḥabīb, *Kitāb adab al-nisāʾ, al-mawsūm bi-kitāb al-ghāyah wa-al-nihāyah*, ed. Abdel Magid Turki (Beirut: Dār al-gharb al-islāmī, 1992), 243–46.

9. Hedaya Hartford and Ashraf Muneeb, *Birgivi's Manual Interpreted: Complete Fiqh of Menstruation and Related Issues* (Beltsville, MD: Amana Publications, 2006), 21 and 25.

10. *Adab al-nisāʾ*, 73–74. Safran, *Defining Boundaries*, 133–40, has an interesting discussion of the ninth-century debate about whether or not dhimmīs could cause impurity. Generally in Islam impurity is caused by prohibited food and drink, impure animals like pigs or dogs, or by bodily excretions, not by people per se.

11. Fattal, 60–69.

12. *Mujeres*, 217.

13. *Adab al-nisāʾ*, 206–10.

14. *Adab al-nisāʾ*, 228–29.

15. See Adrian Wilson, "The Ceremony of Childbirth and its Interpretation," in *Women as Mothers in Pre-Industrial England: Essays in Memory of Dorothy McLaren*, ed. Valerie Fildes (London and New York: Routledge, 1990), 68–107.

16. Hartford and Muneeb, 21–34.

17. *Ṣaḥīḥ al-Bukhārī*, Book 7, nos. 113 and 114.

18. *Ṣaḥīḥ al-Bukhārī*, Book 7, no. 124

19. *Adab al-nisāʾ*, 252–56. See also Ahmed, 79–102.

20. Mālik b. Anas, *al-Muwaṭṭaʾ* (Vaduz, Liechtenstein: Jamʿīyah al-maknaz al-islāmī, 2000), 2 vols.

21. Ed. ʿAbd al-Ghaffār Sulaymān al-Busandārī (Beirut: Dār al-kutub al-ʿilmiyyah, 1988), 12 vols. The section on marriage is in vol. 9.

22. Muḥammad b. Ḥasan Sharhibīlī, *Taṭawwur al-madhhab al-mālikī fī al-gharb al-islāmī ḥattā nihāyah al-ʿaṣr al-mursābiṭī* (Morocco: Wizārah al-awqāf wa-al-shu'ūn al-islamīyah, 2000), 18–23.

23. Sharhibīlī, 90–92, 155–70.

24. See Fierro and Marín, " La islamización de las ciudades andalusíes," and Fierro, "El alfaquí beréber" Yaḥyā b. Yaḥyā al-Laythī (m. 234/848), 'el inteligente de al-Andalus,'" in *Biographías y genero biográfico en el occidente islámico*, ed. María Luisa Ávila and Manuela Marín (Madrid: Consejo Superior de Investigaciones Científicas, 1997), 269–344.

25. *Adab al-nisā'*, 92. For his recruitment see Abū al-ʿAbbās Aḥmad ibn Muḥammad Ibn ʿIdhārī al-Marrākushī, *Al-Bayān al-Mughrib fī akhbār al-Andalus wa al-Maghrib*, ed. G. S. Colin and E. Lévi-Provençal (Beirut: Dār al-kutub al ʿilmīyah, 2009), 4 vols., 2:110–11.

26. Coope, *Martyrs*, 24–27.

27. Judith Romney Wegner explores this tension in "The Status of Women in Jewish and Islamic Marriage and Divorce Law," *Harvard Women's Law Journal* 5 (1982), 1–33.

28. *al-Mudawwanah*, 2:165–66; Ibn Ḥazm, *al-Muḥallā*, 9:26–37.

29. *al-Mudawwanah*, 2:157–59.

30. *al-Mudawwanah*, 2:155–56, 166–68.

31. *al-Mudawwanah*, 2:156, 157–59.

32. 2:165–66. On black women in al-Andalus, see Marín, *Mujeres*, 125–40.

33. Zomeño, "Kafā'a," note 66.

34. 2:156.

35. *al-Muḥallā*, 9:25–26, 35–37.

36. *al-Muḥallā*, 9:33–37.

37. *al-Muḥallā*, 9:36–37. The three freedwomen were Juwayrīyah and Safīyah, who were Jewish captives, and Maria the Copt, who was a gift from an Egyptian leader. He probably means Maria, but I can find no tradition that she was black.

38. Ibn Hishām, *al-Sīrah al-nabawīyah*, ed. Muṣṭafā al-Saqqā (Cairo: Sharikah maktabah wa-maṭbaʿah Muṣṭafā al-Bābī al-Ḥalabī, 1900), 2 vols., 1:187–90.

39. Abū Jaʿfar Muḥammad ibn Jarīr al-Ṭabarī, *The History of al-Ṭabarī (Ta'rīkh al-rusul wa-al-mulūk)*, vol. 6, trans. W. Montgomery Watt and M. V. McDonald (Albany: State University of New York Press, 1988), 47–50.

40. Ahmed, 64–78, contrasts the relative independence of at least some of Muḥammad's wives during the jāhilīyah and early Islamic era with the increasing subordination of women during the conquests.

41. *al-Mudawwanah*, 2:152–55.

42. *al-Mudawwanah*, 2:159–61.

43. *al-Mudawwanah*, 2:216–17.

44. *al-Mudawwanah*, 2:236–38.

45. *al-Mudawwanah*, 2:248.

46. *al-Muḥallā*, 9:83–100.

47. *al-Muwaṭṭa'*, 1:574.

48. *al-Muḥallā*, 9:92–93.

49. *al-Mudawwanah*, 2:216–17. As noted above, this passage prohibits the use for ṣadāq of items that have not reached their potential value; it does not, however, mention dogs or cats.

50. *al-Muḥallā*, 9:21–100.

51. For example *Ṣaḥīḥ al-Bukhārī*, Book 7, nos. 54 and 79.

52. *al-Mudawwanah*, 2:239–41.

53. Ali, 49–62, argues that jurists draw an analogy between marriage and a sale but do not actually equate them.

54. *al-Mudawwanah*, 2:254–56 and 258–63.

55. *al-Muḥallā*, 9:108–13.

56. *Adab al-nisā'*, 203.

57. *al-Mudawwanah*, 2:419–51.

58. *al-Muwaṭṭa'*, 1:636–68.

59. *Adab al-nisā'*, 122–23.

60. *al-Mudawwanah*, 2:291–95.

61. *Adab al-nisā'*, 246–47. Mālikī law generally allowed men to beat their wives, but within limits. See Maribel Fierro, "Ill-Treated Women Seeking Divorce: The Qur'ānic Two Arbiters and Judicial Practice Among the Mālikīs in Al-Andalus and North Africa," in *Dispensing Judgment in Islam: Qadis and Their Judgments*, ed. Muhammad Khalid Masud (Leiden: Brill, 2006), 323–47.

62. Mālik outlines the rules concerning zinā' in *al-Muwaṭṭa'*, 2:15–26.

63. Susan Treggiari, *Roman Marriage: Iusti Coniuges from the Time of Cicero to the Time of Ulpian* (Oxford: Clarendon Press, 1991), 262–64.

64. For the preservation of Jewish law under Islamic rule, see Norman A. Stillman, *The Jews of Arab Lands: A History and Source Book* (Philadelphia: The Jewish Publication Society of America, 1979), 22–63.

65. Norman Roth suggests that the Visigothic *Fuero juzgo* or *Forum iudicum* remained influential in territories newly conquered by Alfonso X (r. 1252–84). "Jewish collaborators in Alfonso X's Scientific Works," in *Emperor of Culture: Alfonso X the Learned of Castile and His Thirteenth-Century Renaissance*, ed. Robert I. Burns (Philadelphia: University of Pennsylvania Press, 1990), 59–71.

66. *The Oriental, the Ancient, and the Primitive: Systems of Marriage and the Family in the Pre-industrial Societies of Eurasia* (Cambridge: Cambridge University Press, 1977), 319–487.

67. Ahmed, 12–13.

68. Treggiari, 323–40.

69. Goody, 347–60. The story appears in Gen. 29–31.

70. *Forum iudicum*, Liber III, titulus I.1, I.6.

71. *Forum iudicum*, Liber IV, titulus V.3.

72. King, 228–33.

73. *Forum iudicum*, Liber III, titulus I.3.

74. *Forum iudicum*, Liber III, titulus IV.

75. Treggiari, 264–90. Sharī'ah does not condone honor killings.

76. *Forum iudicum*, Liber III, titulus VI.2.

77. *Forum iudicum*, Liber III, titulus VI.1.

78. *Forum iudicum*, Liber III, titulus V.7.

79. *Forum iudicum*, Liber III, titulus II.1.

80. *al-Muwaṭṭa'*, 1:644.

81. Marín, *Mujeres*, 186–98, thinks it is probable that middle- and upper-class women veiled.

82. Marín, *Mujeres*, 445–52.

83. Asaf A. A. Fyzee, *Outlines of Muhammadan Law* (Delhi: Oxford University, 1999), 387–440 and 441–67.

84. *al-Muwaṭṭa'*, 1:187.

85. Fyzee, 105–6.

86. Fox, 163–69.

87. Goody, 361–82.

88. *Forum iudicum*, Liber V, titulus I.1 and I.2.

89. *Forum iudicum*, Liber V, titulus I.1.

CHAPTER 5

1. Ibn al-'Aṭṭār, 41–70.

2. Ibn al-'Aṭṭār, 41–44.

3. *al-Muwaṭṭa'*, 1:585–86.

4. Ibn al-'Aṭṭār, Chalmeta and Marugán's introduction, 7–9. Documents in Christian Europe were viewed in much the same light before the thirteenth century; see M. T. Clanchy, *From Memory to Written Record: England 1066–1307* (London: Edward Arnold Ltd., 1979), 253–93.

5. *Al-Muwaṭṭa'*, 1:576.

6. Ali, 72–75, discusses the founding jurists' resistance to shurūṭ.

7. See Marín, *Mujeres*, 403–17. On the Ottoman period see Abdal-Rehim Abdal-Rahman Abdal-Rehim, "The Family and Gender Laws in Egypt During the Ottoman Period," in Sonbol, *Women, the Family, and Divorce Laws*. On women's changing status under Sharī'ah over time see Nikki R. Keddie, "The Past and Present of Women in the Islamic World," *Journal of World History* 1, no. 1 (Spring 1990), 77–108.

8. *Ṣaḥīḥ al-Bukhārī*, Book VII, no. 157.

9. 2:161–65.

10. 2:155–56.

11. Amalia Zomeño, *Dote y matrimonio en al-Andalus y el norte de África: estudio sobre la jurisprudencia islámica medieval* (Madrid: Consejo Superior de Investigaciones Científicas, 2000), 57–60.

12. Zomeño, 64–68.

13. Ibn al-'Aṭṭār, editors' analysis of a marriage contract, 45–51, and Marín, *Mujeres*, 365–79.

14. *Adab al-nisā'*, 102–3.

15. *al-Mudawwanah*, 2:266–68.

16. Marín, *Mujeres*, 354–64.

17. *Adab al-nisā'*, 95.

18. Abū al-Asbagh 'Īsā Ibn Sahl, *Dīwān al aḥkām al-kubrā*, ed. Rashīd b. Ḥamīd al-Nu'aimī, 2 vols. (Riyadh, 1997).

19. Ibn Sahl, 2:730–35, 749–56.

20. Ibn Sahl, 2:818–30.

21. al-Khushanī, Arabic163–73, Spanish 202–14.

22. Ṭāha, 125; Ibn Ḥayyān, ed. Makkī, 79, and Makkī's note no. 205.

23. For general background on the *Ṭawq* see Lois A. Giffen, "Ibn Hazm and the *Tawq al-Hamāmah*," in Jayyusi, *Legacy*, 420–42. The edition I am using is *Ṭawq al-ḥamāmah fi al-ulfah wa-al-ullāf*, ed. 'Abd al-Raḥmān Muṣṭāwī (Beirut: Dār al-ma'rifah, 2004). I will also refer to the English translation by A. R. Nykl, *The Dove's Neck Ring* (Paris: Librairie Orientaliste Paul Geuthner, 1931).

24. James Monroe, among others, suggests that this type of poetry can best be seen as Umayyad court poetry rather than the product of Bedouin culture. See "Zajal and Muwashshaḥa," in Jayyusi, *Legacy*, 398–419, and his note no. 4.

25. See Giffen.

26. *Ṭawq*, 175; Nykl, 135–36.

27. *Ṭawq*, 69–72; Nykl, 38–41.

28. José Miguel Puerta Vílchez, "Abū Muḥammad 'Alī Ibn Ḥazm: A Biographical Sketch," in Adang and Fierro, *Ibn Ḥazm*, 3–24.

29. Adang, "Ibn Hazm on Homosexuality."

30. *Ṭawq*, 53; Nykl, 24–25.

31. Marín, "Marriage and Sexuality," 12.

32. *Saḥīḥ al-Bukhārī*, Book VII, no. 108. Generally the word is used only to describe honor involving women's behavior, but the ḥadīths say that God also has ghayrah, which is offended whenever a human being, male or female, commits a sexual impropriety. See Book VII, no. 148.

33. *Ṭawq*, 96–97; Nykl, 63–64.

34. *Poema del Cid*, ed. Ramón Menéndez Pidal (New York: New American Library, 1959), lay 140.

35. 1:424.

36. Nabih Amin Faris, *The Mysteries of Purity, from al-Ghazali's Iḥyā 'ulūm al-dīn* (Lahore: Ashraf, 1966), 92–93.

37. *Ṭawq*, 89–92; Nykl, 56–59.

38. *Ṭawq*, 170–72; Nykl, 131–32.

39. *Ṭawq*, 130; Nykl, 93–94.

40. *Ṭawq*, 105–8; Nykl, 69–72.

41. *Ṭawq*, 217; Nykl, 178–80.

42. *Ṭawq*, 215–41; Nykl, 176–203.

43. *Ṭawq*, 198–202; Nykl, 157–62.

44. Louis Crompton, "Male Love and Islamic Law in Arab Spain," in Stephen O. Murray and Will Roscoe, *Islamic Homosexualities: Culture, History, and Literature* (New York and London: New York University Press, 1997), 142–57. See page 150.

45. "Male Love."

46. *Ṭawq*, 43; Nykl, 15.

47. See Salvador Peña, "Which Curiosity? Ibn Ḥazm's Suspicion of Grammarians," in Adang and Fierro, *Ibn Ḥazm of Cordoba*, 233–50.

48. *Ṭawq*, 79–80; Nykl, 47–48.

49. "Male Love," 147.

50. Nykl, note 31.3.

51. *Ṭawq*, 215–41; Nykl, 176–203.

52. *Ṭawq*, 220; Nykl, 181. A mi'zar or izār usually means a garment covering the lower half of the body. See Yedida Kalfon Stillman, *Arab Dress: From the Dawn of Islam to Modern Times* (Leiden: Brill, 2003), 7–28.

53. Adang, "Ibn Hazm on Homosexuality."

54. Jayyusi, "Andalusī Poetry: The Golden Period," in Jayyusi, *Legacy*, 317–66, and Cynthia Robinson, "Ubi Sunt: Memory and Nostalgia in Taifa Court Culture," *Muqarnas* 15 (1998), 20–31.

55. Monroe, *Poetry*, 19–21 (introductory material), and 178–86 (his edition and translation of the poem).

56. The scholarly controversy over the origins and nature of the zajal and muwashshaḥah is extensive. See Alan Jones, "Romance Scansion and the Muwashshaḥāt: An Emperor's New Clothes?," *Journal of Arabic Literature* 11 (1980), 36–55, and "Sunbeams from Cucumbers? An Arabist's Assessment of the State of Kharja Studies," *La Corónica* 12 (1983–84), 45–70; James Monroe, "Zajal and Muwashshaḥa," in Jayyusi, *Legacy*, 398–419, and "Pedir peras al olmo? On Medieval Arabs and Modern Arabists," *La Corónica* 10 (1981–82), 121–47; and Samuel L. Stern, "Les vers finaux en espagnol dans les muwassahs hispano-hébraiques: une contribution à l'histoire du muwassah et à l'étude du vieux dialecte espagnol 'mozarabe,'" *Al-Andalus* 13 (1948), 299–346.

57. Monroe, *Poetry*, 41–44 (introductory material) and 260–73 (his edition and translation of the poem). The quotation is from 266–67.

58. Monroe, *Poetry*, 218–19. Monroe's translation follows.

59. Norman Roth, "Deal Gently."

60. Roth, "Deal Gently," 41. Roth's translation.

61. Marín, "Muslim Religious Practices in Al-Andalus (2nd/8th—4th/10th Centuries)," in Jayyusi, *Legacy*, 878–94.

62. López de la Plaza, 102–8.

63. Fierro, "The Polemic about the 'karāmāt al-awliyā'' and the Development of Ṣūfism in al-Andalus (Fourth/Tenth–Fifth/Eleventh Centuries)," *Bulletin of the School of Oriental and African Studies* 55, no. 2 (1992), 236–49.

64. Fierro, "Heresy in Al-Andalus," in Jayyusi, *Legacy*, 895–908; Makkī, *Al-tashayyu' fī al-Andalus mundhu al-fatḥ ḥattā nihāyah al-dawlah al-umawīyah* (Cairo: Maktabah al-thaqāfah al-dīnīyah, 2004), 13–14. For Ibn Qiṭṭ see also Ibn Ḥayyān, *Al-Muqtabas*, ed. P. Melchor M. Antuña (Paris: Paul Geuthner, 1937), 133–39, and Kennedy, *Muslim Spain*, 71. See also Lévi-Provençal, *Histoire*, 1:383–85.

65. *Sufis of Andalusia: The Rūḥ al-quds and the Durrat al-fākhirah of Ibn Al-Arabi*, trans. R. W. J. Austin (London: George Allen & Unwin, 1971). For his accounts of female mystics, see 108–10, 142–46, and 154–55.

66. *Abenmasarra y su escuela: orígenes de la filosofía Hispano-Musulmana* (Madrid: Imprenta Ibérica, 1914).

67. Asín Palacios, *Abenmasarra*, 40–54.

68. Asín Palacios, *Abenmasarra*, 92–106. Asín Palacios and Makkī also believe that Ibn Masarrah was influenced by the Ismāʿīli Shīʿism of North Africa; see Makkī, *Al-tashayyuʿ*, 21–22.

69. For an overview of the various theories about Ibn Masarrah's teachings see Kirstin Sabrina Dane, "Power and Discourse in Al-Andalus: The Case of Ibn Masarra" (MA thesis, McGill University, 2006), 68–91.

70. Garrido Clemente, 155–58.

71. Garrido Clemente, 38–51.

72. *al-Faṣl*, 4:198–99.

73. See Hodgson, 1:384–86, and Lapidus, *Muslim Societies*, 106–9.

74. The Qarmatian movement in Islam, for example (ca. 900), was later depicted as holding women in common, a distortion of the community's actual practices, which probably included monogamous marriage and socializing between men and women. See Ahmed, 98–99.

75. See also Addas, "Andalusī Mysticism and the Rise of Ibn ʿArabī," in Jayyusi, *Legacy*, 909–33.

76. William C. Chittick, *Imaginal Worlds: Ibn al-Arabi and the Problem of Religious Diversity* (Albany: State University of New York Press, 1994), 15–29, 123–36; Chittick, *The Sufi Path of Knowledge* (Albany: State University of New York Press, 1989), 33–76, 127–32; Ibn al-Arabī, *The Bezels of Wisdom*, trans. R. W. J. Austin (New York: Paulist Press, 1980), 172–86, 269–84.

77. Ibn al-ʿArabī, *Sufis of Andalus*, 143–46.

78. Ibn al-ʿArabī, *Kitāb mawāqiʿ al-nujūm* (Cairo: Maṭbaʿah al-saʿādah, 1907), 123–30. He also refers to the pen and tablet various times in the *Futūḥāt al-makkīyah*, ed. ʿUthmān Yaḥyā (Cairo: al-Hay'ah al-miṣrīyah al-ʿāmmah li-l-kitāb, 1972–83), 14 vols.; see especially 1:46–49, 2:182–83, 2:313–17, and 2:350–51.

79. *al-Futūḥāt al-makkīyah*, 2:313.

80. *al-Futūḥāt al-makkīyah*, 1:48.

81. *Kitāb mawāqiʿ al-nujūm*, 123.

82. *al-Futūḥāt al-makkīyah*, 2:314.

83. See also Murata, *Tao of Islam*, 188–202.

84. Murata, 12–14, 153–69.

85. *al-Futūḥāt al-makkīyah*, 2:313.

86. Al-Shāfiʿī, *Kitāb al-umm*, quoted in Ali, 178.

CHAPTER 6

1. Scales, 117–31, speculates that many of the Arabs who arrived at the time of the conquest settled in rural areas and lost their connection with the Umayyad leadership.

2. Maribel Fierro, "Les généalogies du pouvoir en Al-Andalus," in *Islamisation et arabisation de l'occident musulman médiéval (Viie-Xiie siècle)*, ed. Dominique

Valérian (Paris: Publications de la Sorbonne, 2011), 265–94; Ibn al-Qūṭīyah, editor's introduction, 67–69.

3. Fierro, "El alfaquí beréber."

4. Michael Brett and Elizabeth Fentress, *The Berbers* (Oxford: Blackwell, 1996), 88–92.

5. For economic ties, see Mostapha Taher, "Les rapports socio-économiques entre al-Andalus et le Magrib al-Aqsa aux Xe et XIe siècles," in Philippe Senac, ed., *Le Maghreb, al-Andalus et la Méditerrané occidentale (Viie–Xiiie siècles)* (Toulouse: Université de Toulouse-Le Mirais, 2007), 183–99.

6. Brent, 87–88; 'Abd al-Raḥmān ibn 'Abd Allāh Ibn 'Abd al-Ḥakam, *Conquête de l'Afrique du Nord et de l'Espagne*, trans. Albert Gateau (Alger: Éditions Carbonel, 1947), 126–45.

7. Muḥammad Ḥaqqī, *Al-barbar fī al-Andalus: dirāsah li ta'rīkh majmū'ah ithnīyah min al-fatḥ ilā suqūṭ al-khilāfah al-Umawīyah* (Casa Blanca: Sharikah al-nashr wa al-tawzī' al-madāris, 2001), 200–204; Kennedy, *Muslim Spain*, 23–26; Lévi-Provençal, *Histoire*, 1:41–44.

8. Ḥaqqī, 31–44.

9. On Shī'ī influences, see Makkī, *al-tashayyu'*, 9–14.

10. Salah Alouani, *Tribus et Marabouts: A'rāb et walāya dans l'intérieur de l'Ifriqiya entre le Vie/Xiie siècles* (Helsinki: Academia Scientiarum Fennica, 2010), 81–93.

11. Manzano Moreno, *La frontera de Al-Andalus en época de los omeyas* (Madrid: Consejo Superior de Investigaciones Científicas, 1991), 238–49. For the revolt of al-Kāhinah, see Mohamed Sadok Bel Ochi, *La conversion des berbères à l'Islam* (Tunis: Maison Tunisienne, 1981), 76–80.

12. Ibn Ḥayyān, ed. Antuña, 133–39; Lévi-Provençal, *Histoire*, 1:383–85; Makkī, *al-Tashayyu'*, 13–14; Manzano Morena, *La Frontera*, 253–57.

13. 'Abdul-Qādr Būbāya, *Al-barbar fī al-Andalus* (Beirut: Dār al-kutb al-'ilmīyah, 2011), 142–48.

14. Fierro, "Los cadíes de Córdoba de Abd al-Rahman III (r. 300/912–350/961)," in Rachid El Hour and Rafael Mayor, eds., *Cadíes y cadiazgo en Al-Ándalus y el Magreb medieval* (Madrid: Consejo Superior de Investigaciones Científicas, 2012), 69–98.

15. Kennedy, *Muslim Spain*, 3–4; Manzano Morena, *La Frontera*, 233–38.

16. Bel Ochi, 43–45, 92–93.

17. Ibn Ḥayyān, ed. Antuña, 17–18.

18. Ibn 'Idhārī, 3:276–77. See also Helena de Felipe, *Identidad y onomástica de los beréberes de al-Andalus* (Madrid: Consejo Superior that Investigaciones Científicas, 1997), 39–51.

19. Ibn Ḥayyān, ed. Antuña, 18–19.

20. Ḥamdī 'Abd al-Mun'im Muḥammad Ḥusayn, *Thawrāt al-barbar fī al-Andalus fī 'aṣr al-imārah al-umawīyah, 138–316 H 756–928 M* (Alexandria: Mu'assasah shabāb al-jāmi'ah, 1993), 55–66.

21. Ibn 'Idhārī, 3:276–77; Lévi Provençal, *Histoire*, 1:386–87.

22. D. M. Dunlop, "The Dhunnunids of Toledo," *Journal of the Royal Asiatic Society of Great Britain and Ireland* 2 (April 1942), 77–96

23. Ḥusayn, 60–66.

24. Guichard and Soravia, *Les royaumes de taifas*, 33–34.

25. Ibn 'Idhārī, 3:276–77.

26. Ibn 'Idhārī, 3:277–85.

27. For the history of the revolt see Manuel Acién Almansa, *Entre el feudalism y el Islam: 'Umar Ibn Ḥafṣūn en los historiadores, en las fuentes, y en la historia* (Granada: Universidad de Jaén, 1994); Fierro, *Abderramán III*, 79–93; Ibn 'Idhārī, 2:104–99; Kennedy, *Islamic Spain*, 67–87; Lévi-Provençal, *Histoire*, 1:300–10, 338–48, 368–80, and 2:6–24; Marín Guzmán, "Social and Ethnic Tensions in Al-Andalus"; and Marín Guzmán, "The Revolt of 'Umar Ibn Ḥafṣūn in al-Andalus: A Challenge to the Structure of the State (880–928)," PhD thesis, University of Texas at Austin, 1994.

28. Thomas Glick describes the complex of castle and village (ḥiṣn and qaryah) in *From Muslim Fortress to Christian Castle*, 13–29. See also Marín Guzmán, "Revolt of 'Umar Ibn Ḥafṣūn," 230–313.

29. Ibn 'Idhārī, 2:106; Lévi-Provençal, 1:301–6.

30. Abū 'Abd Allāh Ibn 'Askar and Abū Bakr Ibn Khamīs, *A'lam Mālaqa*, ed. 'Abd Allāh al-Murābiṭ al-Targhī (Beirut: Dār al-gharb al-Islāmī, 1999), 325. David Wasserstein, "Inventing Tradition and Constructing Identity: The Genealogy of Umar Ibn Ḥafṣūn between Christianity and Islam," *Al-Qantara* 23 (2002), 269–98, argues that the whole genealogy is a fiction created at the time of Ibn Ḥafṣūn's conversion to Christianity.

31. Ibn al-Qūṭīyah, 125–26.

32. Lévi-Provençal, *Histoire*, 1:368–69.

33. Ibn 'Idhārī, 2:105; Ibn al-Qūṭīyah, 125–27.

34. Ibn 'Idhārī, 2:117–18.

35. Ibn 'Idhārī, 2:139; Lévi Provençal, *Histoire*, 1:376–78. Lévi-Provençal says his conversion is proof of an unstable character.

36. 2:106.

37. Ibn 'Idhārī 2:114–15; Kennedy, *Muslim Spain*, 73–81; Marín Guzmán, "Revolt of 'Umar ibn Ḥafṣūn," 314–421.

38. Marín Guzmán, "Revolt of 'Umar Ibn Ḥafṣūn," 315–39.

39. Acién Almansa, 64–70.

40. Ibn Ḥayyān, ed. Antuña, 127; Marín Guzmán, "Revolt of 'Umar ibn Ḥafṣūn," 379–81.

41. 2:106.

42. Simonet, writing in the late nineteenth century, emphasizes the Christian identity of Ibn Ḥafṣūn and his family; see *Historia de los Mozárabes*, 566–67, 588–89, 595–98. Cagigas focuses on the rebellion as a nationalist movement in *Los Mozárabes*, 1:235–61.

43. Acién Almansa, 111–19; Glick, *Muslim Fortress*, 62–63.

44. 2:114–15.

45. Virgilio Martínez Enamorado, "Sobre las 'cuidadas iglesias' de Ibn Ḥafṣūn: Estudio de la basílica hallada en la ciudad de Bobastro (Ardales, Málaga)," *Madrider Mitteilungen* 45 (2004), 507–31.

46. *Una crónica anónima de 'Abd al-Rahmān II al-Nāsir*, ed. and trans. E. Lévi-Provençal and Emilio García Gómez (Madrid: Consejo Superior de Investigaciones Científicas, 1950), 149–51.

47. 2:139. Ibn 'Idhārī seems to be quoting Ibn Ḥayyān here; see *al-Muqtabas*, ed. Antuña, 128.

48. See Simonet, 588–89 and 596–98.

49. Flórez, *España Sagrada*, 10:564–70.

50. It is interesting that Flórez, working from the *Vita*, does not identify her father as 'Umar Ibn Ḥafṣūn. *España Sagrada*, 10:465–71.

51. See Ann Christys, *Christians in al-Andalus (711–1000)* (Richmond: Curzon Press, 2002), 101–7.

52. Coope, *Martyrs*, 27–29.

53. *Thawrah 'Umar Ibn Ḥafṣūn za'īm al-muwalladīn fī al-junūb al-Andalusī* (Cairo: Dār al-kitāb al-jāmi'ī, 1982), 7–8, 48–50, and 129–35.

54. For general background on the movement and on the Khārijīs in North Africa see Abun-Nasr, 37–50; Elizabeth Savage, *A Gateway to Hell, a Gateway to Paradise: The North African Response to the Arab Conquest* (Princeton, NJ: Darwin Press, 1997), 1–14; and Joseph Schacht's article, "al-Ibāḍīya," in the *Encyclopedia of Islam.*

55. Lévi-Provençal, 1:372–73; Marín Guzmán, "Revolt of 'Umar ibn Ḥafṣūn," 341–42. For the Aghlabids see Abun-Nasr, 53–59.

56. Zaghrūt, 47–48.

57. 2:114.

58. Ibn Ḥayyān, ed. Antuña, 51.

59. Acién Almansa, 64–70.

60. Savage, *Gateway*, 89–105.

61. 2:14–15.

62. *A'lam Mālaqa*, 325.

63. Ahmed, 70–71.

64. Savage, "Survival Through Alliance: The Establishment of the Ibadiyya," *Bulletin (British Society for Middle Eastern Studies)* 17, no. 1 (1990), 5–15.

CHAPTER 7

1. Kennedy, *Muslim Spain*, 56–59; Manzano Moreno, *La Frontera*, 50–60.

2. Chalmeta, "El concepto de ṯagr," in *La Marche supérieure d'al-Andalus et l'Occident chrétien*, ed. Philippe Sénac (Madrid: Casa de Velásquez, 1991), 15–28.

3. Ibn 'Idhārī, 2:219–20, shows the Banū Dhī al-Nūn participating in a raid against Castile.

4. Manzano Moreno, *La Frontera*, 50–60.

5. Manzano Moreno, *La Frontera*, 60–69.

6. Kennedy, *Muslim Spain*, 67–74; Lévi-Provençal, *Histoire*, 1:295–99. See also Ibn Ḥayyān, ed. Makkī, 343–61, and Makkī's note 567.

7. Joseph F. O'Callaghan, *A History of Medieval Spain* (Ithaca: Cornell University Press, 1983), 163–90; Khalīl Ibrāhīm al-Sāmarrā'ī, *Ta'rīkh al-'Arab wa ḥaḍāratihim fī al-Andalus* (Beirut: Dār al-kitāb al-jadīd al-muttaḥidah, 2000), 134–40.

8. Kennedy, *Muslim Spain*, 60–62; Lévi-Provençal, "Du nouveau sur le royaume de Pampelune au Ixe siècle," *Bulletin Hispanique* 55, no. 1 (1953), 5–22.

9. Lévi-Provençal, *Histoire*, 1:313–14.

10. For an overview of the Banū Qasī see Alberto Cañada Juste, "Los Banu Cassi (714–924)," *Principe de Viana* 41 (1980), 5–95; Kennedy, *Muslim Spain*, 15, 56–69; Lévi-Provençal, *Histoire*, 1:154–60, 1:310–329.

11. Ibn Ḥazm, *Jamharah*, 502–3.

12. Cañada Juste, 11–12.

13. Cañada Juste, 38–39.

14. See Fierro, "El conde Casio, los Banu Qasi y los linajes godos en al-Andalus," *Studia Histórica: Historia medieval* 27 (2009): 181–89.

15. Manzano Moreno, *La Frontera*, 110–24.

16. Fierro, "Hostages and the Dangers of Cultural Contact: Two Cases from Umayyad Cordoba," in *Acteurs des transferts culturels en Méditerranée médiéval*, ed. Rania Abdellatif et al. (Munich: Oldenbourg Verlag, 2012), 73–83.

17. For this narrative see primarily Cañada Juste and Lévi-Provençal, *Histoire*, as cited in note 10.

18. Most of the narrative that follows is from Lévi-Provençal, "Royaume de Pampelune."

19. Ibn Ḥayyān, ed. Makkī, 4, and Makkī's note 28.

20. Ibn Ḥayyān, ed. Makkī, 331–32 and Makkī's note 547.

21. Ibn al-Qūṭīyah, 130–31.

22. Ibn Ḥayyān, ed. Makkī, 4, and Makkī's note 30.

23. Ibn Ḥazm, *Jamharah*, 503.

24. Lévi-Provençal, *Histoire*, 1:333–34, suggests that she was a wife rather than an umm walad.

25. See Lévi-Provençal, "Royaume de Pampelune," and al-Sāmarrā'ī, 145–46.

26. Wasserstein, "Inventing Tradition."

27. "Royaume de Pampelune."

28. There is some question as to how deeply Christianized Basque areas were by the time of the Muslim invasions. Roger Collins, *The Basques* (Oxford and New York: Basil Blackwell, 1986), 145–57, argues that Christianity had thoroughly penetrated the region by the late Visigothic period.

29. Fierro, "Hostages."

30. Ibn al-Qūṭīyah, 127.

31. Clèment, 205–18.

32. Translated by James T. Monroe, *The Shu'ūbiyya in Al-Andalus: The Risāla of Ibn García and Five Refutations* (Berkeley and Los Angeles: University of California Press, 1970), 23–29.

33. For the relationship between the Andalusī shu'ūbīyah and earlier versions of the movement, see Roy P. Mottahedeh, "The Shu'ūbīyah Controversy and the Social History of Early Islamic Iran," *International Journal of Middle Eastern Studies* 7 (1976), 161–82.

34. Based on Yusuf Ali's translation.

35. See Mottahedeh.

36. Monroe, *Shuʿūbiyya*, 1–15.
37. Monroe, *Shuʿūbiyya*, 12.
38. *Ibn García's shuʿūbiyya Letter: Ethnic and Theological Tensions in Medieval al-Andalus* (Leiden: Brill, 2003), 167. Larsson's detailed analysis of the *Risālah* can be found on pages 155–208.
39. Wasserstein, *Party Kings*, 168–74.
40. "On the Eunuchs in Islam," *Jerusalem Studies in Arabic and Islam* 1 (1979), 67–124.
41. Also translated in Monroe's book.
42. Monroe, *Shuʿūbiyya*, 15–19.
43. Monroe, *Shuʿūbiyya*, 30–62.
44. Monroe, *Shuʿūbiyya*, 42.
45. Monroe, *Shuʿūbiyya*, 38–39.
46. Reuven Firestone, "Prophethood, Marriageable Consanguinity, and Text: The Problem of Abraham and Sarah's Kinship Relationship and the Response of Jewish and Islamic Exegesis," *Jewish Quarterly Review* 83, no. 3/4 (January–April 1993), 331–47.
47. Wasserstein, *Party Kings*, 174 and note 26.

CONCLUSION

1. *Islamic and Christian Spain*, 186–90.
2. Scales, 38–109.
3. Glick, *Islamic and Christian Spain*, 282–84.
4. Kennedy, *Muslim Spain*, 179–88; Watt, 95–102.
5. O'Callaghan, 204–7.
6. *Las Siete Partidas*, ed. Gregorio Lopez (Madrid: Boletín Oficial del Estado, 1985), Partida 7, leyes 23 and 24. See also Dwayne E. Carpenter, *Alfonso X and the Jews: An Edition of and Commentary on Siete Partidas 7.24, "De los judíos"* (Berkeley and Los Angeles: University of California Press, 1986).
7. Burns, "Christian-Islamic Confrontation in the West: The Thirteenth-Century Dream of Conversion," *American Historical Review* 76 (1971), 1386–1424; J. M. Col, "Escuelas de lenguas orientales in los siglos XIII y XIV," *Analecta sacra tarraconensia* 18 (1945), 59–89.
8. Albert Sicroff, *Los estatutos de limpieza de sangre* (Madrid: Taurus, 1985).

Bibliography

PRIMARY SOURCES

Abu Nuwas. "The Wretched Pause," translated by Nancy Coffin, Princeton Online Arabic Poetry. Princeton University. http://www.princeton.edu/~arabic/poetry

Akhbār majmū'a fī fatḥ al-Andalus, edited by Lafuente y Alcántara, Emilio. Madrid: Bibliofilo, 1984.

Alphonsi, Petrus. *Dialogi*. In *Patrologia Latina*, edited by Migne, J. P. Vol. 157, 527–672. Paris: Garnier Frères, 1854.

Asín Palacios, Miguel. *Abenhazm de Córdoba y su historia crítica de las ideas religiosas*. Vols. 1–5. Madrid: Ediciones Turner, 1984.

al-Bukhārī. *Ṣaḥīḥ Al-Bukhārī*, http://sunnah.com

Corpus scriptorum muzarabicorum, edited by Gil, Juan. Vols. 1–2. Madrid: Instituto Antonio de Nebrija, 1973.

Una Crónica anónima de 'Abd Al-Rahmān II Al-Nāsir, edited by Lévi-Provençal, E., and Emilio García Gómez. Madrid: Consejo superior de investigaciones científicas, 1950.

Crónica mozárabe de 754, edited by López Pereira, José Eduardo. Zaragoza: Anubar, 1980.

Einhard. *The Life of Charlemagne*. In Einhard and Notker the Stammerer: *Two Lives of Charlemagne*, edited by Thorpe, Lewis, 49–90. New York: Penguin, 1981.

Faris, Nabih Amin. *The Mysteries of Purity, from Al-Ghazali's Iḥyā 'ulūm al-dīn*. Lahore: Ashraf, 1966.

Fuero juzgo en latin y castellano, edited by Real Academia Española. Madrid: Ibarra, 1815.

Gregory of Tours. *The History of the Franks*, edited by Thorpe, Lewis. London: Penguin, 1974.

The Holy Quran, translated by Ali, Abdullah Yusuf. Elmhurst, NY: Tahrike Tarsile Qur'an, 1988.

Ibn ʿAbd al-Ḥakam, ʿAbd al-Raḥmān ibn ʿAbd Allāh. *Conquête de l'Afrique du nord et de l'Espagne*. Translated by Gateau, Albert. Algiers: Éditions Carbonel, 1947.

Ibn Anas, Mālik. *Al-Mudawwanah al-kubrā*. Vols. 1–6. Beirut: Dār al-Sādir, 1990–99.

Ibn Anas, Mālik. *Al-Muwaṭṭaʾ*. Vols. 1–2. Vaduz, Liechtenstein: Jamʿīyah al-maknaz al-islāmī, 2000.

Ibn al-ʿArabī, Abū Bakr Muḥammad ibn ʿAbd Allāh. *The Bezels of Wisdom*. Translated by Austin, R. W. J. New York: Paulist Press, 1980.

Ibn al-ʿArabī, Abū Bakr Muḥammad ibn ʿAbd Allāh. *Futūḥāt al-makkīyah*, edited by Yaḥyā, ʿUthmān. Vols. 1–2. Cairo: al-Hayʾah al-miṣrīyah al-ʿāmmah li-l-kitāb, 1972.

Ibn al ʿArabī, Abū Bakr Muḥammad ibn ʿAbd Allāh. *Kitab mawāqiʿ al-nujūm*. Cairo: Maṭbaʿah al-saʿādah, 1907.

Ibn al-ʿArabī, Abū Bakr Muḥammad ibn ʿAbd Allāh. *Sufis of Andalusia: The Rūḥ Al-Quds and the Durrat Al-Fākhirah of Ibn Al-Arabi*. Translated by Austin, R. W. J. London: George Allen & Unwin, 1971.

Ibn ʿAskar, Abū ʿAbd Allāh and Abū Bakr Ibn Khamīs. *Aʿlam Mālaqa*, edited by Al-Targhī, ʿAbd Allāh al-Murābiṭ. Beirut: Dār al-gharb al-islāmī, 1999.

Ibn al-ʿAṭṭār. *Formulario notorial y judicial andalusí del alfaquí y notario cordobés m. 399–1009*, edited by Chalmeta, Pedro, and Marina Marugán. Madrid: Fundación Matritense del Notariado, 2000.

Ibn Ḥabīb, ʿAbd al-Malik. *Kitāb adab al-nisāʾ, al-mawsūm bi-kitāb al-ghāyah wa-al-nihāyah*, edited by Turkī, Abdel Magid. Beirut: Dār al-gharb al-islāmī, 1992.

Ibn Ḥabīb, ʿAbd al-Malik. *Kitāb al-taʾrīkh*. Beirut: Dār al-kutub al-ʿilmīyah, 1999.

Ibn Ḥayyān al-Qurṭubī, Abū Marwān Ḥayyān ibn Khalaf. *Al-Muqtabas III*, edited by Antuña, P. Melchor M. Paris: Libraire Orientaliste Paul Geuthner, 1937.

Ibn Ḥayyān al-Qurṭubī, Abū Marwān Ḥayyān ibn Khalaf. *Al-Muqtabas min anbāʾ ahl al-Andalus*, edited by Makkī, Maḥmūd ʿAlī. Beirut: Dār al-kitāb al-ʿarabī, 1973.

Ibn Ḥazm, ʿAlī ibn Aḥmad. *Al-Akhlāq wa al-siyar fī mudāwāt al-nufūs*, edited by Makki, Ṭahir Aḥmad. Cairo: Dār al-maʿārif, 1981.

Ibn Ḥazm, ʿAlī ibn Aḥmad. *The Dove's Neck Ring*. Translated by Nykl, A. R. Paris: Librairie Orientaliste Paul Geuthner, 1931.

Ibn Ḥazm, ʿAlī ibn Aḥmad. *Al-Faṣl fī al-milāl wa al-ahwāʾ wa al-niḥal*, edited by al-Sahrastānī, Muḥammad ibn ʿAbd al-Karīm. Beirut: Dār al-maʿrifah, 1975.

Ibn Ḥazm, ʿAlī ibn Aḥmad. *Al-Iḥkām fī uṣūl al-aḥkām*, edited by ʿAbd al-ʿAzīz, Muḥammad Aḥmad. Cairo: Maktabah ʿĀtif, 1978.

Ibn Ḥazm, ʿAlī ibn Aḥmad. *Jamharah ansāb al-ʿarab*. Beirut: Dār al-kutub al-ʿilmīyah, 2001.

Ibn Ḥazm, ʿAlī ibn Aḥmad. *Al-Muhallā bi al-āthār*, edited by al-Busandārī, ʿAbd al-Ghaffār Sulaymān. Beirut: Dār al-kutub al-ʿilmiyyah, 1988.

Ibn Ḥazm, ʿAlī ibn Aḥmad. *Naqṭ al-ʿarūs*. Translated by Seco de Lucena, Luis, edited by Seybold, C. F. Valencia: Universidad de Valencia, 1974.

Ibn Ḥazm, ʿAlī ibn Aḥmad. *Ṭawq al-ḥamāmah fī al-ulfah wa-al-ullāf*, edited by Musṭāwī, ʿAbd al-Raḥmān. Beirut: Dār al-maʿrifah, 2004.

Ibn Hishām. *Al-Sīrah al-nabawīyah*, edited by al-Saqqā, Muṣṭafā. Vol. 1. Cairo: Sharikah maktabah wa-maṭba'ah Muṣṭafā al-Bābī al-Ḥalabī, 1900.

Ibn 'Idhārī al-Marrākushī, Abū al-'Abbās Aḥmad ibn Muḥammad. *Al-bayān al-Mughrib fī akhbār al-Andalus wa al-Maghrib*, edited by Colin, G. S., and E. Lévi-Provençal. Vols. 1–2. Beirut: Dār al-kutub al 'ilmīyah, 2009.

Ibn Khaldūn al-Ḥaḍramī, Abū Zayd 'Abd al-Raḥmān. *Al-Muqaddimah*. Translated by Rosenthal, Franz. Vol. 3. New York: Pantheon Books, 1958.

Ibn Maḍā', Aḥmad ibn 'Abd al-Raḥmān. *Kitāb al-radd 'alā al-nuḥāh*, edited by Ḍayf, Shawqī. Cairo: Dār al-ma'ārif, 1982.

Ibn Masarrah, Abū 'Abd Allāh Muḥammad ibn 'Abd Allāh. *Kitāb khawwās al-ḥurūf.* In *Estudio, traducción y edición de la obra de Ibn Masarra de Córdoba: La ciencia de las letras en el sufismo*, edited by Garrido Clemente, Pilar, 272. Salamanca: Ediciones Universidad de Salamanca, 2008.

Ibn al-Qūṭīyah al-Qurṭubī, Muḥammad ibn 'Umar. *Ta'rīkh iftitāḥ al-Andalus*, edited by al-Ṭabbā', 'Umar Fārūq. Beirut: Mu'assasah al-ma'ārif, 1994.

Ibn Sahl, Abū al-Asbagh 'Īsā. *Dīwān al aḥkām al-kubrā*, edited by al-Nu'aimī, Rashīd b. Ḥamīd. Vol. 2. Riyadh: R. Na'īmī, 1997.

John, Abbot of St. Arnulf. "Vita Johannis Abbatis Gorziensis." In *Monumenta Germaniae Historica, Scriptores . . . in Usum Scholarum*, Vol. 4, edited by Pertz, George H., 335–77. Hanover: Hahn, 1841.

al-Khushanī, Muḥammad ibn al-Ḥarīth. *Historia de los jueces de Córdoba por Aljoxani*, edited by Ribera y Tarragó, Julián. Madrid: Imprenta Ibérica, 1914.

Liutprand of Cremona. "Antapodosis." In *Monumenta Germanica Historica, Scriptores . . . in Usum Scholarum*, edited by Becker, Joseph, 1–158. Hanover: Hahn, 1915.

Muslim. *Ṣaḥīḥ Muslim*. http://sunnah.com

Poema del Cid, edited by Menéndez Pidal, Ramón. New York: New American Library, 1959.

al-Razī, Ahmad ibn Muhammad. *Crónica del moro Rasis*, edited by Catalán, Diego. Madrid: Editorial Gredos, 1974.

Samson. *Apologeticus*. In *Corpus scriptorum muzarabicorum*, edited by Gil, Juan, Vol. 2, 506–658. Madrid: Instituto Antonio de Nebrija, 1973.

"Santa Argentea, Actos Del Martirio," in *España Sagrada*, edited by Flórez, Enrique. Vol. 10, 564–70. Madrid: Real Academia de la Historia, 1792.

Siete Partidas, edited by Lopez, Gregorio. Madrid: Boletín Oficial del Estado, 1985.

al-Ṭabarī, Abū Ja'far Muḥammad ibn Jarīr. *The History of Al-Ṭabarī (Ta'rīkh al-rusul wa-al-mulūk)*. Translated by Watt, W. Montgomery, and M. V. McDonald. Vol. 6. Albany: State University of New York Press, 1988.

SECONDARY SOURCES

Aasi, Ghulam Haider. "Muslim Understanding of Other Religions: An Analytical Study of Ibn Hazm's *'Kitab Al-Fasl Fi Al-Milal Wa-Al-Ahwa' Wa Al-Nihal'*." Temple University, 1987.

Abdal-Rehim, Abdal-Rehim Abdal-Rahman. "The Family and Gender Laws in

Egypt during the Ottoman Period." In *Women, the Family, and Divorce Laws in Islamic History*, edited by Sonbol, Amira El Azhary. Syracuse, NY: Syracuse University Press, 1996.
Abun-Nasr, Jamil M. *A History of the Maghrib in the Islamic Period.* Cambridge: Cambridge University Press, 1987.
Acién Almansa, Manuel. *Entre el feudalism y l Islam: 'Umar Ibn Ḥafṣūn en los historiadores, en las fuentes, y en la historia*. Granada: Universidad de Jaén, 1994.
Adang, Camilla. "Ibn Hazm on Homosexuality: A Case-Study of Záhiri Legal Methodology." *Al-Qantara* 24, no. 1 (2003): 5–31.
Adang, Camilla. *Muslim Writers on the Hebrew Bible: From Ibn Rabban to Ibn Hazm*. Leiden: Brill, 1996.
Adang, Camilla. "Some Hitherto Neglected Biblical Material in the Work of Ibn Hazm." *Al-Masaq* 5 (1992): 17–28.
Addas, Claude. "Andalusī Mysticism and the Rise of Ibn 'Arabī." In *The Legacy of Muslim Spain*, edited by Jayyusi, Salma Khadra, 909–33. Leiden: Brill, 1992.
Ahmed, Leila. *Women and Gender in Islam*. New Haven: Yale University Press, 1992.
Ali, Kecia. *Marriage and Slavery in Early Islam*. Cambridge, MA: Harvard University Press, 2010.
Alouani, Salah. *Tribus et marabouts: A'rāb et walāya dans l'intérieur de l'Ifriqiya entre Le VIe/XIIe siècles*. Helsinki: Academia Scientiarum Fennica, 2010.
Amīn, Sharaf al-Dīn 'Abd al-Ḥamīd. *Ibn Ḥazm al-andalusī wa naqd al-'aql al-uṣūlī*. Kuwait: Dār Su'ād al-Ṣabaḥ, 1995.
Appleby, Joyce, Lynn Hunt, and Margaret Jacob. *Telling the Truth about History*. New York: Norton, 1994.
Arnaldez, Roger. *Grammaire et théologie chez Ibn Hazm de Courdoue: Essai sur la structure et les conditions de la pensée musulmane*. Paris: J. Vrin, 1956.
Asad, Talal. "The Idea of an Anthropology of Islam." *Qui Parle* 17, no. 2 (2009): 1–30.
Asín Palacios, Miguel. *Abenhazm de Córdoba y su historia crítica de las ideas religiosas*. Madrid: Ediciones Turner, 1984.
Asín Palacios, Miguel. *Abenmasarra y su escuela: Orígenes de la filosofía Hispano-Musulmana*. Madrid: Imprenta Ibérica, 1914.
Ayalon, David. "On the Eunuchs of Islam." *Jerusalem Studies in Arabic and Islam* 1 (1979): 67–124.
Bachrach, Bernard S. *Early Medieval Jewish Policy in Western Europe*. Minneapolis: University of Minnesota Press, 1977.
Bachrach, Bernard S. "A Reassessment of Visigothic Jewish Policy, 589–711." *American Historical Review* 78, no. 1 (1973): 11–34.
Behloul, Samuel M. "The Testimony of Reason and Historical Reality: Ibn Ḥazm's Refutation of Christianity." In *Ibn Ḥazm of Cordoba: The Life and Works of a Controversial Thinker*, edited by Adang, Camilla, and Maribel Fierro, 457–83. Leiden: Brill, 2013.
Bel Ochi, Mohamed Sadok. *La conversion des berbères à l'Islam*. Tunis: Maison Tunisienne, 1981.
Blankinship, Khalid Yahya. *The End of the Jihād State: The Reign of Hishām Ibn 'Abd*

Al-Malik and the Collapse of the Umayyads. Albany: State University of New York Press, 1994.

Bohas, George. "Aspects of Debate and Explanation among Arab Grammarians." In *The Early Islamic Grammatical Tradition*, edited by Baalbaki, Ramzi, 169–86. Aldershot, UK: Ashgate, 2007.

Bonner, Michael. *Jihad in Islamic History: Doctrines and Practice*. Princeton: Princeton University Press, 2006.

Boswell, John. *Christianity, Social Tolerance, and Homosexuality*. Chicago: University of Chicago Press, 1980.

Boswell, John. *The Royal Treasure: Muslim Communities Under the Crown of Aragon in the Fourteenth Century*. New Haven: Yale University Press, 1977.

Bosworth, C. E., ed. *Encyclopedia of Islam*. Leiden: Brill, 1995.

Bouhdiba, Abdelwahab. *Sexuality in Islam*. Translated by Sheridan, Alan. London and New York: Routledge, 1985.

Bouwsma, William. *A Usable Past: Essays in European Cultural History*. Berkeley and Los Angeles: University of California Press, 1990.

Brett, Michael. *The Rise of the Fatimids: The World of the Mediterranean and the Middle East in the Fourth Century of the Hijra, Tenth Century C.E.* Leiden: Brill, 2001.

Brett, Michael, and Elizabeth Fentress. *The Berbers*. Oxford: Blackwell, 1996.

Būbāya, 'Abdul-Qādr. *Al-barbar fi al-Andalus*. Beirut: Dār al-kutb al-'ilmīya, 2011.

Bulliet, Richard W. *Conversion to Islam in the Medieval Period: An Essay in Quantitative History*. Cambridge, MA: Harvard University Press, 1979.

Cagigas, Isidro de las. *Los Mozárabes*. Vols. 1–2. Madrid: Consejo Superior de Investigaciones Científicas, 1947.

Cañada Juste, A. "Los Banu Cassi (714–924)." *Principe de Viana* 41 (1980): 5–95.

Carpenter, Dwayne E. *Alfonso X and the Jews: An Edition of and Commentary on Siete Partidas 7.24, "De Los Judíos"*. Berkeley and Los Angeles: University of California Press, 1985.

Carter, M. G. *Sībawayhi*. New York: I. B. Taurus, 2004.

Castejón y Martínez de Arizala, Rafael. *Medina Azahara, la ciudad palatina de los califas de Córdoba*. Colección Ibérica. Madrid: Editorial Everest, 1976.

Castro, Américo. *España en su historia: Cristianos, Moros, y Judíos*. Buenos Aires: Editorial Losada, 1948.

Castro, Américo. *The Spaniards: An Introduction to Their History*. Berkeley and Los Angeles: University of California Press, 1971.

Chalmeta, Pedro. "El concepto de tagr." In *La Marche Supérieure d'al-Andalus et l'occident chrétien*, edited by Sénac, Philippe, 15–28. Madrid: Casa de Velásquez, 1991.

Chalmeta, Pedro. *Invasión e islamización: La sumisión de Hispania y la formación de Al-Andalus*. Madrid: Editorial MAPFRE, 1994.

Chittick, William C. *Imaginal Worlds: Ibn Al-Arabi and the Problem of Religious Diversity*. Albany: State University of New York Press, 1994.

Chittick, William C. *The Sufi Path of Knowledge*. Albany: State University of New York Press, 1989.

Choksy, Jamsheed K. *Confict and Cooperation: Zoroastrian Subalterns and Muslim Elites in Medieval Iranian Society*. New York: Columbia University Press, 1997.

Christys, Ann. *Christians in Al-Andalus (711–1000)*. Richmond, UK: Curzon Press, 2002.
Clanchy, M. T. *From Memory to Written Record: England 1066–1307*. London: Edward Arnold, 1979.
Clément, François. *Pouvoir et légitimité en Espagne musulmane à l'époque des taifas, Ve-Xie Siècle: L'imam fictif*. Paris: Editions L'Harmattan, 1997.
Cohen, Jeremy. *The Friars and the Jews: The Evolution of Medieval Anti-Judaism*. Ithaca: Cornell University Press, 1982.
Cohen, Mark R. *Under Crescent and Cross: The Jews in the Middle Ages*. Princeton: Princeton University Press, 1994.
Colbert, Edward. *The Martyrs of Córdoba (850–859): A Study of the Sources*. Washington, DC: Catholic University of America Press, 1962.
Collins, Roger. *The Basques*. Oxford and New York: Basil Blackwell, 1986.
Collins, Roger. *Early Medieval Spain: Unity in Diversity, 400–1000*. London: Macmillan, 1983.
Combs-Schilling, M. E. *Sacred Performances: Islam, Sexuality, and Sacrifice*. New York: Columbia University Press, 1989.
Coope, Jessica. *The Martyrs of Córdoba: Community and Family Conflict in an Age of Mass Conversion*. Lincoln: University of Nebraska Press, 1995.
Coope, Jessica. "With Heart, Tongue, and Limbs: Ibn Hazm on the Essence of Faith." *Medieval Encounters* 6 (2000): 101–13.
Crompton, Louis. "Male Love and Islamic Law in Arab Spain." In *Islamic Homosexualities: Culture, History, and Literature*, edited by Murray, Stephen O., and Will Roscoe, 142–57. New York: New York University Press, 1997.
Crone, Patricia. *Roman, Provincial and Islamic Law: The Origins of the Islamic Patronate*. Cambridge: Cambridge University Press, 1987.
Crone, Patricia. *Slaves on Horses*. Cambridge: Cambridge University Press, 1980.
Dallal, Ahmad. "Science, Medicine, and Technology." In *The Oxford History of Islam*, edited by Esposito, John L., 155–214. Oxford: Oxford University, 1999.
Dane, Sabrina. "Power and Discourse in Al-Andalus: The Case of Ibn Masarra." Master's thesis, McGill University, 2006.
Darnton, Robert. *The Great Cat Massacre and Other Episodes in French Cultural History*. New York: Vintage Books, 1985.
Donner, Fred M. *The Early Islamic Conquests*. Princeton: Princeton University Press, 1981.
Donner, Fred M. "From Believers to Muslims: Confessional Self-Identity in the Early Islamic Community." *Al-Abḥāth* 50–51 (2002–3): 9–53.
Donner, Fred M. *Narratives of Islamic Origins: The Beginnings of Islamic Historical Writing*. Princeton, NJ: Darwin Press, 1998.
Dozy, Reinhardt. *Histoire des Musulmans d'Espagne*. Leiden: Brill, 1932.
Dunlop, D. M. "The Dhunnunids of Toledo." *Journal of the Royal Asiatic Society of Great Britain and Ireland* 74, no. 2 (April 1942): 77–96.
Epalza, Mikel de. "Mozarabs: An Emblematic Christian Minority in Islamic Al-Andalus." In *The Legacy of Muslim Spain*, edited by Jayyusi, Salma Khadra. Leiden: Brill, 1992.

Esposito, John L. *Unholy War: Terror in the Name of Islam*. Oxford: Oxford University Press, 2002.
Fattal, Antoine. *Le Statut des non-musulmans en pays d'Islam*. Beirut: Imprimerie catholique, 1958.
Felipe, Helena de. *Identidad y onomástica de los beréberes de al-Andalus*. Madrid: Consejo Superior de Investigaciones Científicas, 1997.
Fierro, Maribel. *Abderramán III y el califato omeya de Córdoba*. Donostia-San Sebastián: Nerea, 2011.
Fierro, Maribel. "El Alfaquí beréber Yaḥyā b. Yaḥyā Al-Laythī (m. 234/848), 'el inteligente de al-Andalus.'" In *Biographías y genero biográfico en el occidente Islámico*, edited by Ávila, María Luisa, and Manuela Marín, 269–344. Madrid: Consejo Superior de Investigaciones Científicos, 1997.
Fierro, Maribel. "Los Cadíes de Córdoba de Abd Al-Rahman III (r. 300/912–350/961)." In *Cadíes y cadiazgo en Al-Ándalus y el Magreb medieval*, edited by El Hour, Rachid, and Rafael Mayor, 69–98. Madrid: Consejo Superior de Investigaciones Científicas, 2012.
Fierro, Maribel. "El conde Casio, los Banu Qasi y los linajes godos en al-Andalus." *Studia Histórica: Historia medieval* 27 (2009): 181–89.
Fierro, Maribel. "Les Généalogies du pouvoir en Al-Andalus." In *Islamisation et arabisation de l'occident musulman médiéval (VIIe-XIIe Siècle)*, edited by Valérian, Dominique, 265–94. Paris: Publications de la Sorbonne, 2011.
Fierro, Maribel. "Heresy in Al-Andalus." In *The Legacy of Muslim Spain*, edited by Jayyusi, Salma Khadra, 895–908. Leiden: Brill, 1992.
Fierro, Maribel. "Hostages and the Dangers of Cultural Contact: Two Cases from Umayyad Cordoba." In *Acteurs des transferts culturels en Méditerranée médiéval*, edited by Abdellatif, Rania, and Yassir Benhima, 73–83. Munich: Oldenbourg Verlag, 2012.
Fierro, Maribel. "Ibn Ḥazm and the Jewish Zindīq." In *Ibn Ḥazm of Cordoba: The Life and Works of a Controversial Thinker*, edited by Adang, Camilla, and Maribel Fierro, 497–509. Leiden: Brill, 2013.
Fierro, Maribel. "Ill-Treated Women Seeking Divorce: The Qur'ānic Two Arbiters and Judicial Practice among the Mālikīs in Al-Andalus and North Africa." In *Dispensing Judgment in Islam: Qadis and their Judgments*, edited by Masud, Muhammad Khalid, 323–47. Leiden: Brill, 2006.
Fierro, Maribel. "Mawālī and Muwalladūn in Al-Andalus (Second/Eighth–Fourth/Tenth Centuries)." In *Patronate and Patronage in Early and Classical Islam*, edited by Bernards, Monique, and John Nawas, 195–245. Leiden: Brill, 2005.
Fierro, Maribel. "The Polemic about the 'karāmāt Al-Awliyā'' and the Development of Ṣūfism in Al-Andalus (Fourth/Tenth–Fifth/Eleventh Centuries)." *Bulletin of the School of Oriental and African Studies* 55, no. 2 (1992): 236–49.
Fierro, Maribel, and Manuela Marín. "La Islamización de las ciudades andalusíes a través de sus ulemas (s. II/VIII-Comienzos s. IV/X)." In *Genese de la ville islamique en Al-Andalus et au Maghreb occidental*, edited by Cressier, Patrice, and Mercedes García-Arenal, 65–97. Madrid: Casa de Velázquez, Consejo Superior de Investigaciones Científicas, 1998.

Firestone, Reuven. "Prophethood, Marriageable Consanguinity, and Text: The Problem of Abraham and Sarah's Kinship Relationship and the Response of Jewish and Islamic Exegesis." *Jewish Quarterly Review* 83, no. 3/4 (1993): 331–47.

Fox, Robin. *Kinship and Marriage: An Anthropological Perspective*. London: Penguin, 1974.

Freidenreich, David M. "Christians in Early and Classical Sunnī Law." In *Christian-Muslim Relations: A Bibliographical History: Volume I (600–900)*, edited by Thomas, David, 99–114. Leiden: Brill, 2009.

Fuente Pérez, María Jesús. *Velos y desvelos: Cristianas, Musulmanas, y Judías en la España medieval*. Madrid: Esfera de los libros, 2006.

Fyzee, Asaf A. A. *Outlines of Muhammadan Law*. Delhi: Oxford University Press, 1999.

Garrido Clemente, Pilar. *Estudio, traducción y edición de la obra de Ibn Masarra de Córdoba: La ciencia de las letras en el sufismo*. Salamanca: Ediciones Universidad de Salamanca, 2008.

Geertz, Clifford. *The Interpretation of Cultures*. New York: Basic Books, 1973.

Gerber, Jane S. *The Jews of Spain: A History of the Sephardic Experience*. New York: The Free Press, 1992.

Giffin, Lois A. "Ibn Hazm and the *Tawq al-Hamāmah*." In *The Legacy of Muslim Spain*, edited by Jayyusi, Salma Khadra, 420–42. Leiden: Brill, 1992.

Glick, Thomas. *From Muslim Fortress to Christian Castle: Social and Cultural Change in Medieval Spain*. Manchester: Manchester University Press, 1995.

Glick, Thomas. *Islamic and Christian Spain in the Early Middle Ages*. Princeton: Princeton University Press, 1979.

Glick, Thomas, and Oriol Pi-Sunyer. "Acculturation as an Explanatory Concept in Spanish History." *Comparative Studies in Society and History* 11, no. 2 (1969): 136–54.

Goody, Jack. *The Oriental, the Ancient, and the Primitive: Systems of Marriage and the Family in the Pre-Industrial Societies of Eurasia*. Cambridge: Cambridge University Press, 1977.

Grabar, Oleg. "The Meaning of the Dome of the Rock." In *The Medieval Mediterranean: Cross-Cultural Contacts*, edited by Chiat, Marilyn, and Kathryn Ryerson, 1–10. St. Cloud, MN: North Star Press, 1988.

Grabar, Oleg. "The Umayyad Dome of the Rock in Jerusalem." *Ars Orientalis* 3 (1959): 33–62.

Guichard, Pierre. *Al-Ándalus: Estructura antropológica de una sociedad islámica en Occidente*. Granada: University of Granada, 1995.

Guichard, Pierre. *Al-Andalus frente a la conquista cristiana: los Musulmanes de Valencia*. Valencia and Madrid: Biblioteca Nueva, Universitat de València, 2001.

Guichard, Pierre. *La España musulmana: Al-Andalus omeya (siglos VIII-XI)*. Madrid: Historia 16: Temas de Hoy, 1995.

Guichard, Pierre. "El Problema de la existencia de estructuras de tipo 'feudal' en la sociedad de Al-Andalus." In *Estructuras feudales y feudalismo en el mundo mediterráneo*, edited by Bonnaisse, Pierre, 117–45. Barcelona: Crítica, 1984.

Guichard, Pierre. "Le Problème des structures agraires en Al-Andalus avant la conquête chrétienne." In *Andalucía entre oriente y occidente (1236–1492): Actas del V coloquio internacional de historia medieval de Andalucía*, edited by Cabrera, Emilio, 161–70. Córdoba: Diputación Provincial de Córdoba, Servicio de Publicaciones, 1988.

Guichard, Pierre. *Structures Sociales "orientales" Et "occidentales"dans l'Espagne musulmane*. Paris: Mouton, 1977.

Guichard, Pierre. "Une Méditerranée berbère durante le haut moyen âge?" In *Le Maghreb, Al-Andalus et la Méditerranée occidentale (VIIIe—XIIIe siècles)*, edited by Senac, Philippe, 9–18. Toulouse: Université de Toulouse–Le Mirail, 2007.

Guichard, Pierre, and Bruna Soravia. *Les Royaumes de Taifas: Apogée culturel et déclin politique des émirats andalous du XIe siècle*. Paris: Geuthner, 2007.

Haeri, Niloofar. *Sacred Language, Ordinary People*. New York: Palgrave, 2003.

Halm, Heinz. *The Empire of the Mahdi: The Rise of the Fatimids*. Leiden: Brill, 1996.

Ḥamūd, Khaḍr Mūsā Muḥammad. *Al-Naḥū wa al-nuḥāt: al-madāris wa al-khaṣā'is*. Beirut: 'Ālam al-kutub, 2003.

Ḥaqqī, Muḥammad. *Al-Barbar fī Al-Andalus: dirāsah li ta'rīkh majmū'ah ithnīyah min al-fatḥ ilā suqūṭ al-khilāfah al-umawīyah*. Casa Blanca: Sharikah al-nashr wa al-tawzī' al-madāris, 2001.

Ḥarīrī, Muḥammad 'Īsā. *Thawrah 'Umar Ibn Ḥafṣūn za'īm al-muwalladīn fī al-junūb al-andalusī*. Cairo: Dār al-kitāb al-jāmi'ī, 1982.

Hartford, Hedaya, and Ashraf Muneeb. *Birgivi's Manual Interpreted: Complete Fiqh of Menstruation and Related Issues*. Beltsville, MD: Amana Publications, 2006.

Hawting, Gerald R. *The First Dynasty of Islam: The Umayyad Caliphate A.D. 661–740*. London and Sydney: Croom Helm, 1986.

Hawting, Gerald R. "Shirk and 'Idolatry' in Monotheistic Polemic." In *Dhimmis and Others: Jews and Christians and the World of Classical Islam*, edited by Rubin, Uri, and David Wasserstein, 107–26. Tel Aviv: Eisenbrauns, 1997.

Hillenbrand, Carole. *The Crusades: Islamic Perspectives*. London and New York: Routledge, 2000.

Hillenbrand, Robert. "'The Ornament of the World': Medieval Córdoba as a Cultural Center." In *The Legacy of Muslim Spain*, edited by Jayyusi, Salma Khadra, 112–35. Leiden: Brill, 1992.

Hodgson, Marshall G. S. *The Venture of Islam*. Vol. 1. Chicago: University of Chicago Press, 1974.

Ḥusayn, Ḥamdī 'Abd al-Mun'im Muḥammad. *Thawrāt al-barbar fī al-andalus fī 'aṣr al-imārah al-umawīyah, 138–316H 756–928M*. Alexandria: Mu'assasah shabāb al-Jāmi'ah, 1993.

Jayyusi, Salma Khadra. "Andalusī Poetry: The Golden Period." In *The Legacy of Muslim Spain*, 317–66. Leiden: Brill, 1992.

"Jihad Watch: 'In 1492 We Lost Everything.'" http://www.jihadwatch.org/2005/03/in-1492-we-lost-everything.html

Jones, Alan. "Romance Scansion and the Muwashshaḥāt: An Emperor's New Clothes?" *Journal of Arabic Literature* 11 (1980): 36–55.

Jones, Alan. "Sunbeams from Cucumbers? An Arabist's Assessment of the State of Kharja Studies." *La Corónica* 12 (1983–84): 45–70.

Katz, Solomon. *The Jews in the Visigothic and Frankish Kingdoms of Spain and Gaul.* Cambridge, MA: Medieval Academy of America, 1937.

Keddie, Nikki R. "The Past and Present of Women in the Islamic World." *Journal of World History* 1, no. 1 (1990): 77–108.

Kennedy, Hugh. *Muslim Spain and Portugal.* London and New York: Longman, 1996.

Kennedy, Hugh. *The Prophet and the Age of the Caliphates: The Islamic Near East from the Sixth to the Eleventh Century.* London and New York: Longman, 1986.

Khoury, Nuha N. N. "The Dome of the Rock, the Ka'ba, and Ghumdan: Arab Myths and Umayyad Monuments." *Muqarnas: Essays in Honor of Oleg Grabar* 10 (1993): 57–65.

King, P. D. *Law and Society in the Visigothic Kingdom.* Cambridge: Cambridge University Press, 1972.

Lapidus, Ira M. *A History of Islamic Societies.* Cambridge: Cambridge University Press, 1988.

Lapidus, Ira M. "The Separation of State and Religion." *International Journal of Middle Eastern Studies* 6 (1975): 363–85.

Larsson, Gören. *Ibn García's Shu'ūbiyya Letter: Ethnic and Theological Tensions in Medieval Al-Andalus.* Leiden: Brill, 2003.

Lazarus-Yafeh, Hava. "Some Neglected Aspects of Medieval Muslim Polemics Against Christianity." *The Harvard Theological Review* 89, no. 1 (1996): 61–84.

Lévi-Provençal, E. *Histoire de l'Espagne musulmane.* Leiden: Brill, 1950.

Lévi-Provençal, E. "Du nouveau sur le royaume de Pampelune au IXe siècle." *Bulletin Hispanique* 55, no. 1 (1953): 5–22.

Lewis, Bernard. *The Jews of Islam.* London and New York: Routledge, 1984.

Lewis, Bernard. *The Muslim Discovery of Europe.* Princeton: Princeton University Press, 1982.

López de la Plaza, Gloria. *Al-Andalus: Mujeres, sociedad, y religión.* Málaga: Universidad de Málaga, 1992.

Makkī, Maḥmūd 'Alī. *Al-tashayyu' fī al-andalus mundhu al-fatḥ ḥattā nihāyah al-dawlah al-umawīyah.* Cairo: Maktabah al-thaqāfah al-dīnīyah, 2004.

Manzano Moreno, Eduardo. *Conquistadores, emires y califas: Los Omeyas y la formación de Al-Andalus.* Barcelona: Crítica, 2006.

Manzano Moreno, Eduardo. *La Frontera de Al-Andalus en época de os Omeyas.* Madris: Consejo Superior de Investigaciones Científicas, 1991.

Marín, Manuela. "Marriage and Sexuality in Al-Andalus." In *Marriage and Sexuality in Medieval and Early Modern Iberia*, edited by Lacarra Lanz, Eukene, 3–20. London and New York: Routledge, 2002.

Marín, Manuela. *Mujeres en Al-Andalus.* Madrid: Consejo Superior de Investigaciones Científicas, 2000.

Marín, Manuela. "Muslim Religious Practices in Al-Andalus (2nd/8th–4th/10th Centuries)." In *The Legacy of Muslim Spain*, edited by Jayyusi, Salma Khadra, 878–94. Leiden: Brill, 1992.

Marín-Guzmán, Roberto. "The Revolt of 'Umar Ibn Ḥafṣūn in Al-Andalus: A Challenge to the Structure of the State (880–928)." University of Texas at Austin, 1994.

Marín-Guzmán, Roberto. "Social and Ethnic Tensions in Al-Andalus: Cases of Ishbīliyah (Sevilla), 276/889–302/914 and Ilbīrah (Elvira) 276/889–284/897—The Role of 'Umar Ibn Ḥafṣūn." *Islamic Studies* 32, no. 3 (1993): 280–318.

Martínez Enamorado, V. "Sobre las 'cuidadas iglesias' de Ibn Ḥafṣūn: Estudio de la basílica hallada en la ciudad de Bobastro (Ardales, Málaga)." *Madrider Mitteilungen* 45 (2004): 507–31.

Marzolph, Ulrich, and Richard van Leeuwen, eds. *The Arabian Nights Encyclopedia*. Vol. 2. Santa Barbara, CA: ABC-CLIO, 2004.

Menocal, Maria. *The Ornament of the World: How Muslims, Jews, and Christians Created a Culture of Tolerance in Medieval Spain*. Boston: Little, Brown, 2002.

Miller, Elaine R. *Jewish Multiglossia: Hebrew, Arabic, and Castilian in Medieval Spain*. Newark, DE: Juan de la Questa, 2000.

Monroe, James. *Hispano-Arabic Poetry*. Berkeley: University of California Press, 1974.

Monroe, James. *Islam and the Arabs in Spanish Scholarship (Sixteenth Century to the Present)*. Leiden: Brill, 1970.

Monroe, James. "Pedir Peras Al Olmo? On Medieval Arabs and Modern Arabists." *La Corónica* 10 (1981–82): 121–47.

Monroe, James. *The Shu'ūbiyya in Al-Andalus: The Risāla of Ibn García and Five Refutations*. Berkeley and Los Angeles: University of California Press, 1970.

Monroe, James. "*Zajal* and *Muwashshahah*: Hispano-Arabic Poetry and the Romance Tradition." In *The Legacy of Muslim Spain*, edited by Jayyusi, Salma Khadra, 398–419. Leiden: Brill, 1992.

Moral, Celia del. *Árabes, Judías, y Cristianas: mujeres en la Europa medieval*. Granada: Universidad de Granada, 1993.

Morony, Michael G. "Religious Communities in Late Sasanian and Early Muslim Iraq." In *Muslims and Others in Early Islamic Society*, edited by Hoyland, Robert, 1–23. Aldershot, UK: Ashgate, 2004.

Mottahedeh, Roy P. "The Shu'ūbīyah Controversy and the Social History of Early Islamic Iran." *International Journal of Middle Eastern Studies* 7 (1976): 161–82.

Murata, Sachiko. *The Tao of Islam: A Sourcebook on Gender Relationships in Islamic Thought*. Albany: State University of New York Press, 1992.

Nirenberg, David. *Communities of Violence: Persecution of Minorities in the Middle Ages*. Princeton: Princeton University Press, 1996.

Noth, Albrecht. "Problems of Differentiation between Muslims and Non-Muslims." In *Muslims and Others in Early Islamic Society*, edited by Hoyland, Robert, 103–24. Aldershot, UK: Ashgate, 2004.

Novikoff, Alex. "Between Tolerance and Intolerance in Medieval Spain: A Historiographic Enigma." *Medieval Encounters* 11, no. 1 (2005): 7–36.

O'Callaghan, Joseph F. *A History of Medieval Spain*. Ithaca: Cornell University Press, 1975.

Oliver Pérez, Dolores. "Una nueva interpretación de 'árabe,' muladí y 'mawla' como voces representivas de grupos sociales." In *Proyección histórica de España en sus tres culturas: Castilla y León, América y el Mediterraneo*, Vol. 3, edited by Lorenzo Sanz, Eufemio, 143–55. Valladolid: Junta de Castilla y León, 1993.

Oliver Pérez, Dolores. "Sobre el significado de 'mawla' dentro de la historia de Al-Andalus." *Al-Qantara* 22 (2001): 321–44.

Owens, Jonathan. *A Linguistic History of Arabic*. Oxford: Oxford University Press, 2006.

Peña, Salvador. "Which Curiosity? Ibn Ḥazm's Suspicion of Grammarians." In *Ibn Ḥazm of Cordoba: The Life and Works of a Controversial Thinker*, edited by Adang, Camilla, and Maribel Fierro, 233–50. Leiden: Brill, 2013.

Pérez de la Lastra y Villaseñor, Manuel. *La Dinastía omeya De Córdoba*. Córdoba: Excma. Diputación de Córdoba, 1993.

Pinault, David. *The Shiites: Ritual and Popular Piety in a Muslim Community*. New York: St. Martin's Press, 1992.

Pinault, David. *Story-Telling Techniques in the Arabian Nights*. Leiden: Brill, 1992.

Pipes, David. "Mawlas: Freed Slaves and Converts in Early Islam." In *Muslims and Others in Early Islamic Society*, edited by Hoyland, Robert, 277–322. Aldershot, UK: Ashgate, 2004.

Puerta Vílchez, José Miguel. "Abū Muḥammad 'Alī Ibn Ḥazm: A Biographical Sketch." In *Ibn Ḥazm of Cordoba: The Life and Works of a Controversial Thinker*, edited by Adang, Camilla, and Maribel Fierro, 3–24. Leiden: Brill, 2013.

Pulcini, Theodore. *Exegesis as Polemical Discourse: Ibn Hazm on Jewish and Christian Scriptures*. Atlanta: Scholars Press, 1998.

Ribera y Tarragó, Julián. *Disertaciones y opúsculos*. Madrid: Impr. de E. Maestre, 1928.

Robinson, Cynthia. "Ubi Sunt: Memory and Nostalgia in Taifa Court Culture." *Muqarnas* 15 (1998): 20–31.

Roth, Norman. "Deal Gently with the Young Man: Love of Boys in Medieval Hebrew Poetry of Spain." *Speculum* 57, no. 1 (1982): 20–51.

Roth, Norman. "Jewish Collaborators in Alfonso X's Scientific Works." In *Emperor of Culture: Alfonxo X the Learned of Castile and His Thirteenth-Century Renaissance*, edited by Burns, Robert I., 59–71. Philadelphia: University of Pennsylvania Press, 1990.

Roth, Norman. "Jewish Reactions to the *'Arabiyya* and the Renaissance of Hebrew in Spain." *Journal of Semitic Studies* 23, no. 1 (1983): 63–84.

Roth, Norman. *Jews, Visigoths and Muslims in Medieval Spain: Cooperation and Conflict*. Leiden: Brill, 1994.

Sáenz-Badillos, Angel. *A History of the Hebrew Language*. Translated by Elwolde, John. Cambridge: Cambridge University Press, 1993.

Safran, Janina M. *Defining Boundaries in Al-Andalus: Muslims, Christians, and Jews in Islamic Iberia*. Ithaca: Cornell University Press, 2013.

Safran, Janina M. *The Second Umayyad Caliphate: The Articulation of Caliphal Legitimacy in Al-Andalus*. Cambridge, MA: Harvard University Press, 2000.

Said, Edward. *The World, the Text, and the Critic*. Cambridge, MA: Harvard University Press, 1983.

al-Sāmarrā'ī, Khalīl Ibrāhīm. *Ta'rīkh al-'arab wa ḥaḍāratihim fī al-Andalus*. Beirut: Dār al-kitāb al-jadīd al-muttaḥidah, 2000.

Savage, Elizabeth. *A Gateway to Hell, a Gateway to Paradise: The North African Response to the Arab Conquest*. Princeton, NJ: Darwin Press, 1997.

Savage, Elizabeth. "Survival through Alliance: The Establishment of the Ibadiyya." *Bulletin (British Society for Middle Eastern Studies)* 17, no. 1 (1990): 5–15.

Scales, Peter C. *The Fall of the Caliphate of Córdoba: Berbers and Andalusis in Conflict*. Leiden: Brill, 1994.

Schippers, Arie. *Spanish Hebrew Poetry and the Arabic Literary Tradition: Arabic Themes in Hebrew Andalusian Poetry*. Leiden: Brill, 1994.

Senac, Philippe, ed. *Le Maghreb, Al-Andalus et la Méditerranée occidentale (Viiie–Xiiie Siècles)*. Toulouse: Université de Toulouse–Le Mirail, 2007.

Shaban, M. A. *The Abbasid Revolution*. Cambridge: Cambridge University Press, 1970.

Shaban, M. A. *Islamic History: A New Interpretation*. Cambridge: Cambridge University Press, 1971.

Sharf, Andrew. *Byzantine Jewry from Justinian to the Fourth Crusade*. New York: Schocken Books, 1971.

Sharhibīlī, Muḥammad b. Ḥasan. *Taṭawwur al-madhhab al-mālikī fi al-gharb al-islāmī ḥattā nihāyah al-ʿaṣr al-Murābiṭī*. Morocco: Wizārah al-awqāf wa-al-shu'ūn al-islamīyah, 2000.

Sherif, Faruq. *A Guide to the Contents of the Qur'an*. Reading, UK: Garnet Publishing, 1995.

Sicroff, Albert. *Los Estatutos de limpieza de sangre*. Madrid: Taurus, 1985.

Simonet, Francisco Javier. *Glosario de las voces ibéricas y latinas usadas entre los Mozárabes*. Madrid: Est. tip. de Fortanet, 1888.

Simonet, Francisco Javier. *Historia de los Mozárabes de España, deducida de los mejores y más auténticos testimonios de los escritores cristianos y árabes*. Madrid: M. Tello, 1897–1903.

Smith, W. Robertson. *Kinship and Marriage in Early Arabia*. London: Cambridge University Press, 1885.

Sonbol, Amira El Azhary, ed. *Women, the Family, and Divorce Laws in Islamic History*. Syracuse, NY: Syracuse University Press, 1996.

Soravia, Bruna. "A Portrait of the ʿĀlim as a Young Man: The Formative Years of Ibn Ḥazm, 404/1013–420/1029." In *Ibn Ḥazm of Cordoba: The Life and Works of a Controversial Thinker*, edited by Adang, Camilla, Maribel Fierro, and Sabine Schmidtke, 25–49. Leiden: Brill, 2013.

Stern, S. L. "Les vers finaux en espagnol dans les muwassahs hispano-hébraiques: une contribution à l'histoire du muwassah et à l'étude du vieux dialecte espagnol 'mozarabe.'" *Al-Andalus* 13 (1948): 299–346.

Stillman, Norman A. *The Jews of Arab Lands: A History and Source Book*. Philadelphia: Jewish Publication Society of America, 1979.

Stillman, Yedida Kalfon. *Arab Dress: From the Dawn of Islam to Modern Times*. Leiden: Brill, 2003.

Ṭāha, ʿAbdulwāḥid Dhanūn. *The Muslim Conquest and Settlement of North Africa and Spain*. London and New York: Routledge, 1989.

Taher, Mostapha. "Les rapports socio-économiques entre Al-Andalus et le Magrib Al-Aqsa aux Xe et XIe siècles." In *Le Maghreb, Al-Andalus et la Méditerranée Occidentale (Viiie—Xiiie Siècles)*, edited by Senac, Philippe, 183–99. Toulouse: Université de Toulouse–Le Mirail, 2007.

Thompson, E. A. *The Goths in Spain*. Oxford: Clarendon Press, 1969.

Togneri, Reyna Pastor de. "Problèmes d'assimilation d'une minorité: Les Mozarabes de Tolède (de 1085 à la fin du XIIIe siècle)." *Annales* 25, no. 2 (1970): 351–90.

Treggiari, Susan. *Roman Marriage: Iusti Coniuges from the Time of Cicero to the Time of Ulpian*. Oxford: Clarendon Press, 1991.

Tritton, A. S. *The Caliphs and Their Non-Muslim Subjects*. London: Frank Cass and Co., 1970.

Turner, Howard R. *Science in Medieval Islam*. Austin: University of Texas Press, 1995.

Vallejo Triano, Antonio. "Madīnat Al-Zahrā': Transformation of a Caliphal City." In *Revisiting Al-Andalus: Perspectives on the Material Culture of Islamic Iberia and Beyond*, edited by Anderson, Glaire D., and Mariam Rosser-Owen, 3–28. Leiden: Brill, 2007.

Versteegh, Kees. *The Arabic Language*. New York: Columbia University Press, 1997.

Versteegh, Kees. "Ibn Maḍā' as Ẓāhirī Grammarian." In *Ibn Ḥazm of Cordoba*, edited by Adang, Camilla, and Maribel Fierro, 207–31. Leiden: Brill, 2012.

Versteegh, Kees. *Landmarks in Linguistic Thought III: The Arabic Linguistic Tradition*. London and New York: Routledge, 1997.

Viguera Molins, María Jesus, Luis Molina Martínez, and Muḥammad Jalāf. *Los reinos de Taifas: Al-Andalus en el siglo XI*. Madrid: Espasa Calpe, 1994.

Wansbrough, John. *Quranic Studies: Sources and Methods of Scriptural Interpretation*. Oxford: Oxford University Press, 1977.

Wasserstein, David. "Ibn Ḥazm and Al-Andalus." In *Ibn Ḥazm of Cordoba: The Life and Works of a Controversial Thinker*, edited by Adang, Camilla, and Maribel Fierro, 69–85. Leiden: Brill, 2013.

Wasserstein, David. "Inventing Tradition and Constructing Identity: The Genealogy of Umar Ibn Ḥafṣūn between Christianity and Islam." *Al-Qantara* 23 (2002): 269–98.

Wasserstein, David. *The Rise and Fall of the Party Kings: Politics and Society in Islamic Spain, 1002–1086*. Princeton: Princeton University Press, 1985.

Watt, W. Montgomery, and Pierre Cachia. *A History of Islamic Spain*. Edinburgh: University of Edinburgh Press, 1965.

Wegner, Judith Romney. "The Status of Women in Jewish and Islamic Marriage and Divorce Law." *Harvard Women's Law Journal* 5 (1982): 1–33.

Wilson, Adrian. "The Ceremony of Childbirth and Its Interpretation." In *Women as Mothers in Pre-Industrial England: Essays in Memory of Dorothy McLaren*, edited by Fildes, Valerie, 68–107. London and New York: Routledge, 1990.

Wolf, Kenneth Baxter. *Christian Martyrs in Muslim Spain*. Cambridge: Cambridge University Press, 1988.

Wolf, Kenneth Baxter. "*Convivencia* in Medieval Spain: A Brief History of an Idea." *Religion Compass* 3, no. 1 (2009): 72–85.

Wolfe, Ronald G. "Ibn Maḍā' Al-Qurṭubī and the Book in Refutation of the Grammarians." PhD diss., Indiana University, 1984.

Ye'or, Bat. *The Dhimmi: Jews and Christians Under Islam.* London: Association of University Presses, 1985.

Ye'or, Bat. *Eurabia: The Euro-Arab Axis.* Madison, NJ: Farleigh Dickinson University Press, 2005.

Zaghrūt, Muḥammad Muḥammad Ibrāhīm. *Al-'alaqāt bayna al-umawīyīn wa al-fāṭimīyīn fī al-andalus wa al-shamāl al-ifrīqī.* Cairo: Dār al-tawzī' wa al-nashr al-islāmīyah, 2006.

Zomeño, Amalia. *Dote y matrimonio en Al-Andalus y el norte de África: Estudio sobre la jurisprudencia islámica medieval.* Madrid: Consejo Superior de Investigaciones Científicas, 2000.

Zomeño, Amalia. "Kafā'a in the Maliki School: A Fatwā from Fifteenth-Century Fez." In *Islamic Law: Theory and Practice*, edited by Gleave, Robert, and Eugenia Kermeli, 194–204. London: I. B. Tauris, 1997.

Zorgati, Ragnhild Johnsrud. *Pluralism in the Middle Ages: Hybrid Identities, Conversion, and Mixed Marriages in Medieval Iberia.* London and New York: Routledge, 2012.

Index

Abbasids: jihād, 145–46; legitimacy, 34–36; rule in Middle East, 1, 9, 20–22, 24–25, 27–30, 77
'Abd Allāh (amīr), 111, 122, 130, 135, 151
'Abd al-Malik (caliph), 23, 27, 64
'Abd al-Raḥmān I, 21–22, 25, 28, 42, 59, 92, 130
'Abd al-Raḥmān II, 29, 92, 129, 136, 148
'Abd al-Raḥmān III, 9, 29–31, 35–36, 58, 80–81, 113, 124, 131–32, 137, 144–46, 149, 159–60
'Abd al-Raḥmān V, 44
Abraham, 156, 157
Abū Bakr (caliph), 28
Abū Hanīfah, 71
Abū Nuwās, 34, 153
Acién Almansa, Manuel, 136
Adam, 53, 68, 83, 91, 126
adībs, 61
adulterium, 100, 102–3
adultery, 99, 103. *See also* sexual misconduct
Afghanistan, 31, 32
Aghlabids, 140
agnatic kin, 45, 104–5, 161
Aḥkām ahl al-dhimma, 71
Ahmed, Leila, 180n40
al-'ajam (non-Arabic speakers), 8
Alfonso III, 150
Alfonso X, 162, 181n65
Algeciras, 133
Algeria, 134
Ali, Kecia, 88, 181n53
'Alī (Muḥammad's cousin), 28, 33, 109
Almoravids, 1, 38, 161, 173n1
al-Qaeda, 18, 31
'āmil (grammatical regent), 54–55
al-'āmmah (ordinary people), 8, 128, 164n17
al-Andalus (Muslim Spain), 7–8; and cultural history, 9–12; northern march, 16, 135, 144–58; and religious history, 12–13; scholarship on, 3–7; social groups, 7–9, 128. *See also* Arab identity; Arab Muslim elite; Berber Muslims; Córdoba; dhimmīs; Muslim identity; muwallads; non-Arab Muslims
'Antarah, 153
apostasy, 78–79, 137–38, 150, 154
Appleby, Joyce, 10

Arabic language, 45–60, 160; colloquial, 45–47, 57–58, 83, 120–21; dialects, 45–47; in Mecca, 47–48; as official language, 27; as superior, 17, 47–57, 83; vernacular, 46–48, 120, 159, 160. *See also* Classical Arabic
Arab identity, 1–2, 13–14, 38–60; as biological, 1–2, 26, 33, 38–41, 60, 155, 160 (*see also* kinship systems); as distinct from Muslim identity, 8–9, 154–62; fluidity of, 159–60; and language, 26, 45–50, 57–60, 153 (*see also* Arabic language; Classical Arabic); as oppressors, 140; as superior, 129, 143, 155–56; of ʻulamāʼ (religious scholars), 61; of Umayyads, 9, 13–14, 25–26, 33, 36; in Valencia, 169n67
Arab Muslim elite (al-khāṣṣah), 7–9, 13–14, 39, 44, 55, 59, 128, 159. *See also* Abbasids; Arab identity; aristocracy; Muslim identity; Umayyads
Aral Sea region, 32
Aramaic, 82
Argentea, 81, 152, 154; *Vita*, 137–39, 188n50
aristocracy, 9, 22, 25–26, 30, 33, 35, 129, 153, 159–60; and biological descent, 39; marriages, 44–45, 150–51; Visigothic, 16, 136, 147. *See also* Abbasids; Arab Muslim elite; Ibn Ḥafṣūn; Umayyads
Arnedo, 147, 148
ʻaṣabīyah (tribal loyalty), 25–26
asceticism, 122–24, 137–39
aṣḥāb (local authorities), 135, 137
Asín Palacios, Miguel, 123, 185n68
Aslam ibn ʻAbd al-ʻAzīz, 58, 60
Asturias-León, 146, 150
Ayalon, David, 157

Badajoz, 146
Baghdad, 3, 27
Balj ibn Bishr al-Qushayrī, 21–22, 129
Banū Dhī al-Nūn, 131–33, 142–43, 145, 188n3
Banū Hūd, 133
Banū Jarrah, 77
Banū Layth, 129
Banū Muzayn, 111
Banū Qasī, 16, 132, 134–36, 144, 146–54; as Arab elite, 152–53; and Arabic language, 153; marriages, 149–51; naming practices, 152; power and territory, 148–49; religions, 150–52
Banū Sālim (Berbers), 149–50
Banū Shuhayd, 44
Barānis tribes, 131
Barcelona, 146–47
Basques, 146–47, 149–52, 156–57, 189n28
Bat Ye'or, 175n35
beards, 89, 115–16
Bedouins: Arabic language of, 47–48, 50, 53; Pre-Islamic Arabic poetry, 47–48, 50, 113, 183n24
Berbers: Banū Sālim, 149–50; Barānis, 131; Butr tribes, 131; jizyha (poll tax) on, 24, 129; kinship, 170n5; Kutāma Berbers, 28; Nafūsah, 139; Nafzah, 122; Zanātah, 139
Berber army, 3, 21–22, 24–25, 30, 129, 159; conquest of al-Andalus, 38; mercenary, 35–36
Berber Muslims, 160; conversion to Islam, 24; honorary Arabs, 7, 61; military service, 3, 21–22, 24–25, 30, 35; revolts against Umayyads, 15–16, 26, 129–33, 151–52; social status, 128–29, 155; support for Arab elite, 130–31
Bezels of Wisdom (Ibn al-ʻArabī), 126
Bible, 65–68, 91
Biblical Hebrew, 82–83
bin Laden, Osama, 4
bint al-ʻamm (paternal uncle's daughter), 25, 40–41, 43
al-Bīrūnī, 66
bishops, 79, 80, 177n76
blood money (diyah), 59

Bobastro, 134–37
Borja, 147
Boswell, John, 176n51, 176n54
Bouwsma, William, 11–12, 18
bride price, 101. *See also* dower
brides, 93–97, 101–2, 108–10, 117; consent to marriage, 93–95; gift from bride's family, 110. *See also* dower; marriage; wives
Bulliet, Richard, 4, 75, 153, 173n1
Burgos, 146
Butr tribes, 131
Byzantine Empire, 131, 156; cultural traditions, 3, 27; governance, 26, 34; infrastructure, 23; law, 71, 74

Cagigas, Isidro de las, 5, 137, 187n42
Cairo (al-Qāhirah), 28
Calatayud, 145
caliphs, 13–14; as amīr al-mu'minīn, 31, 34; and religious scholars, 50; titles of, 27, 31. *See also* Umayyads
Cantabrians, 146
Cantar de mio Cid, 115
capital punishment. *See* death penalty
capitulation agreements, 72, 76
Carthage, 3
Cassius, 147–48
Castro, Americo, 5
Catalonia, 146
Catholic Church, 5, 73
Celto-Romans, 22, 26
Chalmeta, Pedro, 166n13
Christians, 61–85; civil servants, 66, 76–79, 128; day-to-day treatment in al-Andalus, 61–62, 74–81, 84–85; Ibn Ḥafṣūn's identity as, 135–39, 142–43, 152, 187n30, 187n35, 187n42; legal and social status, 2, 14–15, 69–74; marriage, 100, 150–51 (*see also* interfaith marriage); martyrs, 78–81, 85, 92, 137–39; sexuality, 176n54; in Spain, 5, 162, 163n8; in Taifa period, 37, 161–62; treatment of Jews, 70, 72–73, 162. *See also* Catholic Church; conversion to Christianity; conversion to Islam; dhimmīs; People of the Book; polemic
Christian scripture, 174n21. *See also* Bible; Gospels; New Testament
Christian states, 146–47
circumcision, 39, 80, 174n23; of Christians, 178n80; of Jews, 71, 73
civil servants, 61, 66, 76–79, 128
Classical Arabic, 45–60, 156; and Arab identity, 39, 45, 57–60; and Hebrew, 83–84; and Islam, 50–56; as unchanging ideal, 47
Clément, François, 37, 154
clientage (walā'), 59–61, 128–29, 158. *See also* mawālī (mawlā)
cognatic kin, 104–5, 161
Collins, Roger, 166n13, 189n28
Colloquial Arabic, 45–47, 57–58, 83, 120–21
concubines, 41–42, 73, 101, 103, 108–9, 127, 151
conversion to Christianity, 32, 134, 162, 187n30, 187n35; from Islam, 151–52, 176n58
conversion to Islam, 32–34, 59–61, 153, 154, 161; and jizyah, 72; and marriage rights, 94, 100; rates, 153, 173n1; required, 22–23. *See also* muwallads
Coptic, 46
Córdoba: Arab-Muslim culture, 13–14; bishop of, 79, 80; Christian community, 75–76; Great Mosque, 28; Ibn Ḥafṣūn revolt, 135; religious scholars ('ulamā), 51; Umayyad control of, 3, 133, 142; Yeshiva in, 82, 178n90
Crompton, Louis, 118
Crone, Patricia, 165n6
cross-dressing, 8, 89–90
cultural history, 9–12
cultural identity, 1–2; and Islamic law, 13; scholarship on, 6–7. *See also* Arab identity; ethnic identity; Muslim identity; religious identity

Damascus, 3, 23, 27
dār al-ḥarb, 31–32, 145
dār al-islām, 31
Darnton, Robert, 10–12
death penalty: execution of Christian martyrs, 78–81, 92, 139; for homosexuality, 119; honor killings, 181n75; for women, 141–42
Denia, 156
dhimmah (covenant of protection), 69; definition, 14; end of, 18
dhimmīs: conversion to Islam, 161; definition, 8; legal and social status, 8, 14–15, 69–85, 128–29, 159, 175n26, 175n33, 175n35; marriage to Muslims, 70, 73–75 (*see also* interfaith marriage); protection for, 14, 69–72, 87–88; in Sharī'ah, 87–90. *See also* Christians; Jews; People of the Book
diglossia, 83
divorce: in Gospels, 67; in Roman law, 102; in Sharī'ah, 12–13, 89, 93–94, 96, 98–99, 105, 108, 109; ṭalāq (dismissal of wife), 98–99; in Visigothic law, 103
Dīwān al-aḥkām al-kubrā (Ibn Sahl), 111
dīwān system, 30, 34–35, 78, 89, 159
Dome of the Rock (Jerusalem), 23, 27, 64
Donatist Christianity, 141
Donner, Fred, 33, 63–64, 167n40, 174n9
dos (dowry), 101–2
dower, 15, 95–99, 101–2, 104–10, 161; and consummation of marriage, 96–97
dowry, 41, 101
Dozy, Reinhardt, 5–6
dress, regulation of, 72, 175n43
Dūnash ibn Labrāṭ, 81–82

Ebro River, 144–45, 147, 149, 153–54
Egypt, 23, 28, 32, 46
elite. *See* Arab Muslim elite
endogamy, 8, 13–14, 25–26, 40–45, 74–75, 150, 153, 154, 170n7
Epalza, Mikel de, 80, 176n58
ethnic identity, 1–2; determining factors, 38–39; fluidity of, 143–44, 149, 154, 159–62; and geography, 154; and social status, 166n23. *See also* Arab identity; Muslim identity
Eulogius, 79, 138
Europe, 177n77; history, 4, 18–19; sources, 86, 182n4
Eve, 91, 126
executions. *See* death penalty
exogamous marriage, 40

faqīh, 44, 114
al-Farābī, 51–52, 65
Fāṭimah (Muḥammad's daughter), 28, 33, 109
Fatimids, 28, 29, 140
fatwās (legal rulings), 110–11
Fierro, Maribel, 4, 50, 60, 92, 147–48, 153
fitnah (civil war), 35
Flórez, Enrique, 188n50
fornication, 99. *See also* sexual misconduct
Fortún, 148, 149, 152
Fortún Garcés, 151
Frankish law, 72
Franks, 147
freedmen, 59, 94, 158
freedwomen, 94, 101, 115, 156
frontier. *See* northern march
al-Fusṭāṭ, 28

Galicians, 146, 157
Garrido Clemente, Pilar, 123
Gascons, 146–47
Geertz, Clifford, 10
gender: as ambiguous social category, 8; hierarchies, 127; and law, 86–112 (*see also* Sharī'ah); in literature, 112–19; in mystical texts, 124–27; in scripture, 15, 90–91, 94. *See also* brides;

husbands; marriage; men; widows; wives; women
gender studies, 6
genealogies. See *Jamharah* (Ibn Ḥazm); kinship systems
Germanic law, 72
ghayrah (honor), 115–16, 119, 141–42, 183n32
al-Ghazālī, 115
Glick, Thomas, 4, 6, 136, 159
God: as al-ḥaqq, 125; as al-wujūd, 125; ghayrah of, 183n32; in Sufi texts, 122–27
Goody, Jack, 100–102, 106
Gospels, 65–68, 174n12, 174n21
grammar: in homoerotic literature, 118–19; misuse of definite article, 57–58; prescriptive, 47–48
grammarians, 47–57, 118; critics of, 51–57
Granada, pogrom in, 84
The Great Cat Massacre (Darnton), 11
Great Mosque (Damascus), 23
Greek high culture, 24, 25, 36, 51–52
Greek language, 46, 48–49
Guadalquivir Valley, 133–35, 144
Guichard, Pierre, 6, 39–42, 45, 104, 106, 110, 111–12, 132, 150, 161, 169n5, 170n7

ḥadīths, 12, 31; and Arab identity, 155, 160; on Christians and Jews, 64–65, 71, 174n12; on ghayrah (honor), 115, 183n32; on marriage, 97; on women's nature, 91; and Ẓāhirism, 52
Hagar, 156
ḥajj (pilgrimage to Mecca), 58, 88, 108. *See also* Mecca
al-Ḥakam I, 76, 111
al-Ḥallāj, 122
ḥanīfs (Arabian monotheists), 63
Ḥaqqī, Muḥammad, 4
Ḥarīrī, Muḥammad ʿĪṣā, 4, 139–40
Ḥasday ibn Shapruṭ, 81–82
Hāshim ibn ʿAbd al-ʿAzīz, 78, 146, 148, 161
al-Hāshim II, 35
Hawting, Gerald R., 69, 165n6
Hebrew, 53, 81–84, 121
heretics, 65, 71, 124, 178n95
Ḥijāz, 25; Arabic language of, 47–49
ḥilf (alliance), 129
al-Hishām (caliph), 21
Hishām I, 92, 122
Histoire de l'Espagne musulmane (Lévi-Provençal), 6
homoeroticism, 18, 114, 118–22, 127
homosexuality, legal status of, 114, 119
honor: family, 40, 45, 101, 103; ghayrah, 115–16, 119, 141–42, 183n32; honor killings, 181n75
Hostegesis, 77
Huesca, 145, 147
husbands, 70, 168n52; endogamy, 170n7; legal rights, 93–100, 108–9; obligations of, 98, 161; as superior, 90–91. *See also* brides; concubines; marriage; wives

Ibāḍī movement, 139–42
Iberian Christians (al-ʿujmah), 140
Iberian Muslims, 7–9. *See also* muwallads
Iberian Peninsula, 1, 36
Ibn Abī ʿĀmir, 30, 35, 159
Ibn al-ʿArabī, 49, 122–27, 185n78
Ibn al-ʿAṭṭār, 107–10
Ibn al-Qiṭṭ, 122, 130
Ibn al-Qūṭīyah, 60, 128, 153
Ibn al-Rāwandī, 178n95
Ibn Antonian ibn Julian, Qūmis (Count), 77–78, 80, 85, 146, 171n44, 177n66
Ibn ʿAskar, 134, 136, 142
Ibn Gabirol, Solomon, 82, 121
Ibn García, *Risālah*, 155–58
Ibn Ḥabīb, ʿAbd al-Malik, 44, 89, 91, 92, 98–99, 110–11

Ibn Ḥafṣūn, ʿUmar: Christian identity, 135–39, 142–43, 152, 187n30, 187n35, 187n42; Muslim identity, 139–43, 151; revolt against Umayyads, 16, 29, 133–44, 153
Ibn Ḥanbal, 71
Ibn Ḥawqal, 157
Ibn Ḥayyān, 130
Ibn Ḥazm: *al-Muḥallā bi-al-āthār*, 92, 115; on Arab identity, 161; background and writings, 16–18; on Banū Qasī, 148, 150; on community membership, 60; on homosexuality, 114, 118–19; *Jamharah ansāb al-ʿarab* (Arab genealogies), 1, 9, 41–45, 60, 105, 155, 160; on marriage, 92, 94–98; *Naqṭ al-ʿarūs*, 44; polemic on Christians and Jews, 65–69, 114, 174n21; *Ṭawq al-ḥamāmah* (*The Dove's Neck Ring*), 17–18, 112–19, 121, 127; as Ẓāhirist grammarian, 52–54, 56, 172n58
Ibn ʿIdhārī, 131–32, 135–37, 188n3
Ibn Jinnī, Abū al-Fatḥ ʿUthmān, 55
Ibn Khaldūn, 10, 49
Ibn Maḍāʾ, Aḥmad ibn ʿAbd al-Raḥmān, 54–56
Ibn Marwān al-Jillīqī, ʿAbd al-Raḥmān, 146, 148, 153
Ibn Masarrah, 49–50, 123–24, 185n68
Ibn Naghrīlah, Samuel, 69, 82–84, 114
Ibn Qayyim al-Jawzīyah, 71
Ibn Qutaybah, 67
Ibn Quzmān, 120
Ibn Rustam, ʿAbd al-Raḥmān, 139–40
Ibn Sahl, 111, 113
Ibn Shuhayd, Umayyah ibn ʿĪsā, 153
Ibn Taymīyah, 31
Ibn ʿUbāda al-Qazzāz, 121
Ibn Waḍḍāh, 51
Ibn Zaydūn, 120
ʿiddah (waiting period after divorce or widowhood), 98–99, 103
identity. *See* Arab identity; cultural identity; ethnic identity; Muslim identity; religious identity
idolatry, 69, 120
Idrisids, 129
Ifrīqiyah, 134
īmān (faith), 68–69
impurity, 89–90, 179n10
incest regulations, 104–5
India, 32
indigenous languages, 46
infidelity, 99, 103. *See also* sexual misconduct
Iñiga family, 149–52
Inquisition, 73
interfaith marriage, 70–71, 73–75, 100, 150–51, 154, 175n33, 176n49
Interpretation of Cultures (Geertz), 10
intimacy, 112–22. *See also* homoeroticism; sexuality
Iran, 32
Iraq, 23, 32
Isidore of Seville, 24
Islam: and Classical Arabic, 50–56; modern, 70, 175n35; spread of, 31–33, 35; as superior, 69; as universal religion, 14, 25 (*see also* ummah). *See also* conversion to Islam; Muslim identity
Islamic law, 8, 12–13; physical practices, 68. *See also* Mālikī law; Sharīʿah; Sharīʿah courts
Islamic State (radical group), 13, 18
Islamic Studies, 3–7; relevance to modern world, 3, 7, 18–19
Ismāʿīl, 149

Jamharah (Arab genealogies, Ibn Ḥazm), 1, 9, 41–45, 60, 105, 155, 160
Jerusalem, 23, 27, 64
Jesus, 66–67, 174n21, 174n23
Jewish law, 174n23; on marriage, 100
Jewish scripture, 174n17. *See also* Talmud; Torah
Jews, 61–85; bilingual literary culture, 82–84 (*see also* Hebrew); Christians'

treatment of, 70, 72–73, 162; conversion to Islam, 23; day-to-day treatment, 61–62, 74–75, 81–85; elite status, 84–85; Islamic religious polemic on, 65–69, 114; legal and social status, 2, 14–15, 27, 69–74, 128; pogrom in Granada, 84; in Taifa period, 37, 82, 84. *See also* dhimmīs; People of the Book
jihād, 31–33, 130, 137, 145–47, 175n35
"Jihad Watch" (website), 4
jizyha (poll tax), 14, 32, 70, 88; on Berbers, 24, 129; on Christian Arabs, 72; enforcement, 75
John, Bishop of Córdoba, 80
John of Gorze, 29, 80–81
Judah ha-Levi, 82, 83
Justinian's code, 71

kafā'ah (social equality of spouses), 43, 94, 109–10, 170n22, 190n33
kāfir (unbeliever), 69
Kennedy, Hugh, 4, 6, 20
Khadījah, 95
khalīfah (caliph), 31
Khārijism, 33–34, 36, 130, 139–42
al-khāṣṣah. *See* Arab Muslim elite
al-Khushanī, 57–58, 173n72
kinship systems, 40–41; agnatic, 45, 104–5, 161; Arab, 39–45; Arab and Islamic patrilineal, 13–14, 25, 39–40, 42–43, 57, 104–6, 161; Berbers, 170n5; cognatic, 104–5, 161; "Eastern," 40–41, 110–12; Eurasian patrilineal, 100–101, 104–6. *See also* patriliny
Kulthūm ibn 'Iyād al-Qaysī, 129
kūrah, 145
Kutāma Berbers, 28

language: as basis of creation, 125–26; God's creation of, 53. *See also* Arabic language; Classical Arabic; Hebrew
Larsson, Gören, 156
Latin high culture, 24, 36
law: and gender, 86–112; in practice, 107–27. *See also* Mālikī law; Roman law; Sharī'ah (Islamic law); Visigothic law
lawsuits, 111
legitimacy of rule: Abbasids, 34–36; based on piety, 33–34; genealogical legitimation, 33; Umayyads, 9, 21, 23, 26, 28–34, 38, 135, 159
Leon, 146
letter mysticism, 49–50
Lévi-Provençal, Évariste, 5–6, 134, 142, 153, 177n77, 187n35
Lope, 148–49, 152
love, 112–22. *See also* homoeroticism; sexuality

madhhabs (schools of religious law), 172n58; on dhimmīs, 71, 74–75. *See also* Mālikī law
Madīnah al-Zahrā', 29
Maghrib, 1, 3–4, 129
Mahdī (messiah), 122
mahr, 95, 102. *See also* dower; ṣadāq
Maimonides, 82, 83
Malaga, 133–34
Mālik, 129; *al-Mudawwanah al-kubrā*, 92, 94, 97, 109, 124; *Muwaṭṭa*, 92
Mālikī law, 17, 52, 160, 172n58; on dhimmīs, 71, 73, 175n33; inheritance law, 105; on women's marriage rights, 92–101, 107–10, 114, 161, 181n61
al-Manṣūr. *See* Ibn Abī 'Āmir
Manzano Moreno, Eduardo, 130, 147, 166n23
marches (northern frontier), 144–45. *See also* northern march
Maria the Copt, 124, 180n37
Marín, Manuela, 50, 89, 92, 114, 182n81
marriage, 15, 91–112; consummation of, 96–97; endogamous (*see* endogamy); Eurasian systems, 100–104, 106; exogamous, 40; 'iddah (waiting period after divorce or widowhood), 98–99, 103; kafā'ah (social and economic equality of spouses), 43,

marriage (*continued*)
109–10; model contracts, 107–10; mut'ah (temporary), 123; polygyny, 109, 152–53; in Sharī'ah, 87, 91–104, 150, 154; shighār (marriage of exchange), 95–96; status between men and women in, 43, 90–91, 100; stipulations (shurūṭ), 108; thayyibs, 93–96, 99, 110; Visigothic codes, 100–104, 106, 176n49. *See also* brides; dower; husbands; interfaith marriage; widows; wives
martyrdom, Christian, 78–81, 85, 92, 137–39
Marwān ibn Yūnis al-Jillīqī, 146
Marwānids, 36
masculinity, markers of, 8, 89–90, 115–16
mawālī (mawlā), 7, 44, 51, 147, 157–58, 173n79; Banū Qasī as, 152–53; Berber, 24; definition, 7, 59–60; Persian, 41; of Umayyads, 78; Visigothic, 136, 148. *See also* clientage
Mecca, 12, 58, 67–68, 108; Meccan Arabic, 47–48
men: ethnic and religious identity, 2, 7–9 (*see also* Arab identity; Muslim identity); masculinity, markers of, 8, 89–90, 115–16; sexuality, 99–101, 117, 119 (*see also* homoeroticism; homosexuality). *See also* gender; husbands
menstruation, 89–90
mercenary troops, 30, 34–35
Mérida, 130, 146
Merovingians, 24
Middle Arabic, 46–47, 83
Middle East: Abbasid rule in, 1, 9, 20–22, 24–25, 27–30, 77; differences between al-Andalus and, 21–26; Umayyad rule, 20–21
Miller, Elaine, 83, 178n90
Mishnah Torah (Maimonides), 83
Mishnaic Hebrew, 82
Modern Standard Arabic, 45
mohar, 102. *See also* dower
Mongols, 31; sacking of Baghdad, 21, 35
Monophysite Christians, 71
monotheists, 62, 156. *See also* Christians; dhimmīs; Jews; People of the Book
Monroe, James, 157, 183n24
Morocco, 1
Moses, 67, 68
Moses ibn Ezra, 82
Mozarabs, 5
Muḍarīs, 22, 148, 165n6
Mudawwanah al-kubrā, 92, 94, 97, 109, 124
Muḥallā (Ibn Ḥazm), 92, 115
Muḥammad: death of, 22; kinship with Umayyads, 21, 25, 33; monotheism, 63; pious imitation of, 124; predictions of coming of, 65, 68; on second wives, 109; status as prophet, 31, 65; stories about (*see* ḥadīths); wives of, 95, 124, 180n37, 180n40
Muḥammad b. Salmah, 111
Muḥammad I, 77–79, 132, 146, 149, 151, 171n44
Muḥammad ibn 'Abd Allāh Ibn 'Abī 'Īsā, 131
Muḥammad ibn Dāwūd al-Ẓāhirī, *Kitāb al-zahrah* (*Book of the Flower*), 113
Muḥammad ibn Lope, 135
Muḥammad II, 44
multiglossia, 83
mulūk al-ṭawā'if. *See* Taifa period
al-Mundhir (amīr), 134
Mūsā Ibn Dhī al-Nūn, 132
Mūsā ibn Fortún Ibn Cassius, 152
Mūsā ibn Muḥammad Ibn Ziyād al-Judhāmī, 57–58, 173n72
Mūsā ibn Mūsā ibn Fortún ibn Qasī, 147–50
Mūsā ibn Nuṣayr, 38
mushrik, 69
mushrikūn (polytheists), 62

Muslim identity, 1–2, 154–60; as distinct from Arab identity, 8–9, 154–62; dress, regulation of, 72, 175n43; of Ibn Ḥafṣūn, 139–43, 151; men's legal status, 70, 87–88. *See also* Arab Muslim elite; Berber Muslims; Khārijism; mawālī (mawlā); muwallads; non-Arab Muslims; Sharīʻah (Islamic law); Shīʻism; Sunnī Muslims
Muslim Spain. *See* al-Andalus
Muslim Spain and Portugal (Kennedy), 6
Muṭarraf, 149–50, 152
al-Muʻtaṣim (caliph), 30
Muʻtazilīs, 124
muwallads, 37, 41, 123, 128, 157, 160; Arab identity, 61; definition, 7; revolts against Umayyads, 15–16, 26, 133–44; status of, 78. *See also* conversion to Islam
muwashshaḥah, 81, 120–21, 178n87, 184n56
Muwaṭṭa, 92
mysticism, 15, 49–50, 52

Nafūsah Berbers, 139
Nafzah Berbers, 122
Nāṣirids, 35
nationalism, 5–7, 136
Navarre, 146
Neoplatonic thought, 123
Nestorian Christians, 71, 77, 141
New Testament, 65
non-Arab Muslims, 3, 8–9, 15–16, 154–59. *See also* Berber Muslims; muwallads
North Africa, 1; Berber revolts, 129–30; conquest of, 32; Shīʻism, 122, 185n68; Umayyad defensive bases, 29
northern march, 16, 135, 144–58
Noth, Albrecht, 175n43
"Nunīyah," 120
Nykl, A. R., 118–19

Oliver Pérez, Dolores, 166n9, 173n79
Oporto, 146
Otto I, 80

Pact of ʻUmar, 72, 89
pagans, 69, 71, 115, 131, 156
Pakistan, 32
Palestine, 23
Palmer, R. R., 10
Pamplona, 146–47, 149, 151
Party kingdoms. *See* Taifa period
patriliny: Arab and Islamic systems, 13–14, 25, 39–45, 57, 100–101, 104–6, 161; Eurasian systems, 100–101, 104–6, 161. *See also* endogamy; kinship systems
pen (qalam), 125–26, 185n78
Penyafort, Raymond, 162
People of the Book (ahl al-kitāb), 17, 32–33, 62, 138, 150, 174n9. *See also* Christians; Jews; Zoroastrians
Persian empire, 23–28, 32, 34; high culture, 3, 23–25, 36, 51–52, 155–56
Persian language, 46, 58
piety, 33–34, 123–24, 139–40
poetry, 178n87; Arabic, 34, 39, 81, 113, 156, 160, 168n58; gender in, 120–22; Hebrew, 81–83, 121; pre-Islamic Bedouin, 47–48, 50, 113, 153, 183n24
polemic: Christian, 174n17; as genre, 114; Islamic, 65–69, 114, 157, 174n21
polygyny, 109, 152–53
polytheists, 22
poverty, 94, 97, 101
prescriptive grammar, 47–48
protection: for dhimmīs, 14, 69–72, 87–88; for non-Arabs, 59; for women, 15, 87–88, 109, 119

qāḍīs (judges), 50–51, 57–58, 78, 80, 111
Qayrawān, 3
Quran: Arabic language of, 47–50, 52–53, 55; and Arab identity, 155, 160; on Christians and Jews, 62–64, 68, 71, 174n9; education in, as dower, 97;

Quran (*continued*)
on jizyah, 32; pen and tablet, images of, 125–26; on punishment for sexual misconduct, 99; relevance to modern world, 18–19; as source of Islamic law, 12; stability of, 66; on women's status, 90–91, 94; and Ẓāhirism, 52–53, 55
Quranic heirs, 105
Quraysh, 21, 25, 38

Rabbinic Hebrew, 82–83
Rābi'ah of Basra, 122
Rabī' ibn Theodolfo, 76
Rayyah, 133, 135
al-Rāzī, 130
Recemundus, 80–81, 171n44
religion: essentialist theory of, 162; history of, 12–13
religious education, 46
religious identity, 1–2; fluidity of, 143–44, 149, 152–54, 159–62; and geography, 154. *See also* Arab identity; Muslim identity
religious polemic. *See* polemic
religious ritual, 68–69
religious scholars. *See* 'ulamā'
religous toleration, 70
Ribera y Tarragó, Julián, 173n72
Risālah (Ibn García), 155–58
Risālah al-i'tibār (*Letter of Interpretation*, Ibn Masarrah), 123
ritual pollution, 89–90, 179n10
Romance language, 58, 83, 120, 152, 159
Roman Empire, 23–24, 27, 166n13
Roman law, 72, 74; on marriage and divorce, 100–102
Romans, 5, 163n8
Ronda, 133
Roth, Norman, 83, 181n65
al-Ru'aynī, Isma'īl ibn 'Abd Allāh, 123
Rūmī, Jalāl al-Dīn, 122
Rustamid dynasty, 129, 134, 139–40

Sa'adiyah ben Yosef, 83
ṣadāq (dower), 95–99, 105, 108, 110, 181n49
Safran, Janina, 4, 179n10
Sā'id al-Andalusī, 65
Sa'īd b. Muzayn, 111
al-Samḥ, 131–33
Samson (abbot of Pinna Melaria), 76–79, 178n80
ṣaqālibah (slave troops), 8, 30, 34–36, 155–57, 160, 167n43
ṣaqlabī Taifas, 36–37
Sarah, 156, 157
al-Sarrāj, Abū 'Alī, 130
Sasanian Empire, 23, 71, 74
Saudi Arabia, 31
Savage, Elizabeth, 141
Scales, Peter C., 170n7, 185n2
scripture, Islamic: Arabic language of, 52–56; Christians in, 62–65; Jews in, 62–65, 68, 71, 174n9, 174n12; relevance to modern world, 18–19; on women's status, 90–91. *See also* ḥadīths; Quran
Seville, 51, 142, 148, 177n76
sexuality: female, 15, 90, 98, 99–104, 106, 117; male, 99–101, 117, 119 (*see also* homoeroticism; homosexuality); symbolism of, 125–26
sexual misconduct, 40, 119, 183n32; punishment for, 99–100; Visigoth law on, 101–4, 106, 176n49; zinā', 99–100, 102, 119, 176n49
al-Shāfi'ī, 71
Shaqyā al-Miknāsī, 130
Sharī'ah (Islamic law), 12–13, 86–106; and Arab identity, 14; dhimmī status (Christians and Jews), 62, 69–74, 87–90; enforcement, 74–75; family law, 18, 150; on honor killings, 181n75; on intermarriage, 150, 154; language of, 54; on marriage and divorce, 12–13, 87, 89, 91–105, 108, 109, 150, 154; on sexuality, 17, 99–100; subordinate categories of

persons, 87–90; women's inheritance rights, 91–92, 104–6, 161; women's status in, 8–9, 15, 18, 86–106, 108, 117, 161 (*see also* women, legal status of). *See also* Mālikī law
Sharī'ah courts: and Arab identity, 160; execution of Christians, 78–81, 92, 139; women's status, 15, 18, 110–12
Shī'ism, 33–34, 36, 52, 65, 104, 130, 139–40, 151–52; North African messianic movements, 122, 185n68
shu'ūbīyah, 154–58
Sībawayhi, 47–48
Siete Partidas, 162
Simonet, Francisco Javier, 5, 79, 163n8, 177n76, 187n42
Sīrah, 95
slaves, 74, 88; freed, 59, 94, 101, 115, 156, 158
slave troops (ṣaqālibah), 8, 30, 34–36, 155–57, 160, 167n43
slave women, 115–16, 151, 170n7; blonds, 113; dress, 90; male sexual access to, 101, 119
social categories, 7–8. *See also* Arab identity; Arab Muslim elite; Berber Muslims; dhimmīs; Muslim identity; muwallads; non-Arab Muslims
social history, 6. *See also* cultural history
sources, 11, 75–76, 182n4; on gender, 86–87; literary, 112–19
Spain: Christians, 5, 162, 163n8; conquest of, 32; in modern world, 4; Muslim Spain (*see* al-Andalus); nationalist movements, 136, 187n42
Spanish March, 146
spousal abuse, 91, 98–99, 181n61
Sufism, 15, 49–50, 52; gender in Sufi texts, 122–27
Sunnī Muslims, 151; inheritance law, 104; religious law, 33–34, 71 (*see also* madhhabs)
Syria, 23, 147; conquest of, 28, 32
Syriac, 46, 53
al-Ṭabarī, 95
al-Ṭabarī, 'Alī ibn Rabbān, 67
tablet (lawḥ), 125–26, 185n78
Ṭāha, 'Abdulwāḥid Dhanūn, 4
Tāhart, 134, 139–40
taḥrīf (distortion), 66
Taifa period, 36–37, 133, 160; Christians, 75; ethnic and religious identity, 154; Jews in, 37, 82, 84; poetry, 120
ṭalāq (dismissal of wife), 98–99
Talmud, 66, 82–83, 157, 174n17
Tarazona, 147
Ṭāriq ibn Ziyād, 38
Ṭawq al-ḥamāmah (*The Dove's Neck Ring*, Ibn Ḥazm), 17–18, 112–19, 121, 127
Temple Mount (Jerusalem), 23, 27
thaghr (frontier or march), 145–46. *See also* northern march
thayyibs, 93–96, 99, 110
theology, 64–66
theosophy, 124
Toledo, 75, 142, 145, 176n58, 177n76; Banū Dhī al-Nūn control over, 132
Torah, 65–66, 99, 174n17
Torró, Josep, 169n67
Tortosa, 145
Tota (Ṭūṭah), 151
Tudmir, 76
Tuleda, 145, 148, 149
Tunisia, 1, 28

'Ubayd Allāh, 28
'ulamā' (religious scholars), 34, 36, 50–51, 61, 128
'Umar I, 60, 72
Umar II, 72
Umayyads, 20–37; al-Andalus, rule in, 1–2, 20–37; allies of, 131–32, 143, 146–47; Arab identity, 9, 13–14, 25–26, 33, 36; as caliph, 13–14, 26–31, 51; capital in Syria, 27–28; Christians, relations with, 61, 75, 79–81, 84–85 (*see also* Christians); chronology of rule, 20–

Umayyads (*continued*)
21; clients, 7, 61 (*see also* clientage; mawālī); collapse of, 35, 132, 159; court poetry, 120, 183n24; Jewish access to elite status, 84–85 (*see also* Jews); kinship with Muḥammad, 21, 25, 33; as leaders of jihād, 31–33; legitimacy, 9, 21, 23, 26, 28–34, 38, 135, 159; lineage status, 170n7; Middle East, rule in, 20–21; military, 21–22, 24–25, 30, 34–36, 167n43; monumental building, 28–29; Muslim identity, 13–14; opposition to, 15–16, 33–37, 129–43; perceived as impious, 33–34; regional power, 133, 142–43; tax revenue, 135
ummah, 14, 31, 60; equality in, 8, 109, 140; leader of, 33, 140; nature of, 52, 139–40; non-Muslims in, 63; women in, 89
United States: attitudes toward Islamic world, 18–19; jihadist struggle against, 31
universe, creation of, 125–26

Valencia, 169n67
veiling, 104, 161, 182n81
vernacular language, 120, 159; Arabic, 46–48, 120, 160; Hebrew, 82; Romance, 120, 160
Vikings, 148
virgins, 93–94, 96, 108, 110, 137
Visigothic law, 72–73, 161; on divorce, 103; *Forum iudicum*, 100, 106, 176n49, 181n65; *Fuero juzgo*, 181n65; on marriage, 100–104, 106, 176n49; on sexual misconduct, 101–4, 106, 176n49; women's inheritance rights, 106; women's status, 87
Visigoths, 3, 5, 22, 163n8, 166n13; aristocracy, 16, 136, 147; revolts against Umayyads, 16, 133–43; as rulers, 23–24
Vita (Argentea), 137–39
Vita Johannis Abbatis Gorziensis, 80, 82

walā'. *See* clientage
al-Walīd II, 42–43, 147
walīs: governors, 145, 149; role in marriage contracts, 88–89, 93–97, 108, 115, 119; in Sufi context, 122–23
Walladah, 120
Wasserstein, David, 4, 152, 154, 156–57, 178n95, 187n30
Wellhausen, Julius, 20
widows, 93, 95, 103, 105, 111
wives: divorce, 98–99 (*see also* divorce); financial rights, 95–96; husbands' beating of, 91, 98–99, 181n61; obedience and deference, 15, 88–91, 98–99; as party to marriage contract, 17, 93–98; as property, 93–98, 106, 181n53; rights in Mālikī law, 92–101, 107–10, 114, 161, 181n61; second wives, 108–9. *See also* dower; marriage; widows
women: cross-dressing, 8, 89–90; dishonoring men, 115–17 (*see also* honor; sexual misconduct); endogamy, 74, 150–51, 170n7 (*see also* endogamy); ethnic and religious identity, 2, 8; as friends and confidants, 116–17; as links in genealogy, 42; low status, 94; male sexual access to, 99–101, 119, 176n54; mystics, 124; protection for, 15, 87–88, 109, 119; as ritually impure, 89–90; sexuality, 15, 90, 98, 99–104, 106, 117; sharing of, 123–24, 185n74. *See also* brides; concubines; gender; marriage; widows; wives
women, legal status of: inheritance, 40–41, 87, 88, 104–6, 110–11; in practice, 107–12; as subordinate category of person, 87–90, 180n40. *See also* Sharī'ah (Islamic law)

Yaḥyā ibn Yaḥyā Ibn Kathīr al-Laythī, 128–29, 131
Yamanīs, 21–22, 165n6
Yazīd I, 43

Yazīd ibn Abī Muslim Dīnār, 24
Yeshiva, 82, 178n90
Yūsuf al-Fihrī, 22

Ẓāhirism, 52–56, 172n58
zajal, 120, 184n56
Zamora, 130
Zanātah Berbers, 139
Zaragoza, 51, 145, 147–49
zinā' (unpermitted sexual intercourse), 99–100, 102, 119, 176n49
Ziyād b. 'Abd al-Raḥmān Shabṭūn, 92
Zoroastrians, 23, 33, 71, 168n52
al-Zubaydī, Abū Bakr, 51

Cooking with Peter

Your healthy Autumn & Winter Recipes

Published by
Midsea Books Ltd
Carmelites Street
Sta Venera SVNR1724 – Malta
sales@midseabooks.com

First published in 2008

Produced by Mizzi Design & Graphic Services Ltd
Printed by Gutenberg Press Ltd, Malta

ISBN: 978-99932-7-215-1

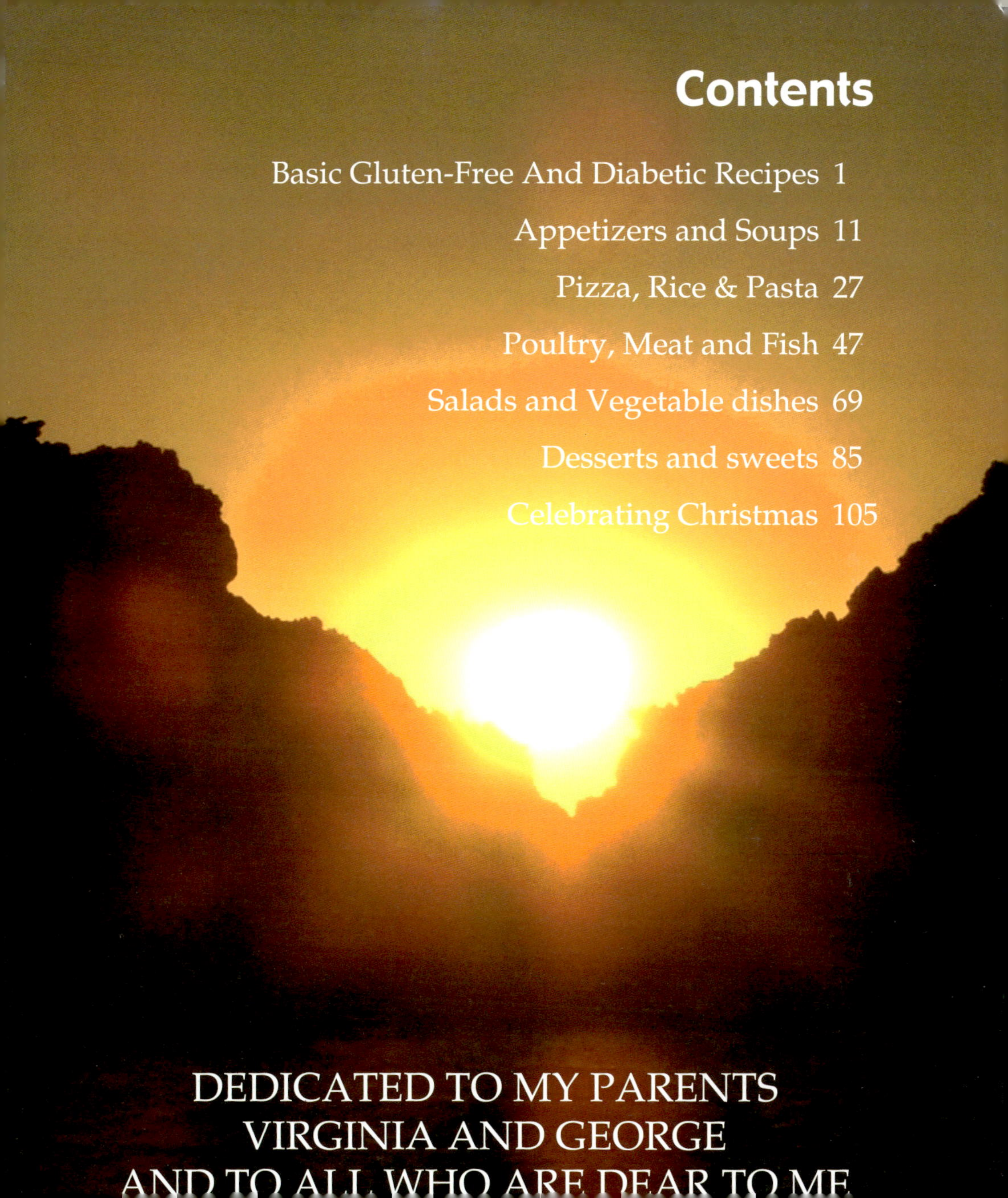

Contents

Basic Gluten-Free And Diabetic Recipes 1

Appetizers and Soups 11

Pizza, Rice & Pasta 27

Poultry, Meat and Fish 47

Salads and Vegetable dishes 69

Desserts and sweets 85

Celebrating Christmas 105

DEDICATED TO MY PARENTS
VIRGINIA AND GEORGE
AND TO ALL WHO ARE DEAR TO ME

Introduction

I was always wary of the food I eat. I was brought up in a family where health and consequently healthy eating were given prime importance. My mother was a diabetic and besides, her cholesterol level was above average. She was an excellent cook and preparing the family meal was one of the highlights of her day. Naturally, what she prepared was also good for her health and therefore her 'no added sugar, low fat and low carbohydrate' meals were what we all ate at home. Looking back, I now realize it was a 'matter of fact' way of eating for us. However it was far from boring and we definitely never felt deprived of a varied and nutritious menu.. We still had our healthy soups, exciting pasta and rice dishes, meats and fresh fish, all accompanied by plenty of vegetables and fresh fruit. What she cooked was Mediterranean and healthy. I remember when it came to pasta or rice dishes, mummy would have a very small helping of it and then compensate for that with her appetizing salads and vegetable dishes. She did prepare desserts and did bake cakes and sweets, but occasionally. They were always very special! I remember she did sometimes 'sin' and take a nibble, much to our consternation.

Now let me come to the purpose of this health book. Two years ago I had issued my first cookery book and then within 5 months I had issued my second one. Cooking with Peter One and Two were found very informative and useful in many a local kitchen and abroad. Subsequently, through my website and mail and through my contributions to local magazines and cookery programmes on local television, I came in contact with a substantial amount of people with health problems. I soon found myself dictating recipes which had a low fat content, had no sugar added or were gluten-free. It wasn't an easy task, and I also had to indulge in quite a bit of research. This is where my growing up in a health conscious environment came to good use as it had given me a good grounding.. The obvious then had to follow, and here is my first Health Book. True to my style I did not want a complicated or medically orientated cookbook. Just a recipe book with attractive and easy Mediterranean recipes good for your health and well being. Most of the recipes in this book are low in fat content. There is also a wide variety of gluten-free recipes and some interesting, handy recipes for diabetics. In this autumn and winter collection I have of course included a chapter, 'Celebrating Christmas'. Apart from some traditional Yuletide fare you will also find a luxury four course dinner ready for you to prepare this Christmas.

And now some advice to my readers with a health problem: When you are first diagnosed with a disease, you may feel as though life will never be the same again. No more eating and enjoying of this and that! What about cooking and where do I start? Don't panic........ Take a step back and look at the wider picture. Being diagnosed with a disease can be a good thing for some people as it can make them realize how much processed foods they

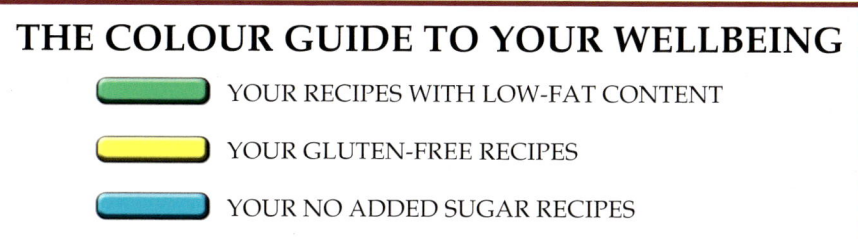

have been consuming! Therefore it's time to get back to basics, using natural ingredients and being responsible for the food we are eating so as to sustain healthy bodies. Healthy eating need not mean boring meals. There is no need to compromise on flavour. It need not lesson your pleasure in cooking and eating. Rather see it as a fresh beginning – an opportunity to try new ingredients and a wide and more exciting range of recipes for your health and enjoyment, for yourself, family and friends.

THE COLOUR GUIDE TO YOUR WELLBEING

YOUR RECIPES WITH LOW-FAT CONTENT

YOUR GLUTEN-FREE RECIPES

YOUR NO ADDED SUGAR RECIPES

Preparing food for a coeliac

Don't be filled with dread at the thought of cooking for a coeliac. The recipes in this book are no more difficult than cooking normally. There is no need to cook two different dishes if you are catering for a coeliac family member. Gluten-free meals can be just as delicious especially when meals are made from naturally gluten-free ingredients. True, some planning is required as you might not be able to get all your gluten-free ingredients from your local food store or supermarket, but you will be surprised at how little extra effort you need. Besides, nowadays most big supermarkets have their gluten-free sections and there are various specialized health shops that sell gluten-free basic foods and ingredients.

There are of course some simple precautions for you to adopt in your own kitchen.

Store and pack all your food separately from all other regular food, whether in your larder or refrigerator. Use separate utensils and equipment such as bread toasters, knives, chopping boards, mixing bowls, cutlery etc. Wash hands and nails thoroughly and even change your apron before you start to cook food for a coeliac.

Terms terms sometimes used by manufacturers that indicate the presence of gluten

Barley starch
Binder
Bran
Bulgar, cracked wheat
Cereal
Cereal protein
Couscous
Durum wheat
Fillers
Flour
Kamut
Malt
Malted Barley
Oat bran
Oat germ
Oatmeal
Pearl Barley
Porridge oats
Rolled oats
Rusk
Rye starch
Semolina
Thickener
Triticale (A mixture of wheat and rye)
Vegetable gum
Vegetable starch
Wheat bran
Wheat germ
Wheat meal
Wheat rusk
Wheat starch

The following food items and drinks may include gluten without your realising it

Baking powder
Holy Communion Hosts
Corn tortillas
Frozen chips
Stock cubes
Stock powder
Vegetable soup
Seasoning mixes
White pepper
Commercial ground almonds
Mustard powder
Packed suet
Cheese spreads
Ready grated cheese
Commercial mayonnaise and dressings
Soy sauce
Dry roasted nuts
Pretzels
Scotch eggs
Bombay mix
Foods deep-fried with other foods
Processed meats
Flavored crisps
Coffee from vending machines
Some fizzy drinks
Malted milk drinks
Beers and ale
Some medicinal tablets
Some children's sweets

Foods that are gluten-free

All fresh meat and fish
All fresh fruit and vegetables
Fresh herbs and individual spices
Maize and sweet corn
Dried peas, lentils, pulses and beans
Rice
Rice bran and noodles
Plain nuts and seeds
Eggs
Natural dairy products
Soya and tofu
Sugar
Honey
Maple syrup
Golden syrup
Treacle
Jams and marmalades
Pure oils
Vinegars
Vanilla essence
Yeast

Gluten-free alternatives

Rice flour
Tapioca flour
Potato flour
Corn flour
Ground cornmeal (polenta)
Soya flour
Chickpea flour
Chestnut flour
Buckwheat flour
Carob flour
Millet flour
Arrowroot

Cooking for a diabetic

There is no getting away from it: Shopping for a diabetic does take a little bit of extra time and effort. Buying fresh meats, fish, vegetables and some fruits is not an issue because you know that these are suitable. However you have to take a little more care over processed foods. Unless clearly stated on the label 'Suitable for diabetics', ready-made sauces, jams and other convenience foods may contain a small proportion of sugar. Nonetheless it is there, so do try to stick to fresh, natural ingredients. Nowadays however, there are many diabetic foods available in supermarkets, specialized health shops and chemists. You will be able to find jams, chocolates, a variety of crackers, biscuits and cakes, flavored creams and custards, jellies, tinned fruits and some delicious ice creams, to mention just a few. What you will need is just a little fantasy and ideas!

Further on in this book (Page) I have given you a recipe for a diabetic sponge cake. You can also make a chocolate version of it. You will also find a recipe for a diabetic sweet pastry (Page). So sit down, and with some thought and imagination you can jot down a whole list of delicious desserts, cakes and sweets all suitable for diabetics. Bake that sponge cake, slice and spread it with jam and stuff it with cinnamon or lemon custard or chocolate cream. Layer the sponge cake with jam, custard, chocolate cream, jelly and grated chocolate. Finish it off with chopped toasted nuts, and there you are: A whopper of a trifle! Serve mini trifles in individual glasses for that elegant touch. Serve them to all your guests. Believe me; they won't realize the dessert is diabetic! Use your diabetic sweet pastry for fruit tarts or just add some chopped toasted nuts to the pastry, then cut and bake it into your favourite biscuits. Mummy used to make a delicious sweet ricotta tart. She mixed her ricotta with some crushed sweetening tablets, beaten eggs, some grated orange zest, a few drops almond essence and coarsely chopped chocolate. She baked it in a sweet pastry case. We would devour her diabetic ricotta tart before she got the chance! Always keep some toasted nuts stored in airtight containers. They come in very handy as a snack or sprinkled over some plain yoghurt or custard. They make all the difference. So as you see, the list could be endless. What you will need is a little imagination and some basic diabetic ingredients available in health shops. However do stick to the basic golden rule: Even though a food item is labelled as 'Suitable for diabetics' or 'Contains no added sugars', always have a little of it per day. It might contain natural fruit sugars anyway. Never miss out on your regular visits to the family doctor and don't make excuses to miss out on your daily walk in the fresh air. Coming back to cooking, what you will need most is common to all good and healthy cooking: Common sense, dedication and love!

Basic
Gluten-Free
and Diabetic
Recipes

Gluten-Free Pizza Base

IYou will never buy another ready-made pizza base after you've made your first gluten-free pizza dough. Pizza appeals to everyone and makes a quick and easy complete meal if served with an interesting crispy salad. There are endless choices of toppings for your pizzas.

Ingredients

Makes 4 pizzas

175 grams rice flour
75 grams potato flour
50 grams tapioca flour
225 Ml. lukewarm water
1 teaspoon sugar
20 grams dried active yeast
25 grams milk powder
1 ½ teaspoons gluten-free baking powder
1 teaspoon xanthan gum
1 teaspoon salt
1 tablespoon olive oil
1 egg
Extra rice flour for kneading

Method

Place the lukewarm water in a small bowl and stir in the sugar and yeast. Cover and stand in a warm place for 15 minutes.

Place the rice flour, tapioca flour, rice flour, milk powder, baking powder, xanthan gum and salt in the bowl of your food mixer. Mix the dry ingredients together. In a separate bowl whisk together the olive oil and the egg and then pour into the flour mixture. Mix at a low speed and then pour in the yeast mixture. Continue mixing for a few minutes until a smooth dough is produced.

Transfer the dough to a rice-floured surface. Coat your hands with the flour, knead slightly and then divide into 4 portions. Form each portion into a ball and then flatten out into a round pizza base shape. Place a sheet of baking paper on a baking tray and place the pizza bases. Cover the tray with a clean cloth and stand in a warm place for 20 minutes. Bake in a moderate to hot oven for 10 minutes before removing and adding the toppings of your choice. Return the pizzas with the toppings to the oven and bake for a further 12 minutes or until golden and bubbly.

Gluten-Free Béchamel Sauce

Ingredients
600 Ml. Milk
60 grams butter
25 grams rice flour
25 grams corn flour
½ teaspoon ground nutmeg
Salt and fresly ground pepper to taste

Method
Melt the butter in a saucepan and stir in the corn flour, rice flour and nutmeg. Combine with a wooden spoon and cook over a low heat for 2 minutes. Gradually pour in the milk whilst whisking continuously. Allow to just simmer and thicken. Season to taste.

Gluten-Free Mushroom Sauce

Mushroom sauce will make a simple grilled fillet very interesting. You can even warm up some left-over roast meat or poultry and top with this delicious sauce, thereby avoiding commercial bottled sauces.

Ingredients
400 grams sliced mushrooms
1 onion finely chopped
1 tablespoon chopped chives
1 tablespoon lemon juice
1 tablespoon olive oil
Salt and freshly ground pepper to taste
Bechamel sauce made with 600 Ml. milk

Method
Heat the oil in a saucepan and saute' the onion until transparent. Add the mushrooms and cook over medium heat for 4 minutes. Stir occasionally.Remove from heat and stir in the chives, lemon juice and Bechamel sauce. Season. Simmer for 3 minutes whilst stirring continuously.

Gluten-Free Tomato Sauce

Tomato sauce is ever so versatile. Serve it as a topping for pasta, as a filling for omlettes, as a basic topping for pizza or as a base for casseroles or bean stews. Always use fresh Mediterranean tomatoes and do not overcook the sauce so as to preserve the natural vitamins.I never run short of this sauce! I store it in sterilized glass jars with tight-fitting lids. The secret lies in filling the jars right to the very top. It will keep for up to 3 weeks in the lower part of your refrigerator.

Ingredients

2 tablespoons olive oil
2 onions chopped
2 garlic cloves finely chopped
1 kilo ripe tomatoes
2 tablespoons fresh basil leaves, hand chopped
Salt and freshly ground pepper to taste

Method

Peel and chop up the tomatoes.
Heat the oil in a saucepan and sauté the onion until transparent. Stir in the garlic and saute' over medium heat for 2 minutes. Add the tomatoes, season and cook covered for 12 minutes. Remove the lid and continue cooking for a further 12 minutes whilst stirring occasionally. Remove from fire and stir in the fresh basil.

Gluten-Free Pancake Batter

Ingredients

175 grams rice flour
175 grams tapioca flour
4 large eggs, lightly beaten
350 Ml. milk
½ teaspoon salt
4 tablespoons butter, melted

Method

Sift the flours and salt into a large bowl. Make a well in the centre and pour in the eggs. Whisk at a low speed whilst gradually pouring in the milk. Whisk until smooth then cover the bowl and refrigerate for 1 hour. Whisk the batter again for 1 minute whilst pouring in the melted butter.

Gluten-Free Savoury Pie Pastry

This recipe is ideal for pies and quiches. Although a pastry made from gluten-free flours could be more difficult to handle, the effort will be well worth it. Try to keep the dough as dry as possible, as a rather 'wet' pastry could end up a bit tough when baked.

Ingredients

75 grams rice flour
75 grams fine corn meal (Polenta)
75 grams potato flour
1 heaped teaspoon xanthan gum
½ teaspoon salt
150 grams butter cut into cubes
1 egg
2 tablespoons water
Extra potato flour for dusting

Method

Combine the egg with the water.
Sift the flours, cornmeal, xanthan gum and salt into a bowl. Add the butter and rub into the flour mixture. Make a well in the centre and slowly add some of the egg mixture. Add just enough to be able to bring the pastry together with a fork. Keep as dry as possible.
Knead for a minute and then transfer to a potato-floured surface and knead until smooth.
Roll up in clingfilm and refrigerate for 30 minutes.
Roll out on a potato-floured surface or better still between 2 sheets of baking paper.

Gluten- Free Sweet Pastry

This pastry is ideal for sweet pies and tarts.

Use the same ingredients as for GLUTEN-FREE SAVOURY PASTRY and follow the same method, but add 50 grams sugar to the mixture after rubbing in the butter.
Use as required.

Diabetic Sweet Pastry

This recipe is ideal for your sweet tarts and pies, such as apple pie. Always have small portions of fruit pies because even though the pastry does not contain sugar, there is the fat content, the flour and the natural sugars of the fruit.

Ingredients
450 grams plain flour
Pinch salt
225 grams unsalted butter
2 tablespoons corn oil
6 tablespoons powdered sugar substitute or 6 tablets sweetner
Grated rind of 1 lemon
Few drops vanilla essence
Cold water to bind.

Method
Sift the flour and salt into a bowl. Add the butter and rub into the flour until the mixture resembles fine bread crumbs. Sir in the oil, vanilla, lemon rind and sugar substitute or the crushed sweetening tablets. Gradually add enough water to form a dough which must be firm but elastic and pliable. Turn onto a floured surface and knead for a few minutes. Wrap in cling-film and leave to rest in a cool place for 30 minutes.
Roll out over a floured surface and use as required.

Diabetic Sponge Cake

This is the basic recipe for a sugar-free sponge cake. Use your fantasy and imagination to create a delicious and interesting dessert!
The sponge cake could be sliced diagonally into three layers. Spread some diabetic strawberry jam on each layer and place some halved strawberries and a little whipped fresh cream. Decorate with some halved strawberries and melted diabetic chocolate.
Melt your chocolate with the 'bain marie' method.

You could turn this sponge cake recipe into a chocolate sponge cake. Omit the lemon juice and use 2 tablespoons water instead. Use 2 tablespoons cocoa powder and sift it with the flour. Continue with the recipe as instructed. When the cake is cool, slice diagonally.
Melt 200 grams diabetic chocolate with the 'bain marie' method, cool slightly and mix in 170 grams tinned cream. Use half the mixture to fill your sponge cake and then use the rest to spread as topping. Decorate with some orange zest, and there you are: Your Choco-Orange Sponge Cake!

Always eat small portions as you must consider your daily intake of fats and carbohydrate.

Ingredients
7 eggs
½ cup sugar-free orange juice
3 tablespoons sugar substitute
2 tablespoons lemon juice
¾ teaspoon cream of tartar
1 ½ cups plain flour
Pinch salt
Extra flour for dusting

Method
Grease a baking pan with butter. Line the bottom and sides of pan with baking paper and then grease the paper.
Separate the eggs. Beat the egg whites with the salt until foamy. Add the cream of tartar and continue beating until stiff.

Sift the flour into a separate bowl and mix in the sugar substitute. Make a well in the centre and add the egg yolks, lemon juice and orange juice. Beat for a few minutes and then carefully fold in the beaten egg whites. Pour mixture into prepared baking pan and smoothen surface of mixture. Bake in a moderate to hot oven for around 40 minutes or until sponge cake is golden in colour and cooked through.
Bring out of the oven and place on a cooling rack.

Gluten-Free Chicken Stock

What is fresh and home-made is definitely tastier and best for your health!
These basic recipes for chicken, beef and vegetable stocks will come in very handy for your soups, stews, pies and many sauces.
Never discard any cooked or uncooked chicken or beef bones. You could also use up your left over uncooked vegetables. Be adventurous but careful in you kitchen!

Ingredients
Around 1 kilo raw or cooked chicken bones
Chicken giblets such as liver, heart and neck
2 large onions
2 cloves garlic
1 leek
2 carrots peeled and sliced
A bunch of fresh celery
A handful fresh parsley
1 teaspoon dried thyme
3.5 litres water
6 pepper corns

Method
Wash peel and chop up the vegetables. Chop up the chicken parts and bones as much as possible.
Place all the ingredients in a large pot, bring to the boil and simmer for 3 hours.
Strain and leave to get cold. Remove any extra fat at the surface.
Do not add salt as at this stage you might not know for what recipe this stock is going to be used. You can also freeze this stock.

Gluten-Free Beef Stock

Ingredients

1 ½ kilos uncooked beef bones
 preferably with some meat on them
2 large onions
4 garlic cloves
2 large carrots
A bunch of fresh celery
Bouquet garni
5 pepper corns
4 cloves
1 tablespoon tomato paste
3.5 litres water

Method

Wash, peel and chop up the vegetables.
Lightly grease a roasting tin with olive oil and place the beef bones.
Roast in a moderate to hot oven for 35 minutes or until nicely browned.
Add the vegetables and continue roasting for 15 minutes.
Transfer the bones and vegetables to a large pot. Pour some of the water into the roasting tin and scrape off the roasting juices. Pour this liquid into the pot. Add the bouquet garni, the spices and the tomato paste together with the rest of the water. Bring to the boil, skim off the fat and simmer gently for 4 hours.
Strain the stock and leave to get cold. Skim off any remaining fat and store.

Gluten-Free Vegetable Stock

Ingredients

2 turnips
2 large onions
3 leeks
A bunch of fresh celery
A handful of fresh parsley
80 grams mushrooms
4 carrots
3 courgettes
1 small fennel bulb
Bouquet garni
5 pepper corns
2.5 litres water

Method

Wash, peel and chop up the vegetables.
Place all the ingredients in a large pot and bring to the boil. Cover and simmer gently for 2 hours. Strain the stock and leave to get cold before storing it in your fridge or freezing it.

Appitizers & Soups

Olive and Anchovy Crispy Bites

Ingredients
Makes about 40

1 ½ cup plain flour
115 grams chilled butter, diced
115 grams grated mature cheddar cheese
60 grams anchovy fillets, chopped
50 grams pitted black olives, chopped
½ teaspoon cayenne pepper
Extra flour for dusting
Sea salt to serve

Method
Sift the flour into a bowl. Add the butter and rub into the flour mixture. Mix in the cheese, anchovies, olives and the cayenne pepper. Knead into a dough. If necessary add a few drops cold water to obtain a firm but pliable dough.
Knead briefly over a floured surface.
Wrap up the dough in clingfilm and chill for 20 minutes.
Roll out the dough thinly over a floured surface and cut into 5cm strips. Cut across in alternate directions to form triangles. Transfer to a baking tray lined with baking paper.
Bake in a moderate to hot oven for around 12 minutes or until golden. Cool on a wire rack.
Sprinkle with sea salt and serve with your favourite drinks.

Pete's Smoked Salmon Loaf

Ingredients

Serves 8 to 10

For the pastry

500 grams plain flour
3 teaspoons dried yeast
2 teaspoons sugar
1 teaspoon salt
310 ml. lukewarm milk
50 ml. olive oil
1 teaspoon dried oregano
3 teaspoons dried dill tops
6 tablespoons capers, drained

For the filling

5 onions peeled and sliced
200 grams smoked salmon
Some olive oil
Freshly ground pepper
1 egg white lightly beaten
1 tablespoon sesame seeds

Method

Heat a little olive oil in a large frying pan and sauté the onions until they change colour.
Leave to cool. Cut the smoked salmon into strips.
Place the lukewarm milk in a small saucepan and mix in the sugar and yeast. Cover and stand in a warm place for 15 minutes.
Sift the flour and salt into a bowl and mix in the oregano, capers and dill. Mix in the oil and yeast mixture. Knead for a few minutes until a firm and elastic dough is produced.
Place in a lightly oiled bowl. Cover and stand in a warm place for 30 minutes.
Flatten out the pastry over a floured surface, using the palm of your hand. Flatten out into a rectangular shape wide enough to fit your baking tray.
Spread the onions over the pastry, keeping 4 cms. away from the edges. Place the smoked salmon over the onions. Drizzle some olive oil over the ingredients and season with pepper. Roll up the pastry carefully but tightly and tuck in the ends under the roll. Place on a greased and lightly floured baking tray and brush with the egg white. Sprinkle with the sesame seeds Bake in a moderate to slightly hot oven for 60 minutes or until golden and cooked through.
Bring out of the oven and stand for 6 minutes. Slice and serve drizzled with some olive oil.

Minted Pea and Yoghurt Dip

Ingredients
200 ml. plain yoghurt
6 tablespoons frozen peas, thawed
2 tablespoons fresh mint leaves chopped
2 tablespoons grated Parmesan cheese
2 tablespoons lemon juice
Salt and freshly ground pepper

Method
Place the yoghurt and mint in a food processor and process briefly. Add all the other ingredients and process to a smooth paste.
Place in a suitable container and serve with your favourite cool crudite'vegetables or savoury crackers.

Tunisian Carrot and Potato Dip

Ingredients
700 grams carrots, peeled
500 grams potatoes, peeled
3 garlic cloves, chopped
3 teaspoons ground cumin
2 tablespoons vinegar
4 tablespoons olive oil
Pinch chilli powder
Salt
Finely chopped parsley to garnish

Method
Slice the potatoes and carrots and place them in a saucepan with the garlic and some salt.
Cover with water and bring to the boil. Simmer until the vegetables are just soft.
Drain and transfer the vegetables to a bowl. Mash with a potato masher until smooth.
Place the puree in a serving bowl and mix in all the other ingredients.
Garnish with the parsley.
Serve with warmed pitta bread or savoury crackers.

Pete's Gluten-Free Mediterranean Loaf

Ingredients
Serves 8

75 grams rice flour
25 grams soya flour
175 grams fine cornmeal
2 teaspoons gluten-free baking powder
1 teaspoon xanthan gum
60 grams sundried tomatoes, chopped
60 grams pitted black olives, halved
2 tablespoons chopped mint
100 grams goat's cheese, coarsely grated
1 teaspoon oregano
3 eggs, beaten
200 ml. lukewarm milk
40 grams butter, melted

Method
Grease a loaf tin with butter and line with baking paper. Grease the paper with butter.
Sift the rice flour, soya flour, cornmeal, baking powder and xanthan gum into a large bowl and mix well. Mix in the sundried tomatoes, olives, mint, goat's cheese and oregano.
Combine the milk, eggs and melted butter in a separate container. Gradually add this mixture to the flour mixture whilst beating . Pour the mixture into the prepared tin and smoothen the surface. Bake in a moderate oven for 60 minutes or until cooked through.
Bring out of the oven and stand for 5 minutes. Place on a wire rack to cool.
Serve sliced with your favourite drinks, as a starter with a colourful crispy salad or as part of your gluten-free buffet.

Gluten-Free Crispy Cheese Biscuits

Ingredients
Makes around 30

120 grams potato flour
100 grams butter, softened
100 grams Cheddar cheese, grated
1 teaspoon dried thyme
1 teaspoon xanthan gum
Pinch salt and pepper
Extra potato flour for dusting

Method
Line a baking tray with baking paper.
Cream the butter until pale and soft. Mix in the potato flour and xanthan gum. Add the grated Cheddar and thyme. Season and mix well into a smooth dough. Place dough on a lightly potato floured surface and form into a sausage shape approximately 4 cms. thick.
Wrap up in clingfilm and refrigerate for 2 hours until firm.
Cut the dough into equal slices of around 8mm. thickness and place onto the baking sheet. Bake in a moderate to slightly hot oven for 10 minutes or until pale golden in colour. Leave to cool on the baking sheet for 3 minutes before transferring to a cooling rack with the help of a palette.
Serve with your favourite cocktails or have ready as a light snack.
Keep stored in an airtight container.

Mediterranean Lentil Soup

Ingredients
Serves 6

2 tablespoons olive oil
2 onions, chopped
3 garlic cloves, crushed
200 grams split red lentils
1 teaspoon ground coriander
1 teaspoon ground cumin
1.5 litres homemade
chicken stock (Page 9)
Juice of 1 lemon
Salt and freshly
ground pepper

Method
Heat the oil in a pot and sauté the onion until soft. Mix in the garlic, coriander and cumin. Cook for 2 minutes whilst stirring and then add the lentils and chicken stock. Bring to the boil and skim off any scum at the surface. Season and simmer for about 45 minutes or until the lentils are broken up and integrated into the soup. Stir occasionally during cooking.
Remove from heat and stir in the lemon juice. Serve hot.

Neapolitan Tomato Soup

Ingredients
Serves 6

1 tablespoon olive oil
1 onion, peeled and finely chopped
2 cloves garlic, crushed
1 potato, peeled and finely chopped
500 grams ripe tomatoes, peeled and chopped
Fresh celery leaves, chopped
½ teaspoon dried oregano
1 tablespoon basil leaves, chopped
Salt and freshly ground pepper
Grated Parmesan cheese to serve

Method
Heat the oil in a pot, add the onion, garlic and potato and sauté until the onion is soft.
Add the tomatoes, oregano, basil and celery. Season and bring to the boil whilst stirring occasionally. Simmer covered for 15 minutes.
Bring off the heat and cool slightly. Process the soup until smooth.
Serve with the grated cheese.

Onion Soup From Santorini

Ingredients
Serves 6

2 tablespoons olive oil
600 grams onions
3 potatoes
1 ½ cups tomato juice
2 cups homemade chicken stock (Page 9)
Salt and freshly ground pepper
150 grams Kefalotiri cheese to serve

Method
Peel and thinly slice the onions. Peel and finely dice the potatoes. Heat the oil in a pot and sauté the onions and potato until soft. Season and mix in the rest of the ingredients. Simmer covered for 25 minutes whilst stirring occasionally. In the meantime dice up the cheese. Remove from heat, stir in the diced cheese and serve immediately.

Meatball Soup from Athens

Ingredients
Serves 6 to 8

2 tablespoons olive oil
500 grams minced beef
2/3 cup rice
1 medium onion, finely chopped
1 tablespoon finely chopped parsley
1 egg, lightly beaten
Salt and pepper
Egg and lemon sauce

For the egg and lemon sauce
2 cups hot homemade chicken broth
3 eggs
Juice of 2 lemons
2 teaspoons corn flour

Method
Place all the ingredients for the meatballs except the oil into a bowl. Mix the ingredients well and form the mixture into small meatballs. Pour the oil into a pot and place the meatballs. Cover the meatballs with water and bring to the boil. Season and simmer covered for 30 minutes.
Meantime prepare the sauce: Mix the corn flour and lemon juice in a small container. Beat the eggs in a small bowl and then beat in the lemon mixture. Gradually add the hot broth whilst beating continually.
When the meatball soup is cooked, remove from fire and pour in the egg and lemon sauce. Stir and serve immediately garnished with some finely chopped parsley.
In Greece this soup is usually served on special occasions. Make your meatballs very small so that your plate of soup will look refined!

Smoky Bacon Vegetable Soup

Ingredients
Serves 6 to 8

1 teaspoon olive oil
8 rashers back bacon
1 onion, peeled and chopped
3 cloves garlic, finely chopped
2 carrots, peeled and chopped
200 grams cabbage, finely shredded
Fresh celery leaves, chopped
1 tablespoon chopped parsley
200 grams tomatoes, peeled and chopped
200 grams red lentils
1.5 litres homemade chicken stock
Salt and freshly ground pepper
Grated parmesan cheese to serve

Method

Remove all the fat from the bacon and chop up. Heat the oil in a pot and fry the bacon until crispy. Mix in the onion, garlic, celery and carrots and stir over a high heat for 3 minutes. Add the lentils and tomatoes and pour in the stock. Bring to the boil and simmer covered for 45 minutes. Mix in the cabbage, season and cook for a further 15 minutes. Remove from fire, cool slightly and process the soup until smooth. Stir in the parsley, and return the soup to the pot. Reheat and serve immediately with the grated cheese.

Aljotta – Maltese fish soup

Ingredients

Serves 6 to 8

1 tablespoon olive oil
1.5 kilos small fresh fish suitable for a soup
1 large onion, peeled and chopped
3 cloves garlic, finely chopped
2 carrots, peeled and chopped
Fresh celery leaves
1 tablespoon chopped basil leaves
1 tablespoon fresh marjoram
1 tablespoon fresh mint leaves
2.5 litres water
1 cup rice
Salt and freshly ground pepper
Lemon wedges to serve.

Method

Wash and clean out the fish. Your fishmonger could do that for you if you smile nicely and tip him! Rinse the fish under running water.
Heat the oil in a pot and sauté the onion and garlic until soft. Add the carrots and cook for 3 minutes. Mix in the rest of the ingredients except the rice. Season and bring to the boil. Simmer covered for 2 hours.
Bring off the heat and pass the soup through a sieve whilst mashing up the ingredients to extract all the juices.
Return the soup to the pot, bring to the boil and add the rice. Simmer until the rice is just cooked and serve hot with lemon wedges.

Martina's Soup

Ingredients
Serves 6

2 tablespoons olive oil
2 tablespoons butter
2 onions, peeled and chopped
2 leeks, peeled and chopped
3 apples, peeled, cored and chopped
1 large celery heart, chopped
1 litre homemade chicken stock
2 tablespoons corn flour
2 tablespoons water
Salt and freshly ground pepper
Some tender celery leaves to garnish
Grated Parmesan cheese to serve.

Method
Heat the oil and butter in a pot and sauté the onions and leeks until soft. Mix in the celery and cook over medium heat for 5 minutes. Add the apples and chicken stock and bring to the boil. Season and simmer covered for 25 minutes.
Mix the corn flour with the water and stir into the pot. Remove from heat, cool slightly and process the soup until smooth. Reheat the soup but do not boil.
Serve hot garnished with fine celery leaves and the grated cheese.

Cream of Carrot Soup

Ingredients
Serves 8

2 tablespoons olive oil
2 onions, peeled and chopped
1 clove garlic chopped
10 carrots, peeled and chopped
4 potatoes, peeled and chopped
1 teaspoon thyme
1 bay leaf
6 cups homemade vegetable stock
1 ½ cups skimmed milk
1 ½ cups grated Emmenthal cheese
Salt and freshly ground pepper

Method
Heat the oil in a pot and sauté the onion until soft. Mix in the garlic and thyme and cook for 2 minutes. Add the carrots, potatoes, bayleaf and stock, stir and bring to the boil. Season, cover the pot and simmer for 25 minutes.
Remove from heat, add the milk and process the soup.
Return the soup to the pot and mix in the cheese. Heat up the soup until the cheese melts and is integrated into the soup.
Serve garnished either with some finely chopped parsley or some crutons.

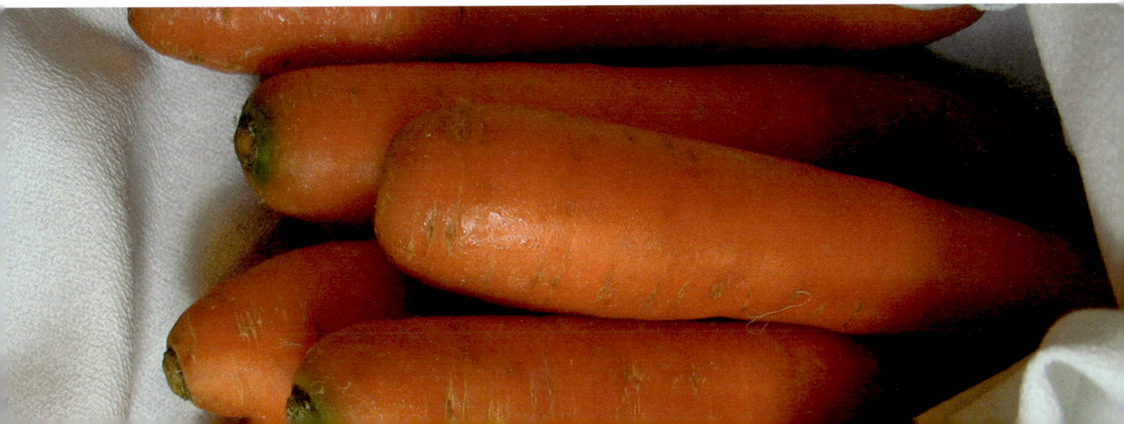

Your Winter Vegetable Soup

Ingredients
Serves 8

3 tablespoons olive oil
2 onions finely chopped
3 carrots, finely chopped
Handful tender celery leaves, chopped
2 parsnips, finely diced
2 turnips, finely diced
2 potatoes, finely diced
1 leek, finely sliced
500 grams tomatoes, peeled and diced
100 grams haricot beans
2 litres homemade vegetable stock (Page 10)
75 grams Basmati rice
Salt and freshly ground pepper
Finely chopped parsley to garnish
Grated Parmesan cheese to serve

Method
Soak the haricot beans overnight.
Heat the oil in a large pot and sauté the onions, carrots and celery until the vegetables are soft. Mix in the parsnips, turnips, potatoes and leeks, season and continue cooking for 5 minutes. Add the tomatoes and haricot beans, stir and cook for 2 minutes. Pour in the stock, bring to the boil and simmer covered for 25 minutes. Mix in the Basmati rice, bring again to the boil and simmer for 8 minutes or until the rice is just cooked. Remove from heat, mix in the parsley and serve hot with the grated cheese.

This is a hearty and very nutritious winter soup. It is a complete healthy meal in itself!

Pizza, Rice & Pasta

A Sicilian Calzone

Ingredients
Serves 4

Pizza dough as for Pizza Peron (Page 30)
450 grams frozen spinach
600 grams ricotta cheese
10 small fresh mozzarella balls, halved
3 eggs, lightly beaten
50 grams anchovy fillets
Salt and freshly ground pepper
Olive oil
1 egg white lightly beaten
3 tablespoons sesame seeds

Method
Thaw the spinach and squeeze out the juices completely. Chop up coarsely.
Place the ricotta in a bowl and mash up with a fork. Season with salt and pepper and mix in the spinach. Add the beaten eggs and mozzarella balls and mix well.
Grease a baking tray with butter and dust with semolina.
Flatten out the pizza dough over a floured surface. Use the palms of your hands to flatten out and form the dough into a rectangular shape, wide enough to fit on your prepared tray. Spread the mixture over the dough keeping 4 cms. away from the edges of the dough. Arrange the anchovy fillets over the mixture. Roll up into a calzone keeping the seam of the dough at the top. Place the calzone on the prepared tray and brush with the egg white. Sprinkle the sesame seeds and drizzle some olive oil. Bake in a moderate oven for 75 minutes. Bring out of the oven and stand for 10 minutes before slicing and serving.

Pizza Peron

Ingredients
Serves 6

For the pastry
3 teaspoons yeast
1 teaspoon sugar
1 cup lukewarm water
3 cups plain flour
2 chilli peppers deseeded and finely chopped
3 tablespoons olive oil
½ tablespoon salt

For the topping
4 tablespoons olive oil
3 onions, peeled and chopped
1 chilli pepper deseeded and finely chopped
300 grams canned sweetcorn, drained
300 grams canned kidney beans, drained
500 grams lean minced beef
4 hard-boiled eggs, chopped
5 tablespoons grated Parmesn cheese
Salt

Method
Add the yeast and sugar to the lukewarm water and mix well. Cover and stand in a warm place for 15 minutes.
Sift the flour and salt into a bowl and mix in the finely chopped chilli. Make a well in the centre and pour in the oil and yeast mixture. Mix, and knead with your hands until a smooth dough is produced. Place the dough on a lightly floured surface and knead for a few minutes. Place the dough in a lightly oiled bowl, cover and leave to stand in a warm place for 30 minutes to prove.
Grease a large pizza pan or baking tray with butter and dust with flour or better still with semolina. Flatten out the pizza dough over a floured surface by using the palms of your hands. Place the pastry on the prepared tray.
Heat the oil in a pan and sauté the onion and chilli until soft. Mix in the beef and cook over a high heat to brown it. Season with salt. Mix in the sweetcorn and kidney beans, remove from heat and cool.
Spread the mixture over the pastry and sprinkle the hard-boiled eggs and the grated Parmesan. Drizzle with some olive oil.
Bake in a hot oven until bubbly and cooked through.
You could make your gluten-free Pizza Peron by using gluten-free pizza bases (Page 2), and cooking the sweetcorn and kidney beans yourself instead of using the canned ones.

Gluten-Free Roasted Vegetable Pizza

Ingredients
Makes 4 pizzas

1 medium aubergine
2 courgettes, sliced
2 red onions, peeled and sliced
2 cloves garlic, sliced
1 red, green and yellow pepper
300 grams pumpkin, diced
200 grams mushrooms, sliced
4 tablespoons olive oil
2 tablespoons hand-chopped basil leaves
1 quantity tomato sauce (Page 4)
4 gluten-free pizza bases (Page 2)
Salt and freshly ground pepper

Method
Cut the aubergine into 1 cm.chunks, sprinkle with salt and leave to drain for 20 minutes.
Rinse the aubergines under running water and leave to drain.
Halve the peppers, remove the seeds and cut into 1 cm. strips.
Place the vegetables in a bowl, drizzle with oil and season with pepper.
Line a baking tray with baking paper and place the vegetables in a single layer. Roast in a hot oven for 35 minutes. Bring out of the oven and season with salt. Mix in the basil leaves.
Have ready 4 pizza bases and bake them for 8 minutes. Bring them out of the oven and spread them with the tomato sauce. Spread the roast vegetables equally over the sauce. Return the pizzas to the oven and bake for a further 15 minutes or until bubbly and cooked through.
You can freeze the pizzas after baking and spreading the topping. When required, you only need to place the filling and bake them for 20 minutes, straight out of the freezer!

Greek Spinach Rice

Ingredients
Serves 4

1 ½ kilos fresh spinach
4 tablespoons olive oil
4 onions, peeled and finely chopped
3 teaspoons dried dill tops
2 tablespoons finely chopped parsley
1 cup rice
2 cups warm water
Juice of 3 lemons
Salt and freshly ground pepper

Method
Pick, wash and blanch the spinach in salty water. Drain the spinach and leave to cool. Squeeze out all the excess liquid and chop up.
Heat the oil in a pot and brown the onions. Mix in the spinach and cook over a moderate heat for 2 minutes. Add the water and bring to the boil. Mix in the rice, dill and parsley. Season, cover the pot and simmer for 16 minutes or until the rice is just cooked. You may need to add a little more water during cooking.
Remove from heat, cool slightly and mix in the lemon juice.
Serve as a starter with some grated Kefalotiri cheese or on its own with meat or fish dishes. A very versatile dish which is also gluten-free!

Classic Risi e Bisi

Ingredients
Serves 6

1 tablespoon olive oil
2 tablespoons butter
2 onions, peeled and finely chopped
1 cup dry white wine
75 grams gluten-free pancetta, diced
1 tablespoon finely chopped parsley
1 tablespoon finely chopped celery leaves
400 grams garden peas
300 grams Vialone Nano rice
1 litre homemade beef stock (Page 10)
Salt and freshly ground pepper
Extra 2 tablespoons butter
60 grams grated Parmesan cheese

Method
Heat the oil and butter in a large pot. Add the onions and sauté until soft. Increase the heat and pour in the wine. Stir and leave to reduce. Mix in the pancetta and cook for 2 minutes and then lower the heat. Add the parsley, celery leaves and the peas. Mix and cook for 1 minute. Mix in the rice, stir and then pour in the beef stock. Season and bring to the boil. Simmer for 18 minutes or until the rice is just cooked. Remove from heat and mix in the extra butter and the grated Parmesan. Serve immediately.
A classic Italian rice dish. Makes an elegant starter to your luncheon party and its gluten-free.

Courgette and Rosemary Rice Bake

Ingredients
Serves 6

350 grams Arborio rice
4 tablespoons olive oil
3 onions, peeled and chopped
4 cloves garlic, peeled and chopped
3 tablespoons fresh rosemary, chopped
500 grams courgettes, coarsely grated
½ teaspoon freshly grated nutmeg
4 eggs, lightly beaten
200 grams Gruyere cheese, coarsely grated
Salt and freshly ground pepper
Some extra grated Gruyere cheese
Gluten-free tomato sauce (Page 4) to serve

Method
Grease a spring-form tin with butter and line the base and sides of the tin with baking paper. Grease over the paper.
Cook the rice in a pot of boiling salty water. Cook for only 8 minutes. Drain the rice and reserve.
Heat the oil in a large pan. Add the onions and sauté until soft. Mix in the garlic and rosemary and cook for 3 minutes. Add the courgettes and nutmeg, stir and cook on a high heat for 4 minutes. Transfer the mixture to a large bowl and leave to cool.
Add the eggs, grated cheese and par-cooked rice to the courgette mixture. Season and mix well. Pour the mixture into the prepared tin and sprinkle the extra Gruyere cheese on top.
Bake in a moderate oven for 50 minutes or until golden brown and cooked through.
Bring out of the oven and stand for 5 minutes. Turn onto a suitable round serving dish and remove tin.
Heat up the tomato sauce and pour it over the rice bake. Serve garnished with some fresh rosemary.

Risotto alla Contadina

Ingredients
Serves 6

3 tablespoons olive oil
2 onions, peeled and sliced
2 cloves garlic, peeled and sliced
150 grams garden peas
150 grams asparagus tips
200 grams mushrooms, sliced
300 grams small courgettes, sliced
150 grams broad beans, skinned
600 grams tomatoes, skinned, deseeded and chopped
3 cups Arborio rice
5 cups homemade chicken stock (Page 9)
5 tablespoons grated Parmesan cheese
Salt and freshly ground pepper
Fresh basil leaves to garnish

Method
Heat the oil in a pot. Add the onions and garlic, and sauté until soft. Mix in all the vegetables except the tomatoes. Stir and cook over medium heat for 3 minutes. Add the tomatoes and the stock, stir and bring to the boil. Mix in the rice, season and simmer uncovered for 17 minutes. Bring off the heat and stir in the grated Parmesan. Cover and stand for 3 minutes.
Transfer the rice to a suitable serving dish, garnish with fresh basil leaves and serve hot.
Another gluten-free and nutritious risotto for you.

Diego's Andalusian Rice Dish

Ingredients
Serves 6

3 tablespoons sesame seeds
4 tablespoons olive oil
120 grams blanched almonds
2 onions, peeled and chopped
4 cloves garlic, peeled and chopped
1 chilli pepper, deseeded and chopped
2 teaspoons fresh rosemary
2 red and 2 yellow peppers
300 grams canned kidney beans, drained
500 grams lean minced beef
400 grams long grain rice
2 teaspoons turmeric
3 tablespoons wine vinegar
Salt

Method
Bring a pot of water to the boil. Add some salt and the turmeric, stir and add the rice.
Cook the rice for just 14 minutes, stirring occasionally. Drain the rice well and return it to the pot. Add 1 tablespoon olive oil and stir to coat the rice with the oil.
Halve the peppers, remove the seeds and cut into strips
Toast the sesame seeds in a non-stick pan until just golden. Reserve.
Heat 3 tablespoons olive oil in a large pan and fry the almonds until golden.
Remove the almonds from the pan and place on a kitchen towel. Reserve.
Add the onions to the pan and sauté until soft. Mix in the garlic, chilli and rosemary and cook for 2 minutes. Increase the heat and add the peppers. Cook until just soft and then mix in the kidney beans. Cook for a while and then mix in the minced beef. Brown the meat with the vegetables and season to taste.
Add the rice and stir it into the rest of the ingredients. Cook for 3 minutes whilst stirring.
Transfer the risotto to a suitable dish and sprinkle it with the vinegar.
Sprinkle the sesame seeds and garnish with some fresh rosemary.

Pete's Pappardelle

Ingredients
Serves 4

500 grams fresh Pappardelle
2 tablespoons olive oil
2 tablespoons butter
100 grams pine nuts
100 grams walnuts, coarsely chopped
3 tablespoons fresh sage, hand-chopped
Salt and freshly ground pepper
Grated Parmesan cheese

Method
Heat the oil in a pan and gently fry the pine nuts until just golden. Remove the pine nuts with a scoop and reserve. Add the butter, and when it melts into the oil, add the chopped sage leaves. Cook the sage over medium heat until it starts to change colour to light golden. Mix in the chopped walnuts, stir and cook for 1 minute. Season with salt and pepper. Bring off the heat and mix in the pine nuts and 3 tablespoons grated Parmesan cheese.
Cook the Pappardelle in abundant salty water. Leave 'al dente'. Drain the pasta and return it to the pot. Mix in the nutty sauce and then transfer it to a suitable serving bowl. Garnish with fresh sage leaves and serve with more grated Parmesan.

Le Lumache di Mamma Lucia

Ingredients
Serves 6

500 grams Lumache
(large snail-shaped pasta)
1 kilo ricotta
150 grams walnuts, shelled
and chopped
50 grams pine nuts
1 teaspoon olive oil
3 tablespoons chopped parsley
3 eggs, lightly beaten
4 tablespoons grated parmesan cheese
Salt and freshly ground pepper
2 tablespoons dry breadcrumbs
Homemade tomato sauce (Page 4)
Grated Parmesan cheese to serve

Method
Grease a baking pan with butter and coat with the breadcrumbs.
Bring a large pot of salty water to the boil. Add the Lumache and cook them very 'al dente', about 11 minutes. Drain the Lumache carefully and reserve.
Heat the olive oil in a non-stick pan and lightly fry the walnuts and pine nuts. Reserve.
Place the ricotta in a bowl and mash it up with a fork. Mix in the eggs, parsley, grated cheese and the nuts. Season with salt and pepper. Stuff the Lumache and place them steadily side by side in the prepared pan. The Lumache must fill the pan in a single layer.
Pour the tomato sauce over the Lumache to cover them completely. Bake in a moderate oven for 45 minutes. Bring out of the oven and stand for 3 minutes.
Serve with the grated Parmesan cheese.

Maglie ai Porri

Ingredients
Serves 4

400 grams Casarecce (Italian pasta)
3 tablespoons olive oil
1 tablespoon butter
2 medium onions, finely chopped
2 cloves garlic, finely chopped
600 grams leeks, peeled and finely sliced
4 tablespoons fresh basil, hand-chopped
2 cups fresh milk
Salt and freshly ground pepper
Grated Parmesan cheese to serve

Method
Heat the butter and olive oil in a large pan and sauté the onion with the garlic until just soft. Mix in the sliced leeks and cook over a medium heat until the vegetables start to change colour. Add the milk, stir and simmer for 8 minutes. Season with salt and pepper.
Bring a pot of salty water to the boil and add the pasta. Cook the pasta but leave it very 'al dente', a little bit more than usual. Drain the pasta and mix it into the sauce. Simmer the pasta with the sauce until the pasta is just done. Mix in the basil leaves and 3 tablespoons grated Parmesan cheese. Bring off the heat and serve immediately with more grated Parmesan.
An unusual wintery pasta dish!

Spaghetti Odori di Sorrento

Ingredients
Serves 4

500 grams spaghetti 3
8 tablespoons olive oil
8 tablespoons lemon juice
1 tablespoon finely grated lemon rind
2 tablespoons finely chopped parsley
3 tablespoons hand-chopped fresh basil
6 tablespoons grated Parmesan cheese
350 grams canned tuna, drained and flaked
Salt and freshly ground pepper
Grated Parmesan cheese to serve

Method
Bring a pot of salty water to the boil. Add the spaghetti and cook them until just 'al dente'. Drain the spaghetti and reserve.

Meantime place the olive oil, the lemon juice and lemon rind, the parley, basil, and grated Parmesan in a food processor. Season with salt and pepper and process until smooth. You might need to add a little warm water from the spaghetti pot to obtain a smooth sauce.

Mix in the flaked tuna.

Place the spaghetti in a large suitable serving bowl, mix in the tuna sauce and garnish with fresh basil leaves. Serve with the grated Parmesan.

I had enjoyed this delicious and unusual pasta dish on the terrace of a friend's home in Sorrento overlooking the gulf of Naples. The view was spectacular to say the least. Sorrento is famous for its olive oil, its lemons and fragrant basil. The spaghetti dish turned out excellent, served just lukewarm!

Fusilli Turriddu

Ingredients
Serves 4

500 grams Fusilli (Italian pasta)
2 medium aubergines
2 green peppers
1 red and 1 yellow pepper
4 tablespoons olive oil
4 cloves garlic peeled and chopped
1 chilli pepper, deseeded and finely chopped
400 grams tomatoes, peeled and chopped
200 grams tomato concentrate
2 teaspoons dried thyme
Salt
Grated Pecorino cheese to serve

Method
Wash the aubergines and cut off the stem. Place the whole aubergines in a hot oven directly on the shelves. Bake for 45 minutes. Bring out of the oven and cool completely.
Peel the aubergines over a bowl to save any juices that might drip. Mash up the resulting pulp with a fork.
Halve the peppers and remove the seeds. Chop up finely.
Heat the oil in a pan and sauté the garlic with the chilli until soft. Mix in the peppers and cook for 3 minutes and then stir in the tomato concentrate with the thyme and cook for 1 minute.Add the aubergine pulp, mix and cook for 1 minute. Mix in the chopped tomatoes, season with salt and leave the sauce to simmer uncovered for 10 minutes.
Meantime cook the Fusilli in boiling salty water, leaving them 'al dente'.
Drain the Fusilli and return them to the pot. Pour in the sauce and 3 tablespoons grated Pecorino.
Give the pasta a good stirring and serve it with more grated Pecorino cheese.

Rigatoni alla Siciliana

Ingredients
Serves 4

500 grams Rigatoni
2 tablespoons olive oil
2 garlic cloves, peeled and finely chopped
1 chilli pepper, deseeded and finely chopped
60 grams capers, drained
350 grams fresh swordfish
250 grams cherry tomatoes, halved
150 grams pitted black olives, halved
2 tablespoons finely chopped parsley
Salt
Extra finely chopped parsley

Method
Wash the swordfish and dice into 3 cm.cubes.
Heat the oil in a large pan. Add the garlic, the chilli and the capers. Sauté for 2 minutes. Mix in the swordfish and cook for 5 minutes over a medium heat. Add the cherry tomatoes, the olives and the parsley. Season with salt and cook for 4 minutes stirring occasionally.
Cook the Rigatoni in abundant salty water and leave very 'al dente'. Drain the pasta well.
Add the pasta to the sauce in the pan and mix well. Cook for 2 minutes and then mix in the extra chopped parsley.
Serve immediately.

Poultry, Meat
and Fish

Pete's Pie

Ingredients
Serves 6

600 grams gluten-free savoury pastry (Page 5)
1 tablespoon olive oil
2 onions, peeled and sliced
600 grams lean minced beef
3 carrots, peeled and diced
3 courgettes, sliced
250 grams mushrooms, sliced
200 grams garden peas
A bunch of tender celery leaves, chopped
Grated zest of 1 lemon
2 tablespoons grated Parmesan cheese
3 eggs, lightly beaten
Freshly grated pepper

Method
Grease a pie dish with a little butter and dust with flour.
Roll out the pastry on a lightly floured surface and use a third of the pastry to cover the base and sides of the pie dish.
Heat the oil in a pan and saute' the onions until soft. Add the meat and brown over a high heat with the onions. Mix in the carrots, lower the heat and cook for 3 minutes. Mix in the rest of the vegtables and the lemon zest. Cover the pan and cook over a low heat for 15 minutes, stirring occasionally. Bring off the heat, season and leave to cool. Mix in the grated cheese and the eggs. Pour the mixture into the prepared pie dish. Roll out the remaining pastry and cover the pie. Seal well and puncture the surface of the pie with a fork in a few places. Bake in a hot oven for 10 minutes then lower the heat and continue baking for 50 minutes in a moderate to hot oven.
Bring out of the oven, stand for 5 minutes and serve.
For a vegetarian version of this pie, substitute the beef with 600 grams diced pumpkin, potato and turnip. Mix in a teaspoon of good curry whilst cooking the vegetables.

Italian Braised Chicken

Ingredients
Serves 4

40 grams butter
2 tablespoons olive oil
4 cloves garlic, halved
A few sprigs of fresh rosemary
1 chicken weighing about 1.5 kilos
200 ml. dry white wine
Salt and freshly ground pepper
Sprigs of fresh rosemary to garnish

Method
Wash and quarter the chicken. Pat it dry with a kitchen towel.
Heat the oil and butter in a large frying pan. Add the garlic and rosemary and sauté gently for 2 minutes. Place the chicken parts in the pan and cook the chicken over a high heat until it browns all over. Turn the chicken occasionally. Pour the wine over the chicken and season with salt and pepper. Cover the pan and simmer for 25 minutes or until the chicken is very tender.
Garnish with fresh rosemary and serve with mashed potatoes and steamed seasonal vegetables.
This simple and quick recipe has always been a great success with my guests.

Moroccan Chicken Tagine

Ingredients
Serves 4

2 tablespoons olive oil
1 big fresh chicken
2 onions, peeled and finely chopped
2 cloves garlic, peeled and finely chopped
1 kilo tomatoes, peeled and chopped
1 teaspoon ground cinnamon
½ teaspoon grated fresh ginger
1 teaspoon turmeric
4 tablespoons good honey
1 tablespoon olive oil, extra
80 grams blanched almonds, chopped
2 tablespoons sesame seeds
Salt and freshly ground pepper

Method
Wash and cut up the chicken into serving pieces. Heat the oil in a tagine or large pan. Add the onions and garlic and cook until the onion changes colour. Increase the heat and mix in all the other ingredients except the honey, almonds, sesame seeds and the extra oil. When the ingredients become bubbly decrease the heat, season and cover the pan. Cook over a low heat for about 45 minutes. Occasionally turn over the chicken pieces to cook evenly.
Remove the chicken pieces from the pan and keep warm. Cook the sauce over a medium heat until it is reduced to a creamy consistency. Stir occasionally. Stir in the honey and add the chicken pieces. Give the ingredients a good stir to heat through and then remove from heat.
Heat the extra oil in a small pan and gently fry the almonds for a few moments. Mix in the sesame seeds and continue frying until just golden. Sprinkle the almond and sesame mixture over the chicken and serve immediately. Serve with plain-boiled rice.

Mum's Chicken Casserole

Ingredients
Serves 4

2 tablespoons olive oil
2 large onions, peeled and thickly sliced
3 cloves garlic, peeled and chopped
4 chicken thigh cutlets
4 chicken drumsticks
Few sprigs fresh rosemary
3 medium potatoes, peeled and cut in chunks
4 tomatoes, peeled and chopped
½ cup homemade chicken stock (Page 9)
150 grams mushrooms, thickly sliced
6 bacon rashers, rinds removed
100 grams whole black olives
Salt and freshly ground pepper

Method
Heat the oil in a large flame-proof casserole dish. Add the onions, rosemary and garlic and sauté until the onions are soft. Add the chicken and cook, stirring, until just browned all over. Add the potatoes, tomatoes and stock. Season with salt and pepper and place uncovered in a hot oven. Bake for 1 hour.
Bring out of the oven and add the mushrooms, bacon and olives. Give the ingredients a good stir and return to the oven. Bake for a further 20 minutes.
A hearty wintery roast!

Lebanese Spiced Chicken

Ingredients
Serves 4

4 tablespoons olive oil
1 red chilli pepper deseeded and finely chopped
4 cloves garlic, peeled and finely chopped
2 onions, peeled and finely chopped
1 small piece fresh ginger, peeled and grated
1 teaspoon ground cumin
1 teaspoon ground coriander
½ teaspoon ground cinnamon
4 tablespoons pistachio nuts
4 skinless chicken breasts, thinly sliced
A bunch of fresh rocket leaves
400 grams couscous
2 tablespoons olive oil
Salt

Method
Wash and trim the rocket and leave to drain.
Bring 400 ml. water to the boil. Stir in 2 tablespoons olive oil and some salt. Mix in the couscous and stand for 8 minutes. Fluff up with a fork.
Combine the chilli, garlic, onions, ginger, cumin, coriander, cinnamon and pistachios in a bowl. Stir in 2 tablespoons olive oil and season with salt.
Heat the rest of the oil in a large pan and add the chicken slices. Brown the chicken on both sides over a high heat. Mix in the spicy mixture and cook for a few minutes. Add the rocket leaves and cook for 1 minute whilst stirring.
Transfer the chicken to a large serving dish and then place the prepared couscous all around the chicken. Serve at once.
For the gluten-free version, serve on a bed of rice. Equally tasty!

A Warm Chicken Salad

Ingredients
Serves 4

2 chicken breasts cut into strips
3 tablespoons olive oil
3 tablespoons sesame seeds
3 tablespoons pine nuts
200 grams tender spinach leaves
1 avocado halved and stoned
100 grams gluten-free Pancetta, cubed
80 grams Parmesan cheese
Salt and freshly ground pepper

For the dressing
4 tablespoons olive oil
2 tablespoons lemon juice
1 teaspoon gluten-free mustard

Method
Wash and trim the spinach leaves and leave to drain well. Cut the avocado halves into slices 1 cm.thick. Place the spinach and avocado slices in a large salad bowl.
Place the ingredients for the dressing in a small jar with a tight-fitting lid. Season with salt and pepper, close the jar and shake well.
Use a potato peeler to shave long strips of Parmesan cheese. Reserve.
Heat 2 teaspoons olive oil in a small pan and gently fry the pine nuts and sesame seeds until just golden. Reserve.
Heat the rest of the oil in a large pan and add the Pancetta cubes. Cook over a medium heat until beginning to turn crispy. Mix in the chicken strips, season and continue cooking until the chicken is done.
Quickly lift the chicken and Pancetta from the pan and toss them with the spinach and avocado in the bowl. Pour over the dressing and toss again. Sprinkle over the pine nuts and sesame and then garnish with the shaved Parmesan. A feast of a winter salad!

Duck Breast with a Citrus Glaze

Ingredients
Serves 4

2 tablespoons olive oil
4 duck breasts
80 grams brown sugar
½ teaspoon ground cloves
Finely grated zest
 and juice of 2 oranges
Finely grated zest
 and juice of 1 lemon
Finely grated zest
 and juice of 1 lime
500 grams baby carrots, peeled
500 grams Mange Tout
Orange wedges
Salt and freshly ground pepper

Method

Boil the baby carrots and mange tout separately in salty water until just done. Drain and keep the vegetables warm.

Choose duck breasts with their skin on. Wash the breasts and use a sharp pointed knife to score the skin of the duck in a criss-cross manner. Rub with salt and pepper.

Place the sugar and ground cloves in a small saucepan. Add enough water to just cover and heat gently until dissolved. Add the zests and juices of the fruit and bring to the boil.

Simmer uncovered until the the liquid is syrupy and then remove from heat.

Heat the oil in a pan. Place the duck breasts skin-side up in the pan. Cook over a high heat until both sides are just done. Remove from heat and keep warm.

Slice the duck breasts diagonally and place on serving plates. Arrange the Mange Tout, the carrots and the orange wedges on each plate. Spoon over the hot glaze and serve immediately.

An easy and healthy way of serving duck in winter.

Sicilian Pork Marsala

Ingredients
Serves 4

4 tablespoons olive oil
2 cloves garlic, peeled and halved
800g pork medallions about 1 cm. thick
300 ml. fine Marsala wine
Grated zest of 1 orange
Salt and freshly ground pepper

Method
Combine the Marsala with the orange zest. Use a kitchen hammer to lightly pound the pork.
Heat the oil in a large pan and gently fry the garlic until just golden. Quickly scoop out the garlic and add the pork medallions. Saute over a high heat until browned on both sides. Season with salt and pepper and pour in the Marsala mixture. Cook uncovered for a few minutes until the meat is done and the gravy reduced slightly.
Serve immediately with some boiled potatoes and steamed seasonal vegetables.
You will be coming back to this recipe quite often!

Pete's Spicy Pork Meatballs

Ingredients
Serves 6

1 kilo lean pork mince
1 small onion, finely chopped
2 cloves garlic, finely chopped
1 teaspoon ground allspice
1 teaspoon ground ginger
½ teaspoon grated nutmeg
½ teaspoon cinnamon
Pinch ground cloves
3 eggs, lightly beaten
70 grams pure ground almonds
Salt and freshly ground pepper
A little olive oil

Method
Place all the ingredients except the oil in a bowl. Mix all the ingredients together well and cover the bowl. Refrigerate for 15 minutes.
Form the mixture into balls and flatten slightly. Place on your grill rack and brush with olive oil. Place under a hot grill until the meatballs are cooked through.
Serve immediately with mashed potatoes and grilled tomatoes.
Could also be your kids' favourite! Will introduce them to the wonderful spices used to enhance appetising dishes and meals.

An Italian Beef Stew

Ingredients
Serves 6

3 tablespoons olive oil
1.5 kilos stewing beef
2 large onions, peeled and chopped
3 carrots, peeled and sliced
200 grams mushrooms, thickly sliced
6 tomatoes, peeled and chopped
4 potatoes, peeled and cut in chunks
2 tablespoons parsley, chopped
200 grams green olives, halved and pitted
200 ml. good red wine
200 ml. homemade beef stock (Page 10)
Salt and freshly ground pepper

Method
Trim the meat of any excess fat and cut into 4 cm. cubes.
Heat the oil in a flameproof casserole. Add the beef cubes and brown on all sides turning frequently. Mix in the onions and the carrots, cover the casserole and let the vegetables sweat with the meat for 8 minutes. Stir occasionally. Mix in the tomatoes, the wine and the beef stock. When the stew starts to boil, add the potatoes, the mushrooms and the parsley. Season with salt and pepper and give the ingredients a good stirring. Cover the casserole and place it in a moderately hot oven. Cook for 90 minutes. Bring out of the oven and mix in the olives.
Bake for a further 5 minutes. Bring out of the oven and serve hot.

Moroccan Beef Tagine

Ingredients
Serves 6

1 tablespoon olive oil
1 kilo beef steak cut into thick slices
2 onions, peeled and chopped
2 cloves garlic, peeled and chopped
2 teaspoons fresh ginger, finely chopped
½ teaspoon cayenne pepper
Good pinch of saffron threads
Juice and grated rind of 1 lemon
4 tomatoes, peeled and chopped
600 grams garden peas
200 grams black olives, halved and pitted
Salt and freshly ground pepper

Method
Trim off any excess fat from the beef and cut it into 3 cm. cubes.
Put the beef in a tagine or large pan with the olive oil. Add the onions, garlic, ginger, cayenne and the saffron threads. Season with salt and pepper. Pour enough water to just cover the meat. Give the ingredients a good stir and bring to the boil. Reduce the heat, cover the pan and simmer for 90 minutes.
Add the peas, tomatoes, the lemon juice and rind, and the olives. Stir well and continue cooking uncovered for another 10 minutes.
Serve hot with fresh bread.
Serve with plain-boiled rice for a gluten-free version.

Camilla's Rabbit Casserole

Ingredients
Serves 4

4 tablespoons olive oil
1 rabbit of around 1.25 kilos, skinned
4 cloves garlic, chopped
300 ml. good red wine
Few sprigs rosemary, chopped
8 tomatoes, peeled and chopped
300 grams black olives, halved and pitted
Salt and freshly ground pepper

Method
Wash the rabbit and cut into serving pieces.
Heat the oil in a large pan. Add the rabbit pieces, the garlic and the rosemary.
Cook the rabbit over a medium heat until it is browned on all sides. Turn frequently. Add the wine and season with salt and pepper. Cover the pan and simmer for 40 minutes. Mix in the tomatoes and olives, cover pan and continue simmering for 20 minutes or until the rabbit meat is tender.
For a gluten-free version serve hot with some sauté potatoes.
My Neapolitan friend Camilla had served this wonderful rabbit stew on a bed of freshly made tagliatelle. Try it the Neapolitan way!

Fathi's Tunisian Lamb Stew

Ingredients

3 tablespoons olive oil
1 kilo boned shoulder of lamb
2 onions, peeled and finely chopped
2 cloves garlic, peeled and finely chopped
1 teaspoon grated fresh ginger
1 teaspoon turmeric
2 teaspoons ground cinnamon
½ teaspoon freshly ground pepper
300 grams pitted prunes, halved
3 tablespoons good honey
2 tablespoons sesame seeds
100 grams blanched almonds, chopped
Salt

Method

Wash the lamb and trim off most of the fat. Cut into 12 portions.
Place the lamb in a big pan. Add the oil, onions, garlic, ginger, turmeric cinnamon, salt and the ground pepper. Add just enough water to cover and then stir the ingredients together. Place on a high heat and bring to the boil. Stir the ingredients and cover the pan. Lower the heat and simmer for 75 minutes or until the meat is very tender.
Add the prunes and continue cooking uncovered for 15 minutes. Stir in the honey and continue simmering for 5 minutes.
Meantime, heat 2 teaspoons olive oil in a small pan. Add the combined almonds and sesame seeds and toast very lightly until just coloured.
Serve the lamb sprinkled with the toasted nuts in a large ceramic dish. A bowl of plain couscous (See page 52), would make an ideal accompaniment to this lamb.

Shepherds' Lamb

Ingredients
Serves 4

3 tablespoons olive oil
1 kilo boned shoulder or leg of lamb
500 grams mushrooms, thickly sliced
500 grams tender spinach leaves
½ teaspoon freshly ground nutmeg
200 ml. dry white wine
Salt and freshly ground pepper

Method
Wash the spinach and trim off the stems.
Wash the lamb and trim off any excess fat.
Heat the oil in a flameproof casserole. Add the meat and cook over a moderate heat until browned on all sides. Add the mushrooms, the spinach leaves and the nutmeg. Season with salt and pepper and pour in the wine. Add enough warm water to just cover the meat and bring to the boil. Cover the casserole and place in a moderate to hot oven. Cook for 1 hour or until the meat is tender, stirring occasionally.
Serve this northern Italian dish with slices of grilled polenta.

Stuffed Cabbage Leaves from Greece

Ingredients

1 large but tender cabbage
2 onions, finely chopped
½ cup rice
1 tablespoon butter
2 teaspoons dried dill tops
1 tablespoon chopped parsley
500 grams minced beef
Salt and freshly ground pepper
Egg and lemon sauce (Page 21)

Method

Remove the stem from the cabbage. Place it in a pot of boiling salty water and boil for 10 minutes. Drain the cabbage and leave to cool.

In a large bowl mix the minced meat, the onions, rice, dill, parsley and the butter. Season with salt and pepper.

Separate the cabbage leaves and cut off any tough parts. Put a spoonful of the filling on each leaf, fold the sides over and roll up tightly.

Line the bottom of a pot with cabbage leaves and place the rolls side by side on the leaves. Place a rather heavy plate on top of the rolls to prevent them opening or moving during cooking. Add enough water to the pot to just cover the rolls and plate. Bring to the boil and simmer for 1 hour over a moderate heat.

Meantime prepare the egg and lemon sauce (Page 21).

Lift the cabbage rolls with a scoop and arrange on a serving dish. Pour the sauce over them and serve hot.

In Greece these cabbage rolls are served as a starter or as a main if accompanied by some seasonal vegetables.

Vitorin's Gozitan Baked Tuna

Ingredients
Serves 4

4 fresh tuna steaks
 of about 250 grams each
Juice of 1 large lemon
4 tablespoons olive oil
4 cloves garlic, finely chopped
6 tomatoes, peeled and chopped
2 tablespoons tomato concentrate
2 teaspoons fresh marjoram
2 tablespoons raisins
2 tablespoons chopped parsley
3 tomatoes, peeled and sliced
2 tablespoons dry bread crumbs
Salt and freshly ground pepper

Method
Wash the fish and pat dry. Place on a plate, season with salt and pepper and pour over the lemon juice. Refrigerate for 1 hour.
Heat 2 tablespoons of oil in a pan and gently fry the garlic. When it starts to change colour, mix in the tomato concentrate and the marjoram. Cook for 2 minutes and then mix in the chopped tomatoes and the raisins. Season with salt and pepper and simmer the sauce for 10 minutes. Remove from heat and cool slightly.
Lightly brush an ovenproof serving dish with oil and place the tuna steaks with the lemon marinade. Pour over the sauce. Place the sliced tomatoes over the sauce and sprinkle the breadcrumbs evenly over the tomatoes. Drizzle the remaining olive oil over the breadcrumbs and place in a moderately hot oven. Bake uncovered for 35 minutes.
Serve hot with lemon wedges and crisp roast potatoes.
Instead of breadcrumbs use 2 tablespoons pure ground almonds for a gluten-free version.

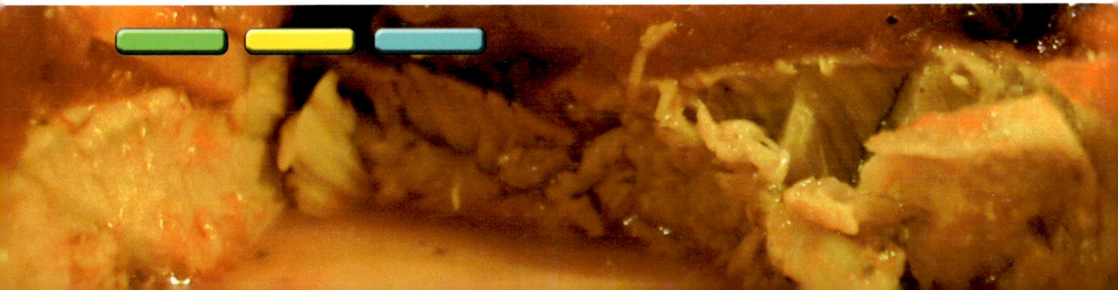

Tuna, Courgette and Pepper Frittata

Ingredients
Serves 4

1 tablespoon olive oil
1 onion, peeled and chopped
2 courgettes, thinly sliced
1 red pepper, seeded and sliced
1 yellow pepper, seeded and sliced
250 grams canned tuna, drained
1 teaspoon oregano
1 teaspoon thyme
75 grams grated Parmesan cheese
6 eggs, lightly beaten
Salt and freshly ground pepper

Method
Heat the oil in a non-stick pan. Add the onion, courgettes and peppers. Cook, stirring frequently for 5 minutes. Mix in the flaked tuna, the oregano and thyme. Season with salt and pepper. Combine the beaten eggs with the cheese. Pour the egg mixture evenly into the pan over the mixture. Cook over a medium heat until the eggs are beginning to set. Pull the sides into the middle to allow the uncooked egg to run on to the pan. Continue cooking until the frittata is set.
Sprinkle the cheese over the frittata and then place the frittata under a medium hot grill.
Cook until the cheese has melted and the surface of the frittata is nicely golden. Serve hot cut into portion-size triangles with a crisp salad.

Prawn Pilafi from Athens

Ingredients
Serves 6

1 kilo peeled fresh prawns
1 tablespoon sea salt
Juice of 1 large lemon
4 tablespoons olive oil
2 onions, peeled and finely chopped
1 clove garlic, peeled and crushed
8 tomatoes, peeled and passed through a sieve
1 tablespoon parsley, finely chopped
1 teaspoon gluten-free paprika
2 cups long-grain rice
Salt and freshly ground pepper
Finely chopped parsley to garnish

Method
Clean and wash the prawns in water to which some sea salt has been added. Drain.
Place 3 ½ cups water in a pot and pour in the lemon juice. Bring to the boil and add the prawns. Cook for 2 minutes only. Scoop out the prawns carefully and reserve the broth.
Heat 3 tablespoons of the oil in a pan and sauté the onions and garlic lightly. Mix in the tomato pulp, the paprika and the parsley. Season with salt and pepper. Let the sauce simmer for 15 minutes, stirring occasionally. Add the cooked prawns to the sauce and simmer for another 5 minutes. Remove from heat.
Meantime add 1 tablespoon olive oil to the prawn broth and bring it to the boil. Stir in the rice. Simmer the rice for 17 minutes or until just done. Remove from heat and stand for 2 minutes.
Place the rice on a round serving dish in the form of a ring. Pour the prawns with their sauce in the centre of the rice ring. Garnish with the parsley and serve hot.
An attractive dinner party dish!

Zev's Baked Salmon

Ingredients
Serves 4

4 salmon fillets of about 200 grams each
120 grams butter, softened
3 cloves garlic, crushed
3 tablespoons fresh dill, chopped
2 tablespoons parsley, chopped
2 teaspoons lemon juice
1 teaspoon finely grated lemon rind
Salt and freshly ground pepper

Method
Brush a low ovenproof serving dish with some olive oil. Place the salmon fillets next to eachother.
Blend together the butter, garlic, dill, parsley, lemon juice and the lemon rind. Season with salt and pepper. Spread the herb butter evenly over the salmon fillets. Cover the dish tightly with an oiled aluminium foil. Bake in a hot oven for around 25 minutes or until the fish is just cooked. Bring out of the oven and stand for 5 minutes.
Serve the salmon fillets with the herb butter. Serve with some boiled baby potatoes and steamed baby carrots and brokkoli.
An easy way of cooking fish for a smart dinner party.

Isabella's Baby Squid

Ingredients
Serves 4

700 grams cleaned baby squid
2 tablespoons olive oil
2 onions, peeled and chopped
2 cloves garlic, finely chopped
Some fresh celery leaves, chopped
1 chilli pepper, deseeded and finely chopped
3 tablespoons parsley, finely chopped
3 teaspoons corn flour mixed in 2 tablespoons water
150 grams mushrooms, thickly sliced
400 grams tomatoes, peeled and chopped
500 grams fresh spinach leaves, chopped
300 ml. dry white wine
Salt and freshly ground pepper
Finely chopped parsley to garnish

Method
Wash the squid and cut into 1cm. pieces.
Heat the oil in a large pan. Add the onions, garlic, chilli and the celery leaves. Mix and cook over a medium heat until the onion changes colour. Add the squid and cook gently for 10 minutes. Stir in the corn flour mixture and then add the tomatoes, mushrooms, spinach, parsley and the wine. Season with salt and pepper and give the ingredients a good stir. Cover the pan and simmer gently for 30 minutes. Cooking the squid quickly over a high heat will result in a rubbery squid!
Uncover the pan and continue simmering gently until the sauce thickens and the squid is tender.
Transfer the squid to a warmed dish, garnish with the chopped parsley and serve hot.

Swordfish Don Giovanni

Ingredients

4 swordfish steaks
of about 200 gramms each
2 tablespoons olive oil

For the marinade
3 tablespoons olive oil
Juice of 1 lemon
1 tablespoon parsley,
finely chopped
Salt and freshly
ground pepper

For the sauce
4 garlic cloves, chopped
1 kilo tomatoes, peeled
and chopped
6 anchovy fillets, chopped
1 tablespoon sage leaves,
chopped
1 tablespoon fresh thyme, chopped
Salt and freshly ground pepper

Method
Wash the swordfish and pat dry. Combine the marinade ingredients in a jug. Place the swordfish in a suitable dish and pour over the marinade. Cover and refrigerate for 1 hour.
Heat the oil in a large pan. Remove the fish steaks from the marinade and fry gently until they are golden in colour on both sides. Remove the fish from the pan and arrange in a warmed serving dish.
Add the garlic to the oil in the pan. Cook until it just changes colour and then mix in the anchovies. Cook for 1 minute and then mix in the tomatoes, sage and thyme. Season with salt and pepper and gently simmer the sauce until it thickens. Pour the sauce over the fish and garnish with some fresh sage leaves.

Salads and Vegetable dishes

Classic French Bean Salad

Ingredients
Serves 6

5 tablespoons olive oil
1 tablespoon wine vinegar
3 teaspoons French mustard
1 red onion, peeled and finely chopped
1 clove garlic, crushed
2 tablespoons capers, drained
800 grams French beans
Salt and freshly ground pepper

Method
Bring a pot of salty water to the boil. Meantime wash the beans and snip off the stalk ends. Add to the boiling water and cook for just 5 minutes. Place the vinegar, mustard, garlic and oil in a jar with a tight fitting lid. Season, close the jar and give it a good shaking.
When the beans are done, drain them and place them in a serving bowl. Pour the dressing over them and mix in the onion and capers. Toss the salad and serve warm.
Ideal with any meat or fish dishes!

A Salad from Santorini

Ingredients
Serves 4

1 red onion, peeled and finely sliced
2 green peppers
6 tomatoes, peeled, deseeded and chopped
420 grams canned chickpeas, drained
2 tablespoons mint leaves, chopped
½ teaspoon oregano
2 tablespoons basil leaves, chopped
200 grams Feta cheese, diced
Juice of 2 lemons
3 tablespoons olive oil
Salt and freshly ground pepper

Method
Wash, halve and deseed the green peppers. Cut into thin strips.
Place the green pepper strips in a salad bowl with the tomatoes and the onion. Mix.
Place half the chickpeas in a bowl. Add 1 tablespoon olive oil and the lemon juice. Mash up with a fork. Mix into the tomato mixture together with the rest of the whole chickpeas.
Sprinkle the dried oregano and mix in the mint and thyme. Season with salt and pepper.
Add the cubed Feta and pour the rest of the oil over the salad. Toss the salad and serve immediately.

Fatma's Moroccan Salad

Ingredients
Serves 4

1 tablespoon olive oil
Juice of 1 large lemon
600 grams tender carrots
3 large winter oranges
3 tablespoons orange juice
75 grams raisins
1 ½ teaspoons
freshly-ground cinnamon
80 grams pine nuts
Salt and freshly ground
pepper

Method
Heat 1 teaspoon olive oil in a non-stick pan and gently toast the pine kernels until just golden. Reserve.
Wash, peel and grate the carrots into a bowl. Peel the oranges and open them up into segments. Toss them with the carrots and season with salt and pepper. Mix in the raisins and sprinkle the cinnamon.
Combine the oil with the orange and lemon juices and pour over the salad. Toss the salad and then scatter over the prepared pine nuts.
Serve chilled with your fish dishes.
Alternatively, you may create a starter by mixing in 800 grams peeled and cooked prawns. Serve in individual containers.

Sofia's Turkish Salad

Ingredients
Serves 4

600 grams tender spinach leaves
1 onion, peeled and coarsely chopped
1 clove garlic, crushed
300 ml. plain yoghurt
1 tablespoon olive oil
100 grams walnuts, shelled and coarsely chopped
2 tablespoons fresh mint, chopped
Salt and freshly ground pepper

Method
Wash the spinach and trim off the stalks.
Heat 1 teaspoon olive oil in a non-stick pan and gently toast the walnuts until just golden.
Bring a pot of salty water to the boil. Add the spinach and onion. Cook for just 8 minutes.
Drain the spinach with the onion and squeeze out all the excess liquid.
Place the spinach and onion in a serving bowl and fluff up with a fork.
Leave to cool and fluff up again.
Combine the yoghurt, oil, crushed garlic and half the mint leaves in a small bowl. Season with salt and pepper. Mix well and pour over the prepared spinach. Scatter over the toasted walnuts and remaining mint.
Serve with grilled meats or fish or on its own as a starter.

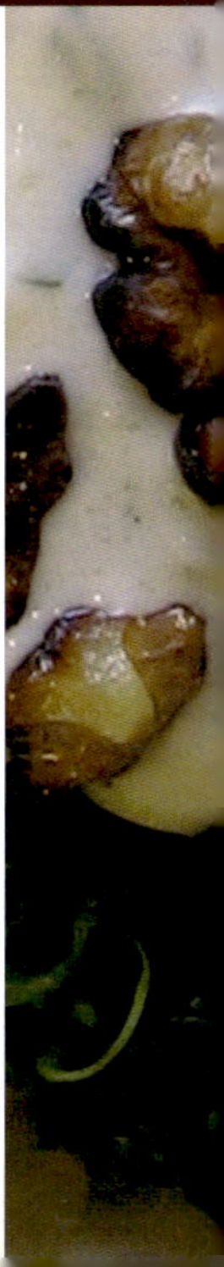

Mum's Ricotta Frittata

Ingredients
Serves 4

600 grams ricotta
4 large eggs
4 tablespoons grated Parmesan cheese
2 tablespoons parsley, finely chopped
Salt and freshly ground pepper
2 teaspoons corn oil

Method
Beat the eggs together until light and foamy. Add the ricotta, season with salt and pepper and beat for 2 minutes. Mix in the parsley and grated Parmesan.
Heat the oil in a non-stick frying pan. Pour in the ricotta mixture and smoothen the surface of the mixture with a spatula. Cover pan and cook over a medium to low heat for 14 minutes. Turn over the frittata onto a large flat plate and then gently slide it back into the pan. Continue cooking for 5 minutes. Serve hot with a crispy green salad.
A quick and healty meal!

Spinach and Rice Frittata

Ingredients
Serves 6

700 grams tender spinach leaves
150 grams long-grain rice
400 ml. skimmed milk
6 eggs
½ teaspoon freshly grated nutmeg
2 teaspoons dried dill tops
Salt and freshly ground pepper

Method
Grease a round, shallow baking dish with olive oil.
Bring a pot of salty water to the boil. Add the spinach and cook until just wilted. This will take just over a minute. Drain the spinach and squeeze out all the excess liquids in a colander over another pot, thereby reserving the liquid. Bring this liquid to the boil and add the rice. Cook for just 10 minutes and drain.
Beat the eggs in a large bowl and gradually add the milk. Season with salt and pepper and mix in the nutmeg and dill. Add the spinach and rice and mix well. Pour into the prepared dish. Bake in a moderate to hot oven for 35 minutes or until cooked through.

Egyptian Potato Frittata

Ingredients
Serves 4

500 grams potatoes
2 onions, peeled and chopped
2 cloves garlic, peeled and chopped
4 eggs, lightly beaten
4 tablespoons parsley, chopped
½ teaspoon freshly grated nutmeg
1 tablespoons olive oil
Salt and freshly ground pepper

Method
Peel and quarter the potatoes. Place them in a pot and cover with water. Add some salt and bring to the boil. Cook until just tender. Drain the potatoes, place them in a bowl and mash them with a masher or fork. Heat ½ tablespoon olive oil in a non-stick frying pan and add the onions. Cook until soft and golden. Add the garlic and cook for one minute. Mix them into the mashed potatoes. Combine the beaten eggs with the parsley and nutmeg. Pour into the potato mixture and mix well. Season. Heat the rest of the oil in the non-stick frying pan and pour in the potato mixture. Smoothen with a spatula. Cook over a low heat for around 14 minutes or until the underneath of the frittata is set. Place under a hot grill and continue cooking until the top is golden coloured and crisp. Turn onto a round serving plate and garnish with some chopped parsley. Serve hot on its own or with meat and fish dishes.

Sfoungato from Crete

Ingredients
Serves 4

2 onions, peeled and finely chopped
500 grams tomatoes
500 grams courgettes, sliced
½ teaspoon oregano
5 eggs, lightly beaten
½ tablespoon olive oil
Salt and freshly ground pepper

Method
Peel, seed and chop up the tomatoes.
Heat the oil in a non-stick frying pan and brown the courgettes with the onions. Season and sprinkle over the oregano. Mix in the tomatoes and cook uncovered over a medium heat until all the liquid has evaporated. Stir occasionally. Add the beaten eggs and simmer for a few minutes.
Serve hot with your toasted bread.
Quick and delicious in winter!

Greek Potato Stew

Ingredients
Serves 6

2 tablespoons olive oil
2 large onions, peeled and chopped
2 garlic cloves, peeled and chopped
500 grams tomatoes
½ teaspoon dried thyme
1 bay leaf
1 kilo potatoes
1 cup water
Salt and freshly ground pepper

Method
Peel the tomatoes and pass them through a sieve. Wash and peel the potatoes, wash again and cut into chunks.
Heat the oil in a pot and brown the onions. Mix in the garlic, thyme and bay leaf. Cook for 2 minutes. Stir occasionally. Add the tomatoes and the water and cook for 2 minutes.
Mix in the potatoes and season. Cover the pot and simmer for 25 minutes or until the potatoes are tender and the sauce has thickened. Stir occasionally. Remove the bay leaf and serve hot with your meat or fish dishes.

Pete's Honeyed Mushrooms

Ingredients
Serves 4

2 tablespoons olive oil
800 grams baby mushrooms
½ teaspoon freshly grated nutmeg
1 tablespoon good balsamic vinegar
2 full tablespoons good honey
Salt and freshly ground pepper

Method
Grease a flame-proof low serving dish with some olive oil.
Wash the mushrooms and pat dry.
Heat the oil in a non-stick pan. Add the mushrooms. Sprinkle over the nutmeg and toss the mushrooms over a high flame for just over 2 minutes. Season and drizzle over with the vinegar. Bring off the heat and drizzle with the honey.
Pour the mixture into the prepared dish and bake in a moderate to hot oven for 12 minutes.
Serve hot with your poultry and meat dishes.

Fragrant Peas

Ingredients
Serves 6

800 grams garden peas
1 tablespoon olive oil
1 tablespoon butter
2 tablespoons fresh sage leaves, chopped
Salt and freshly ground pepper.

Method
Bring a pot of salty water to the boil. Add the peas and cook for just 4 minutes. Drain the peas.
Heat the oil and butter in a pot and add the sage leaves. Cook over a medium flame until the sage leaves start to change to golden in colour.
Add the peas, season and continue cooking for 2 minutes.
Serve hot with poultry and meat dishes.

Baked Butter Beans from Greece

Ingredients
Serves 8

500 grams giant butter beans
8 large tomatoes
2 onions, peeled and sliced
3 cloves garlic, peeled and chopped
3 tablespoons parsley, chopped
2 bay leaves
3 tablespoons olive oil
Salt and freshly ground pepper

Method
Put the butter beans in a large bowl. Fill the bowl with water and leave the beans to soak for 12 hours. Drain the beans.
Put the beans in a pot and add plenty of water. Bring to the boil, and then simmer the beans until they are just done. Drain the beans.
Peel the tomatoes and pass them through a sieve.
Grease a flame proof baking dish with a little olive oil. Arrange the beans in the dish and season with salt and pepper. Combine the tomato pulp with the rest of the ingredients, season and pour the mixture over the beans. Bake in a moderate oven for 55 minutes.
Bring out of the oven and serve hot or even cold.
In Greece this nutritious dish is served as an appetizer or as an accompaniment to grilled meat dishes.

Sicilian Stuffed Courgettes

Ingredients
Serves 4

8 large round courgettes
500 grams ricotta
2 eggs, lightly beaten
2 tablespoons parsley, finely chopped
3 tablespoons grated Parmesan cheese
8 anchovy fillets
2 tablespoons pure ground almonds
Freshly ground pepper

Method
Wash the courgettes and slice off the stalk and tail ends. Bring a pot of salty water to the boil and add the courgettes. Boil for just 9 minutes. Drain the courgettes and leave to cool. Use a teaspoon to gently and carefully remove the insides of the courgettes.
Place the ricotta in a bowl and mash up with a fork. Mix in the beaten eggs and season with pepper. Mix in the parsley and the grated Parmesan. Half fill the hollow courgettes with the ricotta mixture. Place an anchovy fillet in the courgette, and then continue stuffing up the courgettes. Sprinkle the ground almonds over the tops of the courgettes. Grease a flame-proof baking dish with a little olive oil and arrange the courgettes in it. Bake in a moderate to hot oven for 40 minutes. Bring out of the oven and serve hot with some crispy baked potatoes.

Steffie's Vegetable Bake

Ingredients
Serves 4

700 grams potatoes, peeled and sliced
3 leeks, trimmed and sliced
4 tomatoes, sliced
Fresh rosemary sprigs
350 ml. homemade vegetable stock (Page 10)
1 tablespoon olive oil
Salt and freshly ground pepper

Method
Grease a flame-proof dish with a little butter.
Layer the potatoes with the leeks and tomatoes in the dish. Scatter some rosemary in between the layers and season each layer with salt and pepper. End with a layer of potatoes. Pour the stock over the vegetables and brush the top layer of the potatoes with olive oil. Cover with an aluminium foil and bake in a moderate oven for 50 minutes. Remove the foil and continue baking for a further 35 minutes.
Bring out of the oven when the topping is golden and the vegetables are done. Stand for 3 minutes and serve hot. Will make a nice vegetarian dish if served on its own.

Carrots Marsala

Ingredients
Serves 4

500 grams tender carrots
1 tablespoon olive oil
200 ml. good Marsala wine
Salt and freshly ground pepper
2 tablespoons parsley,
 finely chopped

Method
Wash and peel the carrots and cut into thin sticks. Heat the oil in a non-stick frying pan and lightly brown the carrots. Season with salt and pepper and pour over the Marsala.
Cook gently for 12 minutes or until the carrots are just done. Garnish with the parsley and serve hot or cold with your meat or fish dishes. Quick and different!

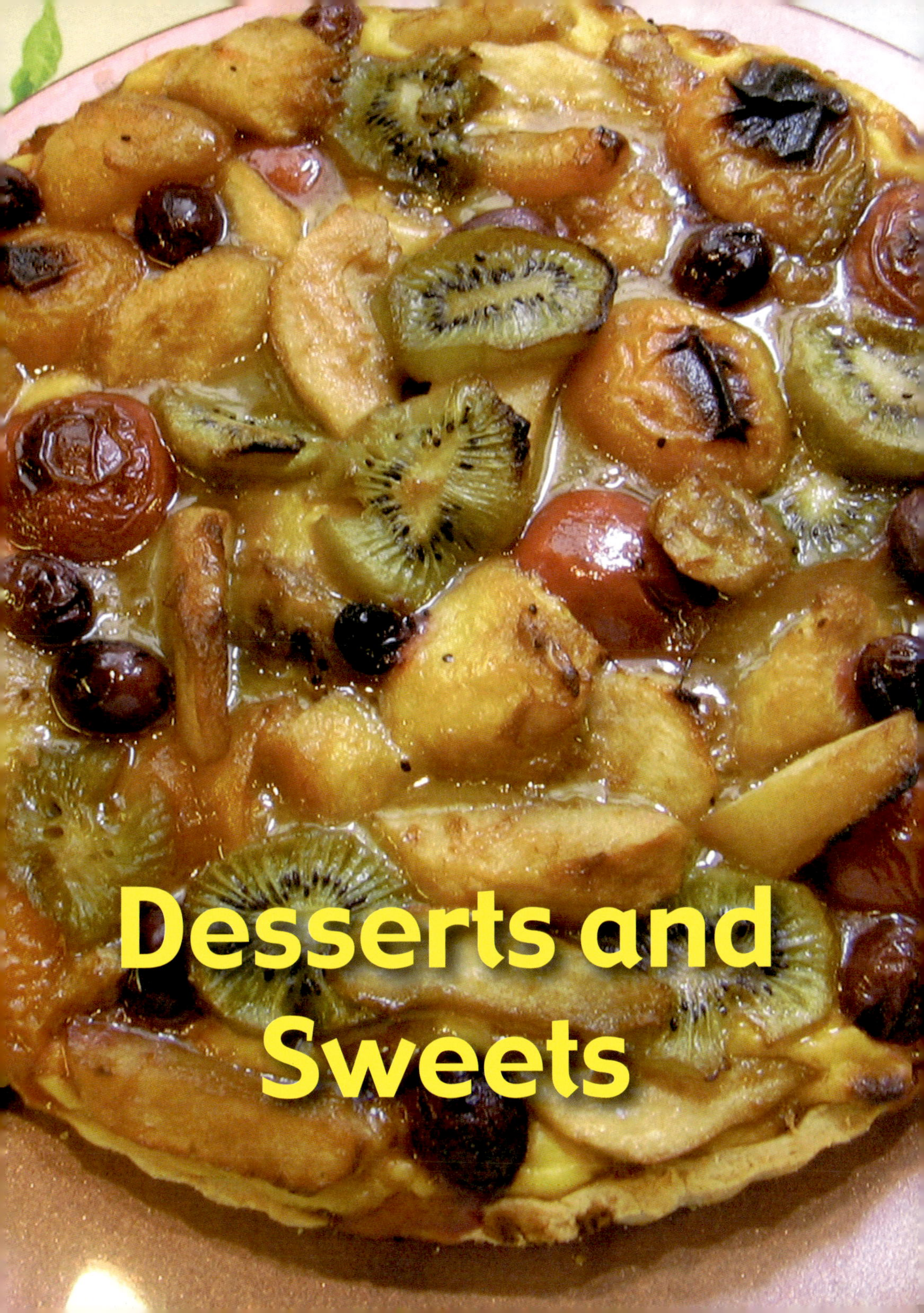
Desserts and
Sweets

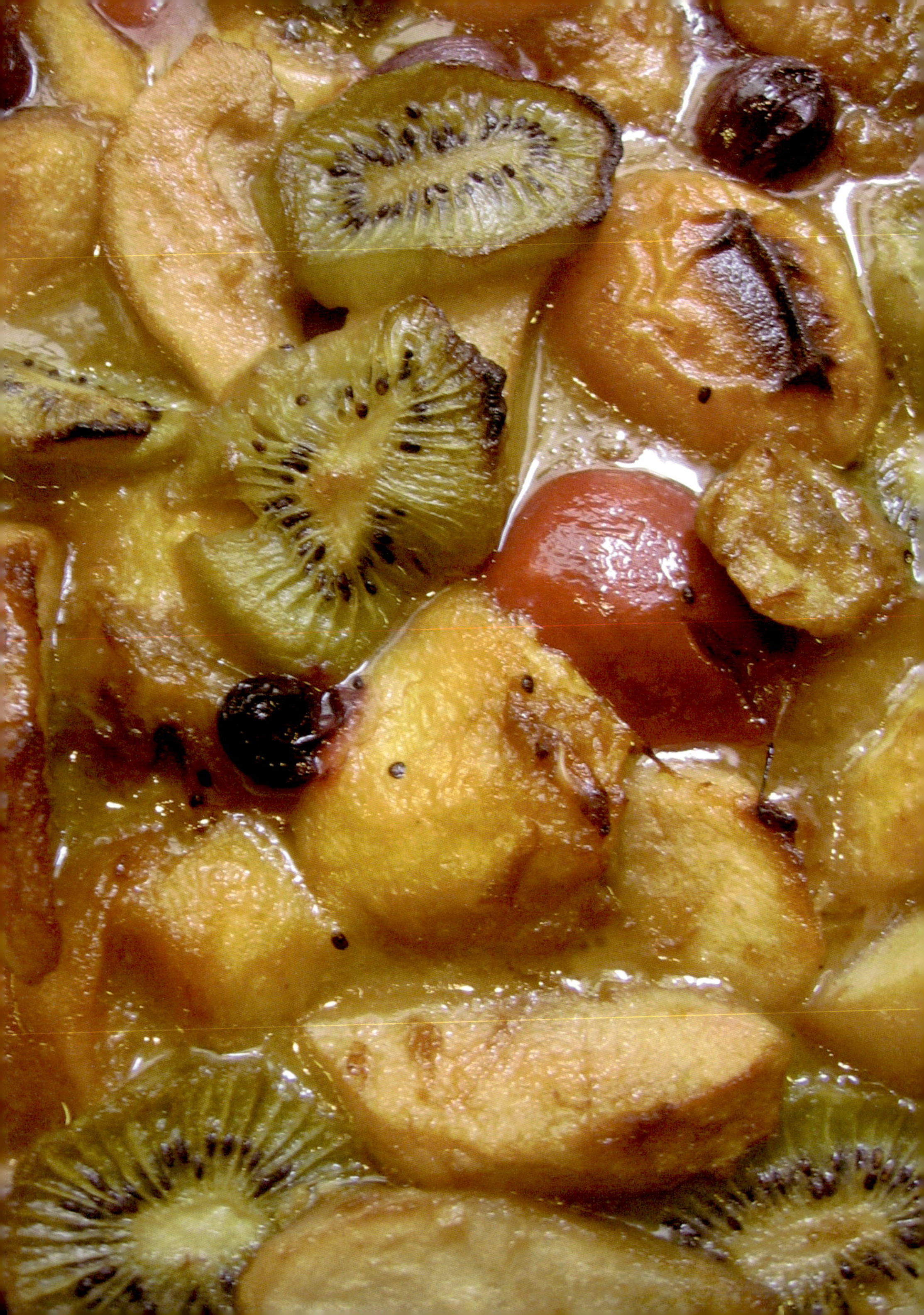

Pete's Gluten-Free Fruit Tart

Ingredients
Gluten-free sweet pastry (Page 6)
40 grams butter
2 teaspoons olive oil
3 tablespoons Demerara sugar
1 apple, peeled, cored and sliced
4 peaches, peeled and halved
5 plums, peeled and halved
5 apricots, peeled and halved
2 pears, peeled and sliced
2 kiwis, peeled and sliced
1 banana, peeled and sliced
Small bunch of grapes

For the pastry cream
2 eggs
50 grams caster sugar
4 teaspoons gluten-free corn flour
300 ml. fresh milk
Few drops vanilla essence
Finely grated rind of half a lemon

Method
Prepare the pastry as instructed on page 6.
Grease a round flan dish (if possible fluted) with a little butter and dust evenly with potato flour. Roll out the pastry on a potato floured surface and line the dish with all the pastry. Prick the pastry with a fork. Have ready a sheet of aluminium foil and grease the shiny side with butter. Place the greased side of the foil over the pastry. Flatten down the foil over the base and sides of the pastry to also cover the sides of the dish. Place dried butter beans over the foil to act as a weight during baking. Place in a moderate to hot oven and bake for 20 minutes. Bring out of the oven, uncover and cool.
Beat the eggs and sugar until pale and thick. Combine the corn flour with 6 tablespoons of the milk and beat into the egg mixture. Heat the

remaining milk until nearly boiling and pour slowly into the egg mixture whilst beating continuously. Transfer the mixture to a clean saucepan and stir over a low heat until the mixture thickens. Add the lemon zest and vanilla and cook for a further 2 minutes. Leave to cool.
Heat the oil and butter in a large pan and add all the fruit. Toss the fruit and sprinkle over the sugar. Gently cook the fruit over a medium heat for 5 minutes whilst stirring occasionally. Leave to cool.
Pour the cream over the baked pastry and arrange the fruit over it. Bake in a moderate to hot oven for around 35 minutes or until the fruit is slightly golden. Serve either lukewarm or at room temperature.
This fruit tart could be prepared with normal sweet pastry unless the gluten-free version is required.

Gluten-Free Almond and Lemon Cake

Ingredients

225 grams pure ground almonds
225 grams butter
225 grams caster sugar
125 grams polenta
1 teaspoon gluten-free baking powder
3 eggs
Grated zest of 3 lemons
Juice of 1 lemon
½ teaspoon vanilla essence

Method

Grease a 20 cm. cake tin with butter. Line the base and sides of the tin with baking paper and then grease over the baking paper.

Beat the butter and sugar until pale and fluffy. Beat in the ground almonds and the eggs, beating well between each addition. Beat in the lemon juice, lemon zest and vanilla. Beat in most of the polenta but reserve 3 tablespoons. Combine the reserved polenta with the baking powder and gently fold into the cake mixture. Pour the mixture into the prepared tin and bake in a moderate oven for 55 minutes or until cooked through.

Bring out of the oven and stand for 5 minutes before removing the tin. Leave to cool on a cooling rack and then decorate with thin slices of lemon.

The Sacher Torte

Ingredients
Serves 8

175 grams good dark chocolate
110 grams butter, softened
110 grams caster sugar
4 large egg yolks
½ teaspoon vanilla essence
110 grams plain flour
½ teaspoon baking powder
5 large egg whites
400 grams good apricot jam

For the topping
200 grams good dark chocolate
175 ml. double cream
2 tablespoons apricot jam

Method
Grease a 20 cm. springform cake tin with butter. Line the base and sides with baking paper. Grease over the baking paper.
Break the chocolate in a heatproof bowl. Place the bowl over a saucepan with simmering water. The bowl must not touch the water. Leave the chocolate to melt.
Cream the butter and sugar until pale and fluffy. Beat in the egg yolks, one at a time. When the chocolate has cooled slightly, gently fold it into the butter mixture and add the vanilla. Sift the flour with the baking powder and gently fold it into the mixture with a metal spoon. Whisk the egg whites in a clean bowl using a clean whisk. Whisk until stiff peaks form. Fold into the mixture with a metal spoon. Pour the mixture into the prepared tin and smoothen the top. Bake in a moderate oven for 1 hour or until cooked through. Bring out of the oven and stand for 10 minutes before turning out of the tin. Leave to get cold on a cooling rack. Slice the cake diagonally and spread the apricot jam. Place the top slice on the jam and press down gently. Brush the top and sides of the cake

with 2 tablespoons jam. Melt the chocolate in a bowl over simmering water and then mix in the double cream. Pour the topping slowly over the cake and with the help of a spatula coat the sides. Leave to set in a cool place. It takes about 2 hours.
The original recipe of the famous Sacher Torte is a very closely guarded secret in the kitchens of the Hotel Sacher in Vienna. A visit to its reputable coffee house is a must for me whenever I visit Vienna. I enjoy every little morsel of this delicious cake. No, I haven't stolen the recipe… lets say yet, but what I gave you is an excellent alternative.

Date and Apple Loaf

Ingredients
Serves 6

150 grams butter
125 grams Demerara sugar
3 eggs
2 tablespoons good honey
225 grams self-raising flour
1 teaspoon ground cinnamon
½ teaspoon ground cloves
1 large apple, peeled, cored and diced
125 grams dried dates, stoned and coarsely chopped

Method
Grease a loaf tin with butter and line with baking paper. Grease over the paper.
Beat together the butter, sugar and the honey. Beat until creamy.
Combine the flour with the cinnamon and cloves. Beat in the eggs alternating with the flour mixture. Gently mix in the apple and dates.
Pour the mixture into the prepared tin and bake in a moderate oven for 50 minutes. Bring out of the oven and stand for 10 minutes before turning out onto a cooling rack.
Serve sliced with a hot cup of tea or coffee. What more would you want on a chilly autumn or winter afternoon?

Gluten-Free Chocolate Brownies

Ingredients
Makes 16

60 grams gluten-free dark chocolate
200 grams caster sugar
100 grams unsalted butter
2 eggs, lightly whisked
75 grams pure ground almonds
1 teapoon vanilla essence
½ teaspoon gluten-free baking powder
110 grams chopped walnuts
Pinch salt

Method
Grease a 20 cm. square tin with butter and line with baking paper. Grease over the paper.
Place the chocolate in a heatproof bowl. Place the bowl over a sauce pan with simmering water. Leave the chocolate to melt. Cream the butter and sugar until light and fluffy. Beat in the lightly whisked eggs, the vanilla and the slightly cooled melted chocolate. Stir in the ground almonds, gluten-free baking powder, salt and the chopped nuts. Spread the mixture in the prepared tin. Bake in a moderate oven for 35 minutes or until well set.
Bring out of the oven and leave to cool completely. Cut into 5 cms. squares for serving.

Gluten-Free Chocolate Orange and Hazlenut Tart

Ingredients
Serves 8

Gluten-free sweet pastry (Page 6)

For the topping
75 grams gluten-free dark chocolate
200 grams hazelnuts, shelled and roasted
75 grams unsalted butter
150 grams caster sugar
2 eggs, lightly beaten
2 teaspoons grated orange rind
25 grams rice flour
3 tablespoons fresh orange juice
Freshly whipped cream to serve

Method
Grease a 23 cm flan dish with butter and lightly dust with potato flour. Roll out the pastry over a potato floured surface and line the base and sides of the flan dish. Prick the pastry with a fork. Have ready a sheet of aluminium foil. Grease the shiny side of the foil with a little butter and press the buttered side of the foil over the pastry. Cover the pastry completely. Place dried butter beans on the foil to act as a weight during baking. Bake in a moderate to hot oven for 20 minutes. Bring out of the oven, uncover and cool.
Chop up the hazelnuts. Chop up the chocolate into very small pieces. Beat the butter and sugar until pale and fluffy. Beat in the eggs and then gently mix in the rest of the ingredients. Spread the mixture onto the cooked pastry. Bake in a moderate oven for 25 minutes. Bring out of the oven and leave to cool.
Serve with a dollop of whipped cream.

Gluten-Free Orange and Almond Cake

Ingredients
Serves 8

2 large oranges
250 grams caster sugar
3 eggs
270 grams pure
 ground almonds
1 teaspoon gluten-free baking powder

For the topping
250 grams mascarpone
50 grams caster sugar
Grated rind and juice of 1 orange
½ teaspoon grated orange rind to decorate.

Method
Grease a 20cm. spring-form tin with butter. Line the base and sides with baking paper and then grease over the paper.
Wash the oranges and place them in a small saucepan. Cover with water, bring to the boil and simmer for 45 minutes. Pour off the water and cover the oranges again with fresh boiling water. Simmer again for 45 minutes.
Halve the oranges, remove the pips and process them in a blender.
Beat the eggs with the sugar until pale and fluffy. Combine the pure ground almonds with the baking powder and fold gently into the egg mixture. Fold in the processed oranges.
Pour into the prepared tin and smoothen the surface of the mixture. Bake in a moderate oven for 1 hour. Bring out of the oven and stand for 10 minutes.
Turn onto a cooling rack and remove the paper. Leave to get cold.
Mix together the mascarpone, the sugar and the orange juice and spread over the cake. Sprinkle the orange rind.
Alternatively, you may prepare a double dose of topping. Slice the cake diagonally and place half the topping on the bottom layer. Place the top layer and press down gently. Continue decorating the cake as instructed above.

Gluten-Free Almond Fingers

Ingredients
Makes 32

175 grams caster sugar
6 eggs
50 grams butter, slightly melted
110 grams pure ground almonds
25 grams rice flour

Method
Grease 2 Swiss roll trays (20x30 cms.) with butter and line with baking paper. Grease over the paper. Combine the rice flour with the pure ground almonds.
Place the eggs and sugar in a bowl and whisk them until pale and fluffy. Gently stir in the melted butter. Gently fold in the almond mixture.
Divide the mixture into 2 and pour into the prepared trays. Bake in a moderate oven for 16 minutes or until golden in colour and firm to the touch.
Bring out of the oven and leave to cool completely. Use a sharp knife to cut 16 fingers out of each tray.
Pack in air-tight containers. You will enjoy them to nibble with a hot cup of tea.

Anna Maria's Gluten-Free Tiramisù

Ingredients
Serves 4

300 ml. strong espresso coffee
3 tablespoons brandy
3 tablespoons dark rum
100 grams gluten-free dark chocolate, grated
3 fresh eggs, separated
4 tablespoons caster sugar
300 grams mascarpone
About 16 gluten-free almond fingers (page 96)
Gluten-free cocoa powder

Method
Have ready a low-sided glass serving dish of around 20x25 cms..
Combine the coffee with the brandy and rum.
Whish the egg yolks with the sugar until light and fluffy. Gently fold in the mascarpone.
Whisk the egg whites until stiff peaks form. Gently fold into the mascarpone mixture.
Line the base of the dish with almond fingers. Now dip some almond fingers quickly into the coffee mixture and arrange them side by side on top of the other almond fingers. Spread half the mascarpone mixture over the soaked almond fingers. Sprinkle half the grated chocolate over the mascarpone. Repeat by placing another layer of almond fingers and another layer of fingers soaked in the coffee mixture. Spread the rest of the mascarpone mixture and sprinkle the rest of the grated chocolate.
Cover the dish with clingfilm and refrigerate for 8 hours.
To serve, remove the clingfilm and sprinkle some gluten-free cocoa over the top.
You may now enjoy this famous, mouthwatering Italian sweet!

Diabetic Choco-Strawberry Pancakes

Ingredients
Serves 8

For the pancake batter
500 ml. milk
2 large eggs
200 grams plain flour, sifted
½ teaspoon salt

For the filling
250 grams strawberries
4 tablespoons diabetic strawberry jam
150 grams diabetic dark chocolate
1 tablespoon butter
3 tablespoons tinned cream

Method
Whisk together the eggs, milk and salt in a bowl. Gradually add the flour whilst whisking continuously. Continue whisking until completely smooth. Let the mixture stand for 15 minutes, and then give it a quick, short whisk.
Heat ½ teaspoon corn oil in a small non-stick pan and when very hot pour in 2 tablespoons of the batter. Tip the pan to the sides so that the batter reaches all the sides of the pan. After about 1 minute, turn over the pancake to cook on the other side. Slide the pancake onto a clean surface to cool. Repeat with the remaining batter.
Wash and hull the strawberries and let them drain. Halve the strawberries and place them in a small bowl. Mix in the diabetic jam and stuff about 8 pancakes with the mixture. Place the pancakes side by side on a serving plate.
You may wrap the rest of the pancakes in clingfilm and freeze them for another time.

Cut the chocolate into pieces and put them in a small bowl. Place the bowl over a saucepan with simmering water and leave the chocolate to melt. Remove the bowl from heat and mix in the butter and then the cream. Pour the sauce over the pancakes and leave to set for a while or refrigerate.

For a gluten-free / diabetic version, use the gluten-free pancake batter (page 4).

Diabetic Apples in Cinnamon Custard

Ingredients
Serves 6

5 apples, peeled, cored
and quartered
5 saccharin tablets
½ teaspoon ground cloves

For the custard
600 ml. skimmed milk
3 tablespoons custard powder
5 saccharin tablets
1 teaspoon ground cinnamon

Method
Place the apples with the saccharin and cloves in a pot. Add enough water to nearly cover the apples. Bring to the boil and simmer covered for 2 minutes. Switch off the heat and leave to stand for 10 minutes. Uncover the pot and leave to get cold.
Place the custard powder and the saccharin in a small saucepan and mix in 3 tablespoons milk. Mix well to combine, and then gradually mix in the rest of the milk. Place the saucepan on a moderate heat and gradually and slowly bring to the boil. Stir continuously. Bring off the heat and leave to cool.
Place the apples with their syrup in individual glass containers. Pour over the custard and then sprinkle over some ground cinnamon.
Serve chilled.

Diabetic Carrot and Walnut Cake

Ingredients
Serves 10

3 cups plain flour
2 teaspoons baking powder
1 teaspoon bicarbonate of soda
Pinch salt
2 teaspoons ground cinnamon
4 large eggs
1 cup sugar substitute
1 cup corn oil
3 medium carrots, peeled and grated
½ cup walnuts, shelled and chopped
1 teaspoon vanilla

Method
Grease a 23 cm. cake tin with butter. Line the base and sides of the tin with baking paper. Grease over the paper.
Sift the flour with the baking powder, bicarbonate of soda, salt and cinnamon into a large bowl. In a separate bowl beat together the eggs, oil, vanilla and sugar substitute. Fold in the grated carrots and the walnuts. Make a well in the centre of the flour mixture and gradually fold in the egg mixture. Pour the mixture in the prepared tin and smoothen the surface. Bake in a moderate oven for around 60 minutes or until cooked through.

Strawberries Virginia

Ingredients
Serves 4

400 grams strawberries
3 tablespoons diabetic strawberry jam
400 ml. plain yoghurt
2 teaspoons freshly ground cinnamon

Method
Wash, hull and halve the strawberries Place them in a small bowl and mix in the diabetic strawberry jam. Divide the mixture between 4 serving glass goblets. Chill.
Combine the yoghurt with the cinnamon in a bowl, cover with clingfilm and chill.
Just before serving, spoon the yoghurt mixture over the strawberries.
You may sprinkle your favourite roasted and chopped nuts over the yoghurt or grate some diabetic chocolate. Treat yourself occasionally, and sprinkle both!
My mother who was a diabetic, simply loved strawberries. As a child, I remember seeing them growing in our garden.

Copenhayi from Athens

Ingredients.
Serves 12

6 eggs seperated
½ cup sugar
4 tablespoons fresh orange juice
½ teaspoon ground cinnamon
1 teaspoon baking powder
2 cups ground unblanched almonds (Shelled almonds but with skin retained)
¾ cup dry toasted breadcrumbs
¼ teaspoon salt
Around 450 grams Phyllo pastry sheets
2/3 cup butter, melted

For the syrup
2 cups sugar
1 cup water
Juice of 1 lemon

Method
Grease a 9 X 13 inch baking pan with butter.

Place the egg yolks and sugar in a bowl and beat until the mixture is thick and creamy. Add the orange juice, cinnamon, almonds and the toasted dry breadcrumbs. Mix well, then add the baking powder and mix lightly.
Beat the eggwhites with the salt until stiff peaks form. Gently fold into the almond mixture.
Line the baking pan with half the amount of Phyllo pastry sheets, brushing each sheet liberally with the butter. Turn almond mixture onto the pastry sheets in the baking pan and smoothen the surface of the

mixture. Place the rest of the phyllo pastry sheets, brushing every sheet with butter. Make 4 long slits in the top layers of pastry. Use a sharp knife and cut the slits across the length of the pan. Bake in a moderate oven for 50 minutes. Bring out of the oven and leave to cool.
Meanwhile, place the water, sugar and lemon juice in a saucepan and leave the mixture to boil for 10 minutes. Pour the hot syrup over the pie and leave to cool completely.
When cold, cut into squares and place on a suitable serving plate.

This almond sweet was created for King George I of the Hellenes, himself a Danish Prince, at the beginning of his reign.

Celebrating
Christmas

Festive Salmon and Prawn Terrine

Ingredients

About 6 large slices smoked salmon
450 grams fresh salmon, chopped
5 eggs
200 ml. tinned cream
2 teaspoons dried dill tops
350 grams giant prawns, shelled and deveined
3 tablespoons parsley, finely chopped
2 teaspoon lemon zest, finely grated
Salt and freshly ground pepper
Finely chopped parsley to garnish
Lemon wedges to serve

Method

Grease a terrine with a little butter. Line the bottom and sides of the terrine with baking paper. Grease over the paper. Lay the smoked salmon slices neatly in the terrine over the baking paper. They must cover the bottom and sides of the terrine.
Place the chopped salmon in a blender. Add the eggs, cream, dill, salt and pepper. Blend until smooth. Pour half the mixture in the terrine and spread out evenly. Arrange the prawns neatly over the salmon mixture. Season with salt and pepper and sprinkle the parsley and lemon zest. Pour the remaining salmon mixture over the prawns and smoothen the top with a spatula. Cover the terrine with foil and seal well. Place the terrine in a baking dish and fill the dish with boiling water until it reaches up to 4 cms. below the rim of the terrine. Place in a moderate oven and cook for 1 hour or until well set. Bring out of the oven and cool completely. Refrigerate for 6 hours.
Turn out the terrine on a suitable serving dish and peel off the paper. Garnish with the parsley and serve with lemon wedges.

The Mushroom Soup

Ingredients
Serves 8

30 grams dried porcini mushrooms
800 grams fresh mushrooms, sliced
1 tablespoon butter
3 tablespoons olive oil
2 onions, peeled and finely chopped
2 cloves garlic, crushed
2 teaspoons fresh thyme leaves
1 tablespoon parsley, finely chopped
4 tablespoons mascarpone cheese
1.25 litres homemade vegetable stock (Page 10)
Salt and freshly ground pepper.

Method
Wash the mushrooms well. Chop up the porcini mushrooms and place in a small bowl. Add boiling water just to cover. Leave to soak.
Heat the butter and oil in a pot and add the onion. Cook over a medium flame until soft. Add the garlic and thyme thyme and cook for 2 minutes, stirring occasionally. Mix in the mushrooms and cook for 2 minutes.
Mix in the porcini mushrooms with the soaking liquid and pour in the vegetable stock. Season and bring to the boil. Cover the pot and simmer for 20 minutes. Bring off the fire, mix in the parsley and cool for a while.
Place half the soup in a blender and process until smooth. Pour it back into the pot with the remaining soup and reheat. Bring off the heat, mix in the mascarpone and serve hot.
For a special occasion such as Yuletide, I usually mix in 150 ml. fine sherry just before serving.

Stuffed Turkey Breasts

Ingredients
Serves 4

2 turkey breast fillets
of around 300 grams each
6 rashers packed streaky bacon,
rinds removed
¼ teaspoon freshly grated nutmeg
60 grams grated Parmesan cheese
2 eggs, lightly beaten
300 grams frozen spinach
30 grams butter
2 tablespoons olive oil
350 ml. dry white wine
1 teaspoon chopped rosemary
Salt and freshly ground pepper to taste

Method
Thaw the spinach and gently squeeze out the excess liquids.
Place the spinach in a bowl and chop up. Mix in the eggs, grated Parmesan cheese and nutmeg. Season and mix well
Place the turkey breast fillets on a clean surface and pound lightly with a kitchen hammer. Arrange 3 rashers of bacon on every turkey fillet. Divide the spinach mixture between the 2 turkey fillets. Spread the mixture over the fillet. Roll up the fillet towards the pointed end of the meat. Secure with toothpicks previously soaked in water, and tie up with clean string.
Heat the butter and oil in a frying pan and brown the turkey on all sides. Transfer the turkey with the juices to a casserole and pour over the wine. Add the rosemary and season.
Bake in a moderate to hot oven for 1 ¼ hour or until turkey is very tender. Bring out of the oven and cool slightly. Place the turkey on a board and remove toothpicks and string. Cut into thick slices and arrange on a warmed serving dish. Pour over the cooking gravy and serve immediately.
Serve with plain steamed vegetables such as Brussels sprouts, carrots and peas.
The turkey fillets may be prepared and stuffed in advance. Keep them refrigerated until cooking time.

Pete's Christmas Veges

Ingredients
Serves 8

800 grams Brussels sprouts
6 courgettes, sliced
400 grams baby carrots, peeled
2 turnips, peeled and diced
3 leeks, peeled and quartered lengthwise
2 cloves garlic, peeled and sliced
1 small chilli pepper, de-seeded and finely chopped
1 small piece fresh ginger, peeled and finely chopped
100 grams walnuts, shelled and chopped
Juice of 1 lemon
3 tablespoons good honey
Salt and pepper
3 tablespoons corn oil

Method
Grease a flame-proof serving dish with butter.
Wash and prepare the vegetables. Heat the oil in a large pan or wok. Add the leeks, garlic, ginger and the chilli. Cook on a high heat for 2 minutes. Mix in the courgettes and Brussels sprouts and cook for 2 minutes. Add the baby carrots and the turnips, season and continue cooking on a high heat for 3 minutes. Stir continuously.
Bring off the heat and place the vegetables in the prepared dish. Sprinkle the lemon juice, scatter the walnuts and drizzle the honey over the vegetables. Pop into a hot oven and bake for 15 minutes. Serve immediately.
This Christmas do away with the potatoes, a few less calories! This delicious vegetable dish goes well with any of your Christmas roasts.

Manuel's Chocolate Truffle Torte

Ingredients
Serves 8

100 ml. fine brandy
1 tablespoonful instant coffee
125 grams good plain chocolate
125 grams good milk chocolate
250 ml. fresh cream
300 grams Bourbon biscuits, crumbed
80 grams unsalted butter
150 grams good plain chocolate, grated
1 tablespoon cocoa powder

Method
Grease a 23 cm. spring-form cake tin with butter. Line the bottom and sides of the tin with baking paper.
Warm the brandy in a small saucepan and mix in the coffee granules. Stir to dissolve and leave to get cold. Mix the biscuit crumbs with the butter. Place in the prepared tin and spread out evenly. Refrigerate.
Break the plain and milk chocolate into pieces and place in a bowl. Place the bowl over a pan with simmering water and leave to melt. Remove from heat and leave to cool slightly. Beat the cream until stiff and then beat in the melted chocolate. Beat for a further 2 minutes. Pour in the coffee mixture and beat for another minute. Pour into the tin over the biscuits and spread out evenly. Refrigerate for 2 hours.
Remove the tin and paper with care. Scatter the grated chocolate over the top and just before serving sprinkle the cocoa through a small sieve.
Just heavenly!

Your Healthy Mince Pies

Ingredients

4 cups raisins
4 cups currants
4 cups sultanas
2 cups freshly ground almonds
2 cups seeded dates, chopped
2 cups seeded prunes, chopped
2 cups dried figs, chopped
2 large apples, grated
2 large carrots, peeled and grated
2 tablespoons grated orange rind
2 tablespoons grated lemon rind
½ teaspoon freshly grated nutmeg
3 cups fresh orange juice
½ cup fresh lemon juice
2 cups brown sugar

Method

Mix all the ingredients in a large bowl, cover and stand overnight. Give the mixture another good stir and pack into clean, dry and sterilized jars. They will keep for 6 months under refrigeration. Prepare your fruit mince early, in November!

For your Gluten-free Mince Pies use Gluten-free Sweet Pastry (Page 6)

For mince pies with a low sugar content, use Diabetic Sweet Pastry (Page 6) and also substitute the 2 cups brown sugar in the Fruit Mince ingredients with 2 cups Diabetic fruit jam.

Grease round disposable baking cases with butter. Roll out the pastry and use a round biscuit cutter to cut the pastry and line the cases. Spoon enough fruit mince to fill the pastry shells. Use a biscuit cutter in the form of a star to cut more pastry. Place the star-shaped pastry over the fruit mince to act as coverings for your Christmas mince pies. Bake in a moderate to hot oven for around 25 minutes or until your mince pies are golden in colour and cooked through. Bring out of the oven and stand for 5 minutes. Remove the mince pies from the cases and place on a wire rack to cool. Store in airtight containers and they will keep for up to 4 weeks.

Marzipan Walnuts

Ingredients
Makes about 60

600 grams pure ground almonds
300 grams icing sugar, sieved
300 grams caster sugar
2 eggs
Juice of 1 lemon
Juice of 1 orange
Few drops almond essence
250 grams walnuts,
  shelled and halved

Method
Mix the ground almonds and sugars in a large bowl. Make a well in the centre and add the eggs, juices and essence. Mix with a spoon and then use your hands to knead the mixture into a sort of dough. Place on a surface dusted with icing sugar and knead for about 3 minutes, or until smooth. Wrap in cling film and stand for 30 minutes.
Take pieces of marzipan and roll into small balls the size of a walnut. Place a walnut halve on each ball. Press the walnut halve into the marzipan with your thumb. Leave to dry for a few hours on a clean surface dusted with icing sugar. Arrange on a suitable serving tray or pack in airtight containers. They will keep for up to a month in winter.
Marzipan is one of my greatest weaknesses. I've tried the above recipe also using different nuts: Pistachios, toasted almonds, toasted hazelnuts, pecans and even glace' cherry halves to add a touch of colour. Try stuffing pitted prunes!
If necessary, use gluten-free icing sugar.

Pete's Christmas Cake

Ingredients

140 grams plain flour
140 grams self-raising flour
220 grams unsalted butter
220 grams Demerara sugar
Grated rind of 1 orange
100 grams pure ground almonds
5 eggs
450 grams mixed sultanas, currants and raisins
100 ml. fine brandy
110 grams candied peel
110 grams glace' cherries, halved
2 tablespoons treacle

To decorate
120 grams blanched almonds
100 grams glace' cherries, halved
350 ml. fine red vermouth
3 tablespoons apricot jam
Marzipan prepared as in previous recipe (Page 114)
1 packet fast setting jelly glaze

Method
Grease a 22 cm. cake tin with butter. Line the bottom and sides of the tin with baking paper and grease over the paper. Sift the flours together. Mix all the fruits together.
Beat together the butter, sugar and orange rind. Beat until pale and fluffy. Beat in the brandy and the ground almonds, and then beat in the eggs one at a time. Fold in the flour in three stages, alternating with the mixed fruit. Add the treacle and give the mixture a light stir. Pour the mixture into the prepared tin and smoothen the top with a spatula. Decorate the cake with blanched almonds and halved cherries as shown. Place in a very moderate oven and bake for 2 ½ hours.
Bring out of the oven and stand for 10 minutes. Place on a cooling rack and leave to get cold.
Carefully place the cake upside down on a large soup plate. Slowly pour the vermouth into the cake. Cover and leave overnight.
Slice the cake diagonally into two. Spread the inner side of the slices

with apricot jam. Roll out just a bit more than half the marzipan over a surface dusted with icing sugar. Roll out in a circular shape as much as possible. Place the marzipan on the bottom slice and trim off any extra marzipan. Place the top slice and press down gently but firmly. Brush the side of the cake with apricot jam.

Roll out the remaining marzipan into a strip as wide as the height of the cake and long enough to go all round the side. I usually cut a piece of baking paper to size and roll out the marzipan over it. I then tilt the paper with the marzipan and slide it towards the cake. Carefully cover the side of the cake with the marzipan strip and trim off any excess. Dampen your fingers and smoothen the seam where the ends meet.

Leave to set for a few hours and then carefully place the cake on a round serving plate.

Prepare the jelly glaze according to the instructions on the packet and brush the top and sides of the cake with the glaze. Leave to set. Keep the glaze handy and give another 3 coatings to get a really glossy look and seal the cake.

Bake and decorate your cake at least 3 weeks before Christmas. It will mature nicely and you will have enough time to enjoy preparing it before the rush sets in.

Greek Almond Shortcakes

Ingredients

1 kilo plain flour, sifted
150 grams caster sugar
500 grams unsalted butter
1 teaspoon orange zest, finely grated
2 egg yolks
300 grams toasted blanched almonds
150 ml. fine brandy
Few drops vanilla essence
About 500 grams icing sugar to coat

Method

Grease 2 baking trays with butter and dust with flour. Coarsely chop the toasted almonds.

Cream the butter and sugar until pale and fluffy. Add the egg yolks, almonds, orange zest, brandy and the vanilla whilst beating constantly. Gradually mix in the flour and knead the mixture into a dough. Have ready a lightly floured surface. Take portions of the dough and hand roll into long sausage-like shapes 3 cms. thick. Use a sharp knife to cut pieces from the rolls 6 cms. long. Place on the prepared trays leaving enough space for swelling during baking. Bake in a moderate to hot oven for exactly 21 minutes. Sift the icing sugar onto a large flat dish. Bring the shortcakes out of the oven and while still very hot place them in batches on the icing sugar. Roll in the sugar and set aside. Give them a second coating when cool.

Place on a suitable serving plate and serve. These shortcakes will keep for up to 6 weeks if stored in airtight containers. Prepare early for Christmas!

Rena's Christmas Loaf

Ingredients

3 teaspoons instant yeast
400 ml. lukewarm milk
175 ml. good honey
2 tablespoons unsalted butter, softened
2 tablespoons olive oil
1 egg, lightly beaten
1 teaspoon salt
1 tablespoon fennel seeds
Zest of 2 lemons, finely grated
450 grams plain flour
A little extra olive oil

For the filling
100 grams raisins
100 grams pitted prunes, chopped
100 grams walnuts, chopped
7 tablespoons good honey

Method
Grease a baking tray with butter and dust with flour.
Combine the yeast with the lukewarm milk in a large bowl. Cover and stand in a warm place for 15 minutes. When the mixture becomes frothy, mix in the honey, butter, olive oil, egg, salt, fennel and lemon zest. Mix well and gradually add the flour whilst stirring. Coat your hands with flour and knead the mixture into a dough. You may need to add a little more flour to obtain a firm dough. Knead for 3 minutes.
Place the dough in a lightly oiled bowl, cover and stand in a warm place for 30 minutes.
Combine the raisins, prunes, walnuts and honey.
Have ready a lightly floured surface. Roll the dough into a large sausage-

like shape. Flatten out with your hands into a 30 cms. rectangular shape. Spread a little more than half the fruit mixture over the dough. Keep 5cms. away from the edges of the pastry. Dampen the edges with a little water. Carefully roll up and seal the side edges whilst stretching them slightly and tucking them underneath. Place the roll on the tray and stand in a warm place for 15 minutes. Bake in a moderate to hot oven for about 40 minutes or until the loaf is nicely golden in colour. Bring out of the oven and spread the rest of the fruit mixture over the loaf. Leave to get cold before serving.

Pastine Siciliane

Pastine di mandorla
Ingredients
350 grams icing sugar
350 grams pure ground almonds
Zest of 1 large lemon
Zest of 1 large orange
2 egg whites
1 tablespoonful good honey
Icing sugar to coat

Method
Grease a baking tray with butter and dust with flour. Process the lemon and orange zests to a paste.
Sift the icing sugar into a bowl and mix in the ground almonds. Add the zests, mix well and then mix in the honey. Gradually mix in the egg whites until the mixture becomes like a pastry. Have ready a surface dusted with icing sugar. Place the mixture over the icing sugar and knead gently until a firm mixture is obtained. Take portions of the mixture and roll into long sausage-like shapes 5 cms. thick. Cut into 7 cms. lengths with a sharp knife and place on the prepared tray. Shape into S shapes with your finger tips. Bake in a moderate oven for 12 to 15 minutes or until slightly golden. Bring out of the oven and leave to cool. Use a small sieve to drizzle the pastine with icing sugar.

Pastine di pistachio
Ingredients
Same ingredients and method as above but instead use 350 grams unsalted pistachio nuts. Grind the nuts in a processor.
Form the mixture into walnut-sized balls and flatten slightly. Bake and coat with icing sugar as for pastine di mandorla.
If necessary use gluten-free icing sugar.